The Olympic Games Effect

The Olympic Games Effect

How Sports Marketing Builds Strong Brands

Second Edition

John A. Davis

WILEY

John Wiley & Sons Singapore Pte. Ltd.

Other Wiley Editorial Offices

John Wiley & Sons, 111 River Street, Hoboken, NJ 07030, USA

John Wiley & Sons, The Atrium, Southern Gate, Chichester, West Sussex, P019 8SQ, United Kingdom

John Wiley & Sons (Canada) Ltd., 5353 Dundas Street West, Suite 400, Toronto, Ontario, M9B 6HB, Canada

John Wiley & Sons Australia Ltd., 42 McDougall Street, Milton, Queensland 4064, Australia

Wiley-VCH, Boschstrasse 12, D-69469 Weinheim, Germany

Library of Congress Cataloging-in-Publication Data

ISBN 978-1-118-17168-4 (Paperback)
ISBN 978-1-118-17169-1 (ePDF)
ISBN 978-1-118-17170-7 (Mobi)
ISBN 978-1-118-17171-4 (ePub)

Typeset in 11.5/14 point Bembo by MPS Limited, a Macmillan Company, Chennai, India
Printed in Singapore by Markono Print Media Pte. Ltd.
10 9 8 7 6 5 4 3 2 1

To Barb!!
Your love and support make me the luckiest guy in the known universe. My life is infinitely better because of you.

Contents

Acknowledgments

When first discussing this second edition with Nick Wall-work, my publisher, I envisioned a relatively straightforward sequel. However, as I dug into the data, I ended up reorganizing and rewriting virtually the entire book. This is good news for fans of the Olympics, corporate chief marketing officers, and companies considering sports sponsorship investments because the 2008 Beijing Olympics, 2010 Vancouver Olympics, and the inaugural Youth Olympic Games held in 2010 in Singapore provided a veritable treasure trove of new Olympic data and sponsorship activities. As I have learned from my experiences writing each edition, it is impossible to analyze the activities of The Olympic Partner (TOP) sponsors without understanding Olympic history and the associated (and countless) stories of success, and failure, that have defined the Games for nearly 3,000 years, thereby elevating them well above being merely a megasports event to serving as a beacon of hope and source of inspiration for billions of people around the world.

There are far too many people to acknowledge properly without creating a 30-page statement of appreciation, but there are a few individuals whose work I admire and whose support has been important to me. They include:

- Dr. Kostas Georgiadis, Dean of the International Olympic Academy in Olympia, Greece, and Vice Rector of the University of Peloponnese.
- Dr. Benoit Seguin, School of Human Kinetics at the University of Ottawa and Supervising Faculty at the International Olympic Academy.
- Dr. Lynn Kahle, Ehrman Giustina Professor of Marketing and Department Head, Lundquist College of Business, University of Oregon.
- Dr. Glenn Hubbard, Dean, and Russell L. Carson, Professor of Finance and Economics, Columbia Business School at Columbia University in the City of New York.
- Dr. Kimio Kase, IESE Business School.
- Richard H. Burton, David B. Falk Professor of Sport Management, David B. Falk College of Sport and Human Dynamics, Syracuse University.
- Dr. Dae Ryun Chang, Professor of Marketing/International Business, Yonsei School of Business, Yonsei University.

Unquestionably, I owe a debt of gratitude to my students from Asia, Europe, and the United States for the past decade, whose energy, enthusiasm, and commitment to conducting fascinating research on sports, sports marketing, and the Olympics have been an ongoing source of inspiration to me. In particular, my Masters students from the International Olympic Academy (a remarkable program held in ancient Olympia), many of whom have been directly involved in Olympic-related activities on behalf of their respective countries for years, gave me terrific new insights about the Olympic movement and the challenges of further enhancing the success of the Olympics for sponsors, host cities, and athletes in the years ahead.

None of my work would see the light of day without the support and ongoing commitment of the great team at my publisher, John Wiley & Sons. Nick Wallwork especially deserves a badge of honor, and an extra beer or two, for being a trusted advisor. The many other wonderful people at Wiley deserve praise and have my eternal gratitude, including Emilie Herman, Jules Yap, Janis Soo, and Paul Dinovo. They are thoughtful, professional, and always encouraging.

Introduction

The first edition of this book was surprisingly well received, generating interest from readers literally all over the world. In the years since the 2008 Beijing Olympics (when the first edition was published), I have been fortunate to speak to audiences all across Asia, in Europe, and in the United States, including the 2011 TED conference in Shanghai, China (TEDxFiveStarSquare), a particularly enjoyable event with a wonderfully diverse range of electrifying speakers with fascinating backgrounds and interests. I was also invited to teach at the International Olympic Academy in their Masters of Olympic Studies, Olympic Education, Organization and Management of Olympic Events program. Being within walking distance of ancient Olympia and the archaeological ruins where the first Olympiads were held was nothing short of thrilling, breathtaking, and humbling. The students, the program team, and the daily visits to the sites of ancient Olympia made for an unforgettable experience.

This second edition of *The Olympic Games Effect: How Sports Marketing Builds Strong Brands* revisits the themes of the first book and adds updated content and data from the 2008 Summer Olympic Games in Beijing, the 2010 Winter Olympic Games in Vancouver, and the first Youth

Olympic Games, held in Singapore in 2010, where I was conveniently living at the time. The content additions in the second edition provide more depth about TOP sponsors (with new case studies and updates to previous cases), social media, fans, host cities and the bidding process, and more. Each chapter has new content and ends with questions designed to test your knowledge and inspire your interest in doing additional research.

The Olympic Games, at their core, are about athletes and athletic competition. But the Olympics have evolved into a much larger phenomenon that extends beyond the boundaries of sport. Propelled by the Olympic movement, the term that describes the interrelationship among athletes, local and national Olympic committees, and related international federations (which are responsible for specific sports around the world), the Olympics have come to represent hope and prosperity—hope, in the sense of a peaceful, better world energized by sport, and prosperity in the economic, social, and political contexts.

Each Olympic Games is a substantial undertaking involving economic and infrastructural resource commitments by host cities and nations. One city, dozens of new venues, hundreds of companies (with thousands of employees), millions of volunteers, and billions of dollars are combined to make the Olympics happen every two years (the Games alternate every two years from Summer to Winter Games, with four years between each Summer Games and four years between each Winter Games). No other sport unleashes such a complex array of activities.

Companies invest as much as $240 million to be TOP (The Olympic Program, the name of the highest level of Olympic sponsorship that gives companies the right to sponsor one quadrennial cycle of both the Winter and Summer Games)[1] sponsors for an event that lasts just over two weeks. To be fair, the $240 million figure is an estimate of the total investment in sponsoring the Olympics; neither the International Olympic Committee (IOC) nor individual sponsors release official figures. But an approximate breakdown shows that TOP sponsors pay a sponsorship fee of roughly $80 to 85 million each and then spend an additional two to four times that amount in activation expenditures. *Activation expenditures* are the cost of the specific marketing programs and tactics in which a sponsor invests to bring the sponsorship to life. These include investing in creative development, media placement, execution and promotion, support services, and postevent review.[2] When one considers that Acer, P&G, Coca-Cola, GE, McDonald's, VISA, Samsung, Dow, Omega, Atos Origin, and Panasonic are the 11 TOP sponsors for the 2012 Olympic Games in London, then one may also assume these companies did not invest their money incautiously or collude in a fit of collective foolishness.[3] In fact, companies that become TOP sponsors have exclusive rights to market in both the Summer and Winter Olympic Games, reaching a potential total viewing audience of more than 4.5 billion people.[4] While the Olympics are a unique and potentially highly beneficial sponsorship opportunity, not everything associated with the Olympics turns into gold, as this book points out. Both the sponsors and the IOC make mistakes.

We will look at the risks and rewards of sponsoring the Olympics, what TOP sponsors are doing to make their Olympic investments productive and value adding, and the impact each Olympics has on the city and nation where the Games are being hosted. The first part of the book's title is "The Olympic Games Effect"—hinting at the potential for a positive brand halo casting a profitable glow over those that are part of such a unique, historical event. As mentioned, there is also a risk as well—a risk that scandal or other significant problems might arise that could tarnish a sponsor's investment. Common sense says that a company's shareholders might be a bit upset at management if $240 million are spent and the result is the proverbial goose egg. Interestingly, many companies have repeatedly sponsored the Olympics, or some portion of it, to great effect. These investments would undoubtedly cease, or decrease dramatically, if the returns weren't promising.

Of course, not everyone or everything related to sports illustrates common sense, such as the penchant for some athletes to use performance-enhancing drugs that give them an athletic edge with unfortunate side effects, like a larger head, smaller genitals, shorter life spans, hair in weird places, and a generally grumpier disposition—not to mention the fact that, when caught, they have to give back their medals, suffer public humiliation, and be banned from the sport for life. For companies, part of the allure of sponsoring sports in general and the Olympics in particular is knowing that the unexpected could and does happen, bringing added attention and interest to that event and their efforts associated with it. Sports marketing is a popular subject in universities around the world for all the reasons people love sports—athletes, teams, clubs, leagues, owners, records, rivalries, dynasties, competing, staying fit, and more. The industry side of sports develops some of the world's most innovative products and offers a stunningly diverse range of events, teams, and contests in different, exotic locales. The industry is huge: Sports apparel, footwear, and equipment alone had sales of more than US$285 billion in 2009–2010,[5] and estimates for the entire industry (including sports events) range up to US$500 billion. The global recession and financial crisis that started in the past decade slowed the industry, as it did most industries. But sports continue to remain popular, and, most important, sports fans are in every country, making sports a form of universal language.

In many societies, success is associated with distinction and greatness by the people and organizations within, based on cultural standards. We look to those who have achieved as role models, figuratively hoisting their accomplishments aloft as the standards to which the rest of us should aspire. As individuals, many of us work hard so that we are noticed and seen as valuable by those who can influence the course of our career. Society's organizations, whether business, not-for-profit, or government, seek visibility and awareness, while also striving to be seen as highly valued by their customers. Of course, our assessments of each other are usually the result of perception born from reputation and/or actual experiences with that person or organization, which ultimately determine whether the perception matches reality. More simply, we try to create a positive image and act accordingly so that others see us favorably. For those companies that see marketing as a strategic asset, having a sharp focus about what they expect to gain from sponsoring the Olympics, communicated properly, can help them win customers and grow profits for years. This book will show the lessons of many companies that have benefited from sponsoring the Olympics, as well as the pitfalls. Furthermore, many of these lessons can be applied to other sports sponsorships as well.

Developing recognizable distinction includes associating your company with other prestigious organizations and events, and few are as powerful or meaningful as the Olympic Games. The Olympics epitomize prestige and distinction, qualities associated with the rare and unique. They are analogous to a limited-edition, exclusive luxury item, never to be offered twice in exactly the same way. Olympic athletes undertake a rigorous, multiyear preparation regimen with no guarantee they will qualify for the Olympics, let alone win their event. Therefore, those who win are seen as extraordinary, heroic individuals who won in an exclusive, even rare, form of international competition against the very best competitors from around the world. The exclusive appeal of the Olympic Games, combined with the unique, even daunting challenges athletes undertake, creates a compelling, irresistible quality that motivates companies to support the Olympics in the hope of benefiting from the associated halo effect.

Beyond the halo cast by the Olympic Games effect are innumerable factors that inspire each of us to watch the Olympics. There is a deep credibility attached to the Olympics that creates a particularly intoxicating appeal. Part of this appeal is witnessing athletes pushing their abilities to the limit, coupled with the element of surprise. No matter how formidable an athlete appears, usually due to dominating performances in competitions leading up to the Olympics, there is always the chance of an unexpected outcome. Physical preparation is crucial to competitive success against rivals, but psychology plays an important role as well. There are many instances in sports where a supposed underdog ends up the victor, vanquishing a previously considered indomitable foe. The gold-medal-winning 1980 U.S. Olympic Hockey team is one such example. Such surprises are part of the allure of any sport. As fans, we know that underdogs may win, no matter how unlikely, because we understand that athletic competitions have numerous complex variables interacting in unique ways, creating unpredictable outcomes. We are inspired by such surprises, just as we are awed by the performance of dominating teams, even if we do not personally like the result. In the case of both the underdog and the favorite, we know that both competitors (whether individuals or teams) worked hard prior to the event and that both also want to win. If an underdog wins, the psychological impact may change the dynamics of future competitions simply because the victor feels more confident, stirring the rest of us to improve our own efforts with the hope that similar outcomes happen for us. If the favorite wins, then we often aspire to reach the same level of consistent dominance, pushing ourselves to improve yet again.

People strive for improvement throughout life. As kids, we always competed. Whether playing in the streets or at school, our goal was to be better than the other kids. Every year we followed our favorite teams, from high school to college to pros, usually those from the city in or near where we grew up, debating how our team would beat the others in the league and, most important, our rivals. As adults, our competitions often shift to encompass business and other professional interests, but the theme of besting a rival, or our own performance, lies close to the surface. Throughout life, competition serves as an energizing force, helping us define who we are while also guiding our objectives (beat my time, this person, this team, or this record next year). If someone chooses not to compete, then we often see that person as weaker and lacking ability. Indeed, we learn to compete on so many levels so often that we attach significant value to the act of competing itself, making almost any competition a vital ingredient of determining worth. We admire competitions that pit one dedicated person or team against another, especially when the commitment is long-standing and reputations have been built accordingly. While rigorous training comprised of relentless practice and repetition is important, indeed vital, to success in any sport, this commitment is motivated by the athlete's ambition to be the best and reach the top of a sport. Winning the sport's premier or championship competition is the athlete's ultimate goal. As fans, we know that a given sport's championship crowns the victor—a status the athlete or team retains for a year until the next championship. As fans we know and understand that our favorite athletes may have only one chance to compete in the Olympics and that the odds of winning are quite small, even if their past achievements suggest superior abilities compared to opponents. The TOP sponsors understand this as well, and they recognize the unique massive audience of 4.5 billion people that each Olympic Games attracts, which, in today's globalizing business world, makes the Games even more commercially valuable and attractive. The challenge for TOP sponsors is determining how to take full advantage of the global exposure afforded by associating with the Olympic Games in a way that enhances their company brand, excites consumers, and grows their business over the long term, yet does not cheapen or undermine the prestigious reputation of the Olympic Games.

How This Book Is Organized

There are five parts to this book. Becoming a corporate sponsor for the Olympics costs a great deal of money well before any effort is put into the activities that actually activate the sponsorship. Imagine buying another company without knowing anything about it and then ignoring it after the purchase—such behavior would be deemed irresponsible. Companies considering a sports sponsorship are well advised to approach it much as one would approach launching a new company, a major product offering, or an acquisition. There are significant operating and marketing complexities, and coordinating them is a 24/7 job. The good news is that the Olympic Games offer a global stage that reaches one of the largest audiences of any event in the world and provides a unique opportunity to create a positive, lasting, and economically valuable relationship with consumers.

Section I: History, Legacy, Tradition—These three words are fundamental to explaining why the Olympics have grown to become the global phenomenon they are today, why there is more to the Olympics than the media spectacle with which we are all familiar today, and why they are more than just a sports event. This section presents a short history of the Olympics and the sociocultural influences that shaped the event at the time of the ancient Greeks. There is a richness to the Olympics that is unlike any other sports event in the world, and much of it is due to the historical legacy from the ancient Greeks. The Games have a formidable reputation as a powerful force for good for people everywhere, and understanding how this reputation was built is instrumental in understanding why they are still revered to this day. There are also interesting parallels between the ancient and modern Olympics that may surprise people. In addition, discussion of the economic impact for Olympic host cities has been expanded.

Section II: Success and Achievement—This part discusses the benefits of associating with the Olympics. Part of the explanation for the ongoing success and popularity of the Olympics lies in the fact that more good things happen than bad. When things go well, whether it's an expected or unexpected performance, people celebrate, and the resulting Olympic Games effect casts a wide glow over those associated with success. An athlete who becomes an Olympian has already achieved something few others can ever experience. Of course, when athletes are medal winners, their performance attains a loftier status, and gold medal winners often become icons, which attracts fans. Fans attract media and sponsors. For companies, associating with Olympic success can have an obvious positive and long-lasting impact on their image.

Section III: Controversy and Challenge—As the 2008 Beijing Olympic Torch Relay illustrated, the visibility of the Olympics has made the Games a magnet for those seeking attention. The Olympics have become one of the best-known brands in the world, which appeals to a wide range of interest groups that know the Games are a useful platform for their own messages. Political issues are often intertwined with the Olympics, despite the Olympic Charter's statements to the contrary. Athletes, too, sometimes find themselves in untenable situations. When controversy hits, the negative impact on all involved can be enormous. We discuss examples of controversies and the potential risks for corporate sponsors.

Section IV: Reputation Development—This part of the second edition features several new chapters, including TOP sponsor case briefs and case studies. The International Olympic Committee (IOC) has developed a series of revenue-generating programs designed to maximize corporate associations while also providing significant funding to support the Olympic movement. The best results come with time, and this part provides details on four select TOP sponsors and the sponsorship programs they have developed over the length of their association with the Olympics.

Section V: Olympic Marketing Victory guides sponsors through how to design their sponsorship program plans based on a clear understanding of fans, creative execution, and marketing communications.

At the end of each part is a chapter of sponsorship preparation questions related to the themes discussed in that part. These questions will help corporate sponsors evaluate their understanding of their own organization and that of the sports event. These questions will be useful to companies considering sponsoring a wide range of sports events, regardless of whether they are Olympic-scale.

I

HISTORY, LEGACY, TRADITION

Chapter 1

The Olympic Dream

Most people harbor dreams in which they overcome seemingly insurmountable odds to achieve something great. For nearly 3,000 years, the Olympics have inspired people from all over the world to overcome adversity and extraordinary challenge in a quest to be recognized as the best in the world. The pursuit of being the best, of being an Olympic athlete, comes with great sacrifice and dedication. The same can be said for companies that sponsor the Olympics. The modern Olympic Games are a singular event, held every two years (each season's Olympics, Summer and Winter, are on alternating four-year cycles). They are busy with people, with dozens of sports, hundreds of events, thousands of athletes, tens of thousands of media people, hundreds of thousands of ticket-holding fans, and billions of viewers. They are complex, with multiple venues and unique rules for every sport and event, held over 17 days, and defined by daunting logistical challenges in coordinating technology platforms, accurately communicating results, adjudicating close calls, addressing controversies small and large, and narrating a storyline that changes every hour of every day of the Games.

There are specific rules governing sponsor rights and responsibilities, as well as clever competitors that attempt to ambush the official sponsors. Protesters target the Games to support their respective agendas, in an effort to change public perception of the Olympics, the host nation, and the corporate sponsors. Athletes, too, find themselves in the spotlight, for their athletic achievements and, on occasion, for their transgressions. In essence, the Olympics are a dynamic, exciting, and unpredictable megasports event. There are no guarantees of success but reasonable assurances that, despite the most careful planning and preparation, surprises can and will occur that test the mettle of all Olympic stakeholders in full view of the world. Given these uncertainties, one may reasonably ask why corporations would want to sponsor such an event, particularly since it occurs infrequently. More specifically, for the purposes of this book, why do TOP (The Olympic Partners) sponsors invest tens or even hundreds of millions of dollars in sponsoring the Olympics? The answer is more complicated than merely stating "because global viewership is so large." Indeed, the size of the audience by itself is an insufficient justification for sponsoring the Olympics since the same money can be invested to reach an equally large audience in many alternative ways. To understand why the Olympics have become such an attractive commercial phenomenon for sponsoring companies requires that we understand more about the important legacy of the Games.

Marketing, at a minimum, is about developing, building, and sustaining a positive reputation for a given offering so that it attracts support from members of the marketplace. In the modern era, this support is in the form of profitable, loyal customers. The Olympic Games of the ancient Greek world built a remarkable legacy of reputable success that lasted for 1,200 years, yet they were not marketed, at least not in the modern sense of marketing. The Games were an integral part of Greek life, known for attracting the best athletes competing and representing their home city-state for the honor and glory of Olympic champion. Victors received rewards, including free food for life, new homes, tax-free status, and long-term fame. Olympic success and the subsequent fame undoubtedly helped foster positive reputations for those involved, spreading the Olympic message through an ancient form of viral marketing—word of mouth. The stories of Olympic competition provided instructive lessons on the virtues of dedication to cause, translated through the tradition of storytelling in which tales of Olympic athletic achievement were spread from one generation to the next, inspiring images of victory and dreams of eternal glory.

"Holding an Olympic Games means evoking history," said Baron Pierre de Coubertin, the founder of the modern Olympics.[1] This is a grand, perhaps even a daunting, sentiment. Evoking history implies a significant responsibility, and, less majestically, a great burden is placed on those who attempt to carry out such lofty ambitions. Failure by any city and its Olympic planners to recognize the importance of the Olympic Games and then organize resources to ensure success risks eternal historical infamy. Given this risk, why do so many companies and cities today vie for a chance to be involved with the Olympic Games? The answer lies partly in understanding the origins of the Olympic Games, since even a rudimentary review will provide a better sense of the traditions and historical context that have helped shape the Olympic reputation as it exists today. There is also the magnetic attraction of the Olympic dream—a concept loaded with vivid imagery and powerful associations like *authenticity*, *mythology*, *mystique*, and the *pinnacle of sport* that are simultaneously positive, motivating, and virtuous. Thomas B. Shepard, former executive vice president, Global Merchant Partnerships & Sponsorship, Visa International, offered this explanation for the appeal and benefits of being a TOP sponsor for the Olympic Games:

> If you look at the Olympics, it is a perfect fit for us. Olympic brand equities include being at the pinnacle of its category; having universal appeal; standing for excellence; having broad-based consumer awareness and acceptance; having global reach with local impact and participation; and standing for leadership. Visa's brand equities of industry leadership; global yet local; accepted everywhere; innovative and modern; and service excellence parallel Olympic brand equities. Visa could probably work on innovativeness, though, because we're not known as the most innovative brand.[2]

Shepard's rationale goes beyond assessing benefits based on return on investment analysis by revealing the strategic rationale and qualitative linkages between the Olympics and Visa. Shepard even describes Visa's weaknesses compared with the Olympics when he discusses the company's need to be more innovative, perhaps implying that an association with the Olympics might provide the catalyst Visa needs to improve its innovativeness.

McDonald's, another TOP sponsor, sees similar benefits. Dean Barrett, senior vice president for global marketing at McDonald's, stated that the Olympics are

> "the ultimate expression of the spirit of McDonald's" because it "directly connects with people of all ages and cultures."[3]

Domestic (or national) sponsors, while not the specific subject of this book, see significant benefit in supporting the Olympics. Bell, a domestic sponsor of the 2010 Winter Games in Vancouver, surprised many, including the Vancouver Organizing Committee (VANOC), when it bid C$200 million for the Games. Their bid was $65 million higher than Telus, a competitor, bid. John McLarty, director of Olympic and Sports Marketing at Bell, explained why:

> You can't really . . . associate yourself with a stronger brand than the Olympics, and allowing us to strengthen our brand by associating with the rings and associate with something as important as Vancouver 2010 is incredibly important for us.[4]

For host cities and corporate sponsors, the premier status of the Olympics offers a unique and highly credible event that captures the imagination of the world and casts a remarkable halo effect over the stakeholders involved. This is not to suggest that the Olympics are without fault because there are well-documented examples of scandals and improprieties that violate the Olympic spirit and rules of conduct that, as a consequence, risk tarnishing the event's reputation and harming the commercial interests of the International Olympic Committee's (IOC's) key corporate sponsors, as discussed later in the book. But interestingly, the scandals have not caused irreparable harm (yet), which suggests that the Olympics enjoy such an exalted status in the eyes of the public that short-term transgressions are forgiven if the integrity of the actual athletic competitions remains intact. Of course, ongoing scandals would be increasingly hard to overcome, so the onus is on the IOC to ensure the highest possible integrity and rules of conduct for all involved.

Authenticity

There is little doubt that the Olympic Games are exciting, unpredictable events, providing fans and competitors with a rich set of experiences. Beyond the excitement, part of the appeal of the Olympics is its image of authenticity, born from centuries of tradition around the purity of honest athletic competition. We expect and trust that the Olympics overall—and the competitions within—will be conducted fairly, with all athletes having prepared by using legitimate training techniques, building their reputations through rigorous and varied competitive events. This simple set of expectations is central to our belief in the Olympics as a pure event free from manipulation, as opposed to, say, professional wrestling, with its implicit and explicit understanding between the wrestling stars and the fans that the entire event is scripted, complete with far-fetched story lines and outsize personas. If the Olympics were ever to resort to rigging or scripting, the entire foundation of the Games would be eroded, and thousands of years of credibility would be wiped out.

The ancient Olympics were a revered religious rite—a celebration and homage to the Greek gods, especially Zeus. Pindar, a famous Greek poet, said in his First Olympian Ode,

> Water is best, and gold, like a blazing fire in the night, stands out supreme of all lordly wealth. But if, my heart, you wish to sing of contests, look no further for any star warmer than the sun, shining by day through the lonely sky, and let us not proclaim any contest greater than Olympia.[5]

Begun in 776 BC, the first Games consisted of one event called the *stade*, a 192-meter foot race. The term *stade* evolved over the centuries into the modern word *stadium*. The stade pitted individual runners against each other, with the outcome determined by physical and mental preparedness and nothing else, suggesting an authentic, unpolluted combination of virtues. Competitors were all male, as women were forbidden from competing or even watching the games. If women were caught, they faced the possibility of death. However, a separate and related women's-only set of races called the Heraea was held, which historians believe were conducted before each men's Olympics. The men wore a simple covering, often just a loincloth, until Orsippus of Megara lost his covering during his Olympic race in 720 BC, yet he still went on to win his event naked. Legend says his victory inspired other competitors, and, thereafter, nudity was common for Olympic athletes.[6] The ancient Olympics were remarkable in another respect: No awards were given for those who did not win. While there was public honor and affection bestowed on victors as described by Pindar, there was little sympathy, nor the pat on the back suggesting "nice try, better luck next time" or similarly supportive sentiments, for those who lost. Losers often suffered shame, humiliation, and social ostracism, as Dion Chrysostomos, a Greek philosopher, observed in contrasting public reaction to victors versus losers,

> The shouts of sections of the crowd differ so much between those which are made with heartiness and praise from the others which are accompanied by irony and often with antipathy.[7]

There were no teams or team events in the ancient Olympics, only individual athletes with their coaches, if the athlete had one. Coaches had to accompany their athlete without a cloak, which may seem like an odd requirement, but it was a practice established after Pherenike, a boxing coach, celebrated her athlete's victory a bit too vigorously, causing her cloak to drop and reveal her gender in front of the surprised male fans and athletes. Her winning athlete was her son Pisodorus, and she herself was the daughter of a famous Olympic boxing champion, Diagoras, who competed in the Games of 464 BC. Ancient Greek tradition punished women who violated the rules of sport by throwing them to their death from Mount Typaeum, but her family's famous athletic accomplishments (her three brothers and a nephew were also Olympic champions) persuaded the judges to pardon her, saving her life. Thereafter, she was called Kallipateira, Greek for "Mrs. Good Father."[8]

With Olympic victory being important for social status, the athletes of the ancient Olympics often sought any advantage they could, from medicinal treatment to financial inducement. They consulted magicians prior to events, seeking spells and potions that might give them an edge, certainly an effort similar in intent to that of today's steroids users. Eupolus of Thessaly, a boxer in the Olympic Games of 388 BC, bribed his opponents to lose. Several hundred years later, the Roman Emperor Nero bribed Olympic officials to include poetry as an official Olympic event (he admired Greek culture and apparently saw his own poetic abilities in a favorable light) and also bribed officials to declare him the victor of the chariot race, even though he fell off his chariot and never finished the event.[9] Athletes who cheated in the ancient Olympics faced beatings, fines, or both. The fines were used to pay for statues that lined pathways leading to the competition venues. The statues were inscribed with a description of the guilty athlete's transgression, serving as a clear, visible reminder to competitors of the penalties they faced, should they cheat.

Such relatively simple themes are simultaneously quaint and hard to imagine, given today's plethora of scientific training techniques (sometimes including the use of performance-enhancing substances), armies of handlers, larger-than-life personas, and commercial incentives. Yet despite the commercialization of Olympic athletes, there is little doubt that a key appeal for the Olympic Games remains, at its core, this notion of authenticity rooted in simple athletic ability, combined with an overriding sense of hope that the world can set aside its differences for 17 days and come together in a show of community and support for the purity of athletic competition.

Companies keen on building and reinforcing an image of trust and integrity invest in sponsoring the Olympics because the event's very authenticity can confer similar credibility on the sponsoring company because of the visibility resulting from the association, not unlike a person who has a photograph taken with a famous person—suddenly, that average Joe gains fame. The sheer novelty of the occasion elevates the unknown temporarily. The challenge is translating this one-time event into longer-term success and benefits. For smart companies, the real advantage of Olympic sponsorship lies in the long-term commitment and associated activities, beyond the temporary excitement surrounding the 17 days of the Games. This rationale of supporting a long-term marketing investment is vital to effective and successful marketing efforts. Stopping sponsorship after one Olympics cycle does not enable a company to leverage its investment or contribute to a longer-term growth plan. Senior management will always be tempted to cancel any program that does not demonstrate direct contribution to company performance immediately, halting potential gains prematurely. Think of it from an athlete's point of view: If a top athlete trains for months or years and then races once to see whether the training paid off, but retires if he or she loses, then little is learned. The real benefit comes from altering race techniques and competing repeatedly to see what nuances are required to achieve consistent success.

Mythology and Mystique

The Olympics inspire mixed emotions and transregional loyalties, fomented by centuries of myth and mystique. Greek city-states vied for the top athletes, offering inducements to persuade top performers to abandon their allegiances.[10] Victory in an Olympic event was a high honor, bestowing riches and virtue upon the winner, and potential ruin upon the losers. The ancient Olympics spanned nearly 12 centuries, from roughly 776 BC to AD 393, when Roman Emperor Theodosius banned the games because he viewed them as a pagan cult. Theodosius's ban may have been political, but it was by no means the only evidence of politics asserting its influence in the Olympics. The Olympics stand out over the ages as a memorable, even mythical event, partly because each Olympiad reveals the stories of athletic success and heroism. Such stories of legendary athletic achievement are passed from one generation to the next, developing society's shared notions of character and virtue, which serve to reinforce the Olympic mythology. We want athletes from our own country to win, but we also want our favorite athletes in specific sports to win, even if they are from another country. The Olympics are unique because they are about the athlete and transcending national boundaries, although nationalism certainly plays an important role as well. Fans around the world look forward to the Olympics because of its reputation, unique structure, and values. Images of the ancient Greek athletes competing purely for honor permeate our collective psyche and ignite our expectations every four years. The Olympic dream, while inspiring virtue in the form of athletic competition, is also an insightful guide to broader social mores and codes of acceptable conduct. We *implicitly* understand what is meant by *sportsmanship* and *fair play*—understandings common across cultures. Consequently, we look forward to the Olympic Games because they bring the world together for just over two brief weeks, reminding us of the importance of harmony and peace as seen through the lens of athletic achievement. In fact, the Olympics can serve as a positive substitute for international conflict, allowing countries to set aside political differences and elevate sports into the role of settler of disputes. These noble associations of sportsmanship and fair play are central to the mystique of the Olympics.

From a business perspective, an important determinant of a marketing program's success is whether the company's own image retained or gained a stronger mystique with its customers. Do not misinterpret the intent here. Mystique is not meant to suggest that companies should strive to be obscure or mysterious. Being understandable and accessible to customers is still important if a company wishes to reduce obstacles to market acceptance. Instead, companies should endeavor to delight their customers with their ability to convey and reinforce uniqueness. As awkward as it may sound, we often attach a vague sense of mystery to success, asking ourselves "what are the secrets to that company's success?" even though those secrets may be painfully obvious (such as superb, high-quality products; clever communications; and extraordinary services). But a key for any successful company versus its less successful competitors is the very fact that it has found a way to more effectively attract customers and convince the market of its uniqueness, often even if the competitors' products are known to be similar if not equal. There is no hidden mystery or deep secret, other than the weight of market expectations motivating company management to focus on consistent successful delivery of promises made. In this sense, well-conceived and well-executed marketing activities, including event marketing, can and should serve not just to win more business and reinforce distinctiveness, but to create competitive *disadvantage* for rivals. By associating with the Olympic Games, sponsorship marketers believe they increase the likelihood their company will be seen as both positive and different vis-à-vis the competition. Since the Olympics often produce stories of amazing athletic prowess and success, the by-product for sponsoring companies is success by association. Such connections add to a company's image, traditions, and history, all of which are quite visible to millions of people around the world.

Pinnacle of Sport

While winning may be an important goal of any athletic competition because it is a common measure of success, the Olympic Games stand for something even greater: They represent an *idea*. The idea, derived in its simplest form from the earliest days of the ancient Greek Olympics, is that achievement is not limited to how one finishes a competition, but how one competes. What is their reputation? What is their strategy? What is their philosophy? What is their character? The present-day equivalent is captured by a popular sports sentiment: *It's not whether you win or lose, it's how you play the game.* Today it is easy to reduce the Olympics to financial gain—after all, the athletes who win have the potential to earn millions of dollars in endorsement fees, and the companies that support them stand to gain by association. But the financial gain does not define the outcome. Instead, the athlete's single-minded determination in pursuit of the *idea* and the dream that the Olympics represent is the true measure of success. Both in ancient times and since 1896, when the modern Olympic era began, the Olympic Games have been considered the pinnacle of sports excellence because they represent athletic competition at its purest level, outside politics, focused only on the skills of the competitors.

Interestingly, this notion of apolitical purity is part of the Olympic mythology, yet it is not entirely accurate historically. According to Stephen Miller, author of *Ancient Greek Athletics* (2004, Yale University Press), despite popular belief to the contrary, the Games were not pure apolitical contests between amateur athletes. Competitions between cities carried the subtext that victory equaled superiority, perhaps more crudely known today as bragging rights. Furthermore, the ancient Greek athletes were not amateurs, at least as we understand the term today. The winners often found themselves the beneficiary of free meals for life, tax exemption, and substantial monetary rewards (in 600 BC, a winning athlete from Athens would be given 500 drachmas, which was an enormous sum on which he could live comfortably for the rest of his life).[11] Certainly these rewards are analogous to the benefits accorded today's athletes, albeit the magnitude of the riches thrust upon today's athletes arguably reflects an even greater largesse. The issue of amateur versus professional athlete did not exist for the ancient Greeks because rewards and prizes were normal for athletes to receive, much as a salary or wage is common today for most jobs.

The idea that the ancient Greeks were beacons of amateur virtue was partially a contrivance of the nineteenth-century Victorian era, a historical revision of sorts from a period when there was significant social and industrial change, with Great Britain the leading influence in the world. In the nineteenth century, many sports were the purview of the wealthy aristocracy, who could afford to spend time competing without worrying about compensation. They believed that for sports to be pure and untainted, one must participate for the love of competing and the thrill of besting another. But the real agenda was to snub the working classes, who were professionals in that they earned a wage for a specialized skill. An organization started by English aristocrats, called the Amateur Athletic Club (AAC), established guidelines for amateur athletes. David Young, a professor of Classics at the University of Florida, is a respected Olympic historian. He delivered a speech prior to the 2004 Olympic Games in Athens, discussing the origins of the modern Olympics and the AAC's efforts to exclude the working class from sports.

> It declared that men who were "mechanics, artisans, or laborers" were de facto "pros," barred from all amateur contests, which were reserved for "gentlemen," that is, people who did no labor for a living.[12]

Young's speech is fascinating, revealing that the first Olympics of the modern era actually preceded the 1896 Athens Olympics by several decades but did not resemble the Games as we now know them. There were separate efforts, first proposed in Greece in 1835, that ultimately inspired an English-led movement in the mid-1850s—a movement that worked initially but sparked resentment among select members of the aristocracy who led the rival formation of the aforementioned AAC. By the mid-1860s, England's Olympic movement dissipated. Interest reemerged in Greece and took a circuitous route that eventually led to the Games of 1896.

The image of Olympic purity confers a certain image of prestige and higher status, an image that sponsoring companies want to promote since such a perception can further separate them from their competitors. Certainly, idealism may play a role in management decisions to sponsor the Olympics, since linking direct results to an Olympic sponsorship can be problematic (for reasons discussed later). Idealism suggests that companies want to associate with the Olympics because doing so is the right thing to do, and it promotes an image of corporate social responsibility, not a bad outcome, certainly. But sponsoring companies still need to grow and generate profits, making altruistic intentions a minority percentage of the overall decision calculus to support the Olympic Games. If a company can convey to the market that it is successful and unique, like the Olympics, then logic dictates that, of the millions of viewers and customers around the world, some percentage of them will increase their purchase of the sponsoring company's products, accelerating that company's performance compared with its competitors. Therefore, the appeal of being directly associated with an event considered the pinnacle of sport is an enticing attraction for sponsoring companies since they, too, wish to be seen as the pinnacle equivalent in their markets.

Questions

1. What benefits are gained by having a deeper understanding of the history of the Olympics?
2. Why is this historical knowledge important for sponsors, and how is it useful?
3. Is an understanding of the historical background of any megasports event important to corporate sponsors? Why or why not?
4. Can the International Olympic Committee (IOC) leverage its history to improve the appeal of the Olympics? If so, how? Which target audiences and stakeholders will benefit from this information?

Chapter 2

The Olympic Experience

At the 2008 Summer Olympic Games in Beijing, German athlete Matthias Steiner captured the imagination of viewers around the world in winning the Gold Medal in weightlifting in the +105-kilogram class. While the German national anthem played during the medal ceremony, tears streamed down his face as he held a picture of his late wife, who had died tragically from injuries related to a car accident the year before. Steiner dedicated the Games to her, telling her in the hospital before she died that he would work hard to keep their Olympic dreams alive.

> She is always with me, in the hours before the competition, she's there. . . . I'm not the superstitious type, don't believe in higher powers, but I hope she saw me. I wish.[1]

Fans around the world relate to these kinds of images because of the unpredictable, emotional nature of each competition. We don't know what surprises may alter the competition directly. We don't know which strategy an athlete or team might employ in their efforts to achieve victory. We don't know how athletes might act when faced with the intensity of the Olympic spotlight. Will they be motivated? Terrified? Sluggish? What we do know is that we will see thousands of well-trained, ambitious athletes hoping to realize their dreams by winning an Olympic gold medal.

The size and scope of the Olympics has changed dramatically over time, as has the composition of the athletes, creating an increasingly dynamic and thrilling mix of competitors and events. While precise figures are not known for the ancient Olympics, games held during the fifth century BC had roughly 300 male athletes from neighboring Greek city-states compete in a total of 14 events. The 1896 Olympic Games in Athens featured 43 events with 280 male athletes from 14 countries. The 1900 Olympics were held in Paris and featured more than 1,000 athletes from 28 countries. Women also competed for the first time in 1900, although their status was considered unofficial. In the 1912 Stockholm Olympics, women were officially allowed to compete in swimming events, and they began competing in all track and field events at the 1928 Olympics in Amsterdam.

From 1896 to 1924, there were no Olympics devoted to winter sports. Instead, the early Olympics of the modern era were held in the summer, and while figure skating was scheduled as part of the 1900 Summer Olympics in Paris, the event was never actually held.[2] It wasn't until the 1908 London Olympics that figure skating finally appeared. In 1924, the Winter Olympics were introduced in Chamonix, France; in fact, these games were originally called "International Sports Week 1924," partly related to objections by modern Olympics founder Baron Pierre de Coubertin. Following the success of this event, it was retro-actively renamed the first official Olympic Winter Games and included 16 medal events in seven sports and 200 athletes from seven countries.[3] By the 2010 Winter Olympics in Vancouver, Canada, the breadth and depth of the Winter Olympics encompassed 2,566 athletes from 82 nations competing for 86 medal events in 15 disciplines and seven sports. (For example, the sport of skiing comprises the disciplines of Alpine skiing, freestyle skiing, cross-country skiing, and snowboarding. Then, the discipline of Alpine skiing has several medal events: downhill, slalom, super G, giant slalom, and combined.[4])

The growth of the Winter Olympics has been remarkable, building from the success of the summer Olympics (both ancient and modern). Three primary themes help explain the growth of the Olympic Games.[5]

1. The Olympic *Brand*
2. The Olympic *Experience*
3. The Olympic *Myths and Heroes*

The Olympic Brand

Definitions of *brand* have evolved significantly in recent years, as companies and marketing have grown more sophisticated. In the best-performing companies, the concept of brand is simply *the entire organization as seen through the eyes of stakeholders.*[6]

In effect, *brand* encompasses every activity and each touchpoint across both tangible and intangible dimensions (touchpoints are discussed further in Chapter 4). Thinking of a brand in this way is useful because one is compelled to consider external points of view, beyond our individual understanding and perception of a brand. "Do others see the brand in the same way?" is a common question. A trap into which companies can fall is to believe their own PR—being so internally focused that leaders assume the market sees the company the same way. As individuals, we try to create a positive outward image. Success is typically predicated on whether such a portrayal is genuine to who we are. But when feedback suggests that we are not what we think, then we seek ways to adjust (or ignore it, perhaps at our own peril). The adjustment is inspired by a combination of external perceptions and disconnects with our own internal sense of self. The most successful organizations develop their brand reputations in much the same way, working hard to authentically reflect their best qualities so that they deliver on their promises, enhancing the company's reputation as a result.

Part of the larger Olympic Games appeal is its reputation for goodwill and also for inspiring a sense of optimism and hope. As fans, we are drawn to the stories of athletes like Matthias Steiner as they unfold, even if we had only learned of them because of the Games. The very fact that from each Olympics a new set of stories emerges about athletes who rise from obscurity to global celebrity reinforces our emotional connection to the Games. As John Furlong, who headed the Olympic Games Organizing Committee (OCOG) for the Vancouver 2010 Winter Olympics and Paralympics said,

> I think people everywhere believe that Olympic values are values to live by. I think through the Olympics people get a sense of hope that they could be better than they are. . . . Everybody's equal, there are certainly great moments where people achieve hero status but for a brief period of time—people of the world are the same.[7]

The Olympic brand as we know it today was not invented recently, nor is it merely the result of some clever marketing communications campaign. Its reputation is the result of thousands of years of traditions supported by societies passing on the heroic stories from one generation to the next, giving the Olympic brand its meaning. Over time, this meaning has shaped our appreciation for Olympic values and transformed the Olympics into a global event on an epic scale. Baron Pierre de Coubertin's vision came to fruition in 1896, but not without trepidation:

> Although the IOC's eager embrace of private enterprise, sponsorship and commercial marketing techniques to fund the games in the latter part of the twentieth century ultimately thwarted his wish to see the Olympics "purify" sport of the "commercial spirit" that he recognized was developing.[8]

> Coubertin was animated by the idea of sports as a driver of social good.

> Sport is not a luxury activity, or an activity for the idle, or even a physical compensation for cerebral work. It is, on the contrary, a possible source of inner improvement for everyone.[9]
>
> Olympism may be a school of moral nobility and purity as well as physical endurance and energy.[10]

Pierre de Coubertin's comments perfectly capture why the modern Olympics are more than just a multiday athletic event. Of course, as the modern Olympics evolved over the past 115 years, pursuing a broader social agenda became increasingly hard without accompanying resources to support such a complex, character-building undertaking. As more countries and athletes were involved, a more professional organization and management structure was required. The Olympics' brand strength and value today is supported by the activities and behaviors of six key influencers:[11]

1. Members of the Olympic movement (anybody connected to the Olympics, volunteers or otherwise, who promotes Olympic values)
2. The IOC (International Olympic Committee)
3. The OCOG (Organizing Committee of the Olympic Games) that works in association with the NOCs (National Olympic Committees)
4. The athletes
5. The broadcasters
6. The consumers

The Olympics are unique because its values of excellence, friendship, and respect are understood around the world, across countries and cultures. Futbol (called soccer in the United States) is the world's biggest and most popular sport, culminating every four years in the World Cup. Its traditions are also well known. But the Olympics still have broader appeal overall due to the variety of events and the many brand associations attached to the Games. People everywhere rally around the Olympics, from volunteers assisting with each Olympiad to kids with dreams of being an Olympian to fans cheering for their favorite athletes. The modern Olympics thrives because of the ongoing interaction among these six factors.

Richard Pound, former vice president of the IOC, describes the Olympic movement's enormous influence, from informal to formal relationships among people and groups around the world, before, during, and after every Olympiad.

There're hundreds of millions of people involved at various levels. Not everybody involved is going to turn into an Olympic athlete. Some are going to be able to play in the street, some are going to play in schools, some on city teams, some on provincial teams.[12]

His comments are not unique. They reflect a common global understanding about what the Olympics are and represent. Any organization, at its core, offers hope in various forms. In effect, it is the promise of something better that inspires people to become loyal customers. In the case of the Olympics, that sense of hope rises well above the athletic competitions themselves to a world filled with virtually unlimited potential in which differences are temporarily set aside. These values are closely associated with the Olympic brand and its history. They were not developed or manufactured by opportunistic marketers. They were and are deeply embedded within the DNA of the Olympics, distinguishing the Games from every other sport.

The Olympic Experience

Experiential marketing has received increasing academic attention since the mid-1990s, although it has been practiced far longer by leading companies such as Nike (particularly their NikeTown stores), Apple, Singapore Airlines, and leading hoteliers like Ritz-Carlton and Four Seasons. The concept is simple: Engage consumers in your brand by actively involving them with multiple programs such as physical environments, products, services, and atmospheric stimulation of the five senses to create a positive and memorable experience. When a customer has a great experience, then the organization has delivered on the promises it made. Of course, the element of surprise in sports is fundamental to our enjoyment of the experience, even if the surprise doesn't always favor our athlete or team. We lament our favorite athlete's and team's lack of success, but we continue to cheer them on while marveling (often with a combination frustration and admiration) at the opposition's performance. True sports events are unpredictable, as opposed to scripted events, such as professional wrestling. One cannot know an outcome for certain, which is a central tenet of fan attraction. The Olympics embody the sense of hope that an athlete can rise to the occasion and win, even against formidable odds. Fans are also attracted to the possibility of inevitability—the likelihood that a dominant performer will continue to dominate, much as Olympic fans continue to watch Michael Phelps. Many will watch such premier athletes in hopes that another dethrones them. The unknown outcome drives this interest.

The Olympics have been creating special experiences for decades, long before the term *experiential marketing* was ever formalized. The Winter Olympics now feature 7 sports and 86 events, versus one sport and one event for most other competitions. The Summer Olympics have 28 sports and more than 300 events. These various events are but one dimension of the Olympic Games experience. Part of the success in any sport is orchestrating the timing, including populating interludes between action with other activities, such as fan giveaways, announcements, statistics updates, and information about other events and/or teams. The Olympics are a highly choreographed entertainment event in which world-class athleticism is the principal focus, but numerous parallel story lines are occurring as well. From the opening Parade of Nations to the closing festivities in which three flags are raised— the Greek flag in the center (recognizing the historical birthplace of the Olympics), the host country flag on the left pole, and the flag of the host country for the next Olympics on the right pole—the Games evoke a celebration of the human spirit, exemplified by athletic competition and a general spirit of cooperation. They are time-honored spectacles in which we know that the athletes involved are the world's best, supported by each host country's efforts to ensure a spectacular overall event, from venues to atmosphere to service to culture.[13]

Olympic Myths and Heroes

Global sports events now take the form of recurring spectacular commercial media festivals. Consumer cultural events take place in which sports stars, and those elevated to an iconic global celebrity status, represent local and/or national communities. The celebrities serve as role models, as objects of adulation and identification, but also increasingly as exemplars of consumer lifestyles to which spectators and television viewers alike are enticed to aspire.[14]

History teaches innumerable lessons, many of which are memorable because of the actions of people who rose to the occasion. Heroes stand out because their accomplishments and achievements were exceptional and often recognized as virtually impossible to duplicate. This infuses legions of athletes and fans with the energy to pursue their own ambitions, whether it is imitating what we have seen or using the effort as a springboard to improve many aspects of our lives. As fans, we gain a feeling of added confidence after our favorite team or athlete has won. When a loss occurs, while discouraging, we also feel frustrated and search for ways to improve.

The many interrelated, unpredictable story lines among athletes and events at each Olympics are a major catalyst propelling fan interest and not the result of an IOC or corporate sponsor's script. The serendipitous nature of every Olympiad is part of the appeal and must always be at the forefront of any sponsor's interest. Readers may wonder why much of this section assertively stresses the importance of spontaneity in the context of the purity of athletic competition with respect to the Olympics, and the answer should be clear: Companies are investing in a wholly uncertain, unscripted set of athletic performances within a structured format, knowing that part of global fan interest is rooted in the utter unpredictability of each event. We watch because we want to see what will *really* happen, versus what we *think* will happen. As the narrative of the Olympics plays out over the 17 days, sponsors stand to benefit, sometimes significantly, from these serendipitous events.

The Games are an amalgam of different activities, emotions, people, and images, each playing an integral part in shaping the Olympic brand, further developing what is arguably the strongest and best-known brand in the world today. The twentieth century saw dramatic growth, with the 1936 Berlin Olympics featuring nearly 4,000 athletes, more than 300 of whom were women, competing from 37 nations in 116 events. The 1972 Munich Olympics saw the number of female athletes break 1,000, out of a total 7,100 athletes from 121 countries competing in 195 events. The 2008 Olympic Games in Beijing had 302 events in 28 sports with 10,942 athletes (4,637 women and 6,305 men).[15] The variety of sports and the diverse mix of athletes continue to make the Olympic Games the world's unique megasports event. The size of both the Summer and Winter Olympics now provides sports fans with hundreds of competitions in which a myriad of factors can affect the outcome, from weather, to sickness, to technique, to fans, to the media, to experience, and more. The Youth Olympic Games (YOG), launched in 2010 with the

Summer in Singapore (and discussed further in Chapter 4), are an extension of the Olympic brand, with many new sports designed to appeal to younger fans and athletes. Each of these variations of the Olympics shares a common theme: top athletes in pursuit of Olympic dreams, yet beholden to the sheer unpredictability of each event's outcome.

Television has been a key driver of fan interest in the Olympics over the years as well, providing access for literally billions of fans around the world. Interest is further stimulated by the athlete profiles that country-specific television networks develop to keep the attention of their home television viewing audience and, hopefully, tell compelling human interest stories. Even though the Greeks of 2,500 years ago lacked the convenience afforded by television, crowds of up to 40,000 people regularly attended the ancient Olympics Games,[16] demonstrating that sports fans are not a modern invention and that the spectacle of sport has been attractive for thousands of years. Aside from being fans of sport, part of their interest was because the ancient games were a religious festival and athletic success was considered a tribute to the gods. Rivalry with other Greek city-states was another reason for intense support and interest. An athlete's victory brought honor to his hometown and conferred heroic status on him, just as defeat brought shame, and when combined with the religious aspects of the Olympics (the ancient Greeks believed that the gods favored the victors), a powerful attraction to the thrill of competition was created.

Famous athletes have a unique appeal that often transcends reason. For example, why do many sports fans support athletes of dubious social character? Partly, the reason is that their questionable nonsport behavior is not seen as a threat to their athletic success. People support those who have accomplished significant athletic feats, even if they are not ideal role models, although our worship typically ends when it is discovered that an athlete's success was achieved by cheating. Perhaps reflecting situational values, while we might forgive marital infidelity, competitor mudsling-ing, or even violence from our favorite athletes (many societies today find the transgressions of the famous humorous and entertaining, whether the famous are film stars, rock stars, or athletes), we find it far harder to forgive sports stars who cheat in preparation for and/or during competition. Competitive malfeasance means that the victory was not achieved honestly and that the violator did not play by the rules that the other competitors—indeed, the rest of society—play by. In many Western societies, we encourage individual expression and inventiveness, as long as it does not unfairly bias the spirit of competition. We celebrate individual achievement, but only if it is attained legitimately. The socially negative consequences of cheating are not exclusive to sports.

The corporate accounting scandals of the early 2000s and the 2008 global financial crisis, triggered partly by ethically questionable lending practices, remind us that profits must be earned responsibly. When financial performances are fabricated and executives receive excessive compensation while falsely propping up their own companies, then we rightfully question the integrity of the individuals involved, the company, and even the system overall. Society rarely celebrates the achievements of those who violate the rules. Furthermore, those who transgress societal norms often face financial penalties and potential lifelong loss of face. Witness the sudden and startling fall from grace of former golfing great Tiger Woods in 2009, when his extramarital affairs were discovered. He went from being described as the greatest golfer of all time, with lucrative endorsement deals and a gold-plated reputation for athletic greatness as well as a societal role model, to ignominy. While it is premature to sentence him to a lifetime of public opprobrium (he may still beat Jack Nicklaus's record for most majors won and concurrently repair some of his reputation), there is no question that he has put a significant and probably permanent dent in his image as a role model. We want our heroes and their performances to be genuine, born of honest effort and sincere intentions. While we will forgive some character flaws, we will shun them the moment they are found to have flagrantly violated our sense of right and wrong.

Every Olympics has had its heroes from whom many fans and observers draw inspiration. Olympic heroes succeed in capturing our imagination through their athletic prowess, determination, and personality. They often represent both our individual and collective ideals, serving as our alter ego in sport and giving us a sense of what is possible. We admire their many talents and cheer for them as they compete, more loudly when they win. We feel their anguish and console ourselves in the face of their defeat, knowing (or certainly hoping) that they will return again one day to capture the victory that eluded them, while reassuring ourselves that not all is lost, despite our hero's failure, because we were fortunate witnesses to stunning performances featuring many gifted competitors.

From the ancient to the modern Olympics, athletes have been coveted by teams and rewarded for their achievements. There were fans of the ancient Greek athletes, just as there are fans of today's stars. Each Olympics attracted large numbers of people who attended to watch the competitions, see speeches and recitals, partake in religious celebrations, and, in an early indication of today's commercialism, sell food and crafts to visitors. The ancient Greeks celebrated the human body as a source of inspiration and beauty, and athletes were immortalized in art and sculpture. Additionally, a physically fit athlete saw his body as a form of intimidation over his competitors, with highly trained and sculpted muscles a sign of ability and prowess. Athletes undertook strict training and nutrition regimens under the watchful eye of trainers—practices that obviously continue today. The ancient Greeks were often soldiers, sometimes military heroes, as well as freeborn Greeks from humble backgrounds, as illustrated in Exhibit 2.1.

Exhibit 2.1   Greek Olympic Athlete

Glaucus, the son of Demylus, was a farmer. "The ploughshare one day fell out of the plough, and he fitted it into its place, using his hand as a hammer; Demylus happened to be a spectator of his son's performance, and thereupon brought him to Olympia to box. There, Glaucus, inexperienced in boxing, was wounded . . . and he was thought to be fainting from the number of his wounds. Then they say that his father called out to him, 'Son, the plough touch.' So he dealt his opponent a more violent blow which . . . brought him the victory."

Pausanias, Description of Greece, 6.10.1[17]

Their accomplishments were considered honorable and an acknowledgment of extraordinary achievement reflecting well on the city-state they represented. Pindar, one of the most respected poets in ancient Greece, wrote many odes celebrating and chronicling athletic achievements and Olympians, including this:

In athletic games the victor wins the glory his heart desires
as crown after crown is placed on his head,
when he wins with his hands or swift feet.
There is a divine presence in a judgment of human strength.
Only two things, along with prosperity, advance life's sweetest prize:

if a man has success and then gets a good name.

Don't expect to become Zeus. You have everything
if a share of these two blessings comes your way.[18]

Isthmian Odes 5.8–15

The performances of the ancient Greeks were as noteworthy for their time as any today. From pure athletic achievement to unusual training habits to lapses of common sense, the ancient Greeks exhibited many of the idiosyncratic tendencies found in the modern era, reinforcing the notion that there is no single prototypical set of qualities, aside from exceptional physical and mental toughness, as illustrated in Exhibit 2.2.

Exhibit 2.2   Selection of Famous Greek Olympic Athletes

Chionis of Sparta was a remarkable athlete, competing as a runner and jumper. As a sprinter, he ran in an event known as the *stade*, a 192-meter race, and another event called the *diaulos*, a two-lap event that equated to 384 meters. Chionis also competed in the equivalent of the long and triple jumps, where some scholars claim he jumped 23 feet and 52 feet, respectively. (The exact measurements are not known, and the claims are still openly debated today.) Chionis's athletic achievements are even more impressive due to their longevity. Both jumping marks would have earned him a gold medal in the 1896 Olympics and a place among the top eight finishers in each Olympics through the 1952 Helsinki Games, and both would be excellent marks in many university competitions around the world today. Certainly, if Olympic success was measured by duration, Chionis stands the test of time and offers a true challenge to today's athletes, whose records rarely last more than a few years. He garnered a well-deserved reputation for extraordinary athleticism, evidenced by the length of his jumps and the duration of the marks, particularly in comparison with today's athletes. At a time when top athletes were often seen as nearly immortal, Chionis of Sparta captured the essence of hero worship.[19]

Melankomas of Caria was the greatest boxer of his day, and his skills were legendary. He won in the 207th Olympic Games in 49 AD by using an unconventional style we would find inconceivable in today's brutal boxing matches. His best skill was avoiding the hits and punches of his opponents, and, even more oddly, he never took a swing in return. He believed that hurting an opponent was a sign of weakness and was not competitively sporting. Instead, he would keep moving, eventually beating his opponents because they would give up out of exhaustion, frustration, or both. He had a reputation for extraordinary physical fitness, resulting from a relentless dedication to training, including reputedly keeping his arms raised for two days straight to condition them for the rigors of his unique boxing style. He died at a young age but had succeeded in earning a reputation for his unmatched, albeit unique, boxing ability. Melankomas's style would suffer heavy criticism in today's boxing world, yet like many leading athletes, he was an innovator, and his success vaulted him to legendary status for 2,000 years, certainly not a bad legacy.[20]

Milo of Kroton won six Olympic wrestling titles in the Olympic Games of 540, 532, 528, 524, 520, and 516 BC. He was known for his enormous strength, which legend suggests he gained by lifting a calf every day. Milo also had a voracious appetite, evidenced by his rumored devouring of a bull after he carried it around the Olympic stadium. His life ended less

(Continued)

glamorously when he chanced upon wedges in a partially cut tree. While attempting to remove the wedges, his hands were caught in the tree, trapping Milo, who was subsequently eaten by wolves later that night. Athletes are sometimes stereotyped as lacking proper mental faculties, and Milo of Kroton may indeed be the first example of brawn over brain. Yet there is little question that Milo was one of the toughest and longest-lasting Olympic champions, competing successfully for 24 years. Winning one gold medal is hard enough, and doing so for six Olympiads in a row suggests that Milo was an impressive and fit competitor, embodying competitive toughness and prolonged accomplishment in the most stressful of contests that symbolize and characterize Olympic competitions to this day. His stature grew as he continued to win, serving as a beacon of athletic virtue, partly because of his longevity.[21]

Leonidas of Rhodes was the most famous of the ancient Olympic athletes. A runner, Leonidas won 12 Olympic events over four Olympics (164, 160, 156, and 152 BC). He remains one of the most decorated athletes to ever compete in the Olympics. His victories were particularly noteworthy given the challenges runners face in sustaining competitive success over many years— simply, it is quite hard to be the best in every race and every Olympics over 12 years. His physical conditioning was undoubtedly outstanding for his time and explains his winning streak. As a model for today's athletes, Leonidas of Rhodes demonstrates that true greatness is achieved when one can sustain extraordinarily high levels of performance over many years, and not just one race or one success, as admirable as one victory is.[22]

These athletes of the ancient Olympics are just a sample of the many who earned favor from their city-states, politicians, and citizens. Their athletic feats were astounding for their time and would have been credible performances in the early Olympiads of the modern era. They received riches, fame, and recognition analogous to the sponsorships, product endorsement deals, and cash bonuses received by the very best of today's athletes. Their accomplishments facilitated their fame, adding to the reputation of the Olympics as a unique event likely to produce extraordinary athletic feats. Had there been corporate sponsors in the ancient Greek world, these athletes and more would undoubtedly have been the Lionel Messi of their day because their athletic achievements were exemplary, elevating them to a higher societal status, just as we have done with top athletes today.

The modern era boasts a long list of Olympic heroes as well—athletes whose accomplishments were extraordinary even if expected. Many went on to greatness in other pursuits, from business to professional sports to broadcasting to politics, which suggests that achievement in one field can affect success in another, although we should not infer direct causation. A few are highlighted in Exhibit 2.3.

Exhibit 2.3   Selection of Famous Modern Olympic Athletes

Jesse Owens is one of the best-known icons of the modern Olympic era. Winning four gold medals in the 1936 Berlin Olympics in the 100-meter dash, 200-meter dash, broad jump, and 4 × 100 relay, he was the first American track athlete to win that many gold medals at one Olympics. His achievements were all the more impressive given the political tension of the times—the Games were held in Hitler's Nazi Germany. Hitler had hoped that the Berlin Olympics would demonstrate the superiority of Aryan people. Instead, Jesse Owens's victories had even German fans cheering him on. Owens eventually went on to a successful speaking career and also represented the United States Olympic Committee. He was awarded the Medal of Freedom in 1976, the highest honor a civilian can receive in the United States. Owens was posthumously awarded the Congressional Gold Medal in 1990. To this day, he serves as a visible symbol of the power of determination and overcoming the most daunting odds.[23]

(Continued)

Bob Mathias won the gold medal in the decathlon at the 1948 Olympics in London at age 18, the youngest winner in track and field in Olympic history at that time, and at the 1952 Olympics in Helsinki. He was an exceptionally talented athlete as suggested by the decathlon, which is a varied test of skill, strength, speed, and stamina. He also attended Stanford University, leading the football team to a 1952 Rose Bowl appearance, making him the first person to compete in both the Rose Bowl and the Olympics in the same year. He retired from Olympic competition at age 22, with nine victories in nine competitions, four U.S. championships, three world records, and two Olympic gold medals.[24] His sports achievements from age 18 to 22, coupled with his scholarly abilities at Stanford, demonstrated Mathias's ability to succeed in multiple domains. Mathias went on to serve four terms in the U.S. House of Representatives. Subsequently, he served as the director of the U.S. Olympic Training Center. Several years later, he was appointed executive director of the National Fitness Foundation. Mathias is an inspiration to those who set out to achieve success in multiple disciplines simultaneously. Mathias once famously observed,

> Years ago, in the days of the Greeks, wars were postponed to make room for the Olympic Games. In modern times, the Games have been postponed twice—to make room for wars.[25]

Jean–Claude Killy was one of the great skiers of his generation, winning three gold medals in the 1968 Olympics in the slalom, giant slalom, and downhill in Grenoble, France. His victory in the slalom came after he was apparently beaten by his rival, Karl Shranz, who had been allowed to redo his run because he said he saw someone appear on the course during his initial run, causing him to stop. While he beat Killy's time in the redo, Schranz was subsequently disqualified by a jury of appeal, awarding the victory to Killy. Killy went on to serve as copresident for the 1992 Albertville, France, Olympics and as an active member of the International Olympic Committee. He succeeded well after his athletic career ended because his personal appeal transcended his obvious athletic accomplishments.[26]

Nadia Comaneci competed for Romania in gymnastics in the 1976 Montreal Olympics at age 14, winning three gold medals, a silver medal, and a bronze medal. Perhaps more impressively, she was the first gymnast to earn a perfect score of 10, a feat she repeated seven times at the 1976 Games. Her accomplishments turned her into an overnight sensation. She then competed in the 1980 Moscow Olympics, winning two gold medals and two silver medals. Nadia escaped from Romania in 1989 shortly before the revolution that brought the collapse of the government. She eventually married American gymnast Bart Connor, and the two of them have a thriving group of gymnastics-related companies, from academies to magazines. She also is a frequent motivational speaker and was recognized as one of the 100 Most Important Women of the 20th Century by ABC News and *Ladies Home Journal*. As the first gymnast to earn perfect scores in Olympic competition, Nadia served as a riveting source of inspiration for gymnasts everywhere, who saw her performances as virtually otherworldly.[27]

Sebastian Coe won the gold medal in the 1,500 meters in both the 1980 Moscow Olympics and 1984 Los Angeles Olympics, the only male to win the 1,500 meters twice. The picture of Coe as he crossed the finish line in 1980 is one of the most famous in the history of the Olympics, showing him with his eyes wide open looking skyward, his mouth agape, and his arms outstretched in a look that combines exhilaration, determination, surprise, and relief. In 1979, prior to his first Olympic success, he set three world records in the 800 meters, 1,500 meters, and mile, establishing himself as one of the great middle-distance runners of all time. In the years 1979, 1981, 1982, and 1986, he was ranked first in the world in the 800 meters. Coe went on to be a Member of Parliament from 1992 to 1997. He was head of the successful

(Continued)

London bid committee for the 2012 Olympics and then moved into the role of chairman of the London OCOG. Coe was a hero not just to his fans in the United Kingdom, but to competitive runners everywhere for his world records, his unique Olympic success at the 1,500 meters, and his postathletic career as a successful and respected politician. He has been mentioned as a possible future president of the IOC. Coe, too, is active in charity, working with and supporting the Helen Rollason Heal Cancer Charity. Finally, he is a worldwide ambassador for Nike and also owns a chain of health clubs.[28]

The Dream Team is a name synonymous with U.S. Olympic basketball. It was the first team comprised of National Basketball Association (NBA) all-stars, and its combination of talent proved dominant in the 1992 Barcelona Olympics, winning the gold medal and each game of the Olympics by an average of 44 points. The players were a who's who of the very best at the time: The biggest names were Magic Johnson, Larry Bird, and Michael Jordan. In addition, the team included Jordan's Chicago Bulls teammate Scottie Pippin, Clyde Drexler, Patrick Ewing, David Robinson, Charles Barkley, the Utah Jazz duo of Karl Malone and John Stockton, Chris Mullin, and Christian Laettner. Their combined success accelerated the popularity of basketball around the world as fans everywhere watched their games knowing that the Dream Team was a unique collection of stars unlikely to be seen again. The Dream Team players continued to excel when they returned to the NBA, setting records, attracting legions of fans, and serving as colorful role models for the rapidly growing NBA. Since then, all of the Dream Team players have gone on to success in business, sports, and/or broadcasting.[29]

Katarina Witt won two gold medals in figure skating at the 1984 Sarajevo Olympics and the 1988 Calgary Olympics, the first skater to win back-to-back gold medals since Sonja Henie in 1932 and 1936. Following her Olympic career, she skated for the "Stars on Ice" show and started a production company called With Witt that produced the skating shows "Divas on Ice" and "Enjoy the

Stars." She won an Emmy Award for her performance in "Carmen on Ice" and was nominated for another Emmy in the production "The Ice Princess." She has her own television show, *Stars auf Eis*, in which celebrities learn to skate on her show, providing for some humorous situations for those less skilled than she (which is almost everyone). She has also endorsed a wide variety of products, including: Diet Coke, Swatch, and Mercedes-Benz.[30]

Michael Phelps is one of the greatest swimmers in Olympic history. He won six gold medals and two bronze medals at the 2004 Athens Olympics and eight gold medals at Beijing in 2008 (beating Mark Spitz's record of seven gold medals from the 1972 Munich Olympics), tying him with gymnast Aleksandr Dityatin (1980 Moscow Olympics) as the only athletes to win eight medals at a single Olympics (although Phelps has now done this twice). He has since founded the Michael Phelps Foundation, which is dedicated to healthy lifestyles and growing the popularity of swimming. He expects to compete in the 2012 Summer Olympics in London, most likely his last.[31]

As marketers, we must pay attention to the traditions and achievements of organizations with which we wish to associate if we are to meaningfully understand how our own company fits alongside them. Over the millennia, Olympic athletes have become heroes and icons, inspiring generations of fans and future athletes to work hard in pursuit of their dreams. Each succeeding generation of athletes strives for Olympic glory because they know competing in the Olympics can have a halo effect that lasts far longer than the actual athletic events themselves. The athletes have the responsibility to shoulder the weight of thousands of years of history, carrying on a tradition that has deep meaning across cultures and offering inspiration to millions of people around the world. Ultimately, the athletes are aware of this at a deeper level. And each Olympic stakeholder, from corporate sponsors to suppliers to host cities to media to fans, has the expectation that the Olympics (and, indirectly, the IOC) will uphold the formidable reputation that has been built over the millennia.

In the context of the Olympic Games, marketers would not invest their marketing dollars to build awareness if the Games did not have the rich traditions from thousands of athletes in hundreds of events all competing for the glory of not just being an Olympic champion, but associating with Olympic virtue. This reasoning is not to suggest that financial benefits ought not to be factored, because clearly businesses must make money to survive. But those companies that invest in the TOP program are spending enormous sums for an event with a 17-day duration. Those sums would not be spent if significant benefits beyond pure profit were unlikely. Part of those benefits are derived from the 2,700 years of Olympic tradition.

Questions

1. Athletes are, in effect, the producers of the Olympic product. What impact do the athletes' stories have on the Olympic product and its brand reputation? Can the product be managed better? If so, how? What would you do?

2. Is too much emphasis in society placed on the success or failure of Olympic athletes? If so, why do you think that is? Is it healthy? If you don't think too much emphasis is placed on the success or failure of athletes, then how would you recommend the Olympics improve recognition of athletes and their performances?

3. How did the Olympics develop its reputation for goodwill? What societal themes are evident in Olympic values and athletic competitions within the Games?

4. Discuss the characteristics of the Olympic brand. Which are most important to the Olympic brand reputation: values, athletes, host cities, competitions/events, sponsors, or the IOC?

5. Is the Olympic experience a legitimate differentiator for the Games, or do all sports use experience to attract fans? What makes the Olympics experience unique as compared with other sports events?

Chapter 3

The Olympic Dynamics

U p to this point, a basic historical backdrop has been introduced to explain the popularity and mystique of the Olympics for fans, athletes, and, ultimately, Olympic sponsors. With more than 2,700 years of Olympic history, the list of iconic athletes is long. Hundreds of thousands of athletes have competed, building and reinforcing the rich and varied traditions that comprise the Olympic ideal, so highlighting the very few always risks excluding other deserving performers. In the modern Olympic era, athletes have undergone a transformation from top athlete into star, a change made easier with the massive growth and popularity of twenty-first-century media and instantaneous communications. With the Olympic Games as a confirmed brand platform, the best athletes can create lifetime opportunities.

Before Olympic Success

Athletes do not have to wait until after the Olympics to gain financial success. Many do so well before an Olympic victory, gaining sponsorship support when their skills and achievements bring them to national and international attention. Qatar is alleged to have paid the Bulgarian weight-lifting federation $1 million in 1999 for eight top weight lifters. Hossein Rezazadeh, a top Iranian weightlifter, was offered $20,000 per month, an exclusive estate, and an additional bonus of $10 million if he were to change nationalities and compete for Turkey's Olympic team during the 2004 Olympic Games in Athens. He turned this generous offer down and still went on to win the gold medal, national pride outweighing financial gain.[1]

Should athletes succeed in winning a medal at the Olympic Games, their home countries often offer financial rewards. Table 3.1 provides reported data on the differing rewards paid to medal-winning athletes.

The figures in this table vary further within some countries, depending on the sport. Japan, for example, has paid, in prior Olympics, $37,750 for a gold medal in canoeing and $236,000 for a gold medal in table tennis. Russia has paid boxers and wrestlers approximately $100,000 for gold, whereas athletes in other sports receive $50,000 for winning plus an additional $50,000 if they break a world record. In Beijing, the United Kingdom paid track and field athletes £5,000 for

Table 3.1   Amounts Athletes Receive for Winning a Medal

	Gold	Silver	Bronze
United States[2]	$25,000	$15,000	$10,000
Canada[3]	$20,000	$15,000	$10,000
Russia[4]	€108,000	€61,000	€40,700
Ukraine[5]	$100,000	$70,000	$50,000
Romania[6]	$157,394	Not known	Not known
Singapore[7]	S$1 million (individuals)	S$500,000	S$250,000
	S$1.5 million (team event)	S$750,000	S$375,000
	S$2 million (team sport)	S$1 million	S$500,000
Japan[8]	$46,000	$27,000	$18,000
China[9]	€1.3 million	Not known	Not known
Australia[10]	AU$15,000	AU$7,500	AU$5,000
Lithuania[11]	$100,000	Not known	Not known
Germany[12]	€15,300	Not known	Not known
South Korea[13]	€28,000	Not known	Not known
UAE[14]	$272,480	$204,360	$136,240

gold, £4,000 for silver, and £3,000 for bronze, whereas judo competitors would have received £20,000 for gold, £10,000 for silver, and £5,000 for bronze. Gold medal winners in sailing would have received £10,000.[15] In addition to the €1.3 million gold medal winners reportedly received in China, they also were given tax-free status on any other payments, and they received a kilogram of gold. This allowed many of their gold medal winners to buy houses, invest, and have a significant amount of financial security following their success. Romania's gold medal gymnasts from the 2004 Athens Olympics each received two new cars, free apartment rent for life, and free university education.[16]

Does this harm the Olympic image of competitive purity? Conceivably, yes. But as discussed in the opening pages of this book, the ancient Greek athletes were not amateurs and were compensated for their performances. After the 1988 Olympics, the IOC decided to allow professional athletes to compete in the Olympics, so the concept of allowing only amateur athletes to compete has disappeared. Furthermore, for many countries, winning an Olympic medal is rare, and the winning athlete inspires national pride and increases recognition, even if it is for only a short period of time. There is a magnetic, captivating attraction to a medal-winning athlete that bestows a measure of glory on the country itself, just as corporate sponsorship of the games and athletes benefits companies. Many of the countries that pay medal winners substantial sums are still developing; consequently, there is a tremendous amount of national pride at stake if an athlete breaks through to win a medal and, thereby, brings added recognition to the country. Larger, developed countries like the United States pay relatively modest sums for winning medals, but athletes in the United States have the potential benefit of lucrative endorsement contracts with leading companies if their performances lead to winning Gold, Silver, or Bronze medals.

During Olympic Success

While Olympic athletes and their achievements are a source of pride celebrated by their home countries, the leap from athlete to marketable star who generates millions of dollars in financial support and a windfall for themselves and their sponsors has become most pronounced in the past 15 to 20 years. The implications are profound because athletes now have an additional motive to compete in the Olympics and, hopefully, win a gold medal—the potential for lucrative financial gain. However, winning a gold medal is a guarantee of neither long-term financial security nor professional success. Marketable success inevitably includes a backstory that reveals more of the personal sacrifice and challenge an athlete has endured to reach ambitious Olympic goals. If today's formal business sponsorships and sophisticated marketing techniques were available to the ancient Greeks, one can easily imagine Milo of Kroton (recall that he was alleged to have eaten a bull) being a spot-on spokesperson for a favorite Greek restaurant or perhaps as an example for a public service announcement about the dangers of being alone in the woods (his unfortunate demise due to being eaten by wolves). Melankomas of Caria might well have had Greek fitness clubs and aerobic trainers for sponsors if such commercial enterprises had existed.

The Olympic athletes of the modern era enjoy a wide array of support choices from sponsors, donors, product companies, and more. This is not unusual in today's sports world, where even athletes who don't win championships make substantial endorsement income. Olympic athletes are different, however, because the title Olympian carries a special stature, and gold medal winners have an even more exclusive claim to fame. Such renown does not guarantee a future filled with lifelong riches and sponsorship deals. But during their Olympic years, top athletes can certainly enjoy life at the top of their sport as a star. Having star-quality branded athletes competing in the Olympics brings additional attention to the Games in terms of both viewers and general world of mouth, or buzz. Sports fans love the stars because these top performers give them somebody to cheer for enthusiastically or to root against with equal passion. Just as with product brands, a branded athlete acts as a filter for attention, separating them from those lesser known. Of course, when those Olympic surprises occur (as discussed in Chapter 8), the competitor vaults from obscurity to star in the process.

Companies that sponsor relatively unknown athletes early in their careers can find themselves in the fortunate position of vastly increased exposure from the media if the athlete succeeds. This can put the athlete in a position of power, even if only temporarily, since their increased fame gives them added leverage to renegotiate with the companies sponsoring them to increase their earning power based on their added value. Corporate sponsors must then decide whether to continue the sponsorship and, if so, how much it is worth. These are not easy questions since the athlete's success may well be fleeting, yet dropping the sponsorship risks losing the increased interest from the public from which the company would benefit.

Exhibit 3.1   Athlete Sponsorships during Olympic Success

Michael Greis won three gold medals at the 2006 Winter Olympics in Torino in the biathlon (a sport combining cross-country skiing with rifle shooting) in the individual, mass start, and relay events. He was named German sportsman of the year. He went on to win gold in the 2007 and 2008 World Championships in the mass start and mixed-relay events, respectively. While the biathlon is not as widely covered as some other Olympic sports, his success attracted numerous corporate sponsors, including Adidas, Powerbar, Excel, DKB Bank, and Erdinger, a maker of nonalcoholic isotonic drinks.[17]

Michael Phelps is sponsored by Speedo, VISA, Omega, Powerbar, and Matsunichi. He also has appeared in TV shows and, in a nod to social responsibility, founded a youth swim program called Swim with the Stars and is deeply involved with Boys & Girls Clubs of America. In 2011, Bloomberg BusinessWeek.com's Power 100 list of the most powerful professional athletes ranked Michael #12, behind #11 LeBron James (Miami Heat) and ahead of perennial stars Kobe Bryant and Roger Federer.[18]

Shaun White has won two Olympic gold medals. As of 2011, he has agreements for more than $10 million in endorsements, including American Express, Target, Oakley, Vail Resorts, Ubisoft, Burton, BF Goodrich, and Cadbury (Stride Gum). He is considered one of the most bankable stars in all of sports, a remarkable feat given the relatively narrow fan base

(Continued)

snowboarding has, compared with more traditional sports. Bloomberg BusinessWeek.com's Power 100 list ranked Shaun #2, behind Peyton Manning (Indianapolis Colts) and ahead of #3 Tiger Woods.[19]

Lindsey Vonn won Olympic gold in Alpine skiing in Vancouver in 2010, displaying fortitude and determination in the face of a significant and painful shin injury. She has garnered more than a dozen endorsement deals, including Under Armour, Head, Oakley, Alka-Seltzer, Procter & Gamble, Rolex, and Red Bull. In 2011, Lindsey was the highest ranked women's athlete (#13 on the overall combined list), ahead of Serena Williams, on BusinessWeek.com's Power 100 list of the most powerful professional athletes.[20]

Usain Bolt won three Olympic gold medals in Beijing in the 100- and 200-meter sprints and the 4×100 relay, setting world records in each event. He has endorsement deals with many leading companies, including Puma, Gatorade, Digital, Regupol, and Hublot. Usain's deal with Puma was renewed in 2010 at a reported $5 million per year for three years, making it the most lucrative track and field endorsement in history. He was ranked as the most marketable athlete in the world in 2011 by SportsProMedia. Estimates of his 2011 net worth range as high as $32 million.[21]

A key challenge for companies is determining how long athletes will be at the peak of their abilities and success. Injury can end an athlete's career well before a long-term relationship can be fostered. So why do companies take the risk to sponsor Olympic stars and pay often substantial sums, knowing there is a very real chance they may not win gold, may get injured, or may even find themselves in ethical trouble (such as performance-enhancing drug use) before the financial investment pays off? Companies sponsor athletes for many of the same reasons they sponsor events—they hope the positive qualities of that athlete will be associated with the company. The logic suggests further that fans of an athlete may become fans of the company sponsoring the athlete. A great deal of marketing work goes into making this association happen, and it usually takes a few years. But just as an Olympics sponsorship can pay dividends over the long run, so, too, can sponsoring an individual athlete.

Post-Olympic Success

Champion athletes have the same appealing qualities that attract companies to the Olympics—prestige, achievement, honor, competition—and this halo can follow them after they retire. Once their competitive years are behind them, they can and often do go on to earn significant incomes from motivational speaking, starting their own companies, serving their countries as politicians or similar leadership roles, and as recurrent spokespersons and sport experts with each subsequent Olympic Games. Companies continue to seek out former Olympic athletes to sponsor or to get involved in their business. Nike is well-known for attracting world-class athletes into their management ranks following their careers. Of course, Nike works with the athletes during the peak of their careers, as well as on new product design, marketing campaigns, and corporate goodwill, as do many of the other leading athletic companies in the world. More than 100,000 athletes have competed in the modern Olympics, so most are not stars. But many have gone on to highly successful post-Olympic careers.

New Sports and Events

The IOC continually reinvents the Olympic Games, adapting the event to meet changing sports interests around the world. Many new sports in the Olympics gained attention through mass media and popular culture, both of which help identify and popularize new trends, including extreme sports. The mix of sports is important to the success of the Olympic program, directly affecting fan and, consequently, corporate sponsorship interest. New sports attract new fan demographics and psychographics, which, for established sponsors such as the TOP partners, may increase their awareness, their reach, and even their sales around the world. Corporate sponsors also gain potential target (or niche) audience opportunities, which can be useful for testing new products and new grassroots marketing campaigns to a smaller market. New sports offerings can also enable a company to link newer products or a different product line altogether to the expanded fan base. Along with customer growth potential comes new partnership opportunities as well, because there may be companies with expertise in attracting a niche audience that could be useful to a large corporate sponsor. The sponsor gains more direct and credible exposure with the partner's customers, and the partner gains from the corporate sponsor's larger overall customer base.

The IOC regularly seeks balance between men's and women's sports to increase the appeal around the world. Once a sport has established a base internationally, with credible athletes and championships recognized by one of the 28 recognized International Federations (IFs), a large fan base, and a history of growing performance and interest overall, it may ultimately find its way into the Olympics. According to the July 8, 2011, edition of the Olympic Charter, the IOC reviews the entire program after each Olympiad. The review includes discussion of sports to add or remove. The total number of sports cannot exceed 28 in any Summer Olympiad (seven sports in the Winter Olympics), so the addition of a sport may also constitute removal of another if the maximum has been reached. As relatively simple as the decision process sounds, the decision itself is governed by a set of IOC bylaws and involves weighing complex data and insights about the current level of success for a sport. A majority vote then approves a program change for the next Olympics.[22]

As new sports are added, the chances of sponsors reaching new audiences increases. Plus, the Olympics maintain a sense of vitality and freshness while adding to the historical traditions of attracting the very best athletes. Table 3.2 outlines the new sports added since 1984.

The 2010 Youth Olympic Games, for participants between ages 14 and 18, added a contemporary dimension to the Olympic brand, including the introduction of new sports and events, and new sports stars, targeted primarily to the youth. Modeled on the format of the regular Olympics, the YOG departs from its more familiar lineage with modifications in several of the typical Olympics sports. Since the YOG are new, changes in sports and disciplines are likely to continue in the years ahead in an effort to maximize appeal to the target youth audience

Table 3.2 New Sports 1984–2008[23]

Olympiad	New Sports Added
1984 Winter Olympics in Sarajevo	Women's 20-km race, Nordic skiing
1988 Winter Olympics in Calgary	Super giant slalom in Alpine skiing
	Nordic combined
	Curling (demonstration sport)
	Short-track speed skating (demonstration discipline)
	Freestyle skiing (demonstration discipline)
1992 Winter Olympics in Albertville	Short-track speed skating
	Freestyle skiing with moguls
1992 Sumer Olympics in Barcelona	Baseball
	Badminton
	Women's judo
1996 Summer Olympics in Atlanta	Beach volleyball
	Mountain biking
	Lightweight rowing
	Women's football
	Professionals were admitted to the cycling events
	Softball (women's-only sport)
1998 Winter Olympics in Nagano	Curling added
	Snowboard giant slalom
	Snowboard half-pipe
	Ice hockey for women
2000 Summer Olympics in Sydney	Triathlon
	Tae kwon do
	Modern pentathlon for women
	Weight lifting for women
2002 Winter Olympics in Salt Lake	Women's two-person bobsleigh added
	Men's and women's skeletons (last time was 1928)
2004 Summer Olympics in Athens	Women's wrestling
2006 Winter Olympics in Torino	Team pursuit speed skating
	Snowboard cross
2008 Summer Olympics in Beijing	Open water swimming
	Women's steeplechase
2010 Olympics in Vancouver	Ski Cross

(Continued)

Table 3.2 Continued

Olympiad	New Sports Added
2012 Summer Olympics in London	No new sports added. Rugby sevens, squash, golf, and karate were under consideration but were not approved. However, both golf and rugby sevens will appear in Rio de Janeiro in 2016.
2014 Winter Olympics in Sochi	Women's ski jumping Men's and women's ski halfpipe Mixed relay in the biathlon Team relay luge Team figure skating

Table 3.3 YOG's New Sports 2010[24]

YOG	Changes from Regular Olympic Games
2010 Singapore	Eliminated synchronized swimming and water polo Added biking disciplines in mountain bike, BMX Eliminated biking disciplines in road, track cycling Changed basketball to three-on-three format
2012 Innsbruck	Hockey added an individual skills challenge Mixed-gender ski teams in Alpine and cross-country events Mixed National Olympic Committees (NOC) teams in figure skating, speed skating, and luge

while also staying true to many of the core activities found in the traditional Summer and Winter Games. In addition to sports, the YOG is distinguished from the traditional Olympic Games by its inclusion of programs in culture and education, designed to emphasize key themes in the world today, including healthy lifestyles, uses of social media, Olympic values, skills development, and social responsibility. For the first edition in Singapore in 2010, global media coverage was not as broad or timely as the regular Olympics, so awareness of the YOG was much lower than the regular Olympics. Table 3.3 describes the main changes in sports introduced by the YOG. Otherwise, the sports found in the traditional Summer and Winter Games still occur.

Like many successful brands, the Olympic Games continues to change and innovate in an effort to stay current with global sports interests. The changes have come in many forms, from allowing professional athletes to compete to modifying the selection of sports to launching entirely new products like the Youth Olympic Games. This dynamism is important for keeping interest in the Olympic movement alive and vibrant from athletes, fans, and, of course, corporate sponsors.

Questions

1. What are the implications of paying athletes who win Olympic medals?
2. What are the risks and rewards companies face when sponsoring Olympic athletes?
3. How should companies evaluate potential endorsees?
4. How do the changes to sports in the regular Olympics affect the Games? How might the changes affect corporate sponsors?
5. Describe and assess the pros and cons of the Youth Olympic Games. What is done well? What changes would you recommend and why? What would the impact of your changes be on corporate sponsors? Athletes? International Federations? Sports?

Chapter 4

The Olympic Host Cities

T he Olympics are arguably the world's largest and most visible sports stage. With more than 4 billion people watching the Summer Games and more than 3 billion viewing the Winter Games, the Olympics clearly provide a unique opportunity for host cities and countries to increase attention and awareness, potentially burnishing their international reputations. One may understandably ask whether placing such significance and emphasis on a singular event might inflate expectations about the potential benefits arising from hosting the Olympics. The answer is less than clear. A further review of the historical legacy, from ancient Greek times, can add depth to our understanding of why the Olympics are perceived to cast a positive glow across all stakeholders, even with the uncertainties surrounding the benefits, particularly economic.

Religion, Politics, Nationalism, and Sports

The ancient Olympics were religious festivals to honor the Greek gods, particular Zeus. The Games were a cause for both celebration and conflict. The Games brought citizens from throughout Greece's many city-states to celebrate and discuss political issues of the day and military victories. Yet the ancient Olympics were also a source of internal conflict and competition. The right to host the Olympics was considered a sacred and prestigious responsibility that brought economic wealth and political power, so disagreements arose occasionally between rival city-states, including soldiers from other city-states taking control of the selected Olympics venue. The Olympic truce was created eventually to protect athletes, citizens, visitors, and dignitaries attending the games from local conflicts. If the truce was violated, then the offenders were punished, as Thucydides, a fifth-century historian, describes in this account:

> In 420 BC the Spartans engaged in a military maneuver in the territory of Elis during the Truce, using 1000 hoplites [an ancient soldier]. As a result, and according to law, the Spartans were fined 200 drachmai per hoplite, a total of 200,000 drachmai. The Spartans refused to pay the penalty, claiming that their maneuver had been completed before the Olympic Truce was officially announced. As a result, the Spartans' participation in the Olympic Games that year was prohibited.[1]

The truce has influence today with the modern belief that, irrespective of conflict, the Olympics must be held and that all sides must cease hostilities during the Games. Of course, as we know, warring nations do not stop their battles. Indeed, the opposite has occurred— World Wars I and II stopped the Olympics. But the truce is a powerful symbol and a key source of inspiration about Olympic values.

In the earliest days, the Olympics were decidedly local and were certainly not the international event with which we are familiar today, yet politics and nationalism played a central role in the ancient Olympic Games. The early Olympics were a closed affair, allowing only Greek male citizens to compete. Foreigners, women, children, and slaves were barred from participating, or even watching. However, aristocratic women were allowed to own chariot teams that could compete in the Olympics as long as they did not drive the chariot themselves. While women did not compete directly in the ancient Olympics, an alternative event for women in honor of Zeus's wife Hera was staged periodically that featured footraces.

Poets were commissioned to write special words of commemoration for the winning athletes, not unlike today's filmmakers turning Olympic success into a full-length movie about the athlete's life story. Pindar, a well-known poet from the fifth century BC, wrote the following piece in honor of Hiero's horse race triumph at the Olympic Games of 476 BC.

> Water is preeminent and gold, like fire burning in the night, outshines all possessions that magnify men's pride. But if, my soul, you yearn to celebrate great games, look no further for another star shining through the deserted ether brighter than the sun, or for a contest, mightier than Olympia where the song has taken its coronal design of glory, plaited in the minds of poets as they come, calling on Zeus' name to the rich radio hall of Hiero.[2]

Fast-forwarding to today shows that the modern Olympics have evolved into a megasports event known worldwide, a remarkable story of long-term brand development and success. Many Olympic athletes are well-known by their fellow home country citizens, and those who climb to the top of their respective sport's world rankings in the years leading up to the Olympics garner additional attention and fame beyond national boundaries. Veteran athletes grow used to the spotlight, and many become celebrity personalities, gaining reputations not just for their athletic accomplishments, but for their personal traits and even quirks as well. There is something powerful and unique about the Olympics that is unlike any other sports event. Part of it is due to scarcity. The Games are held only every two years (the Summer and Winter Games were originally held every four years in the same year, but since 1992 they have been separated by a two-year interval), and they take on the image of a special, limited-edition event. Part of it is due to their centuries-old reputation as the preeminent competition for the world's best athletes. Part of it is due to mass awareness—unlike the ancient Olympics, the modern Games are truly global in stature. Each of these is a contributing factor in the appeal of today's Olympics.

To the victors, whether that is a host city or an athlete, comes the potential for substantial pride, riches, and recognition. Even to athletes who do not win come the respect and honor of having competed against the very best in the world's most visible sports event. But the challenges presented are centuries, even millennia old: achieving success through genuine, hard work and honest effort. The pressures on today's Olympians are intense, but so were those faced by the ancient Greek athletes. However, the glare of the media spotlight and the proverbial fishbowl in which each athlete and Olympic host city lives, coupled with instant global communication, create a wholly more challenging dynamic—staying true to core principles and values, irrespective of the pressure and scrutiny that is part of living under the Olympic microscope, while also training and strategizing the best ways to best the competition ethically.

Olympic Bidding

The process to bid as a host city begins approximately nine years before the Games in question with the submission of a formal application. Following the application submission, the applicant cities are asked a series of questions designed to further understand their ability to successfully host an Olympics. An applicant city favorably reviewed at this stage becomes an official host city candidate. The IOC Evaluation Commission then asks each candidate to submit far more detailed explanations of their plans in response to questions from the commission. Each candidate city is visited by the commission for four days for an in-depth review and inspection. Candidate cities around the world put themselves through a rigorous gauntlet of planning activities that use thousands of people and countless hours as they invest millions of dollars to develop their Olympic bid. Only one city wins. In the year following each Summer and Winter Olympics, the host city for the seasonal Games seven years hence is selected. The process is heavily politicized, subjected to relentless media scrutiny, and invariably far costlier than expected, both in the bidding process and in the operating and capital budget plans for the winning city. Clearly, preparing an Olympic host city bid is not for the fainthearted. The process was not always this intimidating. The early Winter Olympic Games host cities were selected rather informally, based on having an established ski resort of some renown and the desire to boost visitor traffic. Today the effort is grand in scale and ambition, with cities envisioning a winning bid that inspires urban renewal, raises tourism numbers, fosters national pride, and portrays to the world a more updated, modern image.

Cities that wished to bid earlier in the 2000s had to pay a US$100,000 application fee, which simply gave them the right to bid. The 2012 Candidature Procedure and Questionnaire (for cities bidding to host the 2012 Summer Olympics, which were eventually won by London) was 260 pages long, complete with instructions, Olympic vocabulary usage, a detailed host city profile, and 17 themes (topics) that the bidding city had to address in its bid package. Required data ranged from environmental and meteorological reports to security plans to a business plan for the Olympic village. The replies called for not just existing city and organizing committee resources, but extensive volunteer assistance, as well as professional outside services (market research, consulting, accounting, legal) that provided expert input. From the initial pool of bids, the IOC selected a smaller group of the top candidates. To continue, those cities had to pay an additional US$500,000 for the next stage. The 2012 Games in the United States were narrowed down to two cities, New York and San Francisco, for the right to represent the United States during the final bid presentations and selection process. Both cities were required to guarantee $100 million in support of their bid and sign indemnification agreements protecting the IOC and USOC from financial losses or exposure. New York said its final bid effort cost $13 million. New York, along with London, Paris, Madrid, and Moscow, were selected as the final candidates for the July 2005 host city election, held in Singapore, where London was picked as the 2012 host city.[3]

The obstacles to success in both bidding and hosting are formidable, but the rewards are potentially significant politically, economically, socially, and technologically.

Potential Impact (The Olympic Games Effect)

The Olympic Games have a presumed beneficial impact to the host city and, by extension, nation. This potentially positive effect is typically ascribed to tourism increases and the resulting economic impact of their additional spending. Economic impact studies (EISs) are developed as part of most host city bid proposals, relying on a multiplier effect to explain the projected increases in economic activity resulting from hosting the Games. There are legitimate questions, however, surrounding the usefulness of EISs and the multiplier effect, as will be discussed.

These anticipated positive changes are sought by host nations for many reasons, but certainly Olympic prestige can serve to lift the image of a country and bring it the renewed attention of the rest of the world. Host cities and nations invest heavily in infrastructure improvements in the years leading up to the Games. While each city has growth and modernization plans as part of its strategic efforts, the Olympics are used as a catalyst to accelerate the implementation of these plans, partly because city leaders and citizens want to be part of the magical glow that surrounds Olympic Games. Investments from roads to utilities to hotels take on new urgency when a city wins the right to host the Olympics, putting in motion a dynamic economic cycle that creates jobs, rallies citizens, and focuses world attention on the host city well before the Games actually begin. The investments have grown dramatically over the decades as the Olympics have grown in prestige and importance and as global media itself grew. Tables 4.1 and 4.2 summarize the growth of both the Summer and Winter Olympics since the modern era began in 1896.

The Olympic Games are an exceptional event for cities and for corporate sponsors as well. No other sports event catalyzes as diverse a range of related development projects as the Olympics. From local urban renewal projects to global marketing campaigns, the Olympics provide an energy boost for host cities that is often sustained for years after the Games. As the Olympics have grown in size, scope, and popularity, so, too, have the costs to host cities. For corporate sponsors, an important factor to consider is the underlying strength of the sports entity being sponsored. Despite the many known complexities that come with hosting an Olympics, there is little doubt that each Olympiad is a massive undertaking unto its own, not unlike the launch of a new company, the opening of a new market, or the completion of a major public works project. But the complexity implies a certain amount of experienced sophistication: The Olympics are not unprofessional, hackneyed events, so there is some comfort for sponsors in knowing that the money they are investing is part of a respected event with unrivaled

Table 4.1 Summer Olympics[4]

Year	City	Number of Athletes	Number of Nations	Number of Events
1896	Athens	241	14	43
1900	Paris	997	24	95
1904	St. Louis	651	12	91
1906*	Athens	847	20	74
1908	London	2,008	22	110
1912	Stockholm	2,407	28	102
1916	Not held (war)			
1920	Antwerp	2,626	29	154
1924	Paris	3,089	44	126
1928	Amsterdam	2,883	46	109
1932	Los Angeles	1,332	37	117
1936	Berlin	3,963	49	129
1940	Not held (war)			
1944	Not held (war)			
1948	London	4,104	59	136
1952	Helsinki	4,955	69	149
1956	Melbourne	3,314	72	145
1960	Rome	5,338	83	150
1964	Tokyo	5,151	93	163
1968	Mexico City	5,516	112	172
1972	Munich	7,134	121	195
1976	Montreal	6,084	92	198
1980	Moscow	5,179	80	203
1984	Los Angeles	6,829	140	221
1988	Seoul	8,391	159	237
1992	Barcelona	9,356	169	257
1996	Atlanta	10,318	197	271
2000	Sydney	10,651	199	300
2004	Athens	10,625	201	301
2008	Beijing	10,942	204	302
2012	London**	10,500	204	302

*The 1906 games were called the Intercalated Games, designed as international Olympic contests to be held in between the quadrennial Olympic Games. The Intercalated Games were to be permanently housed in Athens. They were dropped after 1906 because the two-year time frame from regular Olympics was considered too tight, among other reasons.
**Estimate.

Table 4.2 Winter Olympics[5]

Year	City	Number of Athletes	Number of Nations	Number of Events
1924	Chamonix	258	16	16
1928	St. Moritz	464	25	14
1932	Lake Placid	252	17	14
1936	Garmisch-Partenkirchen	646	28	17
1940	Not held (war)			
1944	Not held (war)			
1948	St. Moritz	669	28	22
1952	Oslo	694	30	22
1956	Cortina d'Ampezzo	821	32	24
1960	Squaw Valley	665	30	27
1964	Innsbruck	1,091	36	34
1968	Grenoble	1,158	37	35
1972	Sapporo	1,006	35	35
1976	Innsbruck	1,123	37	37
1980	Lake Placid	1,072	37	38
1984	Sarajevo	1,272	49	39
1988	Calgary	1,423	57	46
1992	Albertville	1,801	64	57
1994	Lillehammer	1,737	67	61
1998	Nagano	2,176	72	68
2002	Salt Lake City	2,399	77	78
2006	Torino	2,508	80	84
2010	Vancouver	2,566	82	86
2014*	Sochi	TBD	TBD	98

*Estimate.

historic traditions, international recognition and respect, and a powerful, uplifting message that unites nations.

New York City Deputy Mayor Dan Doctoroff offered this observation in 2004 as Athens was finalizing its preparations for that summer's Olympic Games and as New York was preparing its bid to host the 2012 Olympics (a bid won by London in 2005):

> The Olympic Games are unique in a city's life. I think when you do look back on the Athens experience five, 10 or 20 years from now, the single greatest benefit of the Olympic Games will

be that they acted as a catalyst for the achievement of truly historic changes in the city. Those changes would not have occurred anywhere near the timeframe that they did if it had not been for the Olympics.[6]

The decision to invest in the Olympics Games requires planners to evaluate the costs, risks, and benefits. Each of these evaluation areas imposes structured thinking onto the planning process and helps decision makers debate and assess the big picture rationale and understand the information they will need to effectively tackle the details required for proper planning and implementation.

Costs

There are three primary categories of costs for which each host city must prepare prior to the opening of the Olympics:

1. **Venues**

    Each Olympics is a complicated undertaking, similar to building a small city, but without the luxury of time. Facilities include all athletic and competition venues; the Olympic Village where athletes, coaches, and related staff are housed; and purpose-built commercial establishments for participants, visitors, and fans.

2. **Infrastructure**

    The Olympics significantly impact the demand for infrastructure since tens of thousands of athletes and visitors descend upon the host city for the Games. New roads, expanded utility networks and related power grid expansion, improvement of existing city facilities, technological upgrades, local hospital and health care facility expansion and/or improvements, additional hotel and meetings space, environmental improvements, and new or expanded rail and light rail tracks and related stations are among many infrastructure-related areas to be addressed by host cities.

3. **Organizational**

    The IOC, NOC, OCOG, and host city groups each invest in organizations that ultimately support, run, and promote the

Olympics. The organizational activities include security, community volunteers, events management (athletic and nonathletic), safety and health care, transportation services, and travel, leisure, and tourism.

These three categories are essential for host city bidders to discuss in detail and, upon winning, vital to the eventual success of the Olympics. We know that, as an event, the Olympic Games attract a huge viewing audience and generate substantial media coverage. We also know that for 17 days every two years (through a Winter and Summer Games cycle), the Olympics capture the attention of the world. This combination of media coverage and intense global interest provides an attractive platform for TOP sponsors to associate themselves with the Olympic ideals, launch new products, and further develop their global reputations. But why do host cities invest in the Olympic Games, and what benefits do sponsors derive from a given city's commitment and investment? The answers are not always clear and are sometimes even contradictory.

Economic Impact

Economic impact studies (EISs) are often conducted prior to or in conjunction with a formal megasports project proposal. The analyses are designed to assess how the project is likely to affect the local economy. However, the evidence suggests that both the composition and accuracy of such studies are open to question. The methodology used and the researcher's biases can lead to subjectivity, reducing the credibility of the study's findings. As mentioned earlier in this chapter, EISs use multipliers to project the amount of increased economic activity that will occur as a result of the sports events. The presumption EISs make is that the sports event will generate additional spending above and beyond regular economic activity and that the income generated from this spending will be respent within the same economic region in subsequent periods. The multiplier is always greater than 1, meaning that a $1 in income gen-erated will lead to value creation well above that initial dollar (1.5, 2.0, or even 3.0 times the initial additional income created). Logically, the implication is that a sports event's economic contribution to the local community will be positive and substantial and lead to a permanent, increased level of economic performance. There are a number of problems economists have with multipliers in EISs, and most would agree that EISs tend to be used more for marketing and PR purposes to help sell a project (who would want to promote an EIS that shows a negative economic impact?) than for a rigorous analysis of the impact the sports event would have on true economic factors (e.g., income, employment).[7] Furthermore, the studies may be prone to researcher bias. Since sports entities often hire and use consultants to develop their project plans, the consultants tend to favor positive factors in their analysis, paying scant attention to issues like dislocation, traffic problems, logistics, and inconveniences to the local community. The EISs become tools for showering the sports event with positive, emotional attributes that distract decision makers from the many other changes the event creates in the lives of citizens in the host community.

Therefore, using such studies to argue that hosting an Olympics will lead to an increase and permanent improvement in economic performance for the host city and nation is problematic. While the 1984 Los Angeles Olympic Games resulted in a sizable profit of more than $200 million, suggesting the potential for large-scale sports events to generate positive benefits,[8] translating those short-term gains into lasting economic growth has proven elusive, or at least very hard to conclusively prove. In fact, the economic track record of host cities generating profits from the Olympics since 1984 has been uneven. Thus, even with the Olympics' well-known global reputation as a powerful and symbolic event that generates significant global attention, the 17 days of the Games are simply not capable of sustaining higher, ongoing, post-Games economic activity.

For example, Table 4.3 shows that the GDP growth rate in the host country improves in the Olympic year over the preceding year in 7 of the past 12 Olympic Games (highlighted in bold), yet is not sustained in the year thereafter.

A different study of 12 prior host cities, conducted by the Bank of China, compared the average GDP growth rate in each city in the eight years after they hosted the Olympics to the eight years before. Nine of the host cities witnessed a decline.[9]

Despite the economic uncertainties surrounding host city investments, the ability of the Olympic Games to foster goodwill and associate Olympic values with the host nation holds continued allure for cities and countries around the world. In effect, the Olympics are seen as a

Table 4.3 Host City GDP Growth Rates before/after Olympics[10]

Session	Host Country	Host City	Year of the Event	One Year before the Event	Current Year of the Event	One Year after the Event
18	Japan	Tokyo	1964	8.8	11.2	5.7
19	Mexico	Mexico City	1968	5.9	9.4	3.4
20	Germany	Munich	1972	3.0	4.3	4.8
21	Canada	Montreal	1976	1.8	5.2	3.4
22	USSR	Moscow	1980	1.7	4.3	2.0
23	USA	Los Angeles	1984	4.5	7.2	4.1
24	South Korea	Seoul	1988	11.1	10.6	6.7
25	Spain	Barcelona	1992	2.5	0.9	−1.0
26	USA	Atlanta	1996	2.5	3.7	4.5
27	Australia	Sydney	2000	3.8	2.1	3.9
28	Greece	Athens	2004	4.8	4.7	3.7
29	China	Beijing	2008	11.3	9.0	8.7

proverbial shot in the arm, or even a collective psychic benefit, that can revive and even enhance a country's reputation and brand image. This enthusiasm for using the Olympics to help brand nations has increased in recent decades, partly due to the success of the 1984 Games. However, even the evidence of nation brand success is circumstantial at best, driven by overly optimistic and simplistic assumptions, with actual results at variance with expectations. The reasons are understandable. While consistently branding a single company is challenging enough in its own right, countries are inherently more complicated and unpredictable, with cultures and subcultures, business practice variations, and perception biases all making the effort to convey a singular message and image problematic.[11] Therefore, depending on a single event to brand a nation, even an event with the global impact of the Olympics, is likely to be an overly optimistic, unrealistic expectation.

Risks and Benefits of Hosting an Olympic Games

On an event-specific basis, the Olympics are a challenging financial proposition for host cities and nations due to the absolute and somewhat unpredictable costs involved. But from a broader macroeconomic perspective, the rationale for hosting the Olympics begins to reveal itself and, conceivably, provides a more defensible logic that can help cities in their planning. PEST is a useful framework for strategic and marketing planning because it can help managers assess the larger business environment in which they do and/or will compete by focusing their thinking around each of the framework's four components. These are external environment indicators, often outside the direct control of the organization:

- **P**olitical factors relate to tax, employment, political stability, trade, and environmental issues.
- **E**conomic factors include business and market growth rates, interest rates, inflation, and exchange rates.
- **S**ociocultural factors describe demographics (such as population growth trends, age, and income/wealth), psychographics (such as attitudes and behaviors), and social fabric variables (interactions between and among people within society).

- **T**echnological factors refer to the technological development of the society (R&D investments, technological change and adoption rates, automation).

To complete the context analysis, firm-specific indicators are needed. Organizational and brand factors are therefore added to the framework:

- **O**rganizational factors encompass planning, logistic, and manpower needs.
- **B**rand describes the overall reputation of the organization, whether it is a host city or a corporate sponsor.

Understanding that many resources will be useful and usable after the Olympics and not only expended during the Games with no longer-term potential should compel managers to think carefully about the kinds of marketing activities that can have the maximum Olympics-related life span. Marketing investments are not just about spending money to gain awareness and exposure, but also involve programs that demonstrate an understanding of the broader context in which the Olympics are being held, so that companies can offer customers memorable products and services that can exist long after the Games have ended.

Political

The questions that potential host cities and corporate sponsors need to address include:

1. What is the political climate like for hosting the Olympics? Stable or unstable?
2. What do the changes resulting from the Olympics mean to the local culture?
3. What are the government's trade policies, and how will they affect the Olympic Games decision?
4. Does the government's tax policy affect the Olympic investment decision?
5. Is the government's economic policy direct, indirect, or hands-off?

Each of these questions invites more in-depth research and fact-finding to assess the attractiveness of supporting the Olympic Games. We will now look at the risks and rewards.

Risks The challenging news is that the Olympics also serve as an attractive platform for those with political agendas. This has occurred in numerous Olympiads, but among those that stand out are the 1936 Olympics in Berlin, which Hitler hoped would demonstrate the superiority of the Aryan race (fortunately, he was wrong); the horrific 1972 Olympics in Munich, when a radical Palestinian group called Black September took an Israeli Olympic team hostage and, in an ensuing rescue attempt, the kidnappers and hostages were all killed; the 1980 Olympics in Moscow and the 1984 Olympics in Los Angeles, when the United States and the Soviet Union took turns boycotting the other's Olympics; and the Tibetan protesters who, prior to the 2008 Olympics in Beijing, rioted in Lhasa, disrupted part of the Olympic Torch Relay, and threatened additional protests surrounding the Beijing Olympics. While the Chinese government insisted the Tibet protests were an internal matter and that politics should not play a part in the Olympics, the Games have been a key political tool in presenting China to the world in a new light. The Tibet protests risked undermining this moment of public glory.

The impact for sponsors is potentially devastating if a political message overwhelms the Olympics, since the sponsors' marketing exposure takes on a less visible role compared with the political agenda. The potential problem for sponsors is more than just financial; it is image-related, and since each of the TOP partners is a well-known global brand, part of their reputation is attached to their actions. Protestors can apply pressure on corporate sponsors, either by directly confronting their commercial support of the Olympics (and implying the sponsors are supporting a tainted Olympic Games) or by appealing directly to consumers around the world to boycott any sponsors who do not adequately explain their position on the particular political issue in question. Beijing faced criticism over its policies in Darfur and Tibet, in particular, and more generally its human rights record. Steven Spielberg, the renowned Hollywood director, withdrew as artistic advisor in protest of China's involvement in Sudan. The 2008 Beijing Olympic Torch Relay sponsors were Coca-Cola, Samsung, and Lenovo. Each was a TOP partner (Lenovo did not continue as a TOP partner after the 2008 Olympics), and they paid an additional $15 million each to sponsor the relay.[12] With significant protests in Paris, London, and San Francisco, the three sponsors came under increased media scrutiny, with questions raised as to why they should continue to support an event that was being increasingly subjected to violence by protesters.

Modern Olympic history has also seen the use of boycotts to make a political point. At the Olympics in Melbourne in 1956, two boycotts occurred: Egypt, Iraq, and Lebanon protested the Israeli invasion of Suez; and the Netherlands, Spain, and Switzerland protested the Soviet invasion of Hungary. In Montreal in 1976, 22 African nations boycotted because of New Zealand's national rugby team tour of South Africa earlier in the year. Led by the United States, more than 40 nations boycotted the 1980 Moscow Olympics in protest of the Soviet invasion of Afghanistan. The Soviet Union led a 14-nation boycott of the 1984 Olympics in Los Angeles to retaliate against the 1980 U.S. boycott. The 1988 Olympics in Seoul were boycotted by North Korea because they were still technically at war with South Korea. North Korea was joined by Cuba, Ethiopia, and Nicaragua.[13] Each of these political issues raises important challenges that cities and companies must confront to properly evaluate the attractiveness of the Olympic Games.

Benefits

Host Cities/Nations   For the host city and nation, the Olympics offer the potential for fostering goodwill and generating a more positive feeling from the rest of the world. The challenge, of course, is being cognizant of and prepared for the almost inevitable political agendas and protests that will occur. China and the Beijing Organizing Committee expended considerable effort trumpeting their efforts to produce the best Olympics ever. To be fair, every host city and nation conducts similar promotion of their Olympics' efforts. A successful Olympic Games burnishes the host city's image, demonstrating indirectly the ability of the government to deliver on a complex, highly visible event. The spotlight is intense because it begins shining years before the actual games and for months or even years afterward. As the outside world pays increasing attention to the host city in the run-up to the Olympics, government leaders choreograph the timing of planning updates, venue construction progress, infrastructure improvements, and economic impact to gain favor from the scrutinizing eye of public opinion. This is also when and where challenges arise, since protest groups heighten their own attention on the host city and nation, hoping to receive media attention for their cause while seeking to cast shadows of doubt across the feel-good reports emanating from the NOC and local organizing committee. The host city and nation also seek to inspire their own citizens with regular updates about progress and how the Olympics benefit them and improve their lives. An important objective is rekindling a sense of national pride and patriotism. Properly conceived and executed, a marketing campaign can and should be based on actual activities and the positive contributions these make. A perhaps subtler by-product of hosting the Olympics is that any resulting success can serve to validate government policies. However, the public is generally quite capable of separating the Olympic Games from the politics of the host city and nation, recognizing that having an Olympics is not the same as approving that country's way of life or political institutions.

China again provides a good example. Global concerns over air pollution caused the government to initiate a selection of domestic reforms designed to make the capital environmentally greener during the Olympics. Some factories and government workshops were relocated outside the city to reduce industrial emissions. Automobiles were regulated, with access to the capital allowed on select days of the week based on license plate numbers. There was another incentive as well: IOC President Jacques Rogge had mentioned shifting the competition schedule around to minimize athlete exposure to bad pollution days. A scheduling change during the Olympics would draw unwanted negative attention to Beijing, something that government leaders wanted to avoid.[14] Ideally, the Chinese government's efforts to control pollution during the Games would have been a perfect time to solidify a more permanent and sustained policy of environmental responsibility. This did not occur, however, as the reforms might have slowed China's longer-term economic growth, which is a key priority for government leaders.

Sponsors Companies have an opportunity to affect the political process by being a constructive part of the planning for the Olympics, thereby helping to overcome the perception that their interest is purely commercial. Also, companies can contribute by providing needed jobs in the host city, a politically pleasing activity that can create goodwill for the company with the public while also fostering more positive relations with the local government, which could help the future development of their business interests.

Economic

Host Cities/Nations   The Olympic Games can be an important catalyst spurring economic activity for the host city, nation, and associated sponsors. At the same time, the costs each host city incurs have generally been rising over time. The reasons for the growing expense are low initial budget estimates based on costs at the time of the bid, additional infrastructure challenges and/or needs that arise postbid, and general price inflation associated with the expectations of luxurious spending for any Olympiad.

Host city costs are only part of the Olympics story. While the Summer Olympics have a longer legacy and larger numbers (sports, events, viewers, athletes, revenues), the Winter Olympics have grown rapidly and are just as complex an undertaking. The motivations for host cities include recognition that the Olympics are far more than a sports event.

> The public expects us to deliver more than just a sporting event. Vancouver residents expect the Olympics to be a catalyst for improving their lives.
>
> —*David Cobb, senior vice president of*
> *marketing and communications,*
> *Vancouver Olympic Committee (VANOC)*[15]

Questions to consider:

1. How will the added economic activity affect interest rates?
2. Is inflation a factor (and how will it affect market costs)?
3. How will the Olympics affect the lives of the local community (jobs, prices, business growth, goods availability) in both the short-term and long-term?

Risks   The IOC risks revenue challenges if the Games and related expectations are not properly managed. The members of the IOC and OCOGs must aspire to the highest levels of integrity and credibility for the sponsors, indeed all stakeholders, to have confidence in each specific Olympiad. Scandals, such as the bribery cases associated with Sydney and Salt Lake City Olympiads (and allegedly with the 1996 Atlanta Olympics as well), can be potentially devastating since such activities make sponsors nervous, consumer groups upset, and the general public disenchanted. The net effect can be a severe reduction in economic impact from sponsorship and tourism loss should either of those groups believe that the Olympics have lost their integrity. Another risk is overcommercialization, as happened at the 1996 Summer Olympics in Atlanta, offending those who believe the Olympics stand for something far more significant than commercial gain. Any faltering risks losing key funding sources, including sponsors, without which the Olympics would not be able to support the wide range of nations that compete in every Olympiad. Many teams do not have sufficient individual funding sources and depend on the IOC and its marketing-related revenues to provide the necessary support for their athletes.

Benefits The increased activity from consumer and tourism, in particular, benefits local governments by boosting the host city's income and sale tax bases. Yet consumer-led revenue gains are only part of the potential economic benefits. Investments and construction related to infrastructure improvements can yield important, decades-long benefits by upgrading and developing more efficient utilities, improved transportation, and enhanced local services, thereby creating a more favorable perception of the host city by the world community. Capital contributions on behalf of infrastructure improvements come from each host city's organization committee, trickled down from the IOC's total revenue pool. Additional external funding, such as cash contributions or in-kind trade, spurs the local economy as well. Favorable perceptions, while intangible, can have lasting or, certainly, longer-term economic impact. Salt Lake City enjoyed significant economic increases as a direct result of the boom in tourism, conventions, and hotel occupancy increases. One hotel executive in Salt Lake City commented:

> You simply cannot buy this type of publicity. The potential implications to the hotel industry are tremendous.[16]

The Olympics can have a projective impact as well. The 2010 Vancouver Winter Olympics generated substantial new interest in the city. Tourism Vancouver commissioned research that showed

24% of consumers were more likely to visit Vancouver, 43% of the travel trade was more likely to book business for Vancouver, and 25% of meeting planners were more likely to book meetings in Vancouver.[17]

The combination of these different tangible and intangible factors can lead to positive, long-term benefits, as the Barcelona description in Exhibit 4.1 illustrates.

Exhibit 4.1   Barcelona's Transformation[18]

The 1992 Olympic Games in Barcelona generated significant, positive economic benefits to the city, which was literally transformed as a result of the Olympic Games. As shown in Table 4.4, "Investment Related to the Olympic Games," the total Olympic investment supporting Barcelona was nearly $7 billion, second only to the 1964 Tokyo Olympics, up to that time. Urban planning projects invested in revitalizing an old industrial area that had been built in the nineteenth century near the old city. This area was transformed into the Olympic Village, but it was designed with the intent to blend with the existing city so that following the Olympics, it would become a fully integrated neighborhood, with the living spaces rented and sold on the open market, and not an unusable white elephant. Railroad tracks that originally lay between the city and the beaches were rerouted elsewhere, including underground, so that there was access to the beaches and the seafront. The beaches were also cleaned up. A new underground highway was built to divert traffic away from key city areas, connected to a ring road that moved traffic around the perimeter of the city. Old parks were renovated and new ones built. Private investment saw hotel space expand by 38 percent, enabling the potential of more than 420,000 tourist visits during the Olympics.

Barcelona has since witnessed enormous growth in several economic and business sectors. The city has become one of the top destinations in Europe. The number of overnight hotel stays nearly tripled, from 3.8 million in 1990 to more than 10 million in 2004. The average length of stay increased from 2.8 days to 3.6 from 1990 to 2004. The number of tourists visiting grew from 1.7 million in 1990 to more than 4.5 million in 2004 as well. Infrastructure improvements that had been planned but not enacted previously were accelerated as a result of the inspiration provided by winning the Olympic bid.

Construction for the 1992 Barcelona Olympic Games[19]

Investment between 1986 and 1993	Accumulated Values in 1995 Pesetas	Distribution
Road Construction	343,804,115,503	35.9%
Construction at Poble Nou Olympic Area	212,681,960,000	22.2%
Construction at other Olympic areas of Barcelona	117,973,650,000	12.3%
Montjuic Area	58,138,020,000	6.1%
Vall d'Hebron Area	29,425,740,000	3.1%
Diagonal Area	30,409,980,000	3.2%
Other Projects in Barcelona	182,449,775,658	19.1%
New Western urban axis	7,979,130,000	0.8%
New Eastern urban axis	16,395,880,000	1.7%
Remodelation of Old Port	6,890,000,000	0.7%
Service Galleries	10,071,325,658	1.1%
Other Facilities (cultural, sanitary, and other)	21,229,090,000	2.2%
Improvement of hotel facilities	119,884,350,000	12.5%
Projects in Olympic subsites	69,916,420,000	7.3%
Other Sports Infrastructure projects	29,804,169,039	3.1%
Total	956,630,090,000	100%

Budgets from candidate city proposals are regularly understated. While it is widely recognized that hosting an Olympics is expensive, it is surprising how little actual information exists about the precise, final costs to host cities, beyond general budget figures. In fact, historical tracking of host city costs has proven to be problematic, as no official post–Games reports of actual costs have been consistently produced. A 1993 research report by Frank Zarnowski in the *International Journal of Olympic History* uncovered select financial data from several of the Olympiads for the first 100 years of the modern era, but the numbers were inconsistent, partly owing to poor budget tracking and record keeping. Sometimes the costs reflected operating budgets only, other historical cost estimates reflected infrastructure improvements, and some were a combination of both. In a few Olympic years, no firm numbers exist at all. According to records, the cost of the 1896 Athens Olympics was estimated at $448,000, and the 1936 Olympics in Berlin cost roughly $30 million (in 1936 dollars).[20]

Tables 4.4 and 4.5 present different cost analyses of select Olympiads. Table 4.4 highlights finances for select Summer Olympics between Tokyo in 1964 and Barcelona in 1992, and Table 4.5 offers approximate costs from 1992 forward. The variation is as much due to the unique characteristics of each city as it is a reflection of cost escalation. Ferran Brunet, author of the report behind Table 4.4, explained the distinction between expenditures and investments in the analysis:

> There was considerable sensitivity to questions of "cost," the necessary resources, and the "financing" of a social event of the importance of the Olympic Games. Thus a distinction was made between organizational expenditures (those for aspects not usable after the event) and project expenditures (those usable after the event). The expenditures in projects were made up of direct investments (or those necessary for the development of the event), indirect investments, and investments induced by the event. The organizational expenditures were the true "cost," the net cost, of which nothing would remain afterwards. For this reason effort was made to minimize them. On the other hand, the investment expenditures are the legacy, what remains. For this reason the effort was made to maximize them.[21]

Brunet's analysis provides an insightful look at the range of costs (expenditures and investments) of host cities. Since host city financials related to the Olympics are challenging to consistently gather, evaluating across multiple Olympiads is not an apples to apples comparison and

Table 4.4 Investment Related to the Olympic Games[22]

Millions of US$	Tokyo 1964		Montreal 1976		LA 1984		Seoul 1988		Barcelona 1992	
	M of $	%	M of $	%	M of $	%	M of $	%	M of $	%
Direct expenditures	452,116	2.7%	2,824,863	89.0%	522,436	100.0%	1,467,853	46.5%	2,460,855	26.2%
Operational expenditures	169,510	1.0%	411,857	13.0%	450,394	86.2%	478,204	15.2%	1,361,156	14.5%
Direct investments	282,605	1.7%	2,413,006	76.0%	72,042	13.8%	989,649	31.4%	1,099,699	11.7%
Indirect expenditures	6,373,372	97.3%	350,012	11.1%			1,687,423	53.5%	6,915,274	73.8%
Indirect investments										
Total Olympic investments	6,825,488	100.0%	3,174,875	100.0%	522,486	100.0%	3,155,276	100.0%	9,376,129	100.0%

Table 4.5   General Cost of Recent Olympic Games[23]

City (Year)	Bid Cost	Games Cost	Results
Barcelona (1992)	$10 million	$10.7 billion	*See endnotes*
Albertville (1992)	$2–3 million	$2 billion	($57 million)
Lillehammer (1994)	$3 million	$1.6 billion	$40–50 million profit
Atlanta (1996)	$7 million	$1.7 billion	Broke even
Nagano (1998)	$11 million	$14 billion	$28 million profit for OC ($11 billion debt to various gov't. groups)
Sydney (2000)*	$12.6 million	$6 billion	Broke even
Salt Lake (2002)	$7.0 million	$1.3 billion	$100 million profit

*The dollar values for Sydney are approximations, based on the 2011 U.S. dollar–Australian dollar exchange rate.

requires interpretation to adjust for the unique characteristics of each host city and their corresponding preparation needs. Note that the Games cost estimate in Table 4.5 for Barcelona is $10.7 billion, comprised of the $9.3 billion infrastructure (or "legacy" investments, as Brunet described them) plus $1.4 billion for the Olympic Organizing Committee.

As described later in this chapter, economic impact studies tend to convey a more attractive (and sometimes unrealistic) financial picture, so it is incumbent on Games planners to spend a fair amount of time and analytical rigor on understanding the costs and investments as accurately as possible.

The concern about Olympic development cost overruns factored heavily in the Los Angeles Olympic Organizing Committee's planning for the 1984 Games.[24] The 1984 Olympics in Los Angeles were a bargain compared with Tokyo, due partly to the leadership of Peter Ueberroth, organizer of the Los Angeles Olympics, who was determined to keep costs down and turn a profit while also maintaining the prestige and integrity of the Olympic idea. His efforts led to a nearly $223 million profit, the first Olympics to turn a profit in years. A key to the success of the Los Angeles Olympics was the widespread use of existing facilities—very few new venues were constructed, saving a significant amount of money.[25] The 1988 Winter Olympics in Calgary cost an estimated $636 million, with the government contributing nearly half of this amount. The 1992 Olympics in Barcelona total costs factored in both the new venues and numerous civic and publics works projects that were timed to be completed when the Olympics began.[26] The 1996 Olympics in Atlanta were funded without government support, with capital supplied primarily from sponsorships, ticket sales, and advertising. There was an unfortunate side effect, however. Many observers thought the games were overly commercial, detracting from the prestige of the Olympic movement and from the performance of the athletes.[27] It was the first Olympics in which the IOC president at that time, Juan Antonio Samaranch, did not say that it was the best Olympics ever, which was his usual closing remark. Instead, he said, "Well done, Atlanta. The games were most exceptional."[28] The slight was intentional, signaling disapproval of the overly commercial nature of those Olympics, coupled with the significant safety, transportation, and logistics issues that plagued the Games. The 1998 Nagano Olympics were quite expensive due to a myriad of related infrastructure projects (including a new bullet train line and new highways).[29] The operating budget for the 2000 Sydney Olympics was committed to infrastructure improvements like roads and railways.[30] The wide variation is explained partially by projects attributed directly to Olympics-specific preparation versus projects that were planned or underway anyway that were included in final budget tallies. The 2006 Torino Olympics cost between $3 billion and $3.6 billion.[31] As we will see later in this chapter, the costs for the 2008 Beijing Summer Olympics, the 2010 Vancouver Winter Olympics, and even the new 2010 Youth Olympic Games in Singapore, while varying significantly due to their respective locations, political ambitions, and logistical needs, continued the trend toward final costs exceeding bid budgets.

Sponsors   The economic benefits for sponsors, when planned thoroughly and implemented successfully, can be significant. The sponsorship planning process must include recognition of the likely or assumed commitment to the sponsorship in terms of time, resource investment, and purpose. Knowing the potential length of time will enable the marketing team to plan a sequence of brand-building initiatives that evolve as the company's familiarity with the sponsorship grows and the results come in. Common benefits arising from clear objectives include: market share goals, revenue and profit targets, awareness levels, brand value increases, reputation improvements, and product units sold increases. Visa began its Olympics sponsorship in the 1980s with the basic objective of increasing awareness. With more than 25 years of subsequent Olympic sponsorship experience, the company's objectives changed and grew more sophisticated, designed around a multiplatform marketing approach designed to accomplish specific objectives. However, sponsors that push for overly ambitious objectives and pour substantial additional resources into a concentrated effort for a short period of time are unlikely to produce results consistent with expectations. A long-term strategic, evolutionary point of view, particularly with a globally known brand like the Olympics, offers a better path for achieving substantial benefits.

Sociocultural

Host Cities/Nations The Olympics are a force for good in a broader, more global context. The impact at the local level is important as well:

1. Will the Olympics and our involvement with them foster positive goodwill among the local populace?
2. How will the social dynamic of the community be impacted?
3. What are the attitudes about foreign visitors, organizations, products, and media?
4. Does religion play a role locally, and, if so, how might it be impacted and also affect the success of the Olympic investment?
5. Are citizens actively engaged in the local community?
6. Is there support for environmental causes, and, if so, how would that affect the Olympics?
7. Are leisure and sports actively supported?

Risks The selling of the Olympics to the local population requires sensitivity to the realities of daily life. Disruptions related to construction and added international attention risk alienating the local population and thereby undermining their support. Demands placed on local citizens to put their best foot forward may ring hollow, prompting people to withdraw and eye the Olympics with suspicion, dreading the future influx of visitors whom locals may see as outsiders who can change the local way of life. Host city officials must find ways to overcome these risks through thoughtful, ongoing community meetings and communications.

Benefits Citizens of host cities and nations have historically rallied to support their country's efforts to host the Olympic Games. There are exceptions, such as when citizens of Denver, Colorado, rejected their city's winning bid to host the 1976 Winter Olympics for cost and environmental reasons. Innsbruck stepped in and agreed to host the Games despite having done so in 1964 as well. But for Innsbruck's citizens, the gesture reflected positively on them, generating international goodwill. But cities and countries bid for the Olympics because the overarching benefits and positive image gains serve to boost civic and national pride, helping people believe that they are special.

Sponsors A properly conceived and executed corporate sponsorship campaign can improve the company's standing as a responsible corporate citizen, an issue that is increasingly important today as consumers seek more evidence that the companies whose products they buy offer something more that benefits society.

Technological

Host Cities/Nations The Olympics are a complex logistical and technical event requiring state-of-the-art infrastructure to facilitate proper delivery of essential services (electricity, for example) and support the demands of sophisticated reporting and communications needs. To consider:

1. Are technological services accessible?
2. Are communications channels scalable and open?
3. Are newer technologies, including mobile and digital media, widely supported?
4. Are there any barriers to the use of technology?

Risks and Benefits The risks here are less obvious but can relate to the general quality and state of the host city's technical infrastructure for supporting the increased demands that will be placed on a wide range of the utilities and services on which local citizens survive. Host city officials often use the Olympics as a catalyst for investing in wide-ranging infrastructure upgrades, including technology. For the 2008 Olympics in Beijing, government officials were intent on changing world perceptions favorably toward a view that China's rapid economic growth had fostered technological advancement and a new climate of innovation. The government spent more than $150 million on 450 technology projects specifically linked to the Beijing Olympics. In addition, companies provided another $200 million in support of these projects to ensure that the Olympics were seen as the most technologically advanced.

Sponsors   Corporate sponsors stand to benefit by investing in technology infrastructure (new products, communication sites, local hardware and utility usage and investment, computer-related services) that not only supports the local government's upgrading and modernization of their services but also provides invaluable relationships and partnerships with companies that could provide sustained long-term business opportunities.

Organizational

Host cities and companies will face increased demand for their myriad products and services, not just during the Olympic contests, but well before and after the Games. As demand changes, organizations must be prepared to deliver on expectations.

1. Do we have the competence, skills, and expertise to plan and implement our Olympic efforts? If not, what do we need to succeed, and are those resources easily available and affordable?
2. Who are the key groups we need to coordinate with?
3. Are the various organizations (Olympics, city, companies, other) in approximate alignment on what needs to be done and how to do it?
4. Are there philosophical differences that must be addressed?
5. Do we share a common vision for what needs to be done?
6. Is our infrastructure capable of handling the increased demand?

Risks   Given the inherent complexity of running an Olympic Games, the chance of organizational snafus is reasonably high. Most organizational problems are localized, however, to manageable issues that are rarely the subject of media reports. But there is also the chance of something larger and more significant that can disrupt the Olympics. In 1964 at the Innsbruck Winter Olympics, weather conditions had not yielded a consistent snowpack. The Austrian Army was recruited to carve 20,000 ice bricks out of neighboring mountains and then carry them to the competition area for building the bobsled and luge track. The army also carried 40,000 cubic meters of additional snow from other mountains to the main ski areas. Both of these jobs were monumental organizational challenges that were vital to ensuring a successful Olympics. The 1980 Winter Olympics in Lake Placid faced different organizational challenges that detracted greatly from the enjoyment of the Games for the fans: Poorly coordinated ticketing and transportation left spectators stranded, unable to get to the games. Consequently, many of the events were not full. The 1992 Winter Olympics in Albertville were held in eight different towns, reducing the shared feeling that the Olympics tries to instill in fans and athletes. Only 18 of the 57 total events were actually held in Albertville, creating an organizational and logistical challenge for the organizers, participants, and fans.

The 1996 Summer Olympics in Atlanta illustrated organizational challenges related to security when a bomb exploded in Centennial Olympic Park, resulting in the death of two people and injury to 11 others. Atlanta also confronted organizational challenges with respect to sponsorship transparency when it was learned that the City of Atlanta had negotiated separate commercial sponsorship deals with companies other than the IOC's TOP partners, giving these non–TOP companies direct visibility in and around the Olympic venues, although the practice was against Olympic rules (not to mention generally accepted rules of good faith). This was also a surprise to the Atlanta Organizing Committee, which, along with the IOC, succeeded in stopping some of the unsanctioned activity. The challenge from this situation is not just about the overbearing commercial activity, but that the companies approved by the City of Atlanta were effectively making money at an event with which they had no prior role or involvement nor supported, whereas one of the reasons the TOP partners are so important to every Olympics is because their financial support funds a substantial portion of the Games; they work for years to create a sizable infrastructure that supports both their own efforts and that of the host city on behalf of the Olympics. Organizational issues related to planning and construction have dogged past Olympic Games, notably Montreal, where the construction overrun and organizational issues related to the lack of separation between the operating and infrastructure efforts. The 2004 Olympics in Athens, while successful, were under pressure in the months and days leading up to the opening ceremony, as many of the venues had not been completed. By the time the Olympics started, the venues had been successfully completed, although some design shortcuts were taken to ensure the facilities would be ready in time.

While it is normal for organizations to plan for the worst, the added pressure from being in the spotlight as host of the world's biggest sports event creates its own unique challenges that can affect the spirit and enthusiasm of the Games. In October 2007, tickets for the 2008 Beijing Olympics went on sale via web and telephone. In two hours, 9,000 tickets were sold, but then the system collapsed due to the high demand levels. Consumer response was rapid and overwhelming, with the ticketing web site receiving 8 million hits and the telephone lines bombarded with 2 million calls seeking help. The problem was eventually resolved.

Beyond these event-specific illustrations are organizational issues related to the Olympics construction and preparation activities that precede the Games for several years. Organizational challenges here include disruption to the host city's way of life from infrastructure construction that alters traffic patterns, changes commute times, and affects the real and perceived quality of life for permanent citizens. The host city organizing committee, in coordination with city officials, must work together from the very beginning (even at the earliest bid stage before a city even wins) and subsequently throughout. This effort should include regular, public, transparent town hall meetings with citizens that enable them to air their views on the impact Olympic-related projects are having on their lives. Concurrently, the various Olympic bodies must actively communicate the benefits and upcoming activities related to the preparation for the Games. As each of these issues highlight, organizational coordination and response is a critical component of Olympic planning. For sponsors, organizational planning is vital as well, since their own operating, infrastructure, and marketing activities require similarly complex organizational plans.[32]

Benefits The 1984 Los Angeles Olympics are still considered among the best-run, best-coordinated Games in history. From transportation to venue access to ticketing to customer service, the Los Angeles Olympics garnered widespread praise and recognition, serving as a model for future Olympiads. The positive results were contrary to the pre-Olympics concerns about Los Angeles's notorious traffic problems, air pollution, lack of new facilities, and unappealing urban sprawl undermining financial, fan, and athlete success. The Los Angeles Games faced further complications from the Soviet-led 14-nation boycott and the resulting negative PR, and from the Montreal Olympics of eight years before that fomented global concern about the long-term financial viability of the Olympic movement overall. The Los Angeles Olympic Committee, under the leadership of Peter Ueberroth, actively coordinated with volunteers, city and state officials and agencies, the IOC, corporate sponsors, and myriad support organizations (from utilities to health care to transportation services) to orchestrate a relatively smooth Olympic Games. The net result had both quantitative and qualitative contributions. Quantitatively, the Los Angeles Olympics were a financial success, producing a $220 million profit. Qualitatively, Los Angeles received favorable media coverage, and the vast army of volunteers and paid service providers reinvigorated an Olympic movement that had diminished somewhat following the Montreal financial problems and the more recent Olympic boycotts.[33]

Brand

Reputation is everything. Whether personally or professionally, in business or nonprofit or government work, one's reputation determines success because expectations are developed based on this. Among the questions to consider are:

1. What is our current reputation?
2. How will the Olympics affect our reputation?
3. What are the ingredients/touchpoints that create the brand reputation we have?
4. Are we well-known, or do we have to educate the market about who we are?

5. Are the people who represent us good brand ambassadors?
6. How will the Olympics affect our brand value?

Risks   The Olympics are a chance to present a fresh face to the world. The reputation of every host city and country is at stake. When problems occur, the impact can be immediate (the scandals in Sydney and Salt Lake City demonstrate this), although lasting damage is rare. But sometimes host cities can suffer undue harm to their reputation, even if the Games succeed (and most Olympics are perceived as successful when seen through the lens of goodwill and international cooperation), such as the aftermath of Montreal's cost overruns and budget mismanagement. Other times, attempts to use the Games as a vehicle to demonstrate Olympic values are viewed as contradictory to actual behavior and therefore used for political purposes (such as the boycotts from Moscow in 1980 and Los Angeles in 1984). With *brand* an all-encompassing term describing any entity as seen through the eyes of its stakeholders, there are numerous touchpoints that can directly and indirectly affect a host city's brand. (Touchpoints include any item or service with which people are in contact; with the Olympics, they include athletes, fans, sponsors, sponsor customers, sponsor and Olympics employees, and value chain participants.) Managing these different touchpoints is a fundamental challenge for Olympic Organizing Committees as well as marketers.

Benefits   The Olympics offer the opportunity for organizations to thoroughly map their various touchpoints and determine how they affect people's perceptions. Planners who wish to improve the image of their brand will focus on two key areas: tangible and intangible assets.

Tangible   Tangible assets are physical elements of your brand: products, packaging, advertising, store or destination environments (furniture, fixtures, physical design, layout), people. Relevance and resonance are two key evaluative dimensions of tangible asset success. Asking "are the products *relevant* to my customer's needs, and, if so, do they *resonate* with them?" is vital to creating a positive brand experience. A product's relevance simply means that the offering fills a specific need, and its resonance means that the specific product fits a person's unique situation, connecting with potential customers emotionally and with their lifestyle.

Intangible Intangibles are services, atmosphere, ambience, and attitude. Intangibles can inspire or inflame a person's passions and emotions. Taking great care of customers, while a known sentiment today, is not consistently understood or practiced around the world. This is complicated by cultural differences that can create conflict with the overall perception of the brand. But understanding intangibles and, more important, how to imbue everyone in the organization with delivering extraordinarily well on intangibles presents every organization with a unique and significant opportunity.

The combination of tangible and intangible touchpoints contributes directly toward creating a customer's overall experience. For companies and host cities, having a clear, detailed understanding of their tangible and intangible touchpoints can help identify strengths as well as areas that require additional attention. A useful tool is a brand touchpoints map, as shown in Figure 4.1, which is a visual device created by an organization's managers to aid in seeing the complete range of factors that can affect market perceptions. By drawing these as a chart, managers can also identify those factors whose impact may affect another area of the organization and, consequently, shape consumer beliefs and experiences. The end result is a snapshot of the many individual contributors to an organization's overall brand reputation and the connections among different factors.

Figure 4.1 is a simplified illustration of a touchpoint map. Touchpoints take numerous forms, both tangible and intangible, and trigger a range of associations, from emotional to social to intellectual, that help anchor the brand in the audience's mind. Every circle represents a touchpoint that does or can affect market perception and interaction with the brand. The central circle is the primary branded entity, whether that is a nation, city, company, or even a product. Major thematic groups in the organization represent key themes associated with the brand (some organizations may well have more than the six generic ones shown here). The themes include, but are not limited to, familiar business labels (services, products, organization, brands, experiences, marketing communications, people) to softer labels (empathy, sensitivity, personality, and even humor). The smaller circles are touchpoints and subtouchpoints associated with that theme area. Your diagram does not have to follow this specific design scheme. In fact, the key to using this tool successfully is *not* to copy the diagram in this book. Instead, each

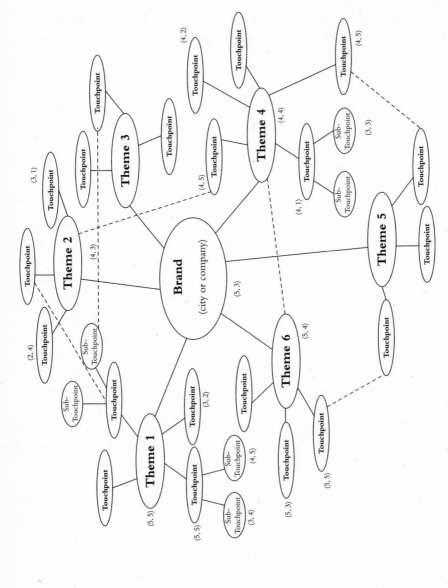

Figure 4.1 Brand Touchpoints Map[34]

organization must create a touchpoints map based on its unique circumstances, offerings, and expertise, developing categories and subcategories accordingly. This tool can be particularly useful when a scoring or evaluation system is applied to each touchpoint. For example, using a 1 to 5 scale (1 = poor, 5 = excellent), organization management can ask two questions about each touchpoint and then score each touchpoint on two dimensions:

1. Brand perspective: How important is this touchpoint to the brand?
2. Audience perspective: Ability of the brand to deliver successfully on this touchpoint?

Once each touchpoint is scored, as illustrated in Figure 4.1, the task then is to identify opportunities and problem areas. An easy way to start is to review each pair of extreme scores and investigate why the discrepancy exists and if fixing it is important to improving the entity's brand value and reputation. As illustrated, let's assume that a Game's organizing committee researches potential audience responses to its Olympic planning and that theme 4 corresponds to proposed Olympic venues. The smaller circle labeled *touchpoint* (representing a specific venue) receives a score of (4, 1) for the two questions (brand, audience). This tells the organizing committee that this venue is very important to the target audience but that the committee's proposal is not viewed positively. This creates a gap that the committee must then determine whether to address, with the attendant repercussions on the Games' brand openly discussed. Working through this exercise requires more than one person with a sheet of paper and a pencil basing it on one opinion. It requires a group of organization leaders openly debating the touchpoints, identifying as many as possible well before organizing them into themes, and, ultimately, creating the diagram and subsequent evaluation. The result will be a more thorough understanding of the organization and its touchpoints, identifying where the organization needs to invest the most resources to ensure it is ready for success on the Olympic stage. While the example here pertains to an Olympic organizing committee, the touchpoints exercise is equally useful for Games' sponsors as well.

Now that we have a clearer understanding of the uses of the PEST framework, let's turn to an overview of host cities and their respective Olympics, from Beijing in 2008 to Sochi in 2014.

2008 Beijing Summer Olympics

Positioning

With its motto "One World. One Dream," the 2008 Olympic Games in Beijing were the culmination of a multiyear effort by China that began before the Games were officially awarded to Beijing in 2001. In fact, Beijing had bid on hosting the 2000 Olympic Games that were eventually awarded to Sydney. In winning the right to host the 2008 Olympics, Chinese leaders had a global stage on which they could introduce modern China to the world.

As with any host city effort, the objectives were ambitious and the planning was complex. The Games had the potential to reshape international perceptions of China and also provide a catalyst for boosting internal pride. China's economy had been growing 8 to 10 percent per year since the 1970s, a growth rate that allows the economy to double roughly every seven years. By the 2000s, China's economy was becoming a serious contender for one of the biggest in the world, on pace to be number two behind the United States by 2010. At the same time, China's self-confidence was growing as well, politically, socially, and economically. The timing of 2008 Olympics turned out to be quite good (arguably even better than had they won the right to host the 2000 Olympics), with a rapidly growing middle class, new wealth being created overall, a seemingly ceaseless appetite from many leading companies in the West to build business opportunities in China, increased tourism, and the continued rapid improvement and success of Chinese athletes competing in international competitions in many sports. The 2008 Olympics had the potential not just to be a launch party, but to serve as confirmation of China's role as a serious and ambitious country economically, culturally, politically, and athletically.

Economic Impact

China envisioned that the 2008 Beijing Olympic Games would have as positive an impact for them as the 1964 Tokyo Olympics had for Japan, in effect showing the world that a new China had emerged and was fully capable of producing the most impressive Olympics ever. A great deal of national pride was at stake. The 2008 Olympics had an operating budget of just under $2.4 billion,[35] but like many other host cities before it, Beijing used the Olympics as a catalyst to complete critical infra-structure projects, with the total budget closer to $40 billion.[36] The range and scale of Beijing's preparation for the 2008 Olympics was impressive. Thirty-one major venues were built from scratch or completely renovated, in addition to a complete overhaul of the city's major transportation systems, including new roads, new airport terminal buildings and runways, new subway lines, and new public buses and taxi services. The new competition venues included the 91,000-seat Beijing National Stadium in which the opening and closing ceremonies and most of the track and field and football events took place, the new Beijing National Aquatics Centre for the water sports events, the Beijing National Indoor Stadium for artistic gymnastics, and the Shunyi Olympic Rowing-Canoeing Park for the rowing- and kayaking-related competitions. Beijing's ambitious plans for the Olympic facilities dwarfed those of prior host cities, with most of the venues designed to be iconic. The Beijing National Stadium was called the "bird's nest" stadium for its novel external steel architecture that resembled the complex interweaving of a bird's nest. The Beijing National Aquatics Centre was called the "water cube" because the exterior looked more like enormous water bubbles than a conventional building. Overall, the Chinese put a great deal of effort into the 2008 Olympics to showcase a positive side to China and accentuate its rapid emergence onto the world stage.

Table 4.6 shows the budget for the Beijing Olympics:

Table 4.6 Projected Costs Beijing Olympics[37]

Expenditure	US$ m	Running Totals US$ m	Percentage (%)
Capital investment			
Sports facilities	102		6.28
Olympic village	40		2.46
MPC and IBC	45		2.77
MV	3		0.18
Total of capital investment		**190**	

(*Continued*)

Table 4.6 Continued

Expenditure	US$ m	Running Totals US$ m	Percentage (%)
Operations expenditures			
Sports events	275		16.92
Olympic village	65		4.00
MPC and IBC	360		22.15
MV	10		0.62
Ceremonies and programs	100		6.15
Medical services	30		1.85
Catering	51		3.14
Transport	70		4.31
Security	50		3.08
Paralympics games	82		5.05
Advertising and promotion	60		3.69
Administration	125		7.69
Pre-Olympic events and coordination	40		2.46
Other	101		6.22
Total of operations expenditure		**1,419**	
Surplus	16		0.98
Total		**1,625**	

Revised budget figures indicated that the official costs exceeded $2 billion. These figures reflect sports venues and related facilities, understating the actual investments significantly.

Given the uncertainty regarding the validity of economic impact statistics, performance claims should be viewed with some skepticism. Nevertheless, various authorities have provided interesting assessments of the economic impact from the Beijing Olympics. The Beijing Organizing Committee for Olympic Games (BOCOG) reported that it had made nearly 21 billion yuan (US$3.3 billion based on exchange rates in 2011) in revenue by March 2009. This was 800 million yuan higher than originally anticipated, based on sharing the sponsorship, merchandising, and ticket sales proceeds with the IOC. A 2008 journal article provided the data summarizing the projected revenues, shown in Table 4.7.

The same report also claimed that the total amount invested for venue upgrades, personnel, living accommodations, and broadcast media

Table 4.7 Projected Revenues, Beijing Olympics[38]

Revenues	US$ m	%
Television rights	709	43.63
TOP sponsorship	130	8.00
Local sponsorship	130	8.00
Licensing	50	3.08
Official suppliers	20	1.23
Olympic coins program	8	0.49
Philately	12	0.74
Lotteries	180	11.08
Ticket sales	140	8.62
Donations	20	1.23
Disposal of assets	80	4.92
Subsidies	100	6.15
Others	46	2.83

centers was 19.43 billion yuan (US$3 billion), and another 19.49 billion yuan was invested in building 102 new venues and related facilities.[39]

The accuracy of the revenue claims is hard to verify. But the cost estimates are substantially lower than those reported by other researchers and media, where the estimates were closer to 257 billion yuan (US$40 billion). Even if the revenue claims are accurate, it would take years for the original investment to break even under either scenario, let alone show a positive financial return. This is not unusual when measuring the economic impact of the Olympics by comparing projections to actual results. One study of the 1994 Winter Olympics in Lillehammer indicated that the projections prior to the event were optimistic, with actual economic contribution smaller and relatively short-lived.[40] Despite the inconsistencies in numbers, as referenced earlier, in June 2009 China's National Audit Office reported that the Beijing Olympics had a profit of $146.4 million.[41]

Lenovo's Winning Olympic Torch Design

One of the interesting story lines of the 2008 Olympics surrounded the IOC's process for awarding the rights to design the Olympic torch. More than 300 companies bid for the rights, with the winner being Lenovo, the only nondesign firm in the process. Lenovo's win, which is discussed further in the Lenovo case study later in this book, yielded many benefits. For Lenovo, being awarded the rights to design the Olympic torch boosted morale at a time when the company was attempting to emerge onto the global stage after its acquisition of IBM's PC division in 2005. Concerns about Lenovo's competence at sustaining IBM's innovation record and quality were among the questions raised in the market at large. Additionally, the challenges of merging several cultures (IBM's, Legend's, Dell's, the Chinese, the U.S.) meant that internal focus was partly on creating a common operating culture that would allow the company to leverage its combination of assets. During acquisition-related transitions, employees were understandably anxious about their jobs, the direction of the company, and how they fit the newer corporate environment. Winning the right to design the Olympic torch injected renewed confidence, revitalizing pride in the company's ability to innovate and providing an added dimension for promoting the company's capabilities. The final design, known as the Cloud of Promise, evoked several themes important to Chinese identity: the invention of paper, use of the auspicious color red, and a design motif reminiscent of both the five Olympic rings and Chinese characters. As not only a TOP sponsor but also a torch relay sponsor, Lenovo would enjoy the fame of being identified as the company that designed the torch, certainly a buzz-worthy attribute, even if the benefit was limited to the time period of the torch relay itself and the 17 days of the Olympic Games.

Torch Relay

The 2008 Olympic Torch Relay began in Ancient Olympia, Greece, on March 24, 2008, and was the longest in Olympic history, with the original planned route covering 137,000 kilometers (85,000 miles) and six continents. The Olympic Torch Relay is, of course, a highly visible and symbolic activity for promoting the Olympics and its sponsors. It is also important for protesters as well. Despite official concerted efforts to quell and even prevent protests in the months leading up to the start of the 2008 Torch Relay, rights groups still emerged, with the protesters using the Olympics to draw attention to human rights issues in China, specifically Tibet, in the hope that media coverage surrounding the

Torch Relay would expand to include reports on the protests, which might then rally global public opinion and thereby inspire support from other governments to pressure China to change its position on Tibet. The IOC and the Chinese were concerned how these protests might affect both public support for the 17 days of the Games themselves and, more immediately the torch relay's three worldwide sponsors: Samsung, Lenovo, and Coca-Cola, especially since the protesters were encouraging these sponsors to boycott the relay to demonstrate their support of the Tibet issue. The protesters also hoped to convince many other Olympic sponsors to withdraw their support and boycott the Games. In the early stages of the torch relay, the protests quickly became a dominant media story in many Western countries, particularly France, the United Kingdom, and, to a lesser extent, the United States. Chinese Olympic authorities countered with publicity designed to position the protesters as fringe members of society, unworthy of the Olympic spirit, and even dangerous.

The costs resulting from the protests were not just related to damaging publicity but also included the added logistics and support expense of protecting the torch along the entire length of the relay route (which was modified and shortened after the start of the relay due to protests, particularly in France, the United Kingdom, and the United States). The security presence was intense, with Chinese bodyguards and security personnel from each country participating in the relay, and the related security expense was significant. In London alone, security cost nearly £750,000, with 1,963 police officers confronting more than 4,000 protesters who were trying to extinguish the Olympic flame. Despite the added security, the protests were not without incident, as more than three dozen arrests were made in London.[42]

Over 3,000 motorcycle police protected the torch as it made its way through Paris. Despite the large security presence, the protesters were relentless, forcing security to extinguish the Olympic flame on a few occasions and, ultimately, compelling Chinese officials to cancel the last third of the planned relay.[43]

Even though the intent of the added security was to protect the torch and the Olympic image, it also served to inhibit public access to the torch, reducing the symbolic and emotional connection that helps make the Olympics special.[44]

In other parts of the world, from Latin America to Australia and the Far East, supporters of the Olympic Torch Relay countered the efforts of protesters. Nevertheless, Jacques Rogge was deeply concerned about the potential for the protests to grow more violent and detract from the goodwill the torch relay and the Olympic Games represent. He even warned athletes not to wear, carry, or display the Tibetan flag as it might lead to their expulsion from the Olympics.

"The torch relay has been targeted," Mr. Rogge said in a speech to the Association of National Olympic Committees, according to Reuters. "The I.O.C. has expressed serious concerns and calls for rapid, peaceful resolution in Tibet. Violence for whatever reason is not compatible with the values of the torch relay and the Olympic Games," he said. "Some people have played with the idea of boycotts. As I speak today, there is no momentum for a general boycott."[45]

Then a massive 7.9 earthquake struck Sichuan on May 12, 2008, and the torch relay's sponsors, as well as other Olympics sponsors, made direct and serious efforts to meaningfully contribute to aiding the victims of the quake. Alice Li, VP of Olympic Marketing in Beijing for Lenovo said,

"We have to take a long-term view," with the hope that Lenovo's support for both the victims of the Sichuan earthquake and the Torch Relay "will convey to consumers that we want to be good corporate citizens."[46]

Lenovo also supported a blood drive and donated computers to schools that were damaged. Other Olympic sponsors provided support as well. Coca-Cola donated nearly 6 million bottles of water and more than $3 million; McDonald's contributed 17,000 meals to those affected by the earthquake, including victims, volunteers, supporters, aid workers, and fire and police officers. General Electric donated more than $2 million of products, including water purifiers and portable ventilators, as well as granted the Red Cross Society of China $1.45 million.[47]

Ultimately, the torch relay continued and was completed on August 8, 2008, with Li Ning, the world-famous Chinese gymnast, carrying it on the final leg that had him ascending the iconic bird's nest stadium on a wire and "running on air" around the rim of the stadium above the thousands of fans and in front of over a billion television viewers around the world. For sponsors, despite the controversy, their commitment to supporting the torch relay throughout gave them significant international exposure. The opening ceremonies alone garnered a viewing audience of more than 1 billion people,[48] and the Olympics overall had a viewing audience estimated at 4.3 billion. While not all of the coverage was positive, their collective support for the victims of the tragic Sichuan earthquake helped soften some of the negative perceptions arising from their support of the torch relay, despite the visible and vocal protests and calls for them to boycott. Furthermore, their support of the Sichuan relief efforts gave them a more human and less overtly commercial image, reinforcing the stated Olympic values of excellence, friendship, and respect.[49]

Media

The 2008 Beijing Olympic Games were an important event not just for the Olympic Movement, but for China and, by extension, China's reputation with the international community. The Games were part of a much larger effort of social, political, economic, and infrastructure progress that had been occurring since Deng Xiaoping's initial reform efforts began in the late 1970s. As a single entity, the Games were not capable of transforming China. But they provided a visible, anchoring focal point for communicating many of the changes that had occurred in China over the preceding 30 years. Arguably, the sizable investments, a reported $40 billion overall, would not have been made, or certainly not made at the accelerated pace that the Games appear to have inspired. While Olympics-specific investments (versus the larger infrastructure investments in new roads, rail transport, the new airport, and upgraded utilities) are hard to consistently verify, it appears that approximately $14 billion was spent on the various venues and associated facilities. Along with the larger infrastructure projects, the Beijing Olympics were the most expensive in history to that time. Was the investment worth it? The answer is complicated, particularly when one considers the various objectives.

The Beijing Olympics were an important event for stoking national pride and support. While surveys show that perceptions of China from

Australia, Canada, Europe, and the United States did not demonstrably shift as a result of the Olympics, the response inside China was quite different and more positively impactful by comparison. Gains in national self-confidence are an important by-product and benefit of hosting the Olympics, even if the perceptions from the rest of the world are less sanguine.[50]

A 2008 Pew survey revealed that 86 percent of Chinese "were satisfied with the way things were going in their country in 2008"[51] and 92 percent were confident about China's growing impact in global affairs, particularly politics.[52] The growth of national pride was concurrent with the ongoing economic success China had enjoyed, and the Beijing Olympics provided a convenient platform for focusing popular opinion within the country.

The IOC's broadcast partners, which are broadcasters around the world tailoring footage to their respective markets, showed a total of 61,700 hours of Olympics coverage. These figures made Beijing the most watched sports event in history at that time. Technological advances allowed the Beijing Olympics to be the first Olympic Games with full digital coverage. The official IOC web site attracted 105 million unique visitors (a *unique visitor* is a measure that counts each visitor only once in the period of time being reported) who watched 21 million video views.

Each Olympics offers a potentially attractive platform for sponsors to associate themselves with the Olympic values and reputation. While the financial picture of the Beijing Olympics was mixed, and the tumult surrounding the torch relay protests and broader human rights issues for the Olympics overall fostered concern and discomfort about China's human rights practices, the key point is that the allure of the Olympics, coupled with the global interest in China (whether positive or negative), offered sponsors one of the most interesting Olympic platforms in years.

2010 Vancouver Winter Olympics

Positioning

"With Glowing Hearts" was the principal theme of the 2010 Winter Olympics in Vancouver. A key subtheme was sustainability. From the design of venues, to minimizing the environmental footprint and impact of the Games, to social responsibility, VANOC (Vancouver Organizing Committee) set forth an ambitious agenda to host one of the most responsible Olympic Games ever.

Economic Impact

The 2010 Vancouver Olympics illustrate the changes that occurred in budgeting and planning as the Games moved from the bid proposal stage to actual construction and execution. The bid budget was US$845 million when the Canadian dollar was worth approximately 62 cents to the U.S. dollar (based on 2002 exchange rates).[53] Table 4.8 shows the VANOC budget that was used in its presentation during the Olympic bidding process.

Table 4.8 Vancouver Organizing Committee 2010 Budget[54]

Revenues	C$ (000)[a]	Expenditures	C$ (000)
IOC Television Contribution	539,681	**Operating Expenditures**	
TOP Sponsorship	131,411	Sports Venues	163,111
Local Sponsorship	396,000	Olympic Village	20,644
Official Suppliers	57,999	Print Media Center	10,250
Ticket Sales	218,223	International Broadcast Center	121,509
Licensing Merchandise	35,001	Games Workforce	231,272
Coin Program	2,771	Technology	208,687
Lotteries	–	Telecommunications	62,022
Donations	20,000	Internet	5,600
Disposal of Assets	10.001	Ceremonies and Culture	84.646
National Government Subsidy	20,000	Medical Services	5,031
Regional Government Subsidy	20,000	Catering	16,568
Other	56,251	Transport	86,789
Total	**1,507,336**	Security	2,199

(*Continued*)

Table 4.8 Continued

Revenues	C$ (000)ᵃ	Expenditures	C$ (000)
		Paralympic Games	42,695
		Advertising and Promotion	51,813
		Administration	123,760
		Pre-Olympic Event and Coordination	18,123
		Other	100,035
		Royalty Payments to IOC	152,580
		Total	**1,507,336**
		Direct Capital Expendituresᵇ	
		Roads and Railways	599,850
		Sports Venues	361,843
		Olympic Village	265,300
		Media Center	14,999
		Other	67,658
		Total	**1,309,649**

ᵃ All amounts shown in 2002 Canadian dollars.
ᵇ Direct capital expenditures were paid entirely by the federal government, the provincial government, or non-VANOC private entities. Direct capital expenditures did not include the Canada Line transit system. Additional noncapital government costs such as security were not included in the VANOC official budget.

In 2007, the budget was updated as in Table 4.9.

Table 4.9 Revised Vancouver Olympic 2010 Budget[55]

Revenue Source	$CAD
IOC Contribution	579,700,000
Less cost of providing Olympic Broadcast Services (OBS)	−178,000,000
IOC Net Contribution	**401,700,000**
Other IOC Revenue	35,000,000
IOC International Sponsorship Program	201,404,000
Domestic Sponsorship	760,000,000
Ticketing	231,854,000

Revenue Source	$CAD
Licensing & Merchandising	46,026,000
Paralympic Revenue	40,000,000
Other IOC Revenue	110,502,000
Total Revenue	**1,826,269,000**
Less: Marketing Rights Royalties	*−197,217,000*
Net Revenue	**1,629,269,000**
Expenditure by Division	**$CAD**
Revenue, Marketing, and Communications	126,427,000
Sport, Paralympic Games, and Venue Management	186,436,000
Service Operations and Ceremonies	548,130,000
Technology and Systems	398,500,000
Human Resources, Sustainability, and International Client Services	153,144,000
Finance and Legal and CEO Office	116,632,000
Project Contingency—Games Operations	100,000,000
Total Expenditures	**1,629,269,000**

In 2007, new construction and developments were given as shown in Table 4.10.

Table 4.10 Venue Construction Costs, Vancouver Olympics[56]

Venue Construction Costs	$CAD
Venue Construction Revenues	
Canada	290,000,000
BC	290,000,000
Total	**580,000,000**
Venue Construction Expenditures	
Venues Constructed by Partners with VANOC $ Contribution	
UBC Ice Hockey Arena (UBC Winter Sports Center)	38,445,000
Richmond Speed Skating Oval	63,110,000
Whistler Olympic and Paralympic (Athletes) Village	37,500,000
Vancouver Olympic and Paralympic (Athletes) Village	30,000,000
Whistler Broadcast and Press Center	3,000,000

(*Continued*)

Table 4.10   Continued

Venue Construction Costs	$CAD
Training Venues/Other Grants	7,400,000
Venues Constructed/Upgraded by VANOC	
Hillcrest Curling Venue	38,000,000
Whistler Athlete Center	16,000,000
Whistler Sliding Center	104,900,000
Whistler Nordic Competition Venue	119,740,000
Cypress Freestyle and Snowboard Venue	15,800,000
Whistler Alpine (Whistler Creekside)	27,635,000
Hastings Park Skating Venue (Pacific Coliseum)	23,700,000
Other	6,270,000
Subtotal	531,500,000
Contingency	55,300,000
Less: Sponsor VIK Contribution	*−6,800,000*
Total	**580,000,000**

A report developed by PricewaterhouseCoopers in 2010 said that through July 2009, just a few months prior to the start of the Winter Games, VANOC's spending was as Table 4.11 shows.

Table 4.11   Revised Vancouver Olympic 2010 Spending[57]

Category	Budget Amount	Spending through July 2009	Remaining Budget in 2009 and 2010
Revenue, Marketing, Communications	$170.4	$72.2	$98.8
Sports and Games Operations	$247.0	$130.5	$116.5
Services and Games Operations	$616.0	$165.5	$450.5
Technology	$391.9	$219.9	$172.0
Workforce and Sustainability	$140.2	$81.5	$58.7
Finance	$126.6	$84.7	$41.9
Subtotal	$1,692.1	$754.3	$937.8
Contingency and Foreign Exchange Loss	$63.8		
Total	**$1,755.9**		

Then in late 2010, VANOC reported the final financial results for the period from September 30, 2003, to July 31, 2010—the preparation and running of the 2010 Winter Olympic Games. Tables 4.12 and 4.13 show the actual financial results.

As these reports illustrate, not only did the budgeted costs and financial projections change, but the actual results were different as well. The total operating budget was closer to C$1.9 billion and approximately C$4 billion was spent on venue construction, infrastructure, and utilities, including closer to C$180 million on the Olympic speed-skating oval.[58]

Costs are only part of the financial picture. Incremental revenues are also an important measure since they account for contributions to economic activity above and beyond what might otherwise have occurred in the absence of the Games. According to a report by consulting firm PricewaterhouseCoopers (PwC), the incremental revenue contributions were generally positive in Vancouver. The PwC report stated that the Vancouver Olympics generated incremental revenues higher than projected: incremental hotel revenues were $130 million more than originally forecast, incremental tourism revenues were $463 million from 2003 through the end of March 2010, and spending for

Table 4.12 Consolidated Statement of Operating Activities and Changes in Fund Balance[59]

Cumulative from September 30, 2003 (incorporation) to July 31, 2010	$ (in thousands of dollars)
Operating Revenues	
IOC contribution *(note a in chapter endnote 60)*	479,742
IOC international sponsorship *(note b in chapter endnote 60)*	173,558
Domestic sponsorship *(note b in chapter endnote 60)*	730,157
Marketing rights royalties *(note c in chapter endnote 60)*	−186,759
Ticketing	269,459
Licensing and merchandising	54,618
Government contributions	
Canada	74,401
British Columbia	113,395
Other	175,558
Total Operating Revenues	**1,884,129**

Table 4.13   Consolidated Statement of Venue Development Activities and Changes in Fund Balance[60]

Cumulative from September 30, 2003 (incorporation) to July 31, 2010	
	$ (in thousands of dollars)
Revenues	
Government contributions	
Canada	290,000
British Columbia	290,000
Sponsorship revenues *(note b)*	11,806
Interest and other	11,515
Total venue development revenues	**603,321**
Expenses	
Cypress Mountain	17,597
Vancouver Olympic/Paralympic Centre	41,386
Pacific Coliseum	18,920
Richmond Olympic Oval	63,679
Training Venues	5,200
UBC Thunderbird Arena	38,216
Olympic and Paralympic Village Vancouver	30,000
Whistler Athletes' Centre	57,809
Whistler Media Centre	3,000
Whistler Creekside	31,312
Whistler Olympic/Paralympic Park	122,467
Olympic and Paralympic Village Whistler	37,500
The Whistler Sliding Centre	104,928
BC Place	12,094
General	15,654
Subtotal expenses	**599,762**
Interest and carrying charges	3,509
Total venue development expenses	**603,271**
Excess of venue development revenues over expenses for the period	**50**
Venue development fund, beginning of period	–
Venue development fund, end of period	**50**

hospitality-related events totaled $90 million. Occupancy rates in both Whistler and Vancouver (the two locales for the Olympics) increased in February 2010. Whistler hotels saw occupancy increase to the mid-80 percent range in February 2010, whereas in prior years the average occupancy was closer to the mid-70 percent range. Vancouver hotel occupancies were close to 90 percent, up from an average of 60 percent from 2004 to 2009. The average daily rate (ADR) in Whistler also increased in February 2010 to more than $450, significantly higher than the $250-plus average from 2004 to 2009. In Vancouver, the ADR zoomed to nearly $250, well above the $110 average from 2004 to 2009.

The 2010 Winter Olympics attracted roughly 325,000 tourists to Vancouver, from other parts of Canada and the world. More than 270,000 were from international locations. Approximately $130 million in incremental hotel revenue in British Columbia was attributable to the 2010 Winter Games. The average length of stay for tourists in Vancouver increased to eight nights, from a historical average of two nights in non-Olympics years. Revenues from food and beverage businesses witnessed a $129 million increase in the first three months of 2010, and retail sales grew $100 million, both above the average for the same time period in the preceding three years. Another $95 million in incremental transportation and recreation spending occurred from January to March 2010. Thus, $455 million in incremental tourism revenues occurred in the January–March 2010 time period.

As the PwC report states,

> The midpoint for the range of real GDP impacts from 2003 to March 31, 2010 is estimated to be $2.3 billion ($2002). Total pre-Games phase economic impacts were estimated at approximately $1.3 billion in real GDP and 30,580 jobs. . . . The estimated economic impact through the first three months of 2010 is $862 million in real GDP and 17,000 jobs generated or supported.[61]

The Vancouver Organizing Committee wanted to be recognized for presenting the greenest and most environmentally responsible Olympics in history. More than $60 million in new business deals related to clean energy and sustainability were confirmed in the three months following the end of the Games. The Canadian Tourism Commission said tourism increased 10 percent in 2010, and the reports from the premier's office in the province said that the local economy benefited by more than $2 billion in increased activity. Another $2 billion in economic activity had been generated by the investment in the Olympic speed-skating oval due to redevelopment, tourism increases, and new jobs in the area around the oval. According to Metro Vancouver Commerce, an initial $60 million benefit in the weeks immediately following the Games grew to more than $300 million in the year that followed. A total of $4.1 billion in economic activity was projected in British Columbia through 2015.[62]

At the same time, there were financial challenges with the Olympic Village complex, which was designed to house the athletes. The mid-2000s during the North American property boom caused the developer to bid too high for the site. Once the Games ended, the flats and apartments of the Olympic Village were to become a model urban residential area, complete with green designs amid beautiful natural surroundings. But as of early 2011, fewer than half of the 737 flats had been sold, the debt on the village stood at C$743 million, and the developer was unable make payments on the loan, forcing the development into receivership. Part of the problem was that the individual residential units were overpriced in the current marketplace, a hangover from the financial recession of the late 2000s. Plans were underway in 2011 to revisit the marketing of the Olympic Village, including repricing the units to reflect the less favorable housing marketing conditions.[63]

From a purely economic perspective, it appears that Vancouver benefited overall from increased economic activity, both in the years leading up to the Olympics and in the 90 days surrounding the Games. This economic vitality would also benefit sponsors, directly and indirectly. Directly, sponsors were exposed to a diverse tourism audience via regular communications throughout the Games. Sponsors may have also benefited through the direct sale of their products and services, particularly in the three months around the Games. Indirectly, sponsors probably would have seen increases in general familiarity and awareness about their companies and products; conceivably, their reputations may have strengthened, or certainly solidified, as a result of their support for the Games.

Media

Sponsors, of course, are interested in the media exposure. Vancouver's TV coverage was substantially greater than either the 2006 Torino or the 2002 Salt Lake City Winter Games. According to the PwC study and IOC reports, a TV audience of more than 3 billion people watched the Vancouver Games. The web also garnered a sizable audience of nearly 74 million unique visitors who watched 38 million hours of online video.[64]

Within Canada, the Olympics were ranked as the number one news story of 2010 by Canadian media editors at leading newspapers, broadcast stations, and web sites throughout Canada. Seventy percent of Canadians felt that the Olympics had created a positive reputation for Canada throughout the rest of the world.[65]

In summary, the 2010 Winter Olympics in Vancouver generated positive results as well as controversy. The facilities, ceremonies, and operations ran smoothly. The economic impact appears to have been more positive than negative, although the legacy of some of the infrastructure, such as the Olympic Village, is less clear. The media coverage was very strong, and Vancouver continued the trend that each Olympics has shown for many years: increased viewership, expanded coverage, increased media choices for following the Games (TV, radio, print, Internet), and ambitious plans for using the Olympics to reshape and enhance the host city and nation's reputation.

Youth Olympic Games

Positioning

The Youth Olympic Games (YOG) were conceived in 2007 by IOC President Jacques Rogge as a sports event to appeal to the world's youth, age 14 to 18, an audience whose interest and participation in sports was decreasing from preceding generations of youth. Similar to the traditional Olympic Games, the Summer and Winter YOG were to be held every four years (Summer in 2010, 2014, and 2018 and Winter in 2012, 2016, and 2020). Like the regular Olympic Games, athletic accomplishment was important. However, Rogge envisioned the Youth Olympic Games as a vehicle to address other global concerns as well, including education, social, and cultural issues. The purpose was to foster a deeper appreciation and understanding of Olympic values and their influence on developing a healthier and more holistic approach to competition, as well as contribution to society. In addition to the athletes, programs for Young Ambassadors and Young Reporters were developed. The role of the Young Ambassadors was to inspire and support Olympic values, particularly in the nonathletic areas of culture and education. The Young Reporters participated in the culture and education programs and also reported on the athletic competitions. At the same time, the YOG were developed to strengthen the connection between the Olympic Movement and the world's youth. The first YOG Summer Games were held in Singapore in 2010, and the first Winter YOG are scheduled for Innsbruck in January 2012.

As Jacques Rogge said to the 3,600 participants during the Singapore YOG,

> The Games will help you learn the difference between winning and being a champion. To win, you merely have to cross the finish line. To be a champion, you have to inspire admiration for your character, as well as for your physical talent. You have to compete in spirit of fair play, respecting your opponents and the rules—without doping or any other unfair advantage. If you can reach that pinnacle, if you are ready to serve as role models for your generation, you will all be champions, irrespective of your rankings.[66]

Three iconic athletes were selected as the first ambassadors for the Singapore YOG: Yelena Isinbayeva, Michael Phelps, and Usain Bolt, lending their well-known reputations and media star power to the Games.[67] Even with such luminaries supporting the inaugural YOG, the IOC's expectations were understated and often not clearly understood. Certainly, athletic performance would continue to be important. But counting medals by country would not occur. Not all top youth athletes would be participating because of the timing of other sports events to which many athletes were already committed. The TV coverage would be global, but the event's newness made a global fan following unlikely, other than as a passing interest. As a means for generating a general sense of goodwill about the importance of Olympic values, the YOG was likely to need multiple iterations and years of experience to determine how effectively such a feeling has been nurtured. The YOG raised more questions than it answered. But every new product, event, or offering, whether from a company or a sports entity, is fraught with risk and uncertainty, and the IOC is well aware of this. The YOG were and are, in effect, a grand experiment.

Economic Impact

The final budget for the 2010 Youth Olympic Games in Singapore was S$387 million, more than three times higher than the S$104 million that was first projected.[68] The additional costs were due to unexpected costs in technology (S$97 million), venue upgrades (S$76 million), and media facilities (S$46 million). More than 70 percent of the S$367 million in contracts went to local Singaporean companies, and another S$45 million was awarded to multinationals with divisions in Singapore.

Table 4.14   Where YOG Money Was Spent[69]

Costs	S$
Technology for score-keeping and start of the art information diffusion system	97,000,000
Upgrading of sports venues and equipment	76,000,000
Live broadcast via multiple media plus staging of opening and closing ceremonies	45,500,000
Logistics such as supply chain management, cleaning, and transport	44,000,000
Security	18,000,000
Operational needs such as language translation, laundry, and catering services	14,300,000
International journey of Youth Olympic Flame	7,000,000
Culture and education program	5,400,000
Other costs*	79,800,000

*Includes office running costs and general administration, marketing and communications, volunteer training, legal and insurance, medical services, and additional logistics such as power requirements.

Media

The IOC reported that 2 billion people watched the YOG from around the world. Coverage was provided by more than 160 rights-holding broadcasters. The official YOG list of broadcasting countries was 185. Both totals were less than those at the traditional Olympics, but this was also an inaugural event. While being officially sanctioned by the IOC and sharing the Olympic reputation, expectations and projections were understandably lower.

As the platform of choice for many youth around the world, the leading social media brands were used by the YOG, including Facebook (3.6 million fans), Twitter, and YouTube. The official YOG web site broadcast many events live; in the first few days of the YOG, there were more than a million visits to the site, and the official IOC web site had more than two million views in August 2010. The YOG developed a Games channel on YouTube, and the uploaded videos were viewed more than 5 million times. More than a third of the YOG audience were under the age of 24, and the channel was ranked as high as third globally among all of YouTube's channels.[70]

How TOP and Other Sponsors Benefited

The Singapore Youth Olympic Games Organizing Committee initially set a sponsorship target of S$50 million, with the government contributing another S$14 million.[71] The actual total was equivalent to S$60 million of in-kind sponsorship. Visa, a TOP sponsor, saw S$154 million in payments during the 12 days of the YOG, nearly 40 percent higher than the same period the year before.[72] Other TOP sponsors provided products to athletes, taking advantage of the market growth of digital technology. Acer supplied limited-edition Olympic-themed laptops to the participants in the Young Reporters and Young Ambassadors programs, Samsung gave out a Digital Concierge portable unit that provided real-time updates on happenings at the Games, and Panasonic supplied digital cameras to the Young Reporters as well.[73] Sponsors used the inaugural YOG as yet another promotional vehicle to connect to a broader, younger, and potentially newer audience, reinforcing their primary sponsorship investments via the TOP program.

Looking Ahead: 2012 Summer Games in London

Positioning

In 2004, more than 67 percent of Londoners polled favored the bid efforts to host the 2012 Olympics. Of the five finalists (New York, Moscow, Madrid, Paris, London), Paris had been considered the favorite until the final 48 hours. Aided by a visit from Prime Minister Tony Blair, a parade of British Olympic and sporting legends, and the articulate, energetic, and persuasive efforts by Lord Sebastian Coe, the bid chairman (including a well-received final presentation before the IOC), London overtook Paris to win the final vote 54 to 50. London's bid proposal emphasized its understanding of the Olympic cause, whereas Paris focused on staging a well-run Olympic Games. While the distinction appears subtle on the surface, particularly when Paris had experience as a three-time recent bidder of Olympic Games, the key to London's successful bid was its focus on inspiring youth (as opposed to hosting well-run Games). In essence, London's bid was about the future of the Olympics and the emotional connection to youth, whereas Paris's bid stressed operational excellence.

An important part of the youth message of the London Olympics is a program called International Inspiration, intended to use sports to transform the lives of 12 million youth in 20 developing countries. With a £40 million budget, and partnerships with UK Sport, UNICEF, the British Council, and organizations in each of the 20 developing countries, Sebastian Coe announced in July 2011 that the program had achieved its objectives a full year before the start of the 2012 Games. Additionally, UK Sport announced that funding for this program would continue through 2015. The potential benefit is both symbolic and significant since the lives of impressionable youth may be positively affected by this program, connecting them more deeply to the Olympic Games and Olympic values.[74]

London intends its Olympics to be the most inclusive and accessible in history, inspiring people to try new approaches and attempt new challenges. The controversial London 2012 logo was targeted to youth, with a jagged, asymmetrical design intended to evoke Internet-type imagery. The initial public reaction was mostly negative when the logo was first revealed in 2007 but has since been muted. In September 2011, the London Olympics were less than a year away and ahead of schedule with venues, sponsorships, and infrastructure development, suggesting a smooth final few months before the opening ceremonies, although riots in August 2011 in London and several other U.K. cities raised concerns about security for the Games.

Economic Impact

London's total anticipated costs are shown in Table 4.15. The EIS projections vary and, as stated previously, must be viewed with a critical eye.

Since the release of this budget, construction costs were revised downward to £7.5 billion, a £51 million decrease from prior estimates.[75] Forecasts suggest that international visitors will spend between £710 and 750 million during the Games, an 18 percent uplift over forecasted spending if the Olympics were not held. This includes a projected £129 million in spending during the Paralympics that follow the regular Games.[76] Increases are projected for high street retailers (£184.8 million), hotels (£122.6 million), entertainment, food, and beverages (£81.5 million), supermarkets (£79.9 million), and airlines and related travel services (£39.7 million). However, other reports suggest a mixed economic picture resulting from the Games, with $15.8 billion in economic output gains against the country's $2.1 trillion economy, a drop in the bucket. Although more than 300,000 jobs will be created in support of the Games, most are temporary, adding approximately 0.1 percent of one year's GDP, equivalent to $2.3 billion.[77]

Medium-term implications, based on the multiplier effect, suggest positive impacts in the two to three years following the Olympics, with expenditures from international visitors expected to rise by £820 million in 2013 with steady increases to £905 million per year by 2015. During this same period, economic output is forecasted to grow from £1.24 billion in 2013 to £1.37 billion in 2015, and an additional 17,900 jobs will be supported as well.[78]

As of July 2011, London 2012 was within a few short weeks of achieving its £700 million sponsorship funding target. Set in 2006, achieving this milestone is significant, given the global economic challenges that followed from 2008 onward. Forty-one domestic sponsors and 11 TOP sponsors have reached agreements to support the Games.[79]

Table 4.15 Anticipated Final Costs for 2012 Summer Olympics in London[80]

		November 2007 ODA Baseline Budget £m	November 2010 Quarterly Economic Report £m	February 2011 Annual Report £m	November 2010–February 2011 Variance £m
Site Preparation and Infrastructure	Power lines	282	285	285	0
	Utilities	256	207	238	31
	Enabling Works	364	382	383	1
	F10 Bridge	89	62	63	1
	Other Structures, Bridges, Highways	740	612	611	−1
	South Park Site Preparation	116	119	111	−8
	Prescott Lock	5	5	5	0
	Other Infrastructure (Landscaping)	243	226	245	19
	Total Site Preparation and Infrastructure	**2,095**	**1,898**	**1,941**	**43**
Venues	Stadium	496	496	486	−10
	Aquatics	214	268	269	1
	VeloPark	72	94	93	−1
	Handball	55	44	43	−1
	Basketball	58	42	42	0
	Other Olympic Park Venues	59	107	107	0
	Non-Olympic Park Venues	101	131	139	8
	Total Venues	**1,055**	**1,182**	**1,181**	**−1**

(Continued)

Table 4.15 Continued

		November 2007 ODA Baseline Budget £m	November 2010 Quarterly Economic Report £m	February 2011 Annual Report £m	November 2010–February 2011 Variance £m
Transport	Stratford Regional Station	119	124	123	−1
	DLR	86	81	80	−1
	Thorntons Field	47	23	23	0
	North London Line	110	107	107	0
	Other Transport Capital Projects	178	140	140	0
	Other Transport Operating Expenditure	357	379	388	9
	Total Transport Projects	**897**	**854**	**861**	**7**
Parkwide Projects	Logistics for Site Construction	337	271	263	−8
	Security for Park Construction	354	300	286	−14
	Section 106 and master planning	127	117	117	0
	Insurance	50	50	50	0
	Parkwide Operations	0	51	213	162
	Security Screening and Operational Areas	0	50	52	2
	Other Parkwide Projects	0	27	28	1
	Total Other Parkwide Projects	**868**	**866**	**1,009**	**143**

Media Centre and Olympic Village				
Stratford City Land and Infrastructure	522	614	613	−1
Stratford City Development Plots	−250	−100	−100	0
Village Construction (Public Sector Funding)	0	698	709	11
Village Receipt	0	−324	−324	0
IBC/MPC	220	301	301	0
Total Media Centre and Olympic Village	**492**	**1,189**	**1,199**	**10**
Program Delivery	647	694	718	24
Taxation and Interest	73	71	25	−46
Total Budget before Contingency	**6,127**	**6,754**	**6,934**	**180**
ODA Program Contingency Available	968	565	439	−126
Total after ODA Program Contingency	**7,095**	**7,319**	**7,373**	**54**

(Continued)

Table 4.15 Continued

	November 2007 ODA Baseline Budget £m	November 2010 Quarterly Economic Report £m	February 2011 Annual Report £m	November 2010– February 2011 Variance £m
Available Program Contingency*	0	−87	−72	15
Retained Savings**	0	0	0	0
Total Potential Anticipated Final Cost (AFC)	7,095	7,232	7,301	69

NOTE: ODA = OLYMPIC DELIVERY AUTHORITY

*Available Program Contingency represents the amount of Program Contingency available in excess of assessed risks.

**Retained Savings represents savings generated that will be used to meet future cost pressures.

Media

The London 2012 Olympics have designated specific areas within each Olympic venue for sponsors to advertise. No outside, non-Olympic sponsors will be allowed. At the same time, Rule 50 of the Olympic Charter stipulates a clean venue policy.

> No form of advertising or other publicity shall be allowed in and above the stadia, venues and other competition areas which are considered as part of the Olympic sites. Commercial installations and advertising signs shall not be allowed in the stadia, venues or other sports grounds.[81]

This rule is to ensure that the Games do not become overtly commercial, thereby keeping the focus of fan interest, whether from their seats in the venues or on TV, on the events and athletes themselves. This rule compels Olympic sponsors to be innovative in their use of Olympic symbolism and messages in their marketing communications. To complement the overall media activities surrounding the 2012 London Olympic Games, the British government is supporting a tourism effort that aims to create the equivalent of £1 billion in marketing and public relations exposure. This will bring additional value to sponsors and serve to further enhance the public's awareness of the London Games.[82]

Looking Ahead: 2014 Winter Games in Sochi

Positioning

Consistent with modern Olympics tradition, the Sochi Olympics are positioned as a "celebration of opportunity . . . human excellence, and aspiration."[83] Blending traditional Olympic themes of athletic performance and cultural traditions, the 2014 Sochi Olympics seek to introduce a unique part of Russia to the world, where the mountains meet the eastern part of the Black Sea. It is the first Winter Olympics hosted by Russia and the first Olympics of any kind hosted in Russia since the 1980 Moscow Olympics hosted by Russia's predecessor, the Soviet Union. Russia hopes that the sizable investments will further enhance

Sochi's reputation as a world-class resort in a unique climatic location. An emphasis on sustainability will animate much of the planning for the 2014 Winter Olympics, much as Vancouver did in 2010. Sochi's objective is for 2014 to be a climate-neutral, zero-waste Games. This is an ambitious objective, to be sure. But every effort made to use innovation in minimizing the carbon and environmental footprint can further the world's understanding and development of even more sophisticated sports event undertakings in the future.

Economic Impact

The Sochi Games have a budget of roughly $12 billion, making it the most expensive Winter Olympics in the modern era. Nearly 60 percent is being funded by the federal government, with the balance coming from private investment. Forecasted marketing revenues are expected to be nearly $500 million, of which $300 million will come from local sponsors and another $125 million from ticket sales. Between 200,000 and 300,000 visitors are anticipated during the Games, and the region's annual tourism is expected to grow from 3 million to nearly 6 million by 2014. Given the uncertainty of economic impact studies, particularly several years before the actual event, these figures will undoubtedly change.[84]

The $300 million local sponsor figure is ambitious, but Gazprom signed a three-year contract valued at $130 million, giving a substantial boost to the domestic sponsorship efforts.[85] Sochi lacks the kind of infrastructure and scale of a Vancouver, requiring the Sochi Organizing Committee of the Olympic Games (SOCOG) to lead the effort in developing a proper infrastructure, indicating one of the reasons that this is to be the most expensive Winter Olympic Games to date.[86]

As a consequence, estimates for developing the Olympic infrastructure range as high as $6 billion. Other projects suggest that nearly $24 billion will actually be invested in the region, beyond what is needed for the Games, in an effort to modernize local transportation, utilities, services, and tourism needs. The introduction of the Olympics is forcing social change on the region as well. Recycling initiatives, common in many parts of the world, are underdeveloped in Russia. The Sochi Olympics are spurring new development and social initiatives in recycling so that it is a more common practice by the time the Games arrive. Even volunteerism is being addressed as a result of the Sochi Olympics, with Russia seeking upward of 30 million people to work regularly on initiatives that will benefit the country for years, even decades, to come.[87]

During an inspection of Sochi's Olympic development progress by the IOC in March 2011, Russian Deputy Prime Minister Dmitriy Kozak commented on the budget, saying,

> Nothing has changed: R195 billion. This is 250 sports sites and the infrastructure sites that ensure their functioning. More than half the money is private investments and about R90 billion is the federal budget.[88]

While his estimate that more than 50 percent of the budget is funded by private investment stands in contrast to the contribution estimate at the start of this section, it is clear that the Sochi Olympics, like Beijing's, represent a significant opportunity for Russia to enhance its image, so the sizable investment is considered worthy. Among the 250 projects referenced by Deputy Prime Minister Kozak are the budget items shown in Table 4.16.

Media

Sochi is expected to continue the Olympic Charter's tradition of ensuring that the venues are free of sponsorship and branding signage and messaging. As stated in the descriptions about London, the Youth Olympic Games, Vancouver, and Beijing, as well as in Chapter 20, investments in and use of social media will continue to grow for both global media companies and sponsors, in addition to the continued use of traditional media, particularly broadcast.

Summary

As we have discussed, being an Olympic host city is not for the faint of heart. Each city's unique characteristics, from cultural nuance to infra-structure sophistication, affect planning in both costs and benefits in the bidding, candidate selection, and actual development phases. Consistent

Table 4.16   Preliminary Budget, Sochi 2014[89]

Project	Investment Volume (000 US$)
Sports Facilities	*806,031*
Biathlon Centre	7,786
Cross Country Skiing Centre	5,173
Roza Khutor Alpine Resort	261,791
Russian National Slide Centre	131,225
Maly Ice Palace	26,227
Sochi Olympic Skating Centre	41,537
Olympic Oval	30,171
Bolshoi Ice Palace	178,588
Sochi Olympic Stadium	55,959
Olympic Curling Centre	12,527
Ski Jumps K-120 and K-90	31,811
Snowboard Park	11,736
Freestyle Center on the trails of "Alpika Service"	11,500
Olympic Villages	*120,908*
Main Olympic Village (Imeretinskaya Valley)	75,545
Mountain Olympic Subvillage	48,363
MPC & IBC	*268,902*
Press Centre (Imeretinskaya Valley)	191,270
International Broadcast Centre	77,632
Total	**1,195,841**

metrics from past Olympiads are challenging to precisely identify, which makes planning by future host cities equally complex. However, many lessons can be gleaned from selected Olympics. Whether it is Los Angeles's pioneering efforts to be profitable by minimizing costs and maximizing sponsorship support, Barcelona's thoughtful approach to sustained development, or Vancouver's efforts to develop an environmentally responsible Olympics, the most successful host cities organize their efforts around focused themes and plan for the long term.

We also know that the Olympics serve as a highly visible platform, not just for the cities, sponsors, sports, and athletes, but for protesters as well. It will always be possible that a particular stakeholder's interests will be at risk if a protest develops sufficient global momentum that it overwhelms the Olympics. For host cities and nations, their reputations are subject to change, hopefully for the better, but certainly not guaranteed, particularly if a scandal or protest dominates the Games. This brings us back to the question of whether hosting an Olympic Games is really worth it, given the significant financial cost, risk of controversy, and uncertain benefits. While this chapter did not conclusively reveal the secrets to ensure host city success or prescribe a singular best path to maximize benefits, the factors that have created areas of success for various host cities are evident. The fact that the complexity and uncertainty surrounding hosting an Olympics has not diminished future host cities' interest in bidding for the Games underscores how highly regarded the Olympics continue to be.

Questions

1. What are the stages in the host city bidding process, and what is the purpose of each stage?
2. In terms of economic performance, what distinguishes the more successful host cities from those that did not perform as well?
3. Why should sponsors care about how host cities plan and execute their Olympic responsibilities?
4. What noneconomic benefits can result from hosting the Olympics?
5. Can host cities prevent protests? How can host cities mitigate the impact of protesters?
6. What can future host cities do to improve the chances of making their Olympics successful?

Chapter 5

Section I Sponsorship Preparation Questions

Section I provided a brief overview of 2,700 years of historical precedent that have helped shape the image and reputation of the modern Olympics as we know it today. Research for this book showed that the best-performing companies succeed partly because they pay attention to the traditions that give them their personality and raison d'être. Understanding both past and current contexts of the Olympics gives us insight into the factors that have elevated the Games to its unique status as a megasports event that rises above others and truly stands for something meaningful in both sports and society. Such a historical examination is useful if one wishes to understand whether an entity has true credibility and authenticity, as opposed to merely being a superficial construction designed for expedient commercial purposes. If an organization's reputation is important, then knowing the Olympics' historical background gives sports marketers a much richer understanding about the values that inspire the global Olympic movement while also helping them identify the personality characteristics and qualities associated with the Olympics that might benefit their company. As a marketer weighing and evaluating the attractiveness of sponsoring the Olympics (and other sports events, for that matter), the following questions can guide the initial evaluation. They are organized into four themes.

Ultimate Dream

The questions in this section are designed to describe the positive, appealing aspects of a sports event by helping marketers understand the event's origins and traditions, more effectively *imagine* the future ahead for their companies, and inspire a road map for achieving their brand vision. In this regard, the ultimate dream of global megasports events differs little from that of any successful business with a premier reputation—in both cases, organizations use their knowledge of past strengths to inspire future gains. There are several explanations for the founding of the ancient Olympics. One suggests that the Games were founded in recognition of Zeus's defeat of his father, Cronus, in a wrestling match, after which Zeus became ruler of the world. As the legend goes, to mark his achievement, Zeus founded the Olympics, perhaps to provide a single event devoted to competitive success. Another story says that the Olympics evolved into one event after generations of athletes and warriors from various city-states had been competing regularly in chariot and foot races as a component of regular religious celebrations. Yet another story says that the ancient Olympics began in 776 BC, when a cook named Koroibos of Elis competed and won in the 600-foot stadion race. Knowing the specific reason for the founding of the first Olympic Games in 776 BC is less important (and isn't possible to identify anyway) than gaining a broader understanding and appreciation for the historical context, especially the role that sports and competition played in ancient Greek life. Contests between city-states, from discus throwing to foot and chariot races, were common, and significant honor and prestige was attached to these competitions. As a marketer, knowing the origins of any sports event provides a clearer understanding of the sport's key associations and the best way to sponsor that sport as a consequence.

For the Olympics, an important component of its long-term success is the continued ability to leverage its historical legacy to generate enthusiasm in the form of sponsorships from the world's leading companies, which provide the financial support needed to fund a significant portion of Olympic activities.

Brand Vision

Brand vision describes any organization's long-term direction as it relates to its ultimate dream. Just as top athletes aspire to win an Olympic medal, and their vision for achieving it helps inform the path required for getting there, the planners of the Olympic Games follow a similar path. My research into the factors that describe what top brands do around the world has identified a vision path, shown in Figure 5.1, that the best organizations pursue.

1. Define why the ultimate dream is important to the organization. The ultimate dream defines the organization's reason to exist, and the vision describes how the organization's leadership anticipates the ultimate dream will be realized. For the organizers of each Olympics, the ultimate dream can be described as a desire to spread Olympic values far and wide so that more people around the world can enjoy and even participate in the Games.

2. Work collaboratively to craft a viable vision. A brand's success over time is the result of leadership's concerted attempts to rally people

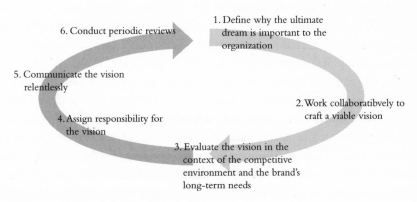

6. Conduct periodic reviews

1. Define why the ultimate dream is important to the organization

5. Communicate the vision relentlessly

2. Work collaboratibvely to craft a viable vision

4. Assign responsibility for the vision

3. Evaluate the vision in the context of the competitive environment and the brand's long-term needs

Figure 5.1   Brand Vision Path[1]

inside the organization around a common cause, seeking their collective input and collaborative effort to achieve something great. This collaboration creates a common buy-in in which everyone feels a sense of ownership for the piece of the brand's success. Because the Olympics have a well-known reputation, educating the organizing committee of each Olympics is less about informing the organizers about the meaning of the Games and more about ensuring they honor and live up to the world's expectations for the event. Each Olympics organizing committee effectively knows they must work collaboratively to achieve success since the eyes of the world are on them.

3. Evaluate the vision in the context of the competitive environment and the brand's long-term needs. The vision for achieving success must be calibrated based on market conditions and trends, as mentioned earlier. Practical considerations, such as financial circumstances, vary significantly from one Olympics to another, based partly on political and social conditions in the host country. China's desire to use the 2008 Beijing Olympics to herald the country's dramatic reemergence on the world stage practically obligated government leaders to invest a significantly larger sum, approximately $40 billion, to properly stage the Olympics and present the country in a favorable light. In contrast, while the 2012 London organizers are investing a substantial amount as well, approximately $11.6 billion, the significantly lower level reflects a practical reality in the United Kingdom to keep costs down to appeal to public interest groups and also to mirror the continued economic austerity that has defined most Western economies since 2007.

4. Assign responsibility for the vision. Senior management is responsible for setting the vision in top brands, which includes a plan for involving the rest of the organization. With the Olympics, the task of assigning responsibility is complicated by the sheer diversity of workers involved: volunteers, salaried management, government officials, sports officials, media, and more.

5. Communicate the vision relentlessly. The leaders of successful brands work hard to gain ongoing buy-in throughout the organization for their vision. The communications and messaging used for this purpose range from formal events and printed communications to informal activities, such as hallway conversations and impromptu meetings. For the organizers of the Olympics, who are working with thousands of diverse helpers both in the host city and around the world, the communications task is even more challenging, requiring consistent messages and a clear understanding of roles, responsibilities, timelines, and measures.

6. Conduct periodic reviews. Today's marketing activities, whether an advertising campaign, sales promotion, or sports sponsorship, are judged on the return gained from the initial investment. The return depends on how realistic the objectives are as well. For example, while being an Olympic sponsor may initially appear to be a powerful way to improve a company's business, an issue would be determining how to actually measure results. Using the Olympics to target a sales and/or market share increase might not be realistic, given the short-term duration of the Games. However, targeting an increase in market awareness, as Visa did when it first began sponsoring the Olympics in the 1980s, could be a reasonable beginning. As the Visa case in this book describes, Visa expanded its marketing objectives over the years as its sponsorship with the Olympics grew. The company had the luxury of time to fine-tune its sponsorship in a way that maximizes its returns and expands its business. The IOC reviews its various marketing objectives as well in an effort to further improve and extend the Olympics brand.

Values

The values theme describes the core values by which the brand/sports event and its organizers live. An organizational imperative is *living* the values, not merely *listing* them. Embedding values deep into an organization's culture means management must find ways to reinforce the values every day. Values are important because of the deeper meaning and resonance they have for any top brand, with both employees and the public at large. We know the values, or can assume we know, of people and organizations with which we are familiar. Familiarity can be viewed from two points of view: either respect or distrust. Those we respect often serve as models of the values to which we subscribe (generosity, selflessness), whereas those we distrust can have negative values (greed, selfishness). Both are recognizable and easily understood, yet one is admirable and the other reprehensible. Marketers must pay attention to the values of the organizations they work with for the simple reason that someone else (a potential customer, for example) may well point out when a sponsor and sports event do not match. (Imagine, hypothetically, a tobacco company sponsoring the Olympics and the fallout for both organizations if this hellish mismatch were to occur, although the repercussions would be far more negative for the Olympics.)

Creating Value

This theme concerns how the brand creates and adds value to its various stakeholders, from suppliers to customers, and, more specifically, the *contribution and impact* the brand hopes to have and the *competencies and skills* needed to support this effort.

Contribution and Impact

Why should the Olympics be concerned with contribution and impact? Identifying contribution and impact provides more tangible guidance for determining long-term strategies and tactical actions.

Contribution can be defined several ways:

1. What advances does the brand hope to make?
2. Does this give new business opportunities to the brand, competitors, market, all?
3. Does it enrich customers' lives? Reduce anxiety or stress? Extend enjoyment?
4. What recognition would provide credibility?
5. What problem(s) should the brand solve?
6. How will the brand extend its success to other markets?

Impact is concerned with the influence the brand will have over time and can be looked at as follows:

1. Who will benefit from this and how?
2. Where will the impact be noticed?
3. How will this affect market share?
4. How will competitors respond?
5. Can the firm support rapid growth if the impact is strong?
6. Will the effect on financials be small or large?

Competencies and Skills

Competencies and skills are the strengths and unique characteristics of the brand that help make it unique. Part of the appeal of the Olympic Games is that they promote peace, goodwill, and sportsmanship. While those may not be directly tied to more traditional business objectives like profit and loss, it is inarguable that the absence of these characteristics would undermine the appeal of the Games. For businesspeople and marketers, creating value can also describe how the event ultimately creates a profitable financial result. But value is not just financial—it is also derived from the enjoyment one feels while watching gifted athletes and compelling athletic contests. In the modern era, the achievements of Jesse Owens at the 1936 Olympic Games in Berlin have transcended everyday records to become legendary. As we think back on the ancient Greek Olympics, we can picture those events, conjuring up colorful images of what it must have been like, which feeds into our positive feeling about the games even today, creating indelible impressions. Sports marketers seeking sponsorship opportunities need to pay attention to how the sports event creates value—that is, if the marketer wants to effectively leverage the associations a company will gain from sponsoring the event.

Personality

The personality theme is the one we most commonly, and unconsciously, experience. Every organization has a personality, just as people do. Highlighting a brand's personality can raise its visibility, reduce its impersonal qualities, and even imbue it with a more *human* quality, thereby potentially making it more appealing to customers. When Olympics TV coverage broadcasts profiles of athletes, they are creating stronger emotional connections between fans and the Games, humanizing the event. The Games themselves can be described as having an energetic *and* competitive personality. There is also an intellectual component to the Olympics' personality, involving strategy elements, since much of the event's success is predicated on long-term planning and preparation from all stakeholders, from athletes to host cities to corporate sponsors. Clearly, emotions factor into the Olympic personality description as well.

The TV profiles of athletes are but one example of how the Olympics, and the media, work to create emotional bonds with viewers around the world. Such an emotional connection makes the Olympics seem less slick and overtly commercial and more accessible. Authenticity, however, may be the single most important aspect of the Olympics' personality. If the Olympics were purely a commercial sports event designed to enrich the president of the IOC or the IOC members, then the centuries-old honor and prestige attached to competing in the Olympics would be greatly diminished, future athletes' interest in competing would probably be reduced, and fans around the world would see the event as far less special. This would negatively impact the overall credibility of the Olympic Games as a sports event of the highest integrity and dissuade its corporate sponsors from future support.

Brands can also use their personality to improve their position and image in the marketplace around the world. As fans, we can describe an event's personality almost like we can describe another person or an animal. The Iron Man Triathlon's personality is tough and extreme. World Cup skiing is fast and aggressive. These are, of course, simplistic illustrations. But understanding an event's personality has ramifications for a marketer's business. Try to picture Apple (innovative, bold, nontraditional) sponsoring a Scottish Games caber-tossing event (unchanging, conservative, tradition). The connection would not be clear or even sensible to target audiences, other than perhaps as a lark or novelty. Personality should be an influential factor when considering sponsorship investments. But personality may not always be a deciding factor, as the dozens of sponsors of EPL (English Premier League), NBA (National Basketball Association), NFL (National Football League), F1 (Formula 1), and other major sports events show. The lack of a clear personality match does not mean the sponsorship should be avoided. Instead, marketers need to decide if the event reaches the right audience and represents the overall values their company espouses. As marketers concerned with proper positioning and alignment between their company and related marketing investments, having a clear sense of the personality fit between the two organizations is a useful, although not rigid, guide to ensuring that the marketplace views the sports marketing effort as consistent with their perceptions of both the company and the sports event.

The audit questions in this section are more qualitative in nature, designed to help sponsors think through the attractiveness of the event from a contextual point of view. Understanding the particular context of an event, its founding, and its development can provide marketers with a clearer sense of the event's fit with their own company.

Questions

Ultimate Dream

1. How or why was the event started?
   a. Who were the founders?
   b. What inspired the original event?
   c. What types of athletes competed?
2. What is the guiding philosophy of the event?
   a. What is the event's ultimate ambition (e.g., biggest, best)?
   b. What does it stand for (e.g., sportsmanship, teamwork)?
3. What are the objectives of the event?
   a. What communities does it attract (local, regional, national, global?)
   b. What are its general aims (e.g., raise money, increase awareness, attract volunteers)?
   c. Is it for-profit or not-for-profit? How does this affect your decision?
   d. Does it benefit a cause (e.g., disease, social/political or economic problems)?
4. What are the event's social connotations?
   a. How is it perceived (e.g., positive, controversial, innovative)?
   b. Does the event enjoy status appeal?

Values

1. What values best represent this event (e.g., virtue, purity, honor, integrity)?
   a. Who associated with this event, past or present, embodies these values (e.g., athletes, fans, community leaders)?
2. Are the event's values widely known?
   a. Who communicates the values?
   b. How are the values communicated?

3. Are the values an authentic, genuine reflection of the event's leaders and their behaviors?
   a. What are the backgrounds of the current and historical leaders and organizers of the event?
   b. Do the leaders live the values in their other work?
4. Does the event consistently uphold its values through its practices (communication, partnership with suppliers and sponsors, reputation with the market)?
   a. Are the event's communications consistent with the event's image and history?
   b. Do the various stakeholders associated with the event uphold the same values? If not, are there any stakeholders whose association might be negative or controversial?

Creating Value

1. How does the event create value (financial, community support, benefit a cause, market exposure, sport reputation enhancement)?
   a. What are its revenue sources?
   b. What are the specific ways the event actually benefits its stated cause (how are the proceeds spent, is there transparency in the use of proceeds, does the event attract media attention, which attracts donors)?
2. Who have been past winners or notable competitors?
   a. Are these athletes well known?
   b. What are their reputations?
   c. Have any of the previous competitors achieved distinction outside this event?
3. Does the event have ongoing awareness? If so, what type?
   a. Does the event enjoy top-of-mind awareness recall (the first event that comes to mind when a person is asked) or dominant awareness recall (the only event recalled)?
   b. Is the awareness recognition-based (meaning that a person has to be prompted before the event comes to mind)?
4. Is this awareness positive or negative?
   a. If positive, are the associations with this event likely to directly or indirectly benefit your company?

   b. If negative, are the associations likely to harm your company's reputation (e.g., scandals, controversies)?

Personality

1. What are the most common associations with this event historically?
2. How would you describe the event's personality (friendly, intense, elitist, accessible, competitive, casual, quirky, predictable)?
3. Do the event's stakeholders (athletes, sponsors, suppliers, fans) share similar personality characteristics?

II

SUCCESS AND ACHIEVEMENT

Chapter 6

The Olympic Stage

The Olympic audience is huge. The 2004 Summer Olympics in Athens attracted 3.9 billion unduplicated viewers (*unduplicated* refers to viewers who watched the Olympics at least once) with a cumulative total of 34.4 billion viewer hours (determined by multiplying the total number of viewers by the duration of the program), and the 2008 Beijing Olympics attracted 4.3 billion viewers. While the IOC did not calculate total viewing hours for Beijing, they did measure the average minute rating (AMR) as 114.3 million (calculated as the number of viewers watching a minute of TV coverage), an increase over the 2004 Summer Games in Athens, which had an AMR of 78 million and the 2000 Summer Games in Sydney's AMR of 113.5 million.[1] The Winter Olympics witnessed impressive viewership as well, with TV coverage of the 2010 Winter Games in Vancouver nearly twice as large as in Turin in 2006, and approximately three times the coverage in Salt Lake City in 2002. Vancouver's viewing audience was calculated as 3.8 billion, a record for the Winter Games.[2]

But the viewership alone is only part of the appeal for corporate sponsors. The Olympic Games generate numerous real-life stories about the athletes and their efforts that add color and depth to the event, beyond the sports events themselves. Much like the stories of the ancient Greek competitors like Chionis of Sparta and Milo of Kroton, the modern athletes are celebrated for years following their Olympic performances. Their stories serve as a point of comparison with the athletes of the modern Olympics, and the surrounding buzz over who will win this time creates a global chorus of interest. This naturally evolving word of mouth adds a raw, more honest voice and an interesting contrast to the slick professionalism of global media. For corporate sponsors, this combination of professionally orchestrated and grassroots enthusiasm is seductive, providing a rich stage on which a viable marketing effort can be implemented.

Olympic Broadcasts

The impact of television on spreading the popularity of the Olympics cannot be overstated. Billions of people in almost every country share in a collective viewing of the Games. Smart marketers and broadcasters have improved their customer targeting, shaping the messages to the tastes and interests of the viewers in each market.

However, television did not create the global fan base for the Olympic Games; the appeal of the Olympics is not an invention of the modern era or due exclusively to the development and proliferation of television. The Olympics have achieved their unique appeal from 2,700 years of experience and tradition building, well before the aid of modern broadcasting. This is an important lesson from my research: The great brands and successful companies have not been products of overnight success from well-financed advertising campaigns. Successful brands, reputations, and companies are institution-building efforts that each succeeding generation of leaders oversees for a limited time. Most traditions are known inside a given institution by those who work there, handed down by their predecessors, versus being the result of some clever marketing campaign. Prior to the development of modern communications, citizens in ancient Greek times learned of the exploits of their favorite athletes through traditional word of mouth. More fans around the world follow the Olympics than ever before because of broadcast coverage, providing an attractive audience for advertisers. The International Olympic Committee (IOC) knows this, of course, and has been able to command higher broadcast revenues from higher fee premiums with each succeeding Olympics because of the significant, positive reputation and ongoing goodwill associated with the Olympic ideal. Figures 6.1 and 6.2 illustrate the dramatic growth in broadcast revenue of the various Olympiads since 1980.[3]

The broadcast revenue growth is impressive and coincides with the increasing sophistication of the Olympic Games as a viable marketing platform for companies. The revenue increases reflect not just the growing global stage that the Olympics command in a commercial sense, but the credibility born of thousands of years of reputation building that reminds fans of the unique values and aspirations closely associated with the Games. When such a reputation is developed over centuries, the associated integrity is almost beyond compare, conferring the mythical, gold-plated status we now associate with almost anything related to the Olympics. The power of this appeal is not lost on the world's countries and companies, hence the continued increases and sophistication of host city bids, rising Olympic sponsorship fees, and the

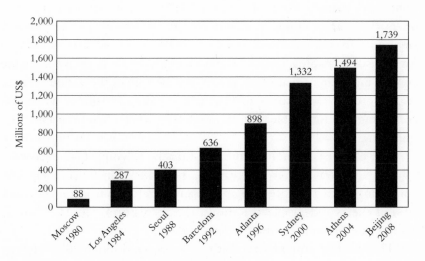

Figure 6.1 Summer Olympic Games Revenues

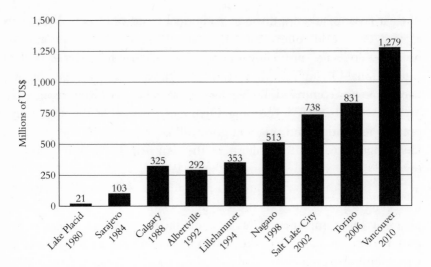

Figure 6.2   Winter Olympic Games Revenues

vigilant protection the IOC exerts over the Olympics and Olympic-related trademarks and intellectual property. Because of the quality associated with the Olympics and the large global audience, companies clamor for the right to reach this attractive and influential group of viewers. Broadcasters around the world, particularly those in the United States (whose broadcast networks invest the largest amounts for both rights and ensuing coverage logistics), know that this vast audience offers tremendous commercial potential to advertisers, bid aggressively large sums for the right to broadcast the Olympics, and know that their own fortunes as broadcasters are tied directly to their ability to create compelling content that offers extensive coverage of the various events, athlete profiles, and stories of Olympic success and failure, while also conveying the intangible appeal and mystique of Olympic values and traditions.

The number of countries broadcasting the Olympic Games and the Olympic Winter Games has grown exponentially in the modern era, coinciding with the technological change and adoption of television around the world. Table 6.1 shows the increase in countries broadcasting the Olympics in the modern era.

The absolute number of countries has grown through 2000, and the broadcast rights fees have increased as well. Furthermore, the broadcast

Table 6.1   Worldwide Broadcast Coverage of the Olympics[4]

Olympic Summer Games		Olympic Winter Games	
Olympic Summer Games	Number of Countries and Territories Broadcasting	Olympic Winter Games	Number of Countries and Territories Broadcasting
1936 Berlin	1	1956 Cortina	22
1948 London	1	1960 Squaw Valley	27
1952 Helsinki	2	1964 Innsbruck	30
1956 Melbourne	1	1968 Grenoble	32
1960 Rome	21	1972 Sapporo	41
1964 Tokyo	40	1976 Innsbruck	38
1968 Mexico City	n/a	1980 Lake Placid	40
1972 Munich	98	1984 Sarajevo	100
1976 Montreal	124	1988 Calgary	64
1980 Moscow	111	1992 Albertville	86
1984 Los Angeles	156	1994 Lillehammer	120
1988 Seoul	160	1998 Nagano	160
1992 Barcelona	193	2002 Salt Lake City	160
1996 Atlanta	214	2006 Torino	200
2000 Sydney	220	2010 Vancouver	220
2004 Athens	220		
2008 Beijing	220		

revenues have grown even though in recent years the number of countries broadcasting has remained steady for both the Olympic Summer Games and Olympic Winter Games. Table 6.2 shows the growth in total revenues from broadcast rights fees, and Table 6.3 shows broadcast fees paid by region.

The structure of the broadcast fees is complex, but the increases over the years are partly explained by the expansion of technology and corresponding broadcast options around the world, in addition to the premium associated with the Olympic movement and the spread of Olympism overall. This premium would be less likely if the Games did not yield positive results for corporate sponsors and country hosts alike, suggesting that the Olympics' brand reputation remains healthy, despite the challenges from scandals and the skyrocketing investments in infrastructure.

Table 6.2   Olympic Games Broadcast Total Revenue History[5]

Olympic Summer Games		Olympic Winter Games	
Olympic Summer Games	Broadcast Revenue	Olympic Winter Games	Broadcast Revenue
1960 Rome	US$1.2 million	1960 Squaw Valley	US$50,000
1964 Tokyo	US$1.6 million	1964 Innsbruck	US$937,000
1968 Mexico City	US$9.8 million	1968 Grenoble	US$2.6 million
1972 Munich	US$17.8 million	1972 Sapporo	US$8.5 million
1976 Montreal	US$34.9 million	1976 Innsbruck	US$11.6 million
1980 Moscow	US$88 million	1980 Lake Placid	US$20.7 million
1984 Los Angeles	US$286.9 million	1984 Sarajevo	US$102.7 million
1988 Seoul	US$402.6 million	1988 Calgary	US$324.9 million
1992 Barcelona	US$636.1 million	1992 Albertville	US$291.9 million
1996 Atlanta	US$898.3 million	1994 Lillehammer	US$352.9 million
2000 Sydney	US$1,331.6 million	1998 Nagano	US$513.5 million
2004 Athens	US$1,494 million	2002 Salt Lake City	US$738 million
2008 Beijing	US$1,739 million	2006 Torino	US$831 million
		2010 Vancouver	US$1,279.5 million

The habit that host cities bid committees have of regularly under-forecasting the construction and preparation costs does not seem to affect the perception of the Games overall or the sponsorship investment of companies, at least as far as fans are concerned. The 2000 Sydney Olympics were originally bid to cost AUS$3 billion (about US$2.7 billion, not including an additional US$4 billion budget by the federal and regional governments to improve transportation and related logistics), but the final tally was closer to AUS$6.6 billion (US$5.9 billion).[7] The 2004 Athens Olympics bid was €4.6 billion (US$6 billion), but the final costs were closer to $10 billion (US$13 billion).[8] The 2008 Beijing Olympics were originally bid at US$1.6 billion,[9] an estimate that quickly rose to US$4 billion. Beijing planners indicated that associated infrastructure projects, such as roads, water treatment plants, pollution controls, public transportation improvements, and a new airport, increased the costs closer to US$40 billion.[10] The 2012 London Olympics bid committee forecasted a budget of £2.4 billion in 2005 (approximately US$4.6 billion

Table 6.3 Olympic Games Broadcast Revenue History Breakdown by Region[6]

AMERICAS

United States

	Olympic Summer Games			Olympic Winter Games		
Host City	Host City	Broadcaster	Rights Fees	Host City	Broadcaster	Rights Fees
1976 Montreal		ABC	US$25.0 million	1976 Innsbruck	ABC	US$10.0 million
1980 Moscow		NBC	US$72.3 million	1980 Lake Placid	ABC	US$15.5 million
1984 Los Angeles		ABC	US$225.6 million	1984 Sarajevo	ABC	US$91.55 million
1988 Seoul		NBC	US$300.0 million	1988 Calgary	ABC	US$309.0 million
1992 Barcelona		NBC	US$401.0 million	1992 Albertville	CBS	US$243.0 million
1996 Atlanta		NBC	US$705.0 million	1994 Lillehammer	CBS	US$295.0 million
2000 Sydney		NBC	US$793.5 million	1998 Nagano	CBS	US$375.0 million
2004 Athens		NBC	US$793.5 million	2002 Salt Lake City	NBC	US$545.0 million
2008 Beijing		NBC	US$893.0 million	2006 Turin	NBC	US$613.4 million

Canada

Host City	Broadcaster	Rights Fees	Host City	Broadcaster	Rights Fees
N/A			1984 Sarajevo	CBC/CTV	US$1.8 million
N/A			1988 Calgary	CBC/CTV	US$3.4 million
1992 Barcelona	CTV	US$16.5 million	1992 Albertville	CBC	US$10.1 million
1996 Atlanta	CBC	US$20.75 million	1994 Lillehammer	CTV	US$12.0 million
2000 Sydney	CBC	US$28.0 million	1998 Nagano	CBC	US$16.0 million
2004 Athens	CBC	US$37.0 million	2002 Salt Lake City	CBC	US$22.0 million
2008 Beijing	CBC	US$45.0 million	2006 Torino	CBC	US$28.0 million

(Continued)

Table 6.3 Continued

AMERICAS

Central/South America

	Olympic Summer Games			Olympic Winter Games		
Host City	Broadcaster	Rights Fees		Host City	Broadcaster	Rights Fees
N/A				1980 Lake Placid	Televisa	US$100,000
N/A				1984 Sarajevo	Televisa	US$250,000
N/A				1988 Calgary	Selected countries	US$310,000
1992 Barcelona	OTI	US$3.55 million		1992 Albertville	Selected countries	US$459,000
1996 Atlanta	OTI	US$5.5 million		1994 Lillehammer	Selected countries	US$501,000
2000 Sydney	OTI	US$12.0 million		1998 Nagano	OTI	US$985,000
2004 Athens	OTI	US$18.0 million		2002 Salt Lake City	OTI	US$1.25 million
2008 Beijing	OTI	US$28.0 million		2006 Torino	OTI	US$1.75 million

Caribbean

	Olympic Summer Games			Olympic Winter Games		
Host City	Broadcaster	Rights Fees		Host City	Broadcaster	Rights Fees
N/A				1984 Sarajevo	Bermuda	US$6,750
N/A				1988 Calgary	No broadcast	
N/A				1992 Albertville	Trinidad & Tobago	US$5,000
1996 Atlanta	CBU	US$190,000		1994 Lillehammer	Selected countries	US$13,500
2000 Sydney	CBU	US$250,000		1998 Nagano	Jamaica CVM	US$12,000
2004 Athens	CBU	US$350,000		2002 Salt Lake City	Jamaica CVM	US$15,000
2008 Beijing	CBU	US$500,000		2006 Torino	No broadcast	

Host City	Broadcaster	Rights Fees		Broadcaster	Rights Fees
2000 Sydney	Teleonce	US$1 million			
2004 Athens	Telemundo	US$1.25 million			
2008 Beijing	Telemundo	US$1.58 million			

ASIA

Asia

Host City	Broadcaster	Rights Fees	Host City	Broadcaster	Rights Fees
N/A			1984 Sarajevo	HK–TVB	US$20,000
N/A			1988 Calgary	ABU	US$278,000
1992 Barcelona	ABU	US$2.2 million	1992 Albertville	ABU	US$471,000
1996 Atlanta	ABU	US$5.0 million	1994 Lillehammer	ABU	US$515,000
2000 Sydney	ABU	US$12.0 million	1998 Nagano	ABU	US$540,000
2004 Athens	ABU	US$15.1 million	2002 Salt Lake City	ABU	US$150,000
2008 Beijing	ABU	US$17.5 million	2006 Torino	ABU	US$600,000

Japan

Host City	Broadcaster	Rights Fees	Host City	Broadcaster	Rights Fees
N/A	Japan Pool	US$19.0 million	1980 Lake Placid	NHK	US$1.05 million
1984 Los Angeles	Japan Pool	US$50.0 million	1984 Sarajevo	NHK	US$2.50 million
1988 Seoul	Japan Pool	US$62.5 million	1988 Calgary	NHK	US$3.90 million
1992 Barcelona	Japan Pool	US$99.5 million	1992 Albertville	Japan Pool	US$9.0 million
1996 Atlanta	Japan Pool	US$135.0 million	1994 Lillehammer	Japan Pool	US$12.7 million
2000 Sydney	Japan Pool	US$155.0 million	1998 Nagano	Japan Pool	US$37.5 million
2004 Athens	Japan Pool	US$180.0 million	2002 Salt Lake City	Japan Pool	US$37.0 million
2008 Beijing	Japan Pool		2006 Torino	Japan Pool	US$38.5 million

(Continued)

Table 6.3 Continued

ASIA

Arab States

Host City	Olympic Games Broadcaster	Rights Fees	Host City	Olympic Winter Games Broadcaster	Rights Fees
1992 Barcelona	ASBU	US$550,000	N/A		
1996 Atlanta	ASBU	US$3.75 million	N/A		
2000 Sydney	ASBU	US$4.5 million	N/A		
2004 Athens	ASBU	US$5.5 million	N/A		
2008 Beijing	ASBU	US$8.5 million	N/A		

Korea

Host City	Olympic Games Broadcaster	Rights Fees	Host City	Olympic Winter Games Broadcaster	Rights Fees
1984 Los Angeles	Korea Pool	US$2.0 million	1984 Sarajevo	KBS	US$180,000
1988 Seoul	KBS	US$2.85 million	1988 Calgary	no broadcast	
1992 Barcelona	Korea Pool	US$7.5 million	1992 Albertville	no broadcast	
1996 Atlanta	Korea Pool	US$9.75 million	1994 Lillehammer	no broadcast	
2000 Sydney	Korea Pool	US$13.75 million	1998 Nagano	KBS	US$50,000
2004 Athens	Korea Pool	US$15.5 million	2002 Salt Lake City	Korea Pool	US$750,000
2008 Beijing	Korea Pool	US$17.5 million	2006 Torino	Korea Pool	US$900,000

EUROPE

Host City	Olympic Games Broadcaster	Rights Fees	Host City	Olympic Winter Games Broadcaster	Rights Fees
1960 Rome	EBU	US$700,000	N/A		
1964 Tokyo	EBU	N/A	1964 Innsbruck	EBU	US$300,000
1968 Mexico City	EBU	US$1 million	1968 Grenoble	EBU	US$500,000
1972 Munich	EBU	US$2 million	1972 Sapporo	EBU	US$1.40 million
1976 Montreal	EBU	US$6.6 million	1976 Innsbruck	EBU	US$1.20 million
1980 Moscow	EBU	US$7.1 million	1980 Lake Placid	EBU	US$3.855 million

Games (Summer)	Broadcaster	Rights Fee	Games (Winter)	Broadcaster	Rights Fee
1984 Los Angeles	EBU	US$22.0 million	1984 Sarajevo	EBU	US$5.6 million
1988 Seoul	EBU	US$30.2 million	1988 Calgary	EBU	US$6.9 million
1992 Barcelona	EBU	US$94.5 million	1992 Albertville	EBU	US$20.3 million
1996 Atlanta	EBU	US$247.5 million	1994 Lillehammer	EBU	US$26.3 million
2000 Sydney	EBU	US$350 million	1998 Nagano	EBU	US$72.0 million
2004 Athens	EBU	US$394 million	2002 Salt Lake City	EBU	US$120.0 million
2008 Beijing	EBU	US$443.4 million	2006 Torino	EBU	US$135.0 million

OCEANIA

Australia

Games (Summer)	Broadcaster	Rights Fee	Games (Winter)	Broadcaster	Rights Fee
N/A			1980 Lake Placid	ATRANSA	US$60,000
1984 Los Angeles	Channel 10	US$10.6 million	1984 Sarajevo	Channel 7	US$750,000
1988 Seoul	Channel 10	US$7.4 million	1988 Calgary	Channel 9	US$1.14 million
1992 Barcelona	TV Olympics	US$34 million	1992 Albertville	Channel 9	US$8.5 million
1996 Atlanta	Channel 7	US$30 million	1994 Lillehammer	Channel 9	US$5.0 million
2000 Sydney	Channel 7	US$45 million	1998 Nagano	Channel 7	US$6.0 million
2004 Athens	Channel 7	US$50.5 million	2002 Salt Lake City	Channel 7	US$11.75 million
2008 Beijing	Channel 7	AUD$78.8 million	2006 Torino	Channel 7	US$12.8 million

New Zealand

Games (Summer)	Broadcaster	Rights Fee	Games (Winter)	Broadcaster	Rights Fee
N/A			1984 Sarajevo	BCNZ	US$25,000
N/A			1988 Calgary	no broadcast	
1992 Barcelona	TVNZ	US$5.9 million	1992 Albertville	TVNZ	US$135,000
1996 Atlanta	TVNZ	US$5 million	1994 Lillehammer	TVNZ	US$500,000
2000 Sydney	TVNZ	US$10 million	1998 Nagano	TVNZ	US$600,000
2004 Athens	TVNZ	US$3.5 million	2002 Salt Lake City	TVNZ	US$600,000
2008 Beijing	TVNZ	US$4.25 million	2006 Torino	TVNZ	US$350,000

in 2005 US$). In 2007, the budget figure had swelled to approximately £7.27 billion (roughly US$11.7 billion in 2011 US$), an increase partly attributed to updated information and data on the logistics and development costs for each of the proposed Olympic venue sites.[11] None of these budget overruns are a cause for celebration, nor should readers construe these comments as an endorsement of underforecasting, whether deliberate or not. If this book were just about the economics of host city bids, the analysis would have a different tone, especially considering the ongoing tax burden such facilities place on citizens just to support maintenance and related expenses in the years following the Olympics. The host city has a responsibility to continue using the Olympic venues for a wide range of cultural activities and megaevents to ensure their economic viability. Host city bids encompass more than venue construction costs; investments in permanent infrastructure improvement, from public transportation to roads to new services to utilities, all of which are designed to benefit the host city, its citizens, and visitors for years if not generations to come, are also factored into bids. While the bid budgets are usually exceeded, the social and economic impact includes the creation of goodwill that has the potential to enhance the reputation and attractiveness of the host city.

The number of broadcast viewers has grown impressively over the years. Approximately 450 million viewers watched the 1972 Munich Olympics, perhaps the first truly live Olympics broadcast (preceding Olympic television coverage was tape-delayed). More recently, 3.6 billion people accessed the 2000 Sydney Olympics, for a total of 36.1 billion viewer hours (determined by multiplying the length of the program by the number of viewers), and 3.9 billion accessed the 2004 Athens Olympics, for a total of 34.4 billion viewer hours.[12] This slight decrease in viewer hours between 2000 and 2004 is not explained by the IOC's available information, but it may be due partly to the first-time use of streaming technology in Athens, transferring viewers from traditional television broadcasts to the newer, nontraditional formats on the Internet and mobile devices. After 2008, the IOC's Marketing Fact Files, which summarize the preceding Games' financial results, stopped using total viewer hours as a metric and turned to average minute rating instead.

Just as the Olympics have grown in broadcast popularity, the IOC's efforts to create successful broadcast partnerships have grown in sophistication. Olympic host broadcast organizations are responsible for covering the entire range of competitive events and redistributing this content to the Olympic broadcast partners for use in their own countries. Each broadcast partner is free to tailor its national broadcast to reflect the interests of their home fans. The broadcast feed hours provided by each host has grown over the years. For example, the 1988 Seoul Olympics broadcast feed hours totaled 2,572, while the broadcast feed hours for the 2008 Beijing Olympics grew to 5,000, a nearly 100 percent increase. The 1992 Albertville Olympic Winter Games had 350 host broadcast feed hours, while the 2010 Vancouver Olympic Winter Games offered more than 1,000 broadcast feed hours.[13]

The number of broadcast feed hours explains only part of the increased popularity and growing audience size for the Olympic Games. Each country's Olympic broadcast partner creates additional content to supplement the host feed content. In Turin, while the host feed hours totaled more than 1,000, the total coverage amounted to 16,000 hours of Olympics-related content when all Olympic broadcast partners' coverages were added together. These additional hours reflect each broadcast partner's efforts to supplement and enhance the core broadcast feed with content specific to each country. Carefully crafted athlete histories and profiles can turn an unknown athlete into a celebrity and a fan favorite, depending on the unique aspects of that athlete's life. The profiles can stretch the broadcast length of an event by several minutes. The broadcasters also create interesting side stories, interview family members and friends, and/or show scenes of the athlete's hometown, with the various chapters of an athlete's life revealed as he or she progresses through the Olympics from qualifying to the finals.

The broadcasters see economic opportunity in their Olympic investment, which is partly why the number of broadcast hours has increased over the years. More coverage can lead to more opportunities for generating advertising revenue. But the increased viewing hours also add logistical and technological complexity to the broadcast rights bids, driving up the costs. The U.S. broadcast network NBC paid US$2 billion for the U.S. rights to the 2010 Winter Olympics in Vancouver and the 2012 Summer Olympics in London.[14] Then, in June 2011, NBC outbid U.S. rivals Fox and ESPN and was awarded the broadcast rights to the 2014, 2016, 2018, and 2020 Olympiads. The bid amount was US$4.38 billion, covering every media platform, and was the most ever paid for Olympic broadcast rights. For each individual Olympics, NBC paid the following:[15]

2014 Sochi Winter Olympics	$775 million
2016 Rio de Janeiro Summer Olympics	$1.226 billion
2018 Pyeongchang Winter Games	$963 million
2020 Summer Olympics	$1.418 billion

The bid amount was enormous, but the multi-Olympics package will enable NBC to amortize its costs more effectively over several Games. Furthermore, the NBC commitment reflects a long-standing belief that TOP sponsors, other broadcasters, the IOC, and fans all know that the Olympics are more than just a modern commercial media event—they are a one-of-a-kind megasports *storytelling* event.

NBC's Olympics web site (www.nbcolympics.com/) offers extensive material devoted to its Olympics coverage, complete with Web profiles of likely U.S. athletes. One can easily foresee these profiles being transformed into full-fledged television vignettes for those athletes who make the final 2012 U.S. Olympic team. The NBC web site also includes a selection of athlete video profiles from past Olympics. The same is true for England's BBC, where athletes from Beijing in 2008 and those likely to make the 2012 London Olympics are featured (see http://news.bbc.co.uk/sport2/hi/olympic_games/default.stm). The creative dimensions to this effort are important because the right selection of imagery and stories about an athlete can create a memorable experience for viewers, turning an athlete from an unknown to a favorite, and also casting a favorable glow onto the Olympics. Olympic advertisers want viewers to watch the additional content because there is a greater chance their own advertisements will be noticed, gaining a powerful association with both the Olympic Games overall and the athletes in particular. The IOC wants each of its broadcast partners to maximize coverage by creating content that is relevant and appealing to their home viewing audience, thereby increasing the chances viewers will watch more coverage. Furthermore, the better the content broadcasters provide, beyond the sheer hours of coverage across as many events as possible, the easier it is for the IOC to retain existing corporate sponsors and broadcast partners while attracting future sponsors and partners as well. Of course, while television remains an important, indeed dominant, media platform, the growth of digital media platforms is creating additional avenues for the Olympics to provide unique marketing opportunities for corporate sponsors, as discussed in Chapter 20 on marketing communications.[16]

Questions

1. Did the growth of television coverage create the global stage for the Olympics, or did the Olympics serve as the catalyst to attract broadcasters?
2. Which is more important to corporate sponsors: the Olympic Games or the television coverage? Why?
3. What are the positive and negative impacts of the Olympics having such a massive television audience?
4. What challenges do broadcasters face in fulfilling their broadcast obligations?
5. How can sponsors take advantage of the growth of global television coverage of the Olympics?

Chapter 7

The Olympic Halo

The concept of the halo effect produced by the Olympics is an important theme throughout this book. To interpret it as merely a way to gain quick exposure underutilizes the sponsorship and would not take full advantage of the global stage the Olympics provide. There are cheaper ways to gain a brief sales increase. Thus far, this book has argued that the keys to success with an Olympic sponsorship include entering into it with an open mind, a deep respect for Olympic history, and an appreciation for one's own company and its relative fit with Olympic values. Assuming this self-analysis confirms that an Olympic sponsorship makes sense, then marketers must determine the most effective and appropriate way to take advantage of it, since any potential halo effect may be fleeting if the sponsorship is executed poorly. Companies must first focus on clarifying the connection between their strategic brand objectives and their Olympic sponsorship. Company leadership can then determine the short-term tactics and marketing programs to use in support of their strategy.

Developing a long-term brand strategy will help companies agree on a common set of growth and development efforts and is far more likely to result in an increase in brand value over time. Most strategic activities tend toward the intangible ("improve our reputation," "build awareness," "increase market share") and require companies to build deep connections with customers and markets. Such connections are not built over the course of 17 days. Measurable short-term gains, such as an increase in sales and/or units sold, will come from the tactics and programs and must be linked to the long-term brand strategy. Certainly, promotions or new product launches, for example, that are tied to the Olympics can be useful tactics that take advantage of the Olympic sponsorship while also helping the company build toward its strategic objectives. The Olympic Games effect, as this book emphasizes, can help TOP sponsors achieve tangible gains through Olympic-themed tactics while also associating the company with the positive values and attributes of the Olympics. Over an extended sponsorship commitment of several Olympiads, sponsors stand to gain significant benefits if they build on the foundation of their earlier efforts.

Long-Term

The questions at the end of Section I provide a good starting point for sponsors in determining the role the sponsorship plays in moving the company closer to its strategic objectives. Recall that the sponsorship preparation questions provided guidance for evaluating the attractiveness of any sports event, organized around four themes:

1. Ultimate Dream
2. Values
3. Creating Value
4. Personality

The questions are important for any sponsoring company because they improve the understanding of the company's strategic intent and how to most effectively take advantage of their sports sponsorship investment, plus the questions will create a common foundation of knowledge for management in its sponsorship decision-making process.

The questions are to be answered as a management team and not by any one individual so that key decision makers debate each of these themes and questions within the group and work collaboratively to arrive at a common view of their firm. Exploring each of these themes can crystallize management thinking about image issues vital to the long-term success and attractiveness of the company. Long-term brand planning includes focusing on three key areas: positioning, awareness, and market growth objectives.

Positioning

Positioning refers to how customers view a company, its products, and/or its services. Marketers expend substantial thinking and creativity on influencing their company's position, but it is important to recognize that a company's position is really more of a reflection of how customers see the company versus any overt, heavy-handed advertising message that attempts to tell the market what to think. Positioning can be affected by choosing the right marketing vehicles, such as sports sponsorships. Indeed, sponsorships can help customers view a company differently or simply more carefully, assuming the other themes of ultimate dream, values, creating value, and personality are consistent with the position communicated.

The Olympics are a prestigious event, and the Olympic Games effect strongly suggests corporate sponsors will have some of this prestige rub off on them, benefiting their position in the market. For example, Visa's brand preference (a measure of loyalty that indicates consumer preference for one brand versus the offerings of competitors) increased to 50 percent in the United States, rating Visa as the "Best Overall Card." While this is not a specific measure of prestige, the connotation of *best* is clear, affording Visa a measure of prestige in the credit card category.

Visa's image as the best overall card did not happen during or immediately after its first Olympic sponsorship in Calgary in 1988. The Visa case study in Chapter 16 discusses Visa's rise in detail, but the improvement has occurred over 25 years, a reasonable indication that Visa took a long-term view of Olympic sponsorship.

Lenovo became a TOP sponsor in time for the 2006 Torino Winter Olympics and 2008 Beijing Olympics. The timing was crucial for the company because it had just acquired IBM's PC division in 2005, changed its name from Legend to Lenovo, and was intent on globally positioning itself as a reputable, innovative computer maker. The effort was challenging, given the compressed two-Olympic, four-year time horizon of their sponsorship. Although Lenovo did not continue its TOP sponsorship after the 2008 Beijing Olympics, the company made positive progress toward its goals, gaining in market share, launching award-winning computers, and innovating in both computer and noncomputer design, as their winning Olympic Cloud of Promise torch design illustrated. Lenovo's case study is an instructive example of a one-quadrennium sponsor (one Winter and one Summer Games) that used the Olympics for a specific and finite purpose at a unique time (and, arguably, a vulnerable time) for the company.

Coca-Cola has been an Olympic sponsor since 1928 (and is now the longest continuous sponsor of the modern Olympics), using the Games to associate its brand with the active lifestyle the Olympics promote. Over the years, Coke has introduced new products, launched an Olympic Pin program, and supported the Olympics with in-kind product support, among many activities. While the Olympics are one of many marketing investments for Coke, the company continues to derive benefit from the sponsorship. As Coca-Cola states,

> The Coca-Cola Company supports the Olympic Games primarily because we share the values of Olympism that, in addition to embracing the vision of a better and more-peaceful world, encourage the discovery of one's abilities and promote the spirit of competition, the pursuit of excellence and a sense of fair play.[1]

More about Coca-Cola's Olympic sponsorship is discussed in its case study in Chapter 15.

Samsung undertook Olympic sponsorship in 1997 as part of a strategic effort to reposition the entire company. Chris Fay, CEO of Saatchi & Saatchi Taiwan, said that Samsung's sponsorship helped boost global sales,

> Prior to the Olympics, Samsung was nowhere on the map in terms of brand awareness.[2]

Acer became an Olympic TOP sponsor in 2007 for a four-year agreement beginning in 2009, taking Lenovo's place as the exclusive worldwide PC sponsors. The agreement encompasses the 2010 Vancouver Winter Olympics and the 2012 London Summer Olympics. While the exact sponsorship fees paid were not disclosed, most estimates suggest Acer paid between $80 and $85 million. Acer President Gianfranco Lanci said,

> (becoming a TOP sponsor) . . . is going to be a big step forward for us in the direction to be a real global company.[3]

Awareness

Companies want to increase their awareness because the more they are known, the greater their chance of acquiring customers. (It is hard to ask for, let alone buy, something one is not aware exists.) Awareness is measured in several ways, but aided and unaided awareness (also known as aided or unaided recall) are most common. Aided awareness is measured by showing survey respondents a product, ad, brand name, or trademark and asking them when they recall last seeing it. Unaided awareness asks respondents to recall *any* product, ad, brand name, or trademark they recall seeing recently.[4] Prior to the 1994 Olympics in Lillehammer, consumers were asked to name brands associated with the Olympics. Coca-Cola was correctly identified as a TOP sponsor, with 22 percent unaided awareness (meaning that consumers did not need product or category prompting). Coke Chairman and CEO Muhtar Kent said that Coke's sponsorship of the 2010 Vancouver Olympics was successful:

> We just concluded our successful Vancouver Olympics program, which helped improve trademark Coca-Cola brand equity scores with Teen in Canada. And these improvements are flowing to the bottom-line as we've grown dollar share for trademark Coca-Cola and system revenue in Canada to their highest levels in years.[5]

Sponsorships have grown in sophistication ever since, in an effort to achieve equivalent top-of-mind recall. Visa has enjoyed important gains in awareness, as one might expect. These increases played a key role in driving the company's financial performance improvements in the past 25 years. The company's unaided awareness grew to 72 percent following the 2000 Olympics in Sydney, for example, although one should not confuse this number with Coca-Cola's because Visa was measuring overall unaided awareness and not any specific association with the Olympics.[6]

In 1996, Samsung senior management set forth a plan to revamp its business and substantially raise its brand value. Samsung has been an Olympic TOP sponsor since 1997 in the wireless communications category. The company's market awareness has increased substantially since, with a 5 percent rise in unaided awareness to 16.2 percent from its sponsorship of the 2000 Sydney Olympics alone. Awareness grew again, from 57 percent to 62 percent, following the 2004 Athens Olympics. Since 1999, brand value has grown over fivefold to $16.8 billion. Samsung has agreed to be a TOP sponsor through the 2016 Olympics. While not all of this brand value or awareness increase is directly attributable to the Olympics sponsorship, Samsung management believes their association with the Olympic movement has been instrumental in reshaping the company's image.[7]

Acer did not specify awareness targets it hoped to achieve from its Olympic sponsorship, but the company did hope to demonstrate the quality of its products by supplying a wide range of technology devices for both the Vancouver and London Olympics. For example, the company expected to supply more than 10,000 monitors, 1,500 touchscreens, 1,500 laptops, 900 servers, five storage area networks (SANs), and 350 trained engineers and technical experts.[8]

Market Growth

Market growth describes changes (increases or decreases) in business year over year, either in units sold or total dollar volume. Market growth can also be measured by reviewing market share (total company sales as a percentage of the total market).[9]

Visa's market share rose from 33 percent in 1986 to 57.3 percent in 2010, with MasterCard the next closest competitor at 31.8 percent, followed by American Express at 8 percent,[10] an increase that coincides with the company's Olympic sports marketing investments. Total transaction volume grew from $111 billion to $5.6 trillion during this time, and the total number of cards issued grew from 137 million to 1.8 billion.[11]

Samsung's mobile phone market share increased from 5 percent in 1999 to 19.2 percent as of mid-2011 (second behind Apple's 20.3 percent share), and sales increased from 17 million units to 280 million units (2010 figures) during that time, surpassing Nokia (the former market leader dropped to third with 16.7 share). As an example of Olympics-specific benefits from sponsorship activation, Samsung saw telecommunications sales increase 44 percent following the 2000 Sydney Olympics.[12]

Acer anticipated growth in select strategic markets. As Wong Chi-man of Hong Kong–based China Everbright Research stated:

> The Olympic sponsorship makes sense for Acer's marketing strategy in light of its recent acquisition of Gateway which supplies computers to North America, and Packard Bell which has a strong presence in Europe. Like Lenovo, which saw a marketing opportunity with the Beijing Olympic Games, Acer sees an effective promotion channel in the geographic markets where it is trying to build its brand.[13]

Coca-Cola's long-standing support of the Olympics has paid dividends, according to the company. The company attributes market share growth in the year following the 2010 Vancouver Olympics to its TOP sponsorship.[14]

Short-Term

As we will see in Section IV, "Reputation Development," and the case briefs in particular, sponsors do have short-term objectives. These vary significantly based on each company. But the important point is not to focus on the differences in the short-term tactics they employ. Instead, short-term tactics depend entirely on a company's business objectives and situation. To increase short-term growth means that a company has to improve the sales and/or profits of its offerings. The Ansoff Matrix[15] shown in Figure 7.1 is a useful device for structuring marketing thinking around product and market growth choices, and the resulting marketing implications.

	Current Products	New Products
Current Markets	A **Grow in Current Markets** Increase market share Increase product usage	B **Product Development** Add product features New-generation products
New Markets	C **Market Development** Expand geographically Identify new segments	D **Diversification** Related Unrelated

Figure 7.1   Growth Choices

Quadrant A

Selecting this quadrant means planning focuses on increasing sales with current products in current markets. There are two ways to accomplish this:

1. Increase market share: To do this requires taking share and customers away from competitors.
   Implications for sports sponsorships
   Company management must have a clear understanding of their strengths and competitor vulnerabilities if competitors' customers are to be convinced to switch.
2. Increase product usage: This means existing customers must buy more of the company's products.
   Implications for sports sponsorships
   Company management must have detailed customer profiles and needs if they are to persuade their own customers to buy more.

Quadrant B

Choosing this quadrant focuses the company on selling new or improved products to current markets. There are two ways to do this:

1. Add product features: R&D attention must focus on improving existing products to appeal to existing customers to increase their purchases.

2. New-generation products: R&D's emphasis is developing wholly new products based on their understanding of existing customers and then hoping the new products are appealing, convincing customers to either supplement their current product purchases or replace them with the new product.

Implications for sports sponsorships

In both cases, company management must commit to a more complex and expensive product strategy since money will be spent on explaining the new product features and/or the new products to existing and/or competitor customers (to increase share) while also implementing the other facets of the sports sponsorship plan.

Quadrant C

This quadrant directs company management attention to finding new markets for current products. This is accomplished in two ways:

1. Expand geographically: Management must select new locations (region, country), preferably where the customers are similar to existing customers in existing markets.

Implications for sports sponsorships

New geographies create new logistical and operational challenges, including possible language and culture differences. Management must be prepared to handle demand and communications issues as interest grows.

2. Identify new segments: New segments can be in existing or new geographies, requiring more extensive knowledge of different customer groups and their associated characteristics. Ideally, preference should be given to those segments with some overlap to existing segments to minimize investment.

Implications for sports sponsorships

New segments can be in existing or new geographies. If the segments are in existing geographies, then management must focus on making the products relevant to the new segments. If the segments are in new geographies, then management has to emphasize product relevance in the cultural and language context.

Quadrant D

Selecting this quadrant means developing entirely new products for entirely new markets. There are two ways:

1. Related: This means the company pursues new products sold to new markets, but within the same industry.

   ### Implications for sports sponsorships

   In this case, companies must be careful not to dilute or erode the company's current brand position or detract from the sports sponsorship effort. This is akin to launching a new company, albeit in a familiar industry, so it is a major effort unto itself, let alone the existing effort to execute on the sports sponsorship properly. It is unlikely a company would do this as a linked growth strategy to the sports sponsorship since they are fundamentally two separate business efforts.

2. Unrelated: This is pure pioneering work in both new products and new markets.

   ### Implications for sports sponsorships

   This is the highest-risk growth choice of all and, as such, requires extraordinary dedication and resources (financial, people, energy, time) to succeed. Given the existing demands on supporting the sports sponsorship, this choice has little or no benefit for the sponsorship and would not make sense unless the company has enormous resources.

The quadrant D choices are the least attractive since growth objectives cannot be clearly tied to the sponsorship. Marketers will want to concentrate on quadrants A, B, or C, which leverage existing knowledge and experience and can conceivably be linked to the sponsorship.

Now that marketers have made a growth choice, attention must be turned to the marketing implications (Figure 7.2), including what marketing mix components should be employed to maximize the growth opportunity in each quadrant.

Quadrant A

To convince existing customers to buy more or to steal customers from competitors, marketing has two tactics at its disposal:

	Current Products	New Products
Current Markets	A **Grow in Current Markets** Heavy marketing and sales Price penetration	B **Product Development** R&D investment Heavy marketing and sales Market research Price skimming or penetration Channel development
New Markets	C **Markets Development** Heavy marketing and sales Market research Channel development	D **Diversification** Heavy R&D investment Heavy marketing and sales Heavy market research Price skimming or penetration Intensive channel development

Figure 7.2   Marketing Implications[16]

1. Heavy marketing and sales: *Heavy* means spending more money and/or increasing the frequency and/or diversity of marketing and selling activities. For existing customers, the marketing message and sales education effort must explain clearly why they should buy more products and what the benefits are. To take customers from competitors, the communications effort will need to persuade customers that your product is different, how that difference is relevant, and why they should care.

2. Price penetration: Increasing share and/or taking competitor customers can sometimes be a function of price—charge less for the same or equivalent products, and more customers will be attracted. The downside is handling complaints from existing customers who paid a higher price previously (as Apple faced when it reduced the price of its first iPhone by $200 just two months after its introduction).

   Implications for sports sponsorships

   Spending more on marketing and sales and price penetration are primarily promotion-focused strategies designed to sharply increase sales over the short term. They are the same as discounting—either the discount is applied directly to the product or the added marketing expense is ultimately deducted from revenues—and both lead to reduced margins. Reduced prices and margins may be counterintuitive or even contradictory, particularly if the sports event is the Olympics with its premier position in the market and the company's long-term brand strategy is to enhance its profile and reputation.

Quadrant B

Convincing existing or competitors' customers to purchase the new or improved products requires marketing to develop a multipart plan:

1. **R&D investment:** In many companies, such as consumer products, marketing may have responsibility for product line development, which means planning each product, extension, and level. Product development expenditures (sourcing, molds, samples, prototypes) are allocated to associated departments, including marketing.

2. **Heavy marketing and sales:** Since this is either an entirely new product launch or an update to a known product, marketing communications programs that explain the products to the market are required. The new product, in particular, will need to be properly positioned, even though the audience is customers from an existing market.

3. **Market research:** Investment in customer data acquisition (updating profile data, trends) will help marketing understand how to position the products.

4. **Price skimming or penetration:** Unlike price penetration as discussed earlier, price skimming targets a very select customer subset, often early adopters, who will pay more for the new product. The term refers to skimming the best customers off the top, knowing that they will pay more and that the rest of the customers will not. The benefit is higher margins and the development of a more exclusive image. The disadvantage is that unit sales and revenues may be lower, as will market share.

5. **Channel development:** Marketing must place the products into the existing company distribution channels, which means convincing channels to accept this new product in addition to existing products, and/or identify new channels that also reach the existing customers but are uniquely qualified with this particular type of product or new feature.

Implications for sports sponsorships
The marketing challenge increases with the addition of new products and/or features since resources and organizational coordination must successfully manage the products in addition to the core sponsorship activities. The company is already expending effort at creating a marketing communications plan to implement the sponsorship investment, so the new products' communication plans have to be carefully incorporated if additional sponsorship leverage is to succeed.

Quadrant C

Selling existing products to new markets through geographic expansion or to new customer groups means marketing has to introduce the company and/or its products since the target audiences may well be unfamiliar with them. Areas of marketing focus should be:

1. Heavy marketing and sales: New audiences require clear communication, just as new products do. Marketing's planning efforts will have to carefully tailor campaigns to each new market, which requires additional coordination with new partners and agencies. Field sales will need to learn about the customer profiles to develop a workable sales plan, which means training investments will be required.
2. Market research: Similar to the market research needs for the quadrant B choice, marketers need to gather useful information and insights about their new target customers if marketing and selling campaigns are to be properly developed.
3. Channel development: New markets may have different distribution channels, so regional management and field sales will need to learn about the differences. The possibility of working with local partners emerges here, which is helpful but can add expense.

   Implications for sports sponsorships
   Marketing to new customers is a different but equally tough challenge. The company may be able to leverage previous investments in marketing communications but would be well advised to ensure proper translation into terms relevant to new markets. This, too, requires additional marketing spending and

resource effort, which must be coordinated with the overall sports sponsorship plan.

Quadrant D

Selling new products into new markets requires an even more comprehensive, expensive, and resource-intensive effort than quadrant C's. This is analogous to Coca-Cola trying to sell surgical tools to doctors under a new brand name (they aren't!). Hypothetically, while research might have suggested this as a good growth opportunity, it would be hard to imagine how this could be linked with Olympic Games sponsorship.

In Section IV, "Reputation Development," TOP sponsor case analyses are presented that describe the actual Olympic sponsorship activities of several TOP partner sponsors. While each company's short- and long-term objectives are discussed, each has an entirely different approach to leveraging its Olympic sponsorship.

Questions

1. Is it possible for a company to successfully reposition itself by sponsoring the Olympics?
2. What do sponsoring companies need to do to ensure that associating with the Olympics can help reposition them?
3. Does improving awareness lead to increased sales, brand value, and market share? Explain.
4. Should sponsors use the Olympics to grow in current markets? Grow via product development? Grow through market development? Grow via diversification? How would you determine the best approach?
5. Would your growth strategy change if you sponsored more than one Olympic Quadrennium? Why or why not?

Chapter 8

The Olympic Spirit

The Olympic spirit is often best seen during surprising moments when competitors arise from seemingly nowhere or overcome substantial challenges. Throughout the history of the Games, an athlete or team comes through with a completely unexpected performance that beats the odds, earning a permanent place in the memories of fans and athletes. Surprises are not always victories, either. Athletes have risen from obscurity to capture the imagination of the public, even if only for a short while. Each Olympic competition is an unknown, even if recognized favorites are competing. There are no guarantees that the presumptive favorite will strike gold. This hint of uncertainty is a fundamental interest driver in most sports, but it takes on special meaning in the Olympics because of the relative infrequency of the Games as compared to the championships of other sports and because of the exalted status accorded Olympic athletes. The term *Olympian* conjures up images of grand performances, even if the athlete does not win. It is used in society to describe particularly impressive or heroic accomplishments in many professions. An Olympian has reached the highest level of a sport and is competing in the most revered event in the world. A few are highlighted here to illustrate the ability of these athletes to inspire and provide added vitality to the Olympic legend.

Vera Caslavska, 1968 Olympics in Mexico City

When surprises occur, the world takes notice, as do companies, because the accomplishment is out of the ordinary. There are many examples of athletes whose Olympic success occurred over multiple Olympiads and in the intervening international competitions between Games. That is not surprising. Al Oerter won gold in the discus over four consecutive Olympics from 1956 in Melbourne to 1968 in Mexico City. People would have been surprised had he not won. But a Czechoslovakian gymnast named Vera Caslavska was the notable one in Mexico City in 1968. She had won three gold medals and a silver medal at the 1964 Olympic Games in Tokyo and was expected to repeat her success in Mexico City. But in the weeks leading up to the Olympics, the Soviet Union invaded Czechoslovakia, and she fled into hiding in the mountains to avoid arrest, where she maintained her fitness by practicing in the trees and fields. She was eventually granted permission to compete in Mexico City, but no one knew what toll her experience might have taken on her abilities. However, she won four gold medals and two silver medals, an amazing accomplishment considering her very recent adverse circumstances.[1]

Miracle on Ice, 1980 Olympics in Lake Placid

The Soviet Union dominated hockey in 1980. The team had well-known government support, superb coaching, and training facilities, and they played consistently well internationally. In the year prior to the Olympics, the Soviet team played several exhibition matches against teams from the NHL, ending with a 5-3-1 record. For NHL fans, their professional hockey players were the best in the world, so being on the losing end of the win–loss record against their archrival (this was during the Cold War, when passions and suspicions between the United States and the Soviet Union were at an all-time high) was difficult to endure. As with prior Olympics, the United States fielded a team of talented young amateurs, some from the college level. But the team was seeded seventh out of 12 and was clearly not considered a favorite to win any medal, let alone gold.[2]

The U.S. team surprised many sports fans by tying Sweden, considered a superior team, 2-2. The U.S. team then defeated the Czechoslovakian team 7-3, a dramatic and impressive win over a team many believed to be as formidable as the one from the Soviet Union. After another three wins, the U.S. team qualified for the medal round of play. The Soviet team crushed most of its competitors en route to the medal round, including a 16-0 blowout of the Japanese team. The Soviets were heavy favorites to win their sixth gold medal, out of the seven previous Olympics.

The U.S. and Soviet teams met in the penultimate game, with the winner moving on to the gold medal game. The game went back and forth and eventually the U.S. team went ahead 4-3 with about eight minutes to play. As the game wound down to its final seconds with the clearly pro-American crowd cheering wildly, an American TV broadcast announcer named Al Michaels, sounding as astonished as everybody else, described the last few seconds of the game and shouted what are now immortal words,

> Eleven seconds, you've got ten seconds, the countdown going on right now! Morrow, up to Silk . . . five seconds left in the game. . . . **Do you believe in miracles? Yes! Unbelievable!**[3]

The U.S. team went on to win the gold medal by defeating Finland 4-2 in the championship. But for U.S. sports fans, the game against the Soviet Union was the sports event of the year. It was a culminating event that translated into a wave of national pride that lasted long after the Olympics ended and serves as a vibrant reminder of why the Olympics are so widely loved.

Eddie the Eagle, 1988 Winter Olympics at Calgary

Michael "Eddie the Eagle" Edwards competed for Great Britain in ski jumping at the 1988 Calgary Olympics. He had no outside financial support, self-funding his training and Olympic journey. His surprising fame was not due to winning the gold medal. Edwards was notable because he finished last (55th and 58th in the two ski jump events) and, in the process, won the hearts of fans. (Edwards contends that he did not finish last in one of his events because he beat a French ski jumper who had broken his leg the day before. As Edwards said jokingly, "I'm going to take it because he's French.") Part of his charm was his relaxed attitude, everyday appearance, and humor. As he recounted in a 2007 interview about how he was able to qualify for the Olympics,[4]

> At the time there was a rule that a country could send one representative to each sport in the Olympics. I loved skiing and as a kid I wanted to be a stuntman, so I decided to put them together. Nobody else applied. I mean, I wasn't completely incompetent: I'd done a 77m jump, which wasn't big by Olympic standards, and I held the record for stunt jumping [10 cars and six buses]. I realised two years before the Olympics that I might be able to get to Calgary because no one else was going to apply and so started training. I got a lot of advice from Austrian and French ski-jumping coaches, but because I can't speak French or German, a lot of it went over my head.[5]

His poor eyesight required Edwards to wear thick glasses during his jumps, and they often fogged up. His equipment was decidedly average compared to that of his competitors, and it was rumored that he had to wear five to six pairs of socks to keep his boots fitting snuggly. Despite his lack of a typical athlete's support or equipment, Edwards was the United Kingdom's best ski jumper and held the British record, although it must be stated that he was also their only ski jumper at the time and the first to have competed in the Olympics. This list of rather unremarkable qualities still enabled him to compete and win the hearts of fans around the world. Whenever he jumped at Calgary, fans chanted his name and cheered his jumps enthusiastically. Eddie the Eagle was even referenced by the president of the Calgary Olympics in his closing remarks when he said that some athletes soared like an eagle. Following the Calgary Olympics, Edwards enjoyed several years of celebrity.

I did things I thought I'd never get chance to do. I sung a few records, opened nightclubs. . . . I did loads of TV and radio work all over the world—travelling by private jet and helicopter from one job to the next. It was great. And the attention from these beautiful women who two weeks before Calgary wouldn't have even noticed me. It was amazing.[6]

Edwards earned a law degree in the 1990s but has since settled into a comfortable life working in construction in the United Kingdom and giving motivational speeches.[7]

Jamaican Bobsled Team, 1988 Winter Olympics at Calgary

The 1988 Winter Olympics in Calgary saw Jamaica enter the four-man bobsled event for the first time. Their entry was unusual to say the least, given the lack of snow in their country. To finance their Olympic training and travel, they sold reggae records, T-shirts, and sweatshirts. Their Olympic debut was marred by crashes and technical glitches, but they became media and fan favorites in Calgary, and their efforts inspired a 1993 movie *Cool Runnings*, starring John Candy. They tried again in Albertville in 1992, where they finished 14th, ahead of teams from Italy, France, Russia, and the United States, surprising fans around the world. They entered a two-man event as well, finishing 10th, ahead of the Swedish national champions. In 2000, the team won the gold medal at the World Push Championships in Monte Carlo. They did not qualify for the 2010 Winter Olympics in Vancouver after unsuccessful efforts in 2002 in Salt Lake City and 2006 in Torino, due partly to poor funding. Despite not winning an Olympic medal as a team, former Jamaican team members have gone on to success. Lascelles Brown, who was the brakeman on the Jamaican team, moved to Canada to train. He became a Canadian citizen one month before the Torino Olympics and went on to win the silver medal in the two-man event (along with Pierre Lueders, not a former Jamaican). The Brazilian team claims an indirect connection to the Jamaican team in that the founder and president of the Brazilian ice sports federation,

Eric Maleson, states that he was inspired to start the Brazilian team after seeing *Cool Runnings*.[8]

The 1994 Russian Winter Olympics Team

The end of the Soviet Union came beginning in August 1991, following a failed coup attempt by a group of former KGB and military leaders. Boris Yeltsin climbed a tank outside the Russian White House, urging people to oppose the coup. By December 1991, Yeltsin and Mikhail Gorbachev (the former Soviet leader) had worked out a transfer of power, and by January 1992, the Soviet Union was no more, and suddenly 15 former Soviet republics were now independent states. As the former republics went their separate ways, so did their athletes. When the 1994 Winter Olympics came along, there was uncertainty about how the Russian team would perform. The Russian team surprised everybody by winning 23 medals, 11 of which were gold—the most of any country, marking a successful and remarkable performance by a country still in the early stages of its new political independence.[9]

Karnam Malleswari

In this era when society tends to celebrate gold medal winners only, we lose sight of the fact that simply qualifying for the Olympics is a significant accomplishment. Most Olympic athletes go home without any medals, let alone winning gold. And while a gold medal is indeed a worthy accomplishment and will always stand for the very best, being an Olympian signifies a level of quality and competitive ability that is *among* the very best. Not winning gold undoubtedly disappoints, yet silver and bronze medal winners deserve praise and recognition. After all, they are among the top three in their specialty of all athletes in the world. Furthermore, their accomplishments represent something important and meaningful to themselves, their family and friends, and their countries. Karnam Malleswari is one such athlete. An accomplished female weight lifter, Karnam competed for India from the mid-1990s to early 2000s. She won a gold medal at the world championships in 1994, and in 1995, she won the Asian championship. Karnam also won a silver medal at the 1998 Asian Games in Bangkok, signaling she was a competitor of global stature. She then went on to win the bronze medal at the 2000 Sydney Olympics. The importance of this bronze medal cannot be overstated. Karnam was the first Indian woman to win an Olympic medal of *any* kind in the Olympic Games. She received numerous national honors as well, including the Rajiv Gandhi Khel Ratna award in 1994–1995, named after India's former prime minister. It is India's highest sports award.[10]

Matthias Steiner

Matthias Steiner was diagnosed with diabetes when he was 18 years old. This did not stop his competitive desire, however. In the 2004 Summer Olympics in Athens, Austrian Matthias Steiner competed in the 105 kilogram category for weight lifting, finishing seventh. In the years between the 2004 and 2008 Olympics, Steiner's life changed in several important ways. He had a falling out with the Austrian Weightlifting Federation; moved to Germany to spend time with his future wife, Susann; and subsequently became a German citizen. Susann and Matthias were saving to support his goal of returning to the Olympics. For 2008, he wanted to compete in the superheavyweight category. To do so, he gained nearly 90 pounds and worked on his strength and technique. Tragically, in July 2007, Susann was in a horrible car accident. While she lay dying in the hospital, Matthias pledged he would make their Olympic dream come true. As the 2008 Olympics unfolded, Steiner was not the favorite. Evgeny Chigishev of Russia and world champion Viktors Scerbatiths of Latvia (who was competing in his fourth Olympics) were favored. Chigishev was in the lead after his final lift, leaving Steiner with one last improbable chance to win. To win, he had to lift 258 kilograms (569 pounds), more than he had ever lifted before. He did it, and the ensuing celebration showed a buoyant superheavyweight jumping up and down effortlessly on the stage as if he were on a trampoline. During the medal ceremony, TV cameras showed Steiner displaying an understandable mix of emotions from smiles of joy to tears, holding his gold medal, flowers, and a picture of his late wife, Susann.[11]

Petra Majdic

Going into the 2010 Vancouver Olympics, Petra Majdic was the favorite to win gold in the Women's Individual Cross Country Sprint, an intense 1.4-kilometer race. She had finished eighth in the 2002 Salt Lake Olympics and sixth in the 2006 Turin Olympics. She had a remarkable season in 2008–2009, winning nine World Cup events. In the 2009–2010 season prior to the Winter Olympics, she won an additional four World Cup events. But her toughness was never tested more than during the 2010 Vancouver Olympics. While warming up for her event, she crashed off course, falling down a hillside into a gully and breaking five ribs. Despite her injuries and tremendous pain, she competed with sheer grit and determination, getting through the qualifying round into the quarterfinals and then the semifinals. During the semifinals, one of the broken ribs punctured a lung, causing it to collapse. Inexplicably, she somehow finished third, earning the bronze medal and the admiration of her teammates and fellow competitors. She was also the first Slovenian woman to win an Olympic medal in cross-country skiing. By the time she retired from competitive cross-country skiing in 2011, she had amassed an impressive record of 24 World Cup wins, placing her fourth in all time.[12]

Joannie Rochette

At the 2010 Vancouver Winter Olympics, Canadian women's figure skater Joannie Rochette earned the bronze medal. Her performance was considered superb, but the most impressive part was not related to her athleticism—it was instead her emotional fortitude. Four days before, her mother, Therese Rochette, died suddenly from a heart attack. The sense of loss was profound for her, but she was determined to finish the competition to honor her mother. Barely keeping her emotions in check during both the short and long programs, with the entire crowd cheering in support and waving the Canadian flag, Joannie turned in one of the most inspiring performances of the entire Olympics.

As she said afterward,

I feel so proud, and the result didn't matter. But I'm happy to be on the podium. That was my goal here. It's been a lifetime project with my mom, and we achieved that.[13]

Joannie was selected by the Canadian Olympic Committee to be the flag bearer for the closing ceremonies, capping a bittersweet Olympic Games for her. Canada had many deserving gold and silver medal winners who could have easily been chosen by the Canadian Olympic Committee for this honor, but she captured the spirit and essence of the Olympic Games. Olympic success is not always about winning gold—it is about overcoming challenges.[14]

The TOP sponsors—indeed, even domestic sponsors—seek the association with the Olympics because of the many different connection points the Games have with fans and viewers around the world. Gold medal winners will of course have the greatest commercial potential, and if some sponsors are lucky enough to have supported an athlete who goes on to win gold, then the added benefits include enhanced awareness and visibility for the brand, even if for just a short period of time. But part of the benefit sponsors gain is the sheer depth of competitor excellence in every sport at the Olympics, which appeals to fans around the world. Companies are not naive enough to assume that their sponsorship of a top athlete prior to the Games will somehow lead to a gold medal, even if that athlete is ranked first in the world in that sport. Instead, sponsors want an Olympics that energizes fans everywhere, provides well-run and exciting competitions, and reveals fascinating new human interest stories that capture the world's imagination. Such stories are not necessarily about gold medal winners, or at least not always the gold medal winners we expect. Often, whether athletes win gold or not, their trials and tribulations add a vital emotional component that serves as a magnetic attraction for fans. Athletes and their unique circumstances become the real story of the Olympics, generating new press coverage, causing chatter and buzz on the Internet and digital media, and attracting more fans through the viral effects of word of mouth who are eager to watch the Games in anticipation of more surprises and compelling stories.

Questions

1. Why would sponsors want to risk their marketing investment on athletes when outcomes are not guaranteed?
2. Evaluate the difference in benefits sponsors might receive from a gold medal winner versus an athlete who does not win but has a more compelling personal story.
3. Are athletes being unfairly taken advantage of by corporate sponsors and broadcast media because of their elite status?
4. How important are individual athlete stories to the overall success of the Olympics, particularly for sponsors?

Chapter 9

Section II Sponsorship Preparation Questions

In this section, we discuss the significant visibility the Olympics has and brings to corporate sponsors. Given the size of the global stage, sports sponsorship marketers must approach their planning and preparation differently than a conventional marketing campaign. While the duration of the Games is a little more than two weeks, the sheer enormity of the spectacle and the variety of events create the potential for unprecedented exposure. Questions to address:

Global Stage

(These questions apply to both TV and in-venue considerations.)

1. What do we want the world to know about us?
   a. Identify two or three key must-haves and ignore the rest.

2. What do we want the world to see?
   a. What are the signage limitations in our sponsorship agreement?
   b. What is our plan for signage?
   c. What is the enduring image we want people to remember?
3. How do we leverage media relationships?
   a. Who do we know at the major broadcasters, and can they help us?
   b. What media kits do we need to provide? What should the content be?
4. Are there conflicting or competing sponsorship agreements that may hinder or inhibit the visibility of our brand (such as official Olympic apparel versus the athlete's individual apparel sponsorship)?
   a. How do we address any potential conflicts?
   b. What do we tell our athletes? The IOC?
5. Are there any partnerships we want to highlight during the Games, either via marketing communications or through providing equipment and supplies?
   a. What is the best way to promote this partnership without diluting our brand?
6. What is the perception of the sports event?

Olympic Games Effect
Long-Term

1. What is the market position we want to own, and how will this sports event help us get there?
   a. What do we consider a reasonable long-term time horizon?
   b. What checkpoints do we need to determine if we are staying on track?
2. What are our awareness objectives, both qualitatively and quantitatively?
3. What are our long-term market growth objectives?
   a. Market share?
   b. Revenue?
   c. Profits?
   d. Number of customers?
   e. Customer loyalty measures?

Short-Term

1. What are the product tactics we want to implement?
   a. Existing or new products? Both?
   b. New features?
2. What are the short-term market growth objectives?
   a. Increase customer usage?
   b. Steal customers from competitors?
   c. Identify new segments?

Overcoming the Odds and Dealing with Surprises

1. Do you have a plan for supporting serendipitous events that may benefit your company (e.g., an athlete you sponsor wins gold, defeating the heavily favored winner)?
   a. How will you handle increased demand?
   b. Who is accountable for taking proper advantage of good news situations?
   c. Are roles clearly understood?
   d. Which people are assigned responsibility for keeping attention focused on the opportunity?
2. Can you leverage the situation to benefit your company, even though you are not affiliated with the athlete or team in the surprising situation?
   a. If so, can you do so genuinely, or will you risk turning off customers?
   b. Who else needs to or should be involved?
3. What will you do to celebrate this success with:
   a. Employees?
   b. Customers?
   c. Stakeholders?
   d. The market?
4. How would you prevent this from turning negative?
   a. Do you have a plan for avoiding overcommercialization?
   b. What if your athlete performs below expectations?
   c. If tragedy strikes, how would you handle it?
5. What performance incentives might enhance your sponsorship?
   a. Will you continue to support an athlete and/or an event and honor your contract, even if they do not achieve success?

III

CONTROVERSY AND CHALLENGE

Chapter 10

The Olympic Challenges

T he Olympics have had their share of challenges, scandals, and switched loyalties throughout history, whether it was because of politics, cheating, financial bribery, or even an ill-considered effort to better one's lot in life.

Astylos of Crotona earned fame as a sprinter, competing and winning in the stade and diaulos in the 73rd, 74th, and 75th Olympiads in 488, 484, and 480 BC, making him famous as he matched the running success of Chionis of Sparta. Besting Chionis, Astylos also competed and won an event called the hoplites, in which competitors raced wearing a suit of armor. He was particularly noteworthy because he first competed for Crotona but then switched to Syracuse in an attempt to gain support from Syracuse Hieron, a tyrant. His switch of loyalties was not a well-received move, angering the people from Crotona who subsequently destroyed his house and statue to demonstrate their hostility and disapproval. In 388 BC, Eupolus of Thessaly bribed three boxers to throw their fights against him, and he was subsequently fined and required to build six bronze statues of Zeus. City-states were known for their efforts to recruit top athletes from rivals by paying substantial sums and asking them to lie about their homes. The ancient equivalent of boycotts occurred when athletes' city-states refused to participate due to ongoing tensions with sister territories.[1]

Much later, Rome's Emperor Nero (AD 37–AD 68) saw himself as artistic and cultured. Finding many of the athletic aspects of the Olympics crude, he eliminated most sports, replacing them with arts contests featuring poetry, singing, and music. As mentioned in Chapter 1, he chose to compete in a chariot race in AD 67 in which he fell off and lost. However, the judges, sensing catastrophic personal harm, declared him the winner anyway, in addition to winner of every other contest in which he participated. His chariot fall was an embarrassment, however, and it served to begin undermining the credibility of the Olympics at this time.[2]

We have seen the direct impact when winners cheat in their efforts to win gold, whether through drugs or other devious means. In 1904, the American Olympic marathon runner Fred Lorz rode in a car for 11 miles on his way to winning the gold. There is an odd admiration one has for such an obvious violation of sportsmanship as we marvel that he had the audacity to pull off such a brazenly offensive maneuver. Yet that admiration is muted by the claxon call of deception and trickery his victory revealed. As it turns out, Lorz's victory was short-lived when officials discovered how he won, and he was subsequently banished from all future competitions. However, he was reinstated within a year after a convincing appeal whereby Lorz persuaded officials that he rode in the car because he suffered severe stomach cramps during the race and did not mean to intentionally defraud—instead, he finished as "a joke."[3] His sense of humor was undoubtedly lost on his fellow competitors and suggested a mild hostility toward the image of Olympic virtue. However, Lorz went on to legitimately win the Boston Marathon in 1905,[4] so he apparently had real athletic talent to go with his talent for comedy.

Controversy surrounded Nancy Kerrigan and Tonya Harding, two competitors in the 1994 U.S. Olympic Trials in figure skating. Kerrigan was clubbed in the leg after skating practice by an assailant who was linked a few days later to Tonya Harding's ex-husband. Harding was not implicated at the time (just prior to the Olympics), denying any involvement, although she did say she had learned after the attack that people close to her were involved, including her ex-husband. With no specific findings of wrongdoing, Harding was allowed to skate in the Lillehammer Olympics, where she finished eighth and Kerrigan earned the silver medal. Because of the attack on Kerrigan, Olympic TV ratings increased dramatically, and the women's short program became the sixth-highest-rated show in U.S. television history. This should not be construed as approval for athletes maiming each other prior to the Olympics to boost their sponsor's financial interests, but it does underscore the unpredictable nature of Olympic competition and how fan interest can be generated by unfortunate circumstances.[5] Less than a month after the Olympics ended, Harding admitted guilt in hindering the investigation, and in June that year, she was stripped of her 1994 National Title and banned for life from the sport. The controversy was one of the most visible at the 1994 Olympics and heightened viewer interest in the Games.

The 2002 Winter Olympics in Salt Lake City saw a pairs figure skating competition marred by controversy. Judges awarded the gold medal to the Russian pairs team who skated a technically difficult but flawed final routine. The Canadian pairs team skated a flawless final routine, which most analysts and observers said was the better routine. But when the final scores for technical merit and artistic impression were given out, the Russian team edged out the Canadians, causing a raucous chorus of boos from fans and obvious dismay from expert analysts commenting on live TV. After the competition, the French judge confessed to having been pressured by the French skating president to score the Russian team higher, then recanted her confession shortly thereafter. However, her controversial remarks sparked a scandal that led to her three-year suspension from the sport and that of the president of the French skating association, who subsequently resigned his position in 2004.[6] As a consequence of the judging scandal, the International Skating Union (ISU) changed the scoring system in 2004. The former system, used for 100 years, scored skating based on a 6.0 scale (6.0 being the top mark). A panel of nine judges from different countries would each render an individual score, which was displayed for all to see, along with the judge's country of origin and the total skating score. The new system gives the judges anonymity. The new system is fairer for the athletes, but it is more confusing for the fans, a potentially unfortunate but necessary by-product of good intentions since the old system allowed fans to cheer and jeer the individual judges' scores, thereby involving the fans more directly in figure skating. Skating analysts are confident that fans will get used to the new system. More important, the new scoring system's anonymity will reduce the chances of judges being pressured or bribed.[7]

Performance-enhancing drugs have become the more common route for athletes seeking an unfair advantage, despite the serious consequences if discovered. Witness Ben Johnson, the Canadian sprinter who was stripped of his gold medal in the 100 meters from the 1988 Seoul Olympics when he tested positive for banned substances. Marion Jones, the American sprinter who won five medals at the 2000 Sydney Olympics (three gold and two bronze), admitted in 2007 to using performance-enhancing drugs. Her confession came after years of denial that she had ever cheated in her track career, despite ongoing suspicion from international sport governing bodies and fellow athletes. Subsequent to her admission, she returned her Olympic medals, even before the International Olympic Committee officially disqualified her Sydney performances and issued its formal demand that she return her medals, and she served a six-month jail sentence in 2008. Authenticity is indeed a vital part of the Olympic appeal.

When athletes are found to have cheated, their integrity is damaged, the credibility of their sport is diminished, and both the athlete's and sport's long-term brand reputation is harmed, often severely and sometimes irreparably. The controversies surrounding professional cycling and exemplified by certain riders in the Tour de France (although not limited to that event) have tarnished cycling's reputation and cast a negative pall over the sport and its more honest participants. The same is true for Major League Baseball in the United States, where a months-long investigation produced a December 2007 report revealing that more than 80 active players were using or had used performance-enhancing substances, including steroids. This proved to be the most damaging situation professional baseball has faced since the 1919 Black Sox scandal, when the favored Chicago White Sox intentionally lost the World Series to the underdog Cincinnati Reds, providing the Chicago players involved in the fix with a financial payout. Such antics cause fans to become skeptical, the commercial appeal declines, and the sport sees its overall reputation diminish as a result. The central appeal of sport as a genuine, authentic, and unscripted event is lost, reducing the competition to a mere staged performance.

Today, with hundreds of millions of dollars of sponsorship money at stake, the fallout from an unexpected, negative surprise can be felt quickly and engulf many stakeholders concurrently. In 1998, a major bribery scandal surrounding the Salt Lake Olympics threatened to irreparably harm the Olympic movement. The Salt Lake Organizing Committee was accused of bribing IOC officials with substantial gifts and money to influence the host city selection process. Subsequently, four IOC members and two Salt Lake City Olympic Committee officials were forced to resign. Corporate sponsors at the time, including Coca-Cola, John Hancock, UPS, Kodak, IBM, and Visa, considered removing their support. Such a move would imperil the Olympic Games, since several hundred million dollars of Games funding is supplied from corporate sponsorships. In 1999, the Australian Olympic Committee announced that US$1.2 million had been paid to 11 African nations in 1993, just a few weeks prior to the 2000 Olympic site selection vote. Both events rocked the IOC and the Olympic movement. As David d'Alessandro, CEO of John Hancock at the time, said,

> The IOC's sponsorships have become radioactive. All corporate Geiger counters are going off the chart. They've got to find a way to make sponsorships safe again. . . . If they fail to do that and something else comes up, the rings won't be tarnished, they'll be broken.[8]

Lance Helgeson, senior editor of the IEG Sponsorship Report, echoed similar sentiments:

> Make no mistake about it, the scandal and the flap surrounding it are not helping the Olympic brand.[9]

Yet many sponsors focused on the historical legacy of the Olympics and the values represented by the Games. The scandal was seen as frustrating and disappointing, but it was viewed in the context of a short-term problem within an event that has thousands of years of positive contribution. Burke Stinson, a spokesman for AT&T, an Olympic sponsor at that time, said,

We've chosen to take the long view. It's an awkward time for the Games, and by inference the sponsors, but it's a time for sponsors to close ranks, not kick someone when they're down.[10]

Ben Deutsch, spokesman for Coca-Cola, agreed:

[Coca-Cola] isn't going to discard that relationship. This is a serious issue and a cause of great concern for us. But we've expressed our concerns to the organizing committees and the IOC, and we've been assured that they will take swift steps to bring the situation to a positive closure.[11]

The IOC either reprimanded officials or forced them to resign, depending on their level of involvement. New ethics guidelines were adopted that prevented IOC members from visiting bid cities and accepting gifts over $150 in value. Juan Samaranch, president of the IOC at the time, was given a vote of confidence in 1999 by the IOC, clearing him of any wrongdoing. His tenure began in 1980 and he is widely credited for the growth of the Olympics and the dramatic increase in corporate sponsorships (he has also been criticized for over-commercializing the modern Olympics). But when his term expired in 2001, he chose not to seek another term.[12]

Two factors have been identified as primary drivers that ultimately led to the corruption and bribery scandal. First, as the 1980s began, Olympic revenues grew dramatically, in part due to Juan Samaranch's efforts to reach out to corporate and commercial interests and seek their support of the Olympics. Second, the IOC was historically a wealthy club of lifelong members. In the 1980s, this began to change, as the IOC sought a broader range of interests in its membership, many of whom did not have the same wealth as the original members. As broadcast interests grew around the world, so, too, did the revenues from broadcast partners. Some IOC members sought ways to increase their wealth. As the money flows increased further, the economic attractiveness to host cities grew. The stage had effectively been set for backroom deals between bid cities and select IOC members that ultimately led to the Salt Lake City scandal.[13]

Other types of less scandalous controversies affect perceptions of the Olympics as well. Michelle Kwan is one of the most successful figure skaters in U.S. history to not win a gold medal, despite winning nine U.S.

championships, five world championships, and two Olympic medals: a silver at the 1998 Nagano Olympics and a bronze at the 2002 Salt Lake Olympics. In January 2006, *Sports Business Daily* conducted a poll of 200 sports executives, and the results said she was the most marketable winter sports athlete. She had and still has a reputation for being an ideal athlete because of her clean image, enthusiastic personality, and famous smile. Michelle had an injury-plagued year in 2005, prior to the 2006 Torino Olympics, and was unable to compete in the U.S. Figure Skating Championships. Normally, this would prevent her, or any athlete, from making the Olympic team, but Michelle applied for a special waiver because of her medical situation. The U.S. Ladies Figure Skating Association approved the waiver as long as she could demonstrate to a special figure skating panel that she was physically capable of competing, which she successfully did. The skating panel's approval was both unorthodox and highly controversial. However, just prior to the start of the Olympics, she withdrew due to yet another injury suffered during practice.[14] The accompanying media coverage was extensive, particularly in the United States. Part of the challenge was the impact on two of her key sponsors, Coca-Cola and Visa, both of which had created television commercials with her as a spotlighted athlete. Her withdrawal caused Coca-Cola to drop the TV commercial featuring her. Visa continued; because several other athletes were featured with her in the advertisements, Visa was less dependent on her image in that campaign.[15]

In the 2004 Athens Olympics, Brazilian Vanderlei de Lima, who was leading the marathon with four miles to go, was tackled by a spectator, surprising and shocking everyone watching. The incident slowed De Lima considerably, and he ended up winning the bronze. Fans who had been watching the event unfold on large-screen monitors in the stadium were understandably horrified, and they cheered enthusiastically when De Lima entered the stadium in a show of affection and support. At the closing ceremony, de Lima was awarded the Pierre de Coubertin Medal, the highest honor given to athletes who exemplify the Olympic spirit. As the IOC said at the time,

> We decided to do this in recognition of de Lima's exceptional demonstration of fair play and Olympic values during this evening's marathon.[16]

David Masse, a media veteran of prior Olympic broadcasts, was asked why this particular event was repeatedly shown. Masse said,

> Athletic accomplishments or a Michael Phelps are incredible but I think the world loves to see someone struggle against something even bigger than the other athletes, so maybe that's what this Brazilian athlete did.[17]

In early 2008, the athletic company Speedo was the center of controversy over the design of their Speedo LZR Racer swimsuit, introduced in February 2008. Over the first few weeks of its competitive use, 22 world records were set, compared to five in the same period prior to the 2004 Olympics in Athens. The world governing body for swimming, FINA (Fédération Internationale de Natation), ruled the suit legal in April 2008, setting controversy in motion. The Italian national team coach, Alberto Castagnetti, said that the Speedo LZR was akin to "technological doping." However, FINA President Mustapha Larfaoui was thrilled that swimming records were falling as athletes prepared for the Olympics. His concern was only that the same technology was available to everybody. This was problematic, given that many leading swimmers around the world were sponsored by Speedo rivals and did not have the same access.[18]

An unfortunate side effect of many of these controversies is the negative brand association, from the concept of a "French judge" describing any untrustworthy or corrupt judging practice, to Salt Lake as the "bribery-tarnished Olympics," illustrating the hazards a negative brand reputation can have, no matter how unfair or exaggerated the claim may be. The impact on corporate sponsors is likely to be far less direct, but companies must pay attention to controversy related to the sports they sponsor and prepare a crisis communications plan, should something overtly negative occur. In the run-up to the Beijing Olympics, the Tibet protests could have had a detrimental impact on sponsors if global protests had continued to grow. Sponsors would have been deemed unresponsive to the controversy. While the decision may seem deceptively simple to observers (i.e., cease the sponsorship), it involves unwinding extensive contractual relationships, eliminating jobs created to support the sponsorship, and harming relations among the various Olympic stakeholders (sponsors, suppliers, partners, customers, fans, athletes, the IOC), making the decision complex both socially and financially. On the other hand, a politically untenable situation may be so severe that the only sensible solution is stopping all sponsorship support immediately, despite the many ramifications. So far, such a severe outcome has not occurred, undoubtedly a by-product of the power of the Olympic brand to stand for something above typical controversies and, therefore, the public's support for keeping politics out of the Olympics whenever and wherever possible.

Questions

1. In the modern era, does controversy sell (is it *acceptable* as a means to generate interest?)? If so, should sponsors seek out controversial athletes?
2. What are the potential ramifications to sponsors if an athlete transgresses ethical, moral, or legal boundaries? Should sponsors vigorously demand morals and ethics clauses in their sponsorship agreements?
3. Is it possible for a sponsor to benefit from an athlete's controversy? What conditions might make controversy acceptable to the sponsor?
4. In what situations might a controversy significantly harm a sponsor? Describe.
5. What can sponsors do to anticipate and prepare for controversy in their sponsorship activation planning?

Chapter 11

Section III Sponsorship Preparation Questions

The range of negative scenarios is quite broad, and a sponsor's response to controversy will depend entirely on the unique dynamics of the situation. The bribery scandals, like those of Sydney and Salt Lake, led to changes in IOC rules regarding member travel to bid cities, encouraged by collective sponsor actions and reactions. But during the unfolding of the revelations of an impending scandal is when companies need to pay particularly close attention to their handling of the crisis. The initial reactions to any crisis are obviously sharper, more intense, and more emotional than later, so the actions taken at the outset will determine whether a company can successfully navigate its way through.

Unexpected, Negative Surprises

1. Do you have a crisis management plan and team?
   a. Who is the main spokesperson?
   b. Are roles clearly understood?
   c. Have firm internal rules been established regarding who can and cannot speak to the media?
   d. Who or what is at risk?
   e. What is the plan for diffusing a crisis?
   f. Which outside groups need to be brought in and/or influenced?
   g. What actions would be taken? (Be as specific as possible.)
2. How do you want the company portrayed?
   a. Is your objective reasonable, practical, and realistic?
3. What is the worst-case impact of a crisis on your company?
   a. How much is at risk?
   b. Can it escalate?
   c. Who would be involved?
   d. What is the spillover effect?
4. Do you have a plan for helping employees and/or victims deal with the negative surprise?
5. How will you monitor the situation?
6. Barring horrible physical tragedy or calamity, can this be turned into a positive over time?
   a. What is your plan for recovery?
   b. What is the event's response to these questions?

IV

REPUTATION DEVELOPMENT

Chapter 12

The Olympic Opportunity

The Olympics have evolved over the decades into a huge economic event for host cities, athletes, and sponsors. General Electric gained $700 million in new contracts from its support of the 2008 Beijing Olympics.[1] Each sponsor plans for the Olympics to improve its financial performance to a certain degree. Yet while the Olympics have certainly grown dramatically in size, scope, and financial power, driven by a more sophisticated funding model with corporate sponsorship at its core, the values associated with the Olympics remain vital to their appeal. Competitive fair play, honor, and integrity are qualities athletes strive for, even if some fall short in the quest for glory. Just as controversy shines the spotlight of scrutiny on bad behavior and practices, it also stirs the calls for keeping the Olympics' centuries-long ideals firmly at the forefront and reminding the world that despite problems, the Olympics are still a force for good. To ensure the broadest possible representation of sports and nations and to keep Olympic values in front of the public's collective imagination requires a professional funding model that can support less financially stable nations while spreading the message of international goodwill.

Official Olympic Sponsorship

The IOC produces the Olympic Marketing Fact File, which contains a detailed breakdown of funding sources. There are six revenue-generating programs:

1. IOC-managed broadcast partnerships.
2. The TOP partners sponsorship program.
3. IOC official supplier and licensing program.
4. Domestic sponsorship programs run by OCOGs (organizing committees for the Olympic Games).
5. Ticketing programs in the host country.
6. Licensing programs in the host country.

Most of the analysis in this book is devoted to the TOP partners program and select sponsors within it (representative of the diversity of sponsor interests in the Olympics) because their multifaceted marketing programs provide useful insights into the inner workings of complex sports sponsorships. The revenues generated by domestic sponsorships are actually larger than those from TOP sponsors (in the 2005–2008 Quadrennium, TOP sponsors generated $866 million in revenue, whereas domestic sponsors accounted for $1.555 billion in revenue). The Olympics domestic sponsorship program is fascinating to study as well, but it involves several times as many companies and is beyond the scope of this analysis, although the lessons from both the TOP and domestic sponsorship programs are similar. Table 12.1 provides a breakdown of Olympic revenue sources since 1993.

The IOC redistributes the revenue to the related Olympic movement organizations: NOCs (national Olympic committees), IFs (international federations), and the OCOGs. Of the total revenue generated, 10 percent is kept by the IOC to cover its operating costs, and the remaining 90 percent is allocated to the NOCs, IFs, and

Table 12.1 Olympic Marketing Revenue Sources[2]

Source	1993–1996	1997–2000	2001–2004	2005–2008
Broadcast	US$1,251,000,000	US$1,845,000,000	US$2,232,000,000	US$2,570,000,000
TOP Program	US$279,000,000	US$579,000,000	US$663,000,000	US$866,000,000
Domestic Sponsorship	US$534,000,000	US$655,000,000	US$796,000,000	US$1,555,000,000
Ticketing	US$451,000,000	US$625,000,000	US$411,000,000	US$274,000,000
Licensing	US$115,000,000	US$66,000,000	US$87,000,000	US$185,000,000
Total	US$2,630,000,000	US$3,770,000,000	US$4,189,000,000	US$5,450,000,000

OCOGs.[3] The OCOGs are responsible for organizing the Games in their city and developing the sponsors from companies in their region.

Domestic Sponsorship Revenues

Table 12.2 provides an OCOG revenue breakdown for the Summer Olympics since 1996.

An interesting trend is the decrease in the number of Summer Olympics domestic sponsor partners since 1996. A possible explanation may be the widespread criticism of the overly commercial nature of the 1996 Atlanta Olympics, a claim seemingly reinforced by IOC President Juan Samaranch's closing ceremony remarks, in which he did not say that the games were "the best ever," interpreted by Olympic observers as a subtle slight against the Atlanta Games. This may have affected the way Sydney, Athens, and Beijing planned and selected domestic sponsorship partners for their respective Games (although Sydney's efforts

Table 12.2 OCOG Sponsorship Programs Summer Olympics (since 1996)[4]

Olympic Games	Number of Partners*	Revenue and Support
1996 Atlanta	111	US$426 million
2000 Sydney	93	US$492 million
2004 Athens	38	US$302 million
2008 Beijing	51	US$1.218 billion

*Domestic OCOG sponsorship programs usually include several tiers of partnership, which may include sponsors, suppliers, and providers. The figures in this column represent total number of marketing partners from all tiers of the domestic program.

Table 12.3 OCOG Sponsorship Programs Winter Olympics (since 1998)[5]

Olympic Games	Number of Partners*	Revenue and Support
1998 Nagano	26	U$163 million
2002 Salt Lake	53	US$494 million
2006 Torino	57	US$348 million
2010 Vancouver	57	US$688 million

*Same description as Summer Olympics.

generated more dollars than Atlanta, the number of partners declined by 18). The dollars per domestic sponsor rose, however, with each subsequent Summer Olympiad, from $3.8 million per sponsor in 1996 to nearly $24 million in 2008.

Table 12.3 is similar to Table 12.2, but the figures are for the Winter Olympics since 1998.

Interestingly, the number of Winter Olympics partners increased during this time, perhaps owing to the growth of the Winter Olympics. The dollars per domestic sponsor rose from $6.3 million at Nagano in 1998 to $9.3 million per sponsor at Salt Lake in 2002, then dropped again to $6.1 million per sponsor in Torino in 2006, a result that could be due to challenges associated with each Winter host city's unique geographic limitations and/or the varied economic conditions for Winter Games cities. However, the dollars per sponsor rose again, to $12 million for the 2010 Vancouver Olympics.

Ticketing Revenues

Each OCOG is responsible for its own ticketing program, with guidance and support provided by the IOC. Ticketing revenues have grown significantly, as Tables 12.4 and 12.5 illustrate.

Let's turn our attention to ticketing examples from recent Olympiads.

London 2012   Each organizing committee plans rigorously for how to develop a ticketing plan that attracts local fans yet also reinforces the prestige associated with the Olympics. Professional sports leagues have grown dramatically in the past 20 years, with players commanding higher salaries, and club owners increasing the marketing activities to

Table 12.4 Summer Olympics Ticketing Revenues (since 1984)[6]

Olympic Games	Tickets Available	Tickets Sold	% of Tickets Sold	Revenue to OCOG
1984 Los Angeles	6.9 million	5.7 million	82%	US$156 million
1988 Seoul	4.4 million	3.3 million	75%	US$36 million
1992 Barcelona	3.9 million	3.021 million	77%	US$79 million
1996 Atlanta	11 million	8.318 million	75%	US$425 million
2000 Sydney	7.6 million	6.7 million	88%	US$551 million
2004 Athens	5.3 million	3.8 million	71%	US$228 million
2008 Beijing	6.8 million	6.5 million	95.6%	US$185 million

Table 12.5 Winter Olympics Ticket Revenues (since 1988)[7]

Olympic Games	Tickets Available	Tickets Sold	% of Tickets Sold	Revenue to OCOG
1988 Calgary	1.9 million	1.6 million	84%	US$32 million
1992 Albertville	1.2 million	900,000	75%	US$32 million
1994 Lillehammer	1.3 million	1.207 million	92%	US$26 million
1998 Nagano	1.434 million	1.275 million	89%	US$74 million
2002 Salt Lake	1.605 million	1.525 million	95%	US$183 million
2006 Torino	1.1 million	900,000	81%	US$89 million
2010 Vancouver	1.54 million	1.49 million	97%	US$250 million

broaden the appeal of their brands. This has come at a cost, however, by increasing ticket prices to the point that average fans are less able to afford tickets to a game, let alone season tickets. Corporate ticket packages, luxury suites in stadiums, and seat licenses have been successful additions to ticketing schemes that create a premium image for select seating, often at the sacrifice of loyal individual fans.

For London 2012, a total of 8.8 million tickets were made available for the Games, with 2.5 million of them priced at £20 or less and 1.2 million allocated for the Pay Your Age promotion. This novel promotion allows those under 16 (their age by the time the Games begin in July 2012) to pay their age, and fans over 60 pay only £16. London's ticket prices varied depending on the event, with some events, like athletics, having six different pricing tiers and others, like canoeing, having three pricing tiers. The variation in pricing was significant, with the least expensive tickets costing £20 and the most expensive £2,012 (opening ceremonies). Table 12.6 summarizes selected highlights of the London ticket prices.

The organizing committee stated that 90 percent of the tickets sold to the public would be £100 or less, 66 percent would be £50 or less, and the remainder £20 or less. As would be expected, the only credit

Table 12.6   London 2012 Ticket Prices[8]

Ticket prices for selected events

Sport/Ceremony	Venue	Stage	Price Range
Opening ceremony	Olympic stadium	n/a	£20–£2,012
Closing ceremony	Olympic stadium	n/a	£20–£1,500
Athletics	Olympic stadium	Preliminary	£20–£150
		Final	£50–£450
		Super-final	£50–£725
Basketball	Basketball Arena/ North Greenwich Arena	Preliminary	£20–£115
		Quarterfinal	£20–£125
		Semifinal	£35–£125
		Bronze	£45–£325
		Final	£50–£425
Boxing	ExCel	Preliminary	£20–£95
		Quarterfinal	£30–£110
		Semifinal	£30–£150
		Final	£50–£395
Cycling (track)	Velodrome	Preliminary	£20–£150
		Final	£50–£325
Football	Various UK-wide venues	Preliminary	£20–£60
		Quarterfinal	£20–£60
		Semifinal	£20–£125
		Bronze	£30–£75
		Final	£30–£185
Gymnastics (artistic)	North Greenwich Arena	Preliminary	£20–£150
		Final	£50–£450
Rowing	Eton Dorney	Preliminary	£20–£95
		Final	£30–£150
Swimming	Aquatics Centre	Preliminary	£20–£150
		Final	£50–£450
Triathlon	Hyde Park	Final	£20–£60

card the Olympics allows for the purchase of tickets is Visa. Fans could also pay by cash, check, or postal order. Non-U.K. residents had to apply for tickets via their country's national Olympic committee (NOC). A further 120,000 tickets were being allocated for school-children in London. Despite the earnest efforts of the London Olympic Committee to develop a fair pricing plan, some politicians were upset that not enough lower-priced tickets were made available, effectively pricing many U.K. citizens out of the Olympics.[9] Sebastian Coe, chairman of the London 2012 Olympics, said,

> "[This is] the daddy of all ticket strategies" adding: "We have three clear principles for our ticketing strategy: tickets need to be affordable and accessible to as many people as possible, tickets are an important revenue stream for us to fund the Games, and our ticketing plans have the clear aim of filling our venues to the rafters."[10]

The organizers had 1.9 million fans apply for tickets, of which 700,000 actually received the e-mail, leaving 1.2 million fans disappointed. The disappointment stemmed from the final sports for which fans received tickets. While fans were told that there were no guarantees they would receive their sport of choice (the application clearly stated the cost of the tickets and that the actual event would be identified later), many were frustrated. As one ticket holder tweeted,

> I got one tkt to beach volleyball. Kids beyond disappointed. Applied for equestrian & gymnastics.[11]

However, some fans did receive their sport or sports of choice, so not all were dissatisfied. The ticket recipient received two to four tickets at an average cost of £275. The 1.2 million fans who were unable to secure tickets were offered a second chance to apply for remaining tickets. For dissatisfied fans, a public exchange was created to facilitate trading between fans and also to sell any last-minute unsold tickets. This example points out a sizable challenge for the organizers of every Olympiad: how to most effectively satisfy the needs of fans while also generating the revenues needed to cover costs and still position the Olympics as a unique, one-of-a-kind event.

Table 12.7   Vancouver 2010 Ticket Prices[12]

Event	Price Range
Alpine skiing	$25–$150
Biathlon	$25–$25
Bobsleigh	$30–$85
Cross-country skiing	$25–$70
Curling	$65–$125
Figure skating	$50–$525
Freestyle skiing	$50–$150
Ice hockey	$25–$775
Luge	$30–$85
Nordic combined	$50–$120
Short-track speed skating	$50–$150
Skeleton	$30–$85
Ski jumping	$80–$210
Speed skating	$95–$185
Opening ceremonies	$175–$1,100
Closing ceremonies	$175–$775

Vancouver 2010   Vancouver's ticket pricing was also based on tiers, covering a price range from a low of $25 to a high of $1,100. Approximately 1.6 million tickets were made available, with a third for members of the Olympic family. However, there was no price difference between the public tickets and those for the Olympic family. Of the 1.6 million tickets, 100,000 were priced at the lowest tier of $25 or less. Approximately half the tickets were priced at $175 or less, and 50,000 complimentary tickets were allocated as well. Fans were required to apply for tickets with allocation based on final availability. To accommodate high-demand events, a lottery was used. Table 12.7 outlines the ticket price ranges for the various sports.

2010 Youth Olympic Games, Singapore   A sense of excitement and trepidation characterized the 2010 Youth Olympic Games (YOG). As a new megasports event in the IOC family, the inaugural Youth Olympic Games in Singapore in 2010 were a renewed effort by the IOC to appeal to the youth of the world, hoping to capture their interest in an age offering a wide range of leisure choices, from gaming to extreme sports to social media. The IOC was hoping the YOG would build a new base of Olympics fans and athletes who would become supporters of the regular Winter and Summer Games as they matured. Pricing tickets for such an event is not easy. The regular Olympics pricing varies significantly from one Games to the next, with the only consistency appearing to be a range of ticket prices and a certain percentage allocated to students and seniors at reduced rates. Another challenge was over-coming the lack of awareness about the YOG and how it differed from the traditional Olympics.

When final ticket pricing was announced in the spring of 2010, a total of 320,000 tickets were made available to the public. The Singapore Olympic Committee was acutely aware of the challenges of structuring pricing to appeal to the broadest range of fans, encourage foreign tourists, and meet the financial needs of the organizing com-mittee. They also knew that as a new event without any history, plus a lack of familiarity in the public's mind, lower prices would encourage higher ticket sales. The organizing committee decided that final pricing needed to be affordable, partly to avoid empty venues for this inaugural event. Also, the YOG was an opportunity to showcase Singapore to the rest of the world as a country with a dynamic and thriving culture able to host complex international sports events, as it demonstrated when it began hosting an F1 race in September 2008.

Pricing was structured in three basic tiers, as shown in Table 12.8.

Singapore's location near the equator means weather is tropical year-round, with temperatures averaging about 30°C to 33°C (86°F to 92°F). Prices were decreased for select venues that had both covered and uncovered seating or viewing areas. See Table 12.9.

Singapore's three simple pricing tiers were an acknowledgment that fan enthusiasm would not develop just by being associated with the Olympics. Despite these good-faith efforts, while official totals of venue

Table 12.8 Singapore 2010 YOG Ticket Prices[13]

Event	Prices
Preliminaries	S$10
Quarterfinals/Semifinals	S$15
Finals	S$30

Table 12.9   Singapore 2010 YOG Decreased Ticket Prices[14]

Event	Prices
Preliminaries	S$5
Quarterfinals/Semifinals	S$7.50
Finals	S$15

occupancy were not released, numerous news agencies and blogs around the world indicated that most venues had many empty seats.

Beijing 2008   A total of 7 million tickets were made available for sale in 2006, ahead of the 2008 Beijing Olympics. Ticket prices ranged from US$4 to as much as $5,000. According to Beijing officials, 58 percent of the tickets were priced at $12.50 or less. Student tickets represented 14 percent of the total tickets allocated, with preliminary tickets sold for as little as US$0.64 for preliminary events to US$1.28 for finals. The Beijing Olympic Committee (BOCOG) limited the number of tickets fans could buy. For both the opening and closing ceremonies, individuals could purchase only one ticket. Two tickets were allowed for fans interested in the most popular events, and fans could purchase two to five tickets for the least popular events. Of the 60,000 opening ceremonies tickets made available to the public, 24,000 were set aside for Chinese citizens, a 7 percent increase over the tickets made available to Europeans for the 2004 Athens Olympics. As with other Olympics, Visa was the only credit card that could be used for credit-based purchases. Table 12.10 summarizes ticket pricing by event.

Irrespective of which Games are examined, empty seats are evident. Depending on the specific ticket plan of each Olympic Games, corporate packages were sold with the understanding that tickets would be used by the company's invited guests. Still, many venues have been seen over the years with a significant percentage of the seats unused or unsold, prompting anger from some fans who had hoped to buy tickets only to be told the Games had sold out. The effort to create ticket exchanges will certainly help ameliorate this problem, but the ongoing challenge for Olympic organizing committees will be determining how to increase venue occupancy during all events, especially in the preliminary and semifinal stages. True sellouts are unlikely, however, given

Table 12.10 2008 Summer Games in Beijing Ticket Prices[15]

Event	Price Range
Opening ceremony	$200–$5,000
Closing ceremony	$150–$3,000
10-km marathon swimming	$30–$30
Archery	$50–$100
Athletics	$50–$800
Badminton	$50–$500
Baseball	$30–$150
Basketball	$50–$1,000
Beach volleyball	$50–$400
Boxing	$30–$400
Canoe/kayak flatwater	$30–$80
Canoe/kayak slalom	$30–$100
Cycling BMX	$50–$100
Cycling mountain bike	$30–$30
Cycling road	Free
Cycling track	$50–$100
Diving	$60–$500
Equestrian	$40–$400
Fencing	$50–$100
Football	$40–$800
Gymnastics artistic	$50–$300
Gymnastics rhythmic	$100–$400
Gymnastics trampoline	$50–$100
Handball	$30–$150
Hockey	$30–$150
Judo	$50–$200
Modern pentathlon	$30–$50
Rowing	$30–$80
Sailing	$120–$600
Shooting	$30–$50
Softball	$30–$120
Swimming	$100–$800
Synchronized swimming	$60–$500
Table tennis	$50–$800
Tae kwon do	$50–$200
Tennis	$100–$600
Triathlon	$50
Volleyball	$50–$800

(Continued)

Table 12.10   Continued

Event	Price Range
Water polo	$30–$400
Weight lifting	$30–$200
Wrestling	$50–$200

the sheer range and variety of sports events—some are simply more popular than others and, therefore, generate the most interest.

Ticketing revenues are a function of Olympic location, proximity of venues, size of venues, transportation, and general destination appeal. The majority of tickets sold of the total available for sale are in the 70 to 80 percent range for the Summer Olympics (with Beijing leaping far ahead with nearly 96 percent of all its tickets sold) and in the 80 to 90 percent range for the Winter Olympics (with Vancouver far ahead with 97 percent of its tickets sold), which can provide Olympic organizing planners and sponsors a reasonable assurance of the numbers of visitors and the potential economic impact. In turn, this general knowledge can assist sponsors as they finalize their location-specific marketing programs and determine financial allocations.

Licensing Revenues

Similar to ticketing, the OCOGs run their own licensing programs with guidance from the IOC. The philosophy is to support local branded companies, reflecting the domestic cultural and business practices of the host city and nation. Summer Olympics license revenues are shown in Table 12.11 and Winter Olympics license revenues in Table 12.12.

Table 12.11   Summer Olympics License Revenues (since 1988)[16]

Olympic Games	Licenses	Revenue to OCOG
1988 Seoul	62	US$18.8 million
1992 Barcelona	61	US$17.2 million
1996 Atlanta	125	US$91 million
2000 Sydney	100	US$52 million
2004 Athens	23	US$61.5 million
2008 Beijing	68	US$163 million

Table 12.12 Winter Olympics License Revenues (since 1994)[17]

Olympic Games	Licenses	Revenue to OCOG
1994 Lillehammer	36	US$24 million
1998 Nagano	190	U$14 million
2002 Salt Lake	70	US$25 million
2006 Torino	32	US$22 million
2010 Vancouver	48	US$51 million

The 1996 Atlanta Olympics saw a doubling of the number of licensees and a quadrupling of revenues over the preceding two Olympiads. The licensee numbers dropped significantly by the 2004 Athens Olympics (again, perhaps due to the overcommercialization effect from 1996), while the revenues per licensee climbed sharply. However, Beijing showed a rebound, with nearly three times as many licenses and an almost tripling of revenues over the 2004 Athens Olympics.

Nagano in 1998 was a busy Olympics with respect to the number of licensees. The dollars per licensee, however, were far lower than in Lillehammer. Since Nagano, the licensing revenues have varied, with a sharp decline in the number of licenses for the 2006 Torino Olympics and then an increase in both licenses and revenues for the 2010 Vancouver Olympics.

It is noteworthy that both the Beijing and Vancouver Olympiads witnessed significant increases in licenses and license revenues over their respective predecessor Olympiads, despite the severe economic conditions that dominated most of the world from 2007 onward, a testament perhaps to the strength, power, and enduring appeal of the Olympics.

The Olympic revenue programs reviewed in this section provide a financial context for understanding the growth and maturation of the Olympic movement funding model. As we saw in Table 12.1, "Olympic Marketing Revenue Sources," the total revenues from all six programs have increased from $2.6 billion to more than $5.4 billion since 1993, a 107 percent increase. This growth has been fueled by the growth of Olympic sponsorships, from both the domestic and TOP programs. Domestic sponsorships grew more than 190 percent since 1993, a substantial increase. However, the increase of TOP program sponsorship revenues has been even more impressive, with 210 percent growth since 1993.

TOP Program Sponsorship

For marketers and their companies, success at sports marketing is more than just a chase for financial gold. While the investment for TOP program sponsors is substantial, many of these companies have been sponsors for several Olympiads, generating financial returns and societal goodwill. Four of the TOP sponsors from the 2008 Beijing Olympics declined to continue their sponsorships: Kodak (which had been associated with the Olympics since 1896), Lenovo, Manulife, and Johnson & Johnson. This put pressure on the IOC to find replacements to not just keep the funding contributions alive and healthy, but to also avoid raising concern that the Olympics were becoming less valuable as a sponsorship investment, a tricky challenge given the global financial meltdown at that time. Fortunately, three new TOP sponsors were recruited: Acer, Dow, and P&G. Table 12.13 shows the 11 companies in the seventh generation of the TOP program for the 2009–2012 Quadrennium (each generation spans one quadrennium, a Winter and Summer Games within that four-year period), which is the most

Table 12.13   TOP Sponsors for 2010 Vancouver and 2012 London Olympic Games[18]

Company	Sponsorship Start Date
Coca–Cola	1928 (longest continuous sponsor)
Omega	Olympic relationship-sponsors and/or official timekeeper since 1932
McDonald's	Involved with Olympics since 1968; sponsor since 1976
Panasonic	Started its Olympic involvement in 1984; sponsor since 1987
Visa	1986
Samsung	1997
Atos Origin	2002
GE	2003
Acer	2009
Dow	2010
P&G	2010

Table 12.14   TOP Sponsors 2008 Olympic Games in Beijing[19]

Company	Sponsorship Start Date
Kodak	Supported Olympics since 1896. Kodak became a TOP sponsor in 1986 and ended following the 2008 Beijing Olympics.
Coca-Cola	1928 (longest continuous sponsor)
Omega	Olympic relationship-sponsors and/or official timekeeper since 1932
McDonald's	Involved with Olympics since 1968; sponsor since 1976
Panasonic	Started its Olympic involvement in 1984; sponsor since 1987
Visa	1986
Samsung	1997
Atos Origin	2002
GE	2003
Lenovo	2004
Manulife	Sponsors since 2004. Manulife merged with John Hancock Financial Services in 2004. John Hancock first became a U.S. Olympic Committee sponsor in 1993, then a TOP sponsor in 1994. Its sponsorship ended after the 2008 Beijing Olympics.
Johnson & Johnson	Sponsor since 2005. Its sponsorship ended after the 2008 Beijing Olympics.

exclusive Olympic sponsorship level and the most expensive. Table 12.14 lists the TOP sponsors from the sixth Quadrennium immediately preceding the seventh generation. While official totals are not announced, TOP sponsorship fees increase at least 10 percent from one four-year cycle to the next, although the pace of increase appeared to accelerate from 2007, when Acer signed on, to 2010, when Dow and P&G joined. Sponsorship fees averaged $70 to $72 million per company in the sixth generation of the TOP program, just for the right to be a sponsor, so one can assume Acer paid approximately $80 million for their 2009–2013 sponsorship.

Reportedly, P&G paid $150 to $200 million in 2010 for its TOP sponsorship for a 10-year deal. It was a domestic sponsor of the 2010 Vancouver Olympics, generating significant new business, including a reported $130 million in revenue as a result of that sponsorship, and the success of their efforts led to the decision to become a TOP sponsor. Dow also signed a 10-year deal in 2010 to become a TOP sponsor, and while the total amount was not disclosed, industry estimates state that

$90 million was paid for the first four years ending in 2014. Dow executives presented this investment internally as a $1 billion sales opportunity, an argument that helped gain final approval for the sponsorship from company leadership.[20] Dow has worked quickly to be more involved than a typical TOP sponsor by agreeing to underwrite the £7 million cost of the wrap around the main Olympic stadium (the wrap is a specially designed exterior cover that surrounds the stadium walls). Dow's TOP sponsorship has not been without controversy; protests from India, in particular, have condemned Dow because of the company's Union Carbide subsidiary's disastrous 1984 gas leak in Bhopal that resulted in thousands of deaths. While Dow was not Union Carbide's parent company at the time of the disaster (Dow did not purchase Union Carbide until 1999), the ramifications from the gas leak linger to this day, evidence of the challenges of overcoming a negative reputation. Beyond the sizable sponsorship fee, another three to four times that amount is then spent by each TOP company on sponsorship *activation*, which includes investments in media buys, creative development, operational logistics, and infrastructure development, to maximize their Olympic exposure.[21]

As TOP partners, companies have exclusive rights in their category to be the official worldwide sponsors in their respective product category for the Winter and Summer Olympics in each four-year period. The program is structured to provide unique benefits to each participating sponsor. These benefits include:[22]

- The rights to use Olympic imagery and identities in approved advertising and company communications
- Hospitality events at Olympic Games sites (tents, receptions)
- Direct marketing (advertising, promotions, broadcast, digital)
- Product promotion opportunities
- Ambush marketing protection
- Regular support acknowledgment via IOC sponsorship PR

As the Olympics have grown, so, too, have the sponsorship revenues for TOP partners. Despite the continued escalation of TOP program fees, the exclusive nature of the TOP program and the associated range of benefits (the most obvious of which is an enormous global audience of billions of people for 17 consecutive days during the Games themselves) continue to make this program attractive to select global

Table 12.15   The Olympic Partners Program[23]

Quadrennial	Games	Partners	NOCs	Revenue
1985–1988	Calgary/Seoul	9	159	$96 million
1989–1992	Albertville/Barcelona	12	169	$172 million
1993–1996	Lillehammer/Atlanta	10	197	$279 million
1997–2000	Nagano/Sydney	11	199	$579 million
2001–2004	Salt Lake/Athens	11	202	$663 million
2005–2008	Torino/Beijing	12	205	$866 million
2009–2012	Vancouver/London	11	205	*

*Estimates indicate this figure may exceed $1 billion.

companies. Table 12.15 shows the revenues generated since the IOC introduced the TOP program, as well as the number of partners (corporate sponsors) and national Olympic committees (NOCs).

Quick calculations show that the nine partners in the 1985–1988 quadrennial paid approximately $10.7 million each for the right to be a TOP partner, and by the 2009–2012 quadrennial, estimates indicate that TOP fees were between $80 and 100 million each. Factor in the triple or quadruple additional investments in sponsorship activation infrastructure, media, creative, and support, and the total TOP expenditures are between $240 and 360 million. TOP and domestic sponsorships provided more than 40 percent of the total Olympic marketing revenue in the 2005–2008 Quadrennium.[24] The IOC has also indicated that fewer than 30 of the more than 200 countries that participate in the Olympic Games can afford to come to the Olympics if required to rely on their own funding, indicating the importance of corporate sponsorship support in ensuring both the continuity and broadest possible representation of countries at every Olympics. The revenues received from TOP partners are redistributed by the IOC to the NOCs and OCOGs, as shown in Figure 12.1.

Given the substantial sums involved, a natural question is whether it's worth it. The answer depends on each sponsor's objectives, plans, and implementation. It is tempting to calculate the ROI for the TOP investment, arrive at a figure, and then decide if that figure is attractive. But the decision to invest in being a TOP partner goes beyond merely measuring the investment return. Marketers must consider how closely

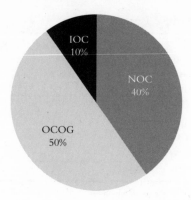

Figure 12.1   Redistribution of TOP Revenues[25]

their company's values and strategic direction align with those of the Olympics, particularly because the Olympics have such a powerful, enduring reputation for goodwill. At the same time, while one could reasonably argue that Omega's long-standing relationship with the Olympics as an official timer are closely linked with the needs of sports, one could equally easily ask how other TOP sponsors' products relate to sports or, more specifically, a healthy lifestyle. The Olympic audience is both large and diverse. Only two sports events command a truly global audience, the FIFA World Cup and the Olympics, and arguably the Olympics has a more universal appeal. (Despite the larger overall audience for the World Cup, with a cumulative audience of more than 26 billion,[26] it is not nearly as widely followed in the United States—still the world's biggest consumer market—as it is in the rest of the world.) The term *Olympian* still stands for the pinnacle of competitive and even life excellence. For the TOP sponsors in the 2009–2012 Quadrennium, the Olympic values of excellence, respect, and friendship extend beyond sports and encompass the pursuit of a quality life overall. In this regard, all TOP sponsors share Olympic values.

To determine whether their company is a good fit for sponsoring the Olympics, marketers must conduct a brand audit of their company and its traditions with the same scrutiny they apply to assessing the value of sponsoring the Olympics (or any event, for that matter). Turning their evaluation inward and applying the same rigor to understanding their own strengths and weaknesses, as they do with potential outside

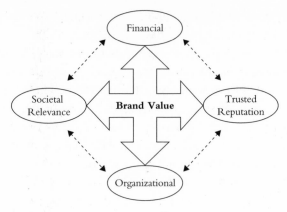

Figure 12.2 Dimensions of Brand Value[27]

investments, is not a natural activity for most companies. Many managers see branding as a narrowly focused, outward-facing activity in creative design, logo development, and sloganeering. But these external activities represent only a fraction of the overall brand-building effort.

A recognized and respected brand can and should be a competitive advantage. In my work with companies, both as an executive and through my academic research, four dimensions of value keep recurring in the stronger companies studied, encompassing both internal and external aspects of a brand (Figure 12.2).

Dimensions of Brand Value Descriptions

Financial   Real value is an important concept to understand because it has different meanings depending on the context in which it is being used. In branding, real value includes financially measurable gain. Classic accounting practice teaches us that the leftover assets we can't easily explain on a balance sheet are goodwill, effectively a crude equivalent of brand value. But business practices have grown in sophistication over the years, just as the components of value have changed over time. David Haigh, CEO of BrandFinance—a global brand consultancy, said in 2008 that 63 percent of the average company's value is intangible, a significant change from a few decades ago, when 90 percent of corporate value was tied up in tangible assets like factories and inventory.[28] There are many methods for measuring brand value, none of them perfect. But they do shed light on the impact brand has on company value.

One of the most popular surveys of brand value is conducted by Interbrand (another brand consultancy). Each year, Interbrand publishes its Top 100 Global Brands survey in *BusinessWeek*. These top 100 brands are based on financial value contributed by the brand. In their 2010 survey, Coca-Cola was the world's most valuable brand at just over $70.4 billion.[29] At the time, Coca-Cola's market capitalization was roughly $150 billion. Thus, Coca-Cola's brand value was more than 47 percent of the company's total value. In another survey, conducted by BrandFinance,[30] Coca-Cola's brand value was cited as just over $34.8 billion. While the $35 billion differential between these two brand values is significant, it is due to differences in calculation methodology. Interested readers can find out more by visiting Interbrand's and BrandFinance's web sites (www.interbrand.com and www.brandfinance .com). There is no universal method for determining brand value because the variables differ depending on your definition of brand (Is it a trademark? Is it goodwill? Is it a product? Is it the entire organization?) and on whether you combine tangible and intangible assets. If intangibles are included, then value determination can get tricky. How does one value leadership or reputation, for example? We know intrinsically that these are important, but calculating a value involves judgment as well as real data—a challenging combination for any precision-driven methodologist. The key takeaway is that the size of the brand value in Coca-Cola's case should impress you, because it means that a significant portion of Coca-Cola's total value is due to factors we cannot touch.

The Olympic Games certainly have a high level of brand value. The tangible components, such as revenue streams from broadcast rights ($2.570 billion, 47 percent), TOP and domestic sponsorships ($2.421 billion, 44 percent), ticketing ($274 million, 5 percent), and merchandise and licensing ($185 million, 3.4 percent), total $5.45 billion.[31] Yet we know that the Olympics are more than just a modern commercial opportunity. The commercial success would not have been possible without its 2,700-year reputation of goodwill and competitive virtue that comprise the Olympic ideal. There is little doubt that the intangible value is *significant*. Financial brand value is clearly important. But it would not be terribly useful or relevant without the other three components of value.

Trusted Reputation Brands are a sign of trust. To earn trust, however, requires businesses to engage in transparent practices that yield quality products, including great service, support, warranties, innovation, and compelling communications, among other customer benefits. With innumerable competitors offering high-quality products in most industries, companies must do more to maintain the market's trust. Thinking through, planning, and offering an experience-based approach to inspiring customers means marketers must carefully consider how to positively affect as many of the elements of the customer's experience as possible. Fortunately, today's marketers have more tools at their disposal for developing relationships with customers, from traditional marketing to new media. But these additional tools also mean there are many more variables to consider, so the complexity of building a trusted reputation has grown commensurately. When trust is consistently developed through the company's multiple touchpoints, the customer's overall experience (before, during, and after usage phases) helps develop a more memorable and meaningful relationship with the brand.

The trusted reputation of the Olympics has been achieved from 2,700 years of experience, encompassing thousands of athletic competitions and competitors, billions of fans, innumerable athletic achievements, and a set of values and principles that silently guide the entire Olympic movement. Over time, more countries have been involved, and the Olympics' reputation has spread commensurately, bringing the Olympic dream to life for billions of people, sharing a common set of values, aspiring to be a part of remarkable human achievement on a world stage.

Organizational Organizational brand value is concerned with company leadership providing all employees with a crystal clear sense of the company's direction, as well as ongoing reminders of the traditions that have made the firm successful over time. Organizational brand value can be particularly powerful when employees believe that they are directly contributing to a cause that benefits customers and even society, as opposed to enhancing shareholder value, which is a financial abstraction relevant to a select few (typically the CEO, CFO, and shareholders). It is challenging to derive inspiration from an abstract concept like enhancing shareholder value. Instead, direction from company leaders ought to reflect the investment made in attracting talent that reinforces competencies and reputations for which the company is known. For example, talented engineers at Apple know they are working for a company driven by a larger purpose—to make, as Steve Jobs once said, *insanely great* products that improve the customer's lifestyle. When a company develops this sense of purpose (or cause, or mission), then it simply *feels* different inside, somehow more meaningful, and everyone within understands how their efforts contribute to the company's overall success.

This concept of organizational brand value is easily seen when watching successful sports teams of talented people with different skills working collectively to win. There is a magical chemistry shared by all the players that goes beyond their individual abilities. Real Madrid, the famous Spanish futbol club, states that since its very early days over a century ago, the organization has always stood for being "*a champion and a gentleman.*"[32] Real Madrid has enjoyed remarkable success during its 100 years of existence, and part of the reason is because their version of organizational brand value describes an ideal (versus quantitative goals, like a specific number of league championships). Its champion and gentleman guideline flows directly through to talent recruiting, from players to management, leading the team to a consistently high performance over time. Similarly, Real Madrid's fierce rival, Barcelona, is another great example of success based on magical team chemistry. In winning the 2011 Champions League 3-1 over Manchester United, Barcelona demonstrated the true art of team play, with its one-touch passing and superb anticipatory defense. Barcelona's 2011 win was their third Champions League title in six years, and they easily rival, if not surpass, Real Madrid, as the world's most successful futbol club. Whereas Real Madrid stands for *a champion and a gentleman*, Barcelona stands for being *more than a club.*[33] The meaning of this phrase varies, but for Barca and its fans, it signifies the club's importance to society, not just to sports, much like the Olympics.

Organizational brand value for the Olympics is wrapped around the entire Olympic movement, from the formal structures represented by the IOC and the various other Olympic committees, to a diverse and dispersed collection of dozens of partnerships with governments, companies, and host cities. If the Olympics were to be more overtly positioned as a revenue-generating commercial enterprise and the IOC organized like a company, for example, then it would lose much of its magic and appeal. We want the IOC to champion the Olympic ideal and stand for the very best in human nature. Put more crudely, the organizational brand value is really a straightforward exercise in not screwing up what thousands of years of tradition have built, and each generation of the Olympic movement's organizers must ensure integrity remains unquestioned.

Societal Relevance   For companies to be successful, they have to be perceived as offering something of value to society collectively and to members within individually. True societal value means that any product or service must be relevant to those who want it. Relevance simply means something is important to us and/or that we want or need it. This is common sense, or at least it should be. Marketers need to translate this common sense into specific solutions (i.e., products or services) that are appealing, both to individual consumers and to other businesses.

As we know, humans are social creatures, and we gain our sense of identity from the way we see ourselves and how others see us. As consumers, we tend to buy products and services that are relevant to our interests and reflect our values and identity. As the world globalizes and a wide range of challenging issues confront us beyond our individual needs, such as threats to our way of life and/or the stability of the society in which we live, we increasingly evaluate society's actors, including companies, based on how their offerings fit our lifestyle and on whether they are good corporate citizens, demonstrated by actively participating in developing solutions to societal problems. Such efforts are called corporate social responsibility (CSR), which has grown because people around the world are learning that many of the business practices of the past 100 years, while yielding growth and higher standards of living for many countries, have also led to significant environmental problems. Company leaders are paying closer attention to the CSR practices of their network of suppliers, distributors, and similar business partners, in addition to their own firm's efforts. Such efforts are becoming a far more important factor in determining successful business performance, well beyond basic financial results. A company may have products we love, such as Starbucks coffee, but many customers would not continue buying Starbucks products if the company stopped selling fair-trade coffee.[34] Boeing's 787 Dreamliner was designed to be a more economical and environmentally friendlier aircraft design, with its unique composite materials. The hope is that we, as airline travelers, will see Boeing more favorably and seek out routes and airlines featuring the 787. Virgin Airways' efforts to test cleaner-burning biofueled commercial airliners reflects Richard Branson's efforts to reduce dependency on traditional fuel, although there is some controversy that biofuels may create another problem (accelerated deforestation to grow specific biofuel-based crops).

For the Olympics, societal relevance relates to the inspiration we derive from watching top athletes compete and the corresponding message implied by athletic success: You can achieve anything if you work hard enough. We may never become Olympic athletes, but we can be world-class in anything we choose to do.

It is against this backdrop of the dimensions of brand value that the decision to invest more than $240 million must be weighed and the opportunity costs assessed. Olympic sponsorship requires an enormous financial sum that can easily be invested in a wide range of marketing activities that benefit the brand without having to concentrate them on a single event like the Olympics.

To illustrate the folly of incautious sports marketing investments, consider the 2000 Super Bowl in the United States, which is the most widely watched U.S. sporting event, with between 90 and 160 million fans tuning in each year.[35] The period of the late 1990s leading up to the 2000 Super Bowl is better known as the dot.com era, when it seemed any entrepreneur could make money doing anything, and common sense was temporarily suspended. More than a dozen Internet companies spent $40 million collectively for 30-second television commercials during the 2000 Super Bowl; the average 30-second Super Bowl TV commercial that year cost $2.2 million. The ads covered a wide range of topics and companies, from Pets.com's infamous sock puppet to E★TRADE Financial's bizarre dancing chimpanzee. Most of those companies are no longer in business today (E★TRADE is one of the remaining few still around, although it has been facing challenges due to large investments in complex bonds tied to the troubled mortgage market),[36] and many went out of business within a year of airing these ads. One of the firms, OurBeginning.com—which specialized in online wedding invitation design—spent more than $4 million on their Super Bowl ads,[37] an amount several times larger than their actual revenues. The dot-coms saw the Super Bowl as a rare and unique event that could serve as a singular platform to market their company. Such shallow reasoning serves as a vivid reminder to companies that their marketing investments ought to be planned with the same rigorous attention applied to R&D budgets, corporate strategic plans, and new product launches, with a keen eye on the long-term potential for developing value and a lasting, responsible brand, not just a short-term spike in awareness and sales.

Beyond the four elements of brand value, the diversity of Olympic sports attracts an equally diverse fan base. The temptation to be avoided is assuming a large audience equates to a good business opportunity. Developing awareness is important, but translating that awareness into measurable financial improvement in the short term is far harder to achieve. Large-scale events like the Olympics are useful marketing opportunities if companies recognize that a critical determinant of marketing success is based on intentionally planning and expecting a longer-term horizon to achieve positive results. Part of the reason is that Olympic audiences are involved more in the athletic contests and are less interested in being sold products, as that blatant commercialism detracts from the Olympic appeal. Less direct appeals, while still intended to create a positive impression with audiences, do not intrude as overtly into the fans' experience of watching the sports. To make the Olympics sponsorship investment useful, marketers must approach it as they would any other marketing effort: Understand the different audiences, identify their needs, create programs that appeal to their interests, and vary the message based on the type of marketing vehicle used.

In 2007, Synovate, a leading market research firm, conducted a survey of 9,500 people in the United States, Asia, and Europe, asking them questions related to the Olympic Games. Respondents were asked generally if they noticed Olympic sponsors, and 63 percent said yes.[38]

Interestingly, China Market Research Group (CMR) conducted its own survey of Chinese citizens around the same time. Nearly 80 percent did not express care or interest in who the Olympic sponsors were, and many simply did not even know, nor was being an Olympic sponsor influential in their product purchase decisions.[39] In another survey, two-thirds of online Chinese consumers could not easily remember Olympic sponsors. However, the same survey measured spontaneous awareness levels (recalling a brand without being prompted) for TOP and domestic sponsors. The TOP sponsors Coca-Cola and Lenovo had the highest spontaneous awareness levels at 38 percent, and domestic sponsors Adidas, China Mobile, and Yili had 28 percent, 23 percent, and 17 percent, respectively. The survey results suggest that sponsor awareness benefits were possible in China.[40] Certainly, the fact that spontaneous awareness was reasonably high for several companies suggests that sponsorship marketing had some level of memorable impact. A different study of 1,500 people from China in 2008 was conducted in two phases, pre- and post-Olympics, to ascertain their recognition of Olympic sponsors. Coca-Cola topped the pre-event survey, with 79.1 percent recognition. Samsung was next with 53.7 percent, then Kodak at 44.4 percent, McDonald's with 44.2 percent, and Panasonic with 42.2 percent. Most surprising was Lenovo, recognized by only 3.4 percent of the survey respondents, despite being a company of Chinese origin. The follow-up postevent survey showed that 68.8 percent of respondents recognized Panasonic, a significant increase. McDonald's was recognized by 66.1 percent, followed by Samsung with 65.7 percent. Lenovo was not mentioned in the postsurvey results analysis.[41] Clearly, each survey in China had different, even somewhat contradictory results, although the CMR research also indicated that spontaneous awareness was positive. In the 2010 Vancouver Olympics, consumer awareness of sponsors showed similar trends to Beijing: The biggest TOP sponsors dominated. In Vancouver, 68 percent of consumers were aware of both Coca-Cola's and McDonald's involvement, followed closely by Visa with 66 percent. Domestic sponsors in Canada had lower consumer awareness levels: AT&T was at 36 percent, P&G was at 27 percent (P&G did not become a TOP sponsor until after the Vancouver Olympics), and other TOP sponsors' consumer awareness levels were below these, with GE at 25 percent, Samsung at 24 percent, and Panasonic at 21 percent.[42] A survey of 1,500 people conducted by News International Track and Field (NITF) in Great Britain in 2011, ahead of the 2012 London Olympics, revealed that Coca-Cola had the highest consumer brand awareness, at 40 percent, and was the most recognized partner of the 2012 London Olympics. McDonald's had the next-highest awareness at approximately 33 percent, followed by Visa with 25 percent awareness. Also, U.K. consumers expressed interest that sponsors should clearly demonstrate how they would support British athletes and healthy lifestyles. Furthermore, the NITF survey findings showed that consumer interest in sponsors would be higher if their sponsorship campaigns were developed around home-country athletes.[43]

Ambush Marketing

Olympic TOP program sponsors treat their respective Olympic investments as a serious strategic asset. Just as the easiest part of a corporate acquisition of another company is the purchase itself (versus the integration, which is far harder and more complex), the easiest part of a sports sponsorship is spending money for exposure. The real challenge, and opportunity, is deciding how to implement the sponsorship so that the event boosts the company's image while simultaneously avoiding undermining or damaging both organizations' reputations. The Olympic TOP program sponsors have planned sophisticated brand-building efforts designed to run for many years using multiple marketing platforms. Among these are the digital and social media tools. Using blogs, social sites, and digital and mobile downloads, companies can have direct, one-on-one communications with consumers. Each of the TOP sponsors establishes multiple criteria for assessing the return on their sponsorship investment, including short-term financial and long-term strategic positioning gains. There are multiple ways to measure sponsorship success. A single formula does not shed necessary light on the contributions of the full range of marketing activities employed. The audit questions throughout this book are designed to help management think through the strategic objectives, tactical choices, and methods of assessment.

When an event is as successful as the modern Olympics, it is little wonder that many companies would want to find a way to take advantage of the Olympic Games effect. Because of the strategic nature of the Olympic investment, and its sheer magnitude, sponsors are understandably interested in protecting their investment. One concern Olympic TOP sponsors have is how to stop ambush marketers from finding ways to gain the benefits of associating with the Olympics without having to pay for the (expensive) sponsorship rights, as discussed in the Samsung Case Brief (but is a concern shared by all TOP sponsors). Protecting official sponsors by policing the activities of ambush (or stealth) marketers is a complex undertaking, and there are more holes than there are plugs in the rules governing sponsor protection. In preparation for the 2004 Olympic Games in Athens, more than $750,000 was spent removing and cleaning billboards throughout the city. The best billboards near the athletic venues were reserved for authorized sponsors only. Despite similar efforts at all Olympics, unauthorized companies do find ways to leverage off the Olympic juggernaut, as Table 12.16 illustrates.

Ambush marketing is not cheap, however. The athlete and team sponsorships independent of the Olympics are expensive. But that money is leveraged across all activities in which that athlete is involved. At a minimum, ambush marketers can create confusion with consumers, as the Beijing examples highlight. If consumers believe nonsponsors are officially part of the Olympics, then it diverts some attention from the TOP sponsors. Many of the ambush marketing examples seen are simply extensions of preexisting business and marketing relationships between the company and the athlete or team, as illustrated by some of the examples. The ongoing challenge for the IOC is finding ways to minimize the effects of ambush marketers without interfering with the normal conduct of business and established contractual relationships for sponsors and nonsponsors alike.

Policing every conceivable location near the venues and watching each individual person carefully is not feasible. However, the London Organizing Committee for the Olympic Games (LOCOG) introduced a strict set of brand protection guidelines.[48] They prescribe precisely which Olympics identities, marks, and related associations are legally protected and cannot be usurped by nonsponsors. In the event of violations, LOCOG can enforce its legal rights by any of several legal means, up to and including injunctions, lawsuits for damages, and demand for payment of the violator's profits to LOCOG.

Table 12.16 Ambush Marketing Examples in the Olympics[44]

Olympic Games	Example
1984	Kodak sponsors TV broadcasts, despite Fuji being Olympics' official sponsor. Fuji returns favor at Seoul 1988 Games.
1992	Nike sponsors news conferences with the U.S. basketball team. Michael Jordan accepts the gold medal for basketball and covers up his Reebok logo.
1994	American Express runs ads claiming Americans do not need "Visas" to travel to Norway (for Winter Olympics).
1996	British sprinter Linford Christie wore contact lenses with Puma's logo on them since he was sponsored by them, even though Reebok was the official sponsor.[45]
2000	Qantas Airlines' slogan "Spirit of Australia" coincidentally sounds like Games' slogan "Share the spirit," to the chagrin of official sponsor Ansett Air.
2008	Anta is a sports products company in China. In 2000, the company had provided attire for the Chinese Olympic team in Sydney. While not an official sponsor for the 2008 Beijing Olympics, the company had TV commercials that featured an ancient Greek temple, fire (similar to the Olympic flame), a past Chinese Olympic athlete, a statue of ancient Greek Olympians, and music reminiscent of composer Vangelis's "Chariots of Fire" theme.[46]
	Other Beijing examples: Pepsi changed its can color to red from blue for the Beijing Olympics, ostensibly because red is an auspicious color in China; Nike has apparel contracts with many athletes who are required to wear the official outfit during medal ceremonies (both Reebok and Adidas have been previous apparel sponsors). Market research firm Ipsos conducted a survey of thousands of Chinese consumers in 2007 that revealed many people thought nonsponsors were "official." According to R3, a Beijing-based consulting firm, 75 percent of Chinese consumers "would prefer to buy products they associated with the Olympics."
2010	MasterCard used catering trucks to serve coffee to passersby at heavily trafficked intersections in Vancouver in an effort to counter Visa's officially sanctioned sponsorship coverage.[47]

Despite ambush marketing challenges, the IOC has been able to make its sponsorship programs perennially attractive, indicating that while not perfect, there is sufficient confidence in the structure of the programs to keep companies interested. When signing a sponsorship deal, even with the brand protection guidelines described earlier, the onus is on the company to ensure that the contract language is clear about how the company's authorized status will be protected and unauthorized companies will be prevented access. An open, up-front exchange of expectations between the event and the sponsor can at least provide strong guidance about what is and is not possible in protecting authorized sponsors from ambush marketers.

For those companies with the financial ability, an Olympic TOP sponsorship can be a powerful and visible platform for enhancing a company's reputation. As a reminder, success as a sports sponsor involves more than giving money to have your name associated with an event. Having a plan that sets clear sponsorship objectives, tactical programs, and evaluation criteria is not a luxury but a requirement, plus a major responsibility and cost. As the Olympics continue to grow and costs accelerate, the complexity of hosting an Olympiad increases. Corporate sponsors may be tempted to offset the increased sponsorship costs by implementing more aggressive product, marketing communication, and merchandising programs to boost revenues. Doing so risks accelerating the pace of overt commercialization of the Olympics, distracting and detracting from the primary purpose of the Olympic Games: pure athletic competition. However, when such situations occur, the ensuing public backlash has led to adjustments by the IOC and improved self-policing by sponsors, quietly guided by the reputation of the Olympic movement and the values its espouses.

The next four chapters examine a selection of TOP program sponsors, chosen because each has been involved with the Olympics for a different length of time, and each has different strategic intentions and tactical implementations. Of the four cases, two are case *briefs* (shorter summaries of those sponsors' Olympics sponsorships) and two are case *studies* (in-depth reviews). Also, all four are in the seventh generation of TOP sponsors. Interested readers are welcome to download two updated case studies of Lenovo and John Hancock, two TOP sponsors from the first edition of this book, since reading their cases will help one further understand how they used their Olympics sponsorships to build their brands (available at www .wiley.com/go/olympiceffect).

TOP VII Sponsors (Seventh Generation of TOP Sponsors)

- Chapter 13. Acer Case Brief: Olympic sponsor since 2009
- Chapter 14. Samsung Case Brief: Olympic sponsor since 1997
- Chapter 15. Coca-Cola Case Study: Olympic sponsor since 1928
- Chapter 16. Visa Case Study: Olympic sponsor since 1986

Questions

1. Describe why sponsorships play an important role in the IOC's funding and overall support of the Games. (Don't just describe the amount; think about what the sponsorship funds enable.)
2. Describe how sponsors can use the dimensions of brand value to evaluate their sponsorship decisions.
3. Can a TOP sponsorship affect brand value directly? Why or why not?
4. Assuming brand value can be impacted, how can an Olympic TOP sponsorship increase brand value? Or decrease it?
5. TOP sponsors require a substantial financial commitment from the sponsoring company. Why do you think TOP sponsors choose to invest in the Olympics, as opposed to allocating the same amount of money to a variety of marketing activities?
6. Given the amount of capital at risk, would a company be better off choosing ambush marketing as its sports sponsoring strategy? Can you think of other protections TOP sponsors should seek to minimize the impact of ambush marketers?

Chapter 13

The Olympic Sponsor Case Brief: Acer

Background

The universality of the Olympic Games has a strong influence on us, as it brings people together, overcomes prejudice and gives full respect to diversity. This principle is the basis of our winning formula to building Acer into a successful global company. We truly believe in it and exercise the principle in our daily operation.

—J. T. Wang, Acer Inc. Chairman and Acer Group CEO[1]

In 2007, shortly after it was known that Lenovo would not extend its Olympic TOP sponsorship, IOC officials announced that Acer would become a TOP sponsor from 2009 to 2013 for the 2010 Vancouver Olympics and the 2012 London Olympics, the first Taiwanese company to become an Olympic sponsor. As part of the agreement, Acer would supply the equipment for the Vancouver and London Olympics, as Lenovo had done in 2006 and 2008. For Vancouver, Acer supplied more than 6,500 computer-related components, plus more than 100 engineers and support staff to ensure the smooth running of the technology infrastructure. The equipment being supplied for London in 2012 is even more impressive: 11,000 desktops, 10,500 monitors, 1,500 laptops, 1,500 touch screens, 900 servers, 5 storage area networks (SANs), an assortment of related supplies and accessories, and approximately 350 technical support professionals.[2]

> "Making an important contribution to the smooth and efficient running of the London 2012 Olympic Games is a very exciting task for Acer as we continue to serve more and more business customers," said Walter Deppeler, Acer EMEA president and chief marketing officer. "We want to prove that as our equipment and engineers can support the biggest sporting event in the world and satisfy the diverse needs of our Olympic customers. There is no doubt that we can also support businesses of any size."[3]

Samsung had served as an example of a company whose fortunes seemed to change for the better because of becoming an Olympic sponsor in 1997. Several industry analysts said that Samsung's brand awareness increased as a direct result of its association with the Olympics. As the Lenovo case online describes, its Olympic sponsorship came at an important time for the company, given its recent (at the time) acquisition of IBM's PC division, its name change to Lenovo from Legend, and its ambition to grow beyond China and become a global PC brand. The 2008 Beijing Olympics, in particular, was an ideal location since China was using the Olympics to reemerge onto the world stage. The questions that arose, however, were how Lenovo would choose to activate its Olympic sponsorship during the Games and then how it would use the Olympic association to build awareness and establish its brand globally. Whereas Visa has been a sponsor since 1986 and has seen important performance gains partly as a result of its Olympic sponsorship, Lenovo sponsored only the 2006 and 2008 Olympics, so the company did not have enough time to fully leverage its Olympic association.

Strategic Ambitions

Acer had its own global ambitions. As the number four PC maker in 2007, Acer's strategy was to compete with, challenge, and ultimately surpass HP, Dell, and Lenovo, using the Olympic sponsorship as a catalyst. When the Olympic sponsorship deal was announced in December 2007, Acer, like Lenovo a few years earlier, had recently completed its own significant acquisition, of U.S. PC maker Gateway (for $710 million). Due to the Gateway acquisition, Acer's 2008 sales were projected to reach $20 billion. The company's goal was to double its U.S. market share to 11.7 percent as well. Soon after their 2007 announcement of becoming a TOP sponsor, Acer estimated that its Olympic association would help propel the company to revenues of over $30 billion by 2012.[4] They also anticipated an increase in brand value and a boost to employee morale.[5] Furthermore, company leaders believed that being associated as a TOP partner alongside venerable global brands like McDonalds, GE, Coca-Cola, Visa, and Samsung would raise its overall visibility and enhance its credibility. Acer Chairman of the Board J. T. Wang, said:

> The careful choice of associating our company with established world leaders in their respective sectors has helped grow the brand perception of Acer around the world.[6]

Of course, associating with the world's leading sports event offers Acer equally compelling potential, as Chairman Wang describes:

> The universality of the Olympic Games has a strong influence on us, as it brings people together, overcomes prejudice and gives full respect to diversity. This principle is the basis of our winning formula to building Acer into a successful global company. We truly believe in it and exercise the principle in our daily operation.[7]

Similar sentiments were offered by President Gianfranco Lanci:

> The experience with the International Olympic Committee will bring a fresh and new approach. It will be like being part of a huge community of men and women who, though sharing

different feelings and emotions, are driven by a common intent to promote an open dialogue built on solidarity and support. Seen in this perspective, differences become beneficial to all parties, something that is in line with Acer's objective to build easy-to-use technological solutions that are shaped around real people and real needs.[8]

Even the analyst community saw opportunity in Acer's Olympic sponsorship, as evidenced from comments by Wong Chi-man, an analyst with Hong Kong–based China Everbright Research.

The Olympic sponsorship makes sense for Acer's marketing strategy in light of its recent acquisition of Gateway which supplies computers to North America, and Packard Bell which has a strong presence in Europe.[9]

Acer's Olympic sponsorship is consistent with earlier sports marketing investments the company made in an effort to improve brand visibility in the United States and Europe, including Formula 1 (the Scoured Ferrari Formula One team), Moto GP (the Ducati Corse team), Spanish football club Barcelona (its sponsorship ended in 2009), and Italian Football club Internazionale Milan.[10]

Marketing Tactics and Challenges

Part of any Olympic sponsorship activation includes numerous advertising vehicles, from print to digital to television, product launches, and more. In Vancouver, Acer showcased its newest PCs, laptops, and state-of-the-art displays.[11]

Acer created Olympic-themed television ads for the 2010 Vancouver Winter Olympics, with uneven results. In Australia, Acer's ads inadvertently created confusion with viewers who mistakenly thought the ads were from Lenovo, the TOP sponsor from 2006 and 2008 that Acer replaced. The Australian ads used freestyle skier Lydia Lassila to convey the toughness of their notebooks, but the message was lost on viewers. Peter Fairbrother, executive director of Ipsos, a leading marketing research company, said:

Using an Olympic theme might get some cut-through, but it's no guarantee of advertising success, and the results validate this point. Coke had a change in tack by not running an Olympics ad [at Vancouver] and used a local execution which worked well for them.[12]

As 2009 drew to a close, Acer's U.S. market share had increased significantly to just over 13 percent. Unfortunately, Acer's U.S. market share declined in 2010 to just under 11 percent and dropped again in the second quarter of 2011 to 8.5 percent.[13]

Executive Turnover

In 2011, a disagreement between Acer CEO Gianfranco Lanci and the board of directors led to Lanci's resignation. Lanci's hope of challenging HP, Dell, and Lenovo was questioned by the board, which thought Acer ought to be more distinctive and not just another PC company, competing for uniqueness with companies like Apple and HTC (a leading mobile phone manufacturer).[14] Soon thereafter, on April 19, 2011, Acer announced that Jim Wong had been appointed the new president, taking Lanci's place. He had previously been corporate senior vice president and president of IT Products Group.[15] Not long afterward, Corporate Vice President of Marketing and Brand Gianpiero Morello left the company. Interestingly, Anton Mitsyuk, Acer's head of the Olympic sponsorship, took Morello's place.[16] As of June 2011, the IOC was in talks with Acer to extend its TOP sponsorship beyond the 2012 Olympics.[17]

Questions

1. Evaluate Acer's motives for becoming an Olympic TOP sponsor. What were the pros and cons at the time of the decision in 2007?
2. Given Lenovo's short tenure as an Olympic TOP sponsor, what lessons might Acer have learned?
3. What recommendations would you make for Acer to take the best advantage possible of its Olympic association?

4. Does the company's advertising in Australia suggest its marketing message was wrong? Visit the Internet and find more examples of Acer's Vancouver Olympics marketing. What do you notice?

5. What impact might the executive turnover have on Acer's performance? How might the Olympic sponsorship be affected?

Chapter 14

The Olympic Sponsor Case Brief: Samsung

Background

Samsung started out in 1938 as a small trading company in grocery products that also produced its own noodles. Over the decades, the company reshaped itself several times, moving into manufacturing, electronics, engineering, and consumer products. The late 1990s proved to be an important time period for Samsung. Following the 1997 Asian financial crisis, Samsung shifted gears again, investing more in R&D and placing greater emphasis on design and innovation. Its transformation from local trading company to global brand powerhouse has been extensively cataloged, but 1997 also marked the year that Samsung became a TOP sponsor for the Olympics, setting in motion a relationship that has helped the company solidify its reputation as one of the leading and most successful brands in the world. At the time, Samsung Chairman Kun-Hee Lee said,

Devise strategies that can raise brand value, which is a leading intangible asset and the source of corporate competitiveness, to the global level. Samsung decided to sponsor the Olympic Movement to strengthen its global corporate image and brand value and has been carrying out a global marketing campaign with the Olympic Games and the Olympic Movement as the single theme.[1]

Increasing Brand Value

The company saw significant value in associating with the Olympic Games. The value of its brand rose from $3.1 billion in 1999 to $19.5 billion in 2010 according to Interbrand, the world's largest brand consulting company.[2] The company's progress since 1997 has been remarkable. Not only did Samsung surpass rival Sony in 2005 to become the world's most valuable consumer electronics brand at that time but also it gained a globally recognized reputation for superior quality and innovation, and it became one of the industry leaders in several markets, including mobile phones.

Olympic Sponsorship

Samsung's Olympic sponsorship planning shifted over time as well, with the company's marketers increasingly using the Olympic Games as a strategic platform for long-term brand positioning, rather than just driving sales. The company's confidence in the Olympics was high, demonstrated in 2007 when it was announced Samsung would extend its sponsorship through the 2016 Olympics in Rio de Janeiro, covering all Winter and Summer Games. Samsung management firmly believed in the power of the Olympics to emotionally capture the world's imagination and said that their Olympic investments had been central to its growth as a brand and its mobile phone business in particular. Official company statements even said,

. . . investing in the Olympic Games means unlimited growth potential.[3]

Beijing 2008

As the 2008 Beijing Olympics approached, the company envisioned its most ambitious sponsorship marketing effort ever. Their activation plans focused on phones and mobile applications, designing their lead product, the F480, to be the official phone of the Olympics. The F480 was a touchscreen phone with a five megapixel camera (significant for a mobile phone at that time) that had face recognition capability. The phone also had a smile shot feature triggered to photograph people whenever they were smiling. The phone offered different colors, including gold, reflecting the Olympic theme. It also had ringtones, wallpaper, and cheer songs, all of which carried an Olympic theme. The company's game plan was to launch the phone in Africa, Europe, and Asia in the months before the Games commenced, including extensive TV advertising in most of those markets.[4]

The Olympics invariably attract their share of controversy. As the world's largest sports event of its kind, the Games have become much more than a series of athletic competitions—it has become a global stage whose spotlight shines on all associated with it, including protesters, activists, and those with a political agenda. Samsung had become a sponsor of the Olympic Torch Relay in 2004, seeing the sponsorship as a highly visible symbol of the world coming together. Each torch relay traverses numerous countries around the world and, over time, has found increasing challenges from protesters who use the relay as a vehicle for elevating their own message. Beijing would be no different, since China's human rights policies, including its handling of Tibet, had raised the ire of rights groups around the world. The demonstrators saw the relay as a way to put pressure on the sponsors to cease their sponsorship and/or align with the cause—perhaps even stop the relay before its completion. None of those things happened, but the relay route was altered in its early stages after severe protests in France and the United Kingdom.[5]

Vancouver 2010

Samsung wanted the Vancouver Winter Olympics to be another platform for branding its reputation in the mobile sector as an innovator. But because of the global financial crisis, questions about Samsung's commitment to its Vancouver sponsorship arose. Gyehyun Kwon,

Samsung vice president and head of worldwide sports marketing, responded to this concern:

> Samsung has worked in tough financial times before and there's no way they'd give up on the Games. Kwon: "We just cut down on the other parts and consolidate to maximize the utility and effect of our sports marketing."[6]

In addition, in an effort to continue bolstering its corporate social responsibility (CSR) image, Samsung Electronics Canada enlisted 10 Canadian youth to use new media to chronicle their experiences and the Games. Using blogs, vlogs, and social and digital media, these young Canadians produced content that was spread virally on YouTube.com, Facebook, Samsung's own web site, and a wide variety of blogs.[7] Samsung created a new campaign for Vancouver in support of its phone and mobile business called "Discover Your Every WOW Moment," with WOW meaning Wireless Olympic Works, a new technology platform designed to deliver event results and to-the-moment updates directly to users' mobile devices as the Games progressed. Reflecting a bit of the spirit of cooperation that the Olympics have always upheld, Samsung partnered with fellow TOP sponsors Atos Origin and Omega to deliver and display the results. The collaboration was a not-so-subtle signal of the technical capabilities of all three companies and their ability to combine resources seamlessly. Samsung's logo for the Vancouver Olympics featured the Vancouver logo inside a mobile phone-like design.[8] Its activation plans also included a two-story pavilion in the Olympic Park that featured its latest mobile devices and appearances by famous Canadian Winter Olympics athletes Jarome Iginla and Hayley Wickenheiser at the company's client dinners. The company's "Get Together for the Game" campaign also used the athletes' celebrity status and the Canadian love of hockey to inspire fans and unite communities around Canada. Samsung used Iginla and Wickenheiser in television ads designed specifically for the Canadian market. Benjamin Lee, president of Samsung Canada, said,

> Hockey is a game that is in Canadians' blood and the passion for the sport unites the country. Samsung is a proud supporter of men's and women's hockey in Canada, and of the Olympic Games, and we look forward to joining with two of Canada's

hockey heroes, Jarome and Hayley to celebrate the game and the excitement leading up to the Vancouver 2010 Olympic Winter Games.[9]

The Run-Up to London 2012

Samsung once again will serve as sponsor of the 2012 torch relay. In June 2011, Samsung designed a new logo for their 2012 Olympic Torch Relay sponsorship, designed by well-known London artist Kate Moross. Similar to the company's logo for Vancouver, the London design looks like a mobile phone, but with widespread arms, signifying the welcoming message of the London Olympics tagline, Everyone's Olympic Games, and a concerted effort to use their Olympic sponsorship to assert the company's exclusive position as the official wireless tele-communications partner. Given Apple's remarkable strength and fast-growing competitors like HTC, Samsung's laser focus on wireless telecommunications in its Olympic sponsorship is clearly important in the company's efforts to become the brand of choice. As Kwon commented,

> Brand awareness was very low when the [Olympic] sponsorship first started—now our marketing has changed from brand awareness to brand preference.[10]

Samsung's sponsorship activation plan for London is ambitious again. Teaming with Visa this time, visitors to the Games, and around the world, will be able to make mobile payments on an exclusive Olympic-themed mobile device. The two companies stated that the partnership will extend beyond London, perhaps signaling a new level of Olympic sponsorship cooperation between sponsors between Olympiads. Such a commitment has the potential for significant positive impact for the sponsors and the Olympics combined, if it succeeds. The collaboration mirrors trends in consumer interest in mobile payments. Convenience is undoubtedly a factor driving consumer interest as well. For the two companies, the alliance could prove to be propitious timing. Michelle Janes, Visa's senior business leader on the mobile team, said,

> The London Olympic games provided Visa and Samsung a perfect opportunity to partner to advance our mobile strategies

and build on technology assets and sponsorship presence. Samsung is active in mobile payments, we're active in mobile payments, and the timing is right, with mobile payments on the upswing.[11]

Like its use of iconic hockey athletes in Vancouver, Samsung announced that David Beckham would be the company's brand ambassador for the London 2012 Olympics, to be featured in the company's Olympic advertising and PR campaigns.[12] The sponsorship plan looked promising and could be even bigger and more sophisticated than its efforts in Beijing and Vancouver. At the same time, the company had grown increasingly concerned in recent years about ambush marketing. Company officials wanted vigorous policing of ambush marketers and decisive actions to stop their activity. The company had committed more than $100 million to support its Olympic sponsorship (beyond the sponsorship fee itself), and the London Olympics were getting two-thirds of the total, 20 percent more than it spent in Beijing. Gyehyun Kwon expressed his concern diplomatically:

We have a high expectation of the London authorities and the organising committee.[13]

Despite the company's increasingly assertive concerns about ambush marketing, they still see the Olympics as a one-of-a-kind marketing opportunity that has paid dividends since 1997. The image transformation of Samsung has been dramatic, and company officials continue to stress that the power of the Olympics has cast a positive and rejuvenating glow over the entire company. The company's confidence in the Olympics as a vital factor in its brand renaissance will be tested in London, particularly since the company confronted allegations of corruption and a management shake-up in recent years.[14] Echoing this optimism about the Olympics sponsorship, Gee-Sung Choi, Samsung board member and president of the company's Digital Media and Communications business, stated simply,

Our brand image has been lifted.[15]

Questions

1. Samsung's confidence in the Olympics suggests the Games have been the most important marketing vehicle in the company's success since 1997. Offer your assessment of the factors that have helped Samsung since that time, and discuss the impact of its Olympics sponsorship. You might want to visit the web and library databases to gain a more complete understanding of the company's milestones since 1997.
2. Evaluate and discuss Samsung's activation strategy. What do you notice that seems particularly noteworthy, either positively or negatively?
3. Samsung has numerous lines of business, from mobile tele-communications to appliances to software to computers, and more. Is Samsung's emphasis on its mobile business a good strategy? What would you do differently, if anything, and why?
4. Is it possible to stop ambush marketing? Is it even reasonable to assume this can be accomplished? If you were Samsung management and ambush marketing continued, how might that affect your Olympic sponsorship?

Chapter 15

The Olympic Sponsor Case Study: Coca-Cola

In August 2005, the IOC announced a new 12-year agreement with Coca-Cola to continue its TOP sponsorship of the Olympic Games. The announcement occurred at the Great Wall of China and included Jean-Claude Killy of France, winner of three gold medals in skiing in 1968, and Wu Min Xia, a Chinese diver who won a gold and silver medal at the 2004 Athens Olympics.[1] The symbolism surrounding the announcement was important because it connected the rich traditions of the past with the promise of the future. Holding it at the Great Wall echoed China's and the Olympics' multithousand-year histories while sparking interest in the 2008 Games and reminding the public of Coca-Cola's long-standing commitment to the Olympic movement. The attendance of Jean-Claude Killy and Wu Min Xia brought wisdom together with youth, underscoring two key themes of the Beijing Olympics while simultaneously associating Coca-Cola with these same characteristics. The deal would commence at the 2010 Vancouver Winter Olympics and encompass six Olympiads. While the deal's financial details were not disclosed, the benefits to the Vancouver Olympic Committee (VANOC) alone would be in the tens of millions. Coca-Cola would also provide in-kind services. Jacques Rogge, president of the IOC said:

> The contribution of Coca-Cola to the Olympic movement has always been the model of a true partnership. The Olympic Games would not be where they are today, and so many athletes over the years could not have competed in the Games, without the extensive corporate support pioneered by Coca-Cola as our longest continuous sponsor.[2]

This new sponsorship agreement was important for the IOC. With Coca-Cola as one of the world's most recognized brands and a supporter of the Olympics since 1928, the deal would affirm Coca-Cola's confidence in the Games as an important part of its global marketing investments, reinforce the attractiveness of the TOP program to future prospective sponsors, and secure a financial annuity and in-kind support for the IOC for years to come. (The relationship for the first few decades was with the Summer Olympics. The company's formal involvement with the Winter Olympics began in 1952 at the Games in Oslo, skipped the 1956 Winter Olympics in Cortina d'Ampezzo, Italy, renewed its involvement at the 1960 Winter Olympics at Squaw Valley, and has continued ever since.) In 2020, near the end of the 12-year agreement, Coca-Cola's partnership with the Olympics will be 92 years old, one of the longest-running corporate marketing programs in the world and a relationship that has provided Coca-Cola with substantial exposure and awareness benefits.

Of course, since the Olympics are one of the most visible stages anywhere, sponsors are not the only ones that can gain recognition. A potential controversy, such as a scandal or protest, could detract from the goodwill the Games foster and the concomitant benefits sponsors enjoy. Sponsors, too, can find themselves the focus of criticism. The 1996 Summer Olympics in Atlanta celebrated the 100th anniversary of the modern Olympics. But the Atlanta Organizing Committee found itself denounced for allowing the Games to be overly commercial and detracting from the integrity of the Olympics. Dubbed by some critics as the Coca-Cola Olympics (although, to be fair, numerous sponsors and companies contributed to the overt commercialism), the Atlanta Olympics were seen by many as crass and not representative of the Olympic ideals. Former IOC President Juan Antonio Samaranch remarked in his closing speech that Atlanta had delivered a "most exceptional" Olympics, a choice of words many Olympic observers interpreted as a snub at the Atlanta Organizing Committee because he had not said his customary "the best Games ever," as he had at previous Olympiads.[3]

For the 2008 Beijing Summer Olympics, several controversial issues arose, and the question was how much traction these would gain in the media and public marketplace. In April 2008 at the annual shareholder meeting, a member of the audience asked Neville Isdell, CEO of Coca-Cola,

> Will you tell the IOC to stop taking the Olympic torch relay into Tibet, because Tibet belongs to Tibetans?

Isdell responded:

> [The torch relay] has symbolized openness, it has symbolized hopes. I don't believe that stopping the torch run is in any way over the long-term going to be the right thing to do.[4]

China was an important market for Coca-Cola, with first-quarter 2008 results showing a 20 percent increase in unit case volume sales and a 19 percent increase in net income to $1.5 billion. Approximately 5 percent of Coca-Cola's revenue came from China at the time. For the year 2008, case unit sales grew 19 percent in 2008. Sponsoring the Beijing Olympics was seen as good for business.[5] As an iconic American brand with a well-known global reputation, the company has historically emphasized intangible objectives as well, including showing it is a responsible corporate citizen and associating the brand with positive lifestyle values and imagery.

Coca-Cola's commitment to Olympic sponsorship underscores the potential for building sustained value. Yet with the highest brand value of all companies according to a 2010 Interbrand survey, and vast global distribution plus loyal consumers, a reasonable question might be why

Coca-Cola would want or need to invest the sizable sums required to be a TOP sponsor. One could argue that the money might be more effectively invested in research and development, acquisitions, vertical or horizontal integration, or alternative marketing investments.

One of the reasons for Coca-Cola's extraordinary brand success over time is the care and attention paid to building the company's brand equity. Coca-Cola's 2010 balance sheet indicated the value of company assets to be $72.92 billion (including short-term assets like cash, syrup, and other inventories and long-term assets like plant and equipment), and their market capitalization was approximately $155 billion,[6] indicating a significantly favorable investor premium, much of which is attributable to brand value. If Coca-Cola were focused merely on selling caramel-flavored, carbonated sugar water, then it is likely that consumer interest would be diminished, as would investor interest and, ultimately, brand value. Instead, over the past 100 years, Coca-Cola has honed a solid, virtually unchanged reputation (with the exception of the well-known New Coca-Cola debacle of the 1980s) as a symbol of American values. As the U.S. economy expanded in the twentieth century, particularly after World War II, so did Coca-Cola. A defining characteristic of this expansion was the company's use of imagery in promoting its namesake flagship cola beverage. People, from everyday consumers to the military to famous stars, were pictured enjoying themselves and their lives. With the Olympics enjoying a similar reputation for celebrating life, Coca-Cola's ongoing Olympic support seems, in retrospect, a natural fit and a logical brand association.

In describing its sponsorship of the Olympic Games, Coca-Cola states that its values are similar to those of the Olympics,

> . . . which embody the discovery of one's abilities, the spirit of competition, the pursuit of excellence, a sense of fair play and the building of a better and more peaceful world.[7]

Certainly, many companies would assert similar sentiments. However, declaring these values is important for putting a stake in the ground and saying, "This is what we stand for." Coca-Cola's sponsorship undertakings strongly suggest a genuine commitment to bringing its values to life, beyond words on paper.

Coca-Cola's Olympic Sponsorship Activities

To take advantage of this unrivaled sports event, Coca-Cola has developed a wide range of marketing activities and innovative programs to foster a long-term brand. Indeed, Coca-Cola has been deeply involved in more than just the commercial aspects of sponsorship. The company was involved in corporate social responsibility (CSR) through its Olympics relationship long before CSR became fashionable. Historically and through present times, the company has been keenly aware of the increasing emphasis consumers, government organizations, community groups, and society overall place on corporate responsibility. Each of Coca-Cola's Olympic sponsorship activities, represented in Figure 15.1, are closely tied with the company's own values and, as company management believes, those of the Olympics.[8]

Olympic Torch Relay

The carrying of the Olympic Flame in modern times started in 1928, and it took several decades for it to evolve into the transcontinental event involving thousands of runners from around the world that we know today. The Olympic Flame symbolizes the ancient Greek tradition of keeping a flame or fire burning throughout the duration of each

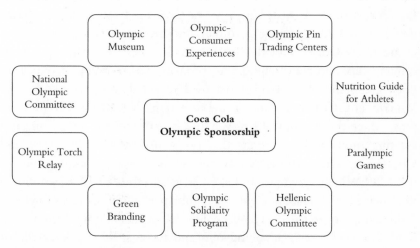

Figure 15.1   Coca-Cola Olympic Sponsorship Activities

Olympiad. The torch relay is a powerful and symbolic event that not only attracts the public but also draws the attention of protesters, who see the flame as a visible means to attract media coverage. Coca-Cola began sponsoring the Olympic Torch Relay at the 1992 Barcelona Olympics, and the 2010 Olympic Torch Relay was Coca-Cola's seventh. Coca-Cola and the other 2010 Olympic Torch Relay sponsors (Royal Bank of Canada, Government of Canada, Bombardier) collectively paid a reported CAD$30 million. In Coca-Cola's case, this was in addition to their TOP sponsorship fee.[9]

Green Branding

In the 2010 Winter Olympic Games in Vancouver, Coca-Cola unveiled its most aggressive sustainability program ever. The company's bottles, furniture, and related hard goods supplies were all made from recyclable materials and reusable energy sources. This required significant cooperation and coordination with its suppliers. Company executives believed the effort was worth it since the company, and all TOP sponsors, are under increasing scrutiny from environmental groups about their green practices.[10] For the 2012 London Olympics, Coca-Cola will further reduce its carbon emissions by outfitting its fleet of delivery trucks to run on biomethane, supplied by fuel extracted from a landfill site in Surrey. A new refueling station has been built near London to support this effort.[11] Coca-Cola used some of the unused steel from the 2008 Beijing Olympics bird's nest stadium construction to create Coca-Cola–branded Olympic trading pins. For this and other sustainability efforts in Beijing, the company was awarded Greenpeace's "first green medal."[12] Coca-Cola used recycled materials in its 2010 Vancouver Olympics trading pins. The benefits are straightforward: The pins reduce the amount of leftover steel by putting it to use, while also creating memorable souvenirs that promote both the Olympics and Coca-Cola. The company developed its first Olympic trading pin for the 1980 Winter Olympics in Lake Placid and then in 1988 established the Olympic Pin Trading Center, a regular part of Coca-Cola's Olympic sponsorships ever since. These centers have been popular with fans, both those who collect trading pins and those seeking a keepsake of their Olympic visit. With global concern over environment issues, repurposing the unused stadium steel matches well with society's needs today while continuing Coca-Cola's long-standing commitment to being a responsible corporate citizen. Interested readers can learn more about Coca-Cola's Olympic sustainability program at www.cocacola .ca/olympics_sustainability_plan.htm.

Support for Hellenic Olympic Committee

Aside from its substantial TOP program participation, in 2007 Coca-Cola donated US$2 million to the Hellenic Olympic Committee to aid in restoring Ancient Olympia, the historic Olympic site. The summer of 2007 brought devastating fires to this area, and the company's donation, along with that of other contributors, contributed toward repair and restoration work.

Minos Kyriakou, president of the Hellenic Olympic Committee, said,

> We cordially congratulate The Coca-Cola Company for its significant initiative and thank the Company and its employees for always demonstrating their commitment to the Olympic values and ideals.[13]

Support for National Olympic Committees

An important piece of Coca-Cola's Olympic sponsorship is its support for more than 200 NOCs around the world. One of the challenges for world-class athletes with the ambition to compete in the Olympics is finding the resources to support their training, and Coca-Cola's sponsorship money (and that of other sponsors) helps support these needs. These resources include:

- Finding proper coaching
- Using the latest approved equipment
- Traveling to and from domestic and international competitions, plus food and accommodation expenses
- Paying competition registration fees

Although many athletes have lucrative endorsement contracts and related support deals, most do not. Consequently, this funding is vital to ensuring athletes have an opportunity to compete in the Olympics.

Olympic Solidarity Program

The Olympic Solidarity Program was started by the IOC in 1983, and a portion of Coca-Cola's sponsorship money funds this program to this day. The funds support training programs for each NOC, as well as scholarships for athletes. In addition, this program helps fund the construction of sports facilities and related infrastructure in NOC countries, particularly those ravaged by war. Academic programs devoted to understanding the Olympic movement and how to host and execute successful sports events provide NOCs with vital knowledge and skills-building insights that can benefit countries for years following an Olympic Games.

Olympic-Consumer Experiences

Coca-Cola has regularly run promotions that give away free tickets to fans around the world in an effort to connect consumers more directly with the Olympic Games. This has included tours of the Olympic Village, meet-and-greet sessions with athletes, and special Coca-Cola Olympic fans centers designed to provide fans a place to rest, have refreshments, and watch live coverage of the Olympics. Large-scale exhibits and targeted investments, some above and beyond their core TOP sponsorship fees, have been made, such as the Coca-Cola Olympic City at the 1996 Atlanta Olympics (an interactive venue adjacent to the Olympics), Coca-Cola RedFest Celebrations at the 2000 Sydney Olympics (featuring live, big-screen broadcasts of the Games, plus live music, entertainment, food, and dancing), Powerade-Aquarius Training Camp in Sydney (behind-the-scenes tours designed for teens), Coca-Cola "On the Ice" at the 2002 Winter Olympics in Salt Lake (including winter sports simulations, luge course, and hockey rink), Coca-Cola Live multimedia shows, and Coca-Cola "O.N. Air in Athens" at the 2004 Olympics (featuring themed entertainment, music, live sports reporting). The Shuang Zone at Chao Yang Park in Beijing was designed for family entertainment and included an area for visitors to take photos with an Olympic Torch, and in Vancouver, the company donated $350,000 to help fund an outdoor sport court for inner-city youth. These are among many examples of Coca-Cola's involvement at each Olympic Games to directly engage with spectators and consumers in the energetic atmosphere of the Olympics while reminding the public that Coca-Cola was the company that made this possible.[14]

Olympic Museum

Coca-Cola sponsors the Olympic Museum in Lausanne, Switzerland, a facility devoted to Olympic history. Coca-Cola was the first sponsor of the museum, donating $1 million in 1987. Coca-Cola's early involvement in this museum reflects another dimension to the company's community involvement, providing the company with a more substantial link to the Olympics than just that of sponsor.

"Nutrition for Athletes" Guide

Coca-Cola's Powerade brand sports drink copublished this guide with the IOC. Within the guide is information about the important connection between fitness and proper nutrition. This guide has the benefit of reminding the market that Coca-Cola produces more than just cola beverages—it makes products the world's leading athletes use to enhance their competitive performance and training.

Paralympic Games

In another display of CSR and concern for the communities it serves, Coca-Cola has also sponsored the Paralympics, which follow the Olympic Games in each host city.

Companies today are expected to be engaged, supportive, and active members of society. The public wants companies to demonstrate their commitment to the greater good, beyond the creation of profits and wealth for a few. Coca-Cola has long seen itself as a responsible corporate citizen, and the broad set of programs it rolls out for each Olympic Games is a purposeful and very public demonstration of its values and that the company is serious about its role in the world as a company that offers more than a famous beverage.

Coca-Cola's Olympic sponsorship is a key part of a broad-based effort to connect with the lives of consumers. Coca-Cola has evolved and expanded its Olympic sponsorship activities to make certain the company stays relevant to consumers. Through the Olympics, Coca-Cola has been able to extend the brand's presence in both tangible ways, through the introduction and sale of products including giveaways and new launches, Olympic Pin Trading Centers, and interactive exhibits in Olympic venues, and intangible ways, through support of the Olympic Torch Relay, the Olympic Solidarity Program, and extensive consumer-experience touchpoints designed to foster strong emotional ties. The Games provide a unique setting to convey the positive, uplifting lifestyle values Coca-Cola believes its consumers associate with the company.

Each of Coca-Cola's marketing activities directly serves the company's desire to bring people closer to the Olympics. With the Games representing peace among nations and competitive goodwill, Coca-Cola has had more than 80 years of Olympic association that has benefited the company's image, brand reputation, and product sales. Over the years, as the Olympics have changed and grown, so, too, has Coca-Cola.

Questions

1. Coca-Cola has used its Olympic sponsorship over the years to do more than just sell its products. Is this an effective way for the company to leverage its sponsorship? If you were in charge of the company's Olympic sponsorship, what would you do? Explain.
2. While each of Coca-Cola's Olympic sponsorship activities is intended to be positive, what are the risks to the company of its Olympic sponsorship? What potential risks exist for the IOC?
3. Explain why Coca-Cola and the Olympics are a match or a mismatch.
4. Was the criticism of Coca-Cola over the 1996 Summer Olympics in Atlanta fair? If so, explain. If not, discuss why the IOC is so restrictive about sponsor signage and advertising in competition venues, unlike, for example, the World Cup.

Chapter 16

The Olympic Sponsor Case Study: Visa

Visa illustrates one of the most detailed examples of sports sponsorship. When Visa began sponsoring the Olympics in 1986, it was one of the three primary competitors in the payment services industry, along with MasterCard and American Express, in addition to lower-tier competitors like Diners Club and Discover. Visa had a good, if unspectacular, reputation for reliable and convenient cashless payment products. Company marketers had a basic objective driving their early Olympic sponsorship activities in the 1980s—to build awareness through advertising—and the Olympics provided a solid and recognizable vehicle for doing so. Building awareness was only a starting point, however. As Sports Marketing Group IMG Managing Director Andrew Hampel said,

Sports sponsorship may give you the right to talk to customers, but if you want to say anything worthwhile about your brand, you have to engage them at a number of levels.[1]

As Visa gained experience from its early Olympics sponsorships, the company's objectives changed, becoming more ambitious, and they adjusted their marketing efforts accordingly, reflecting Andrew Hampel's observations about meaningful brand development. This included organizing its sponsorship investments according to three stages of market development:

1. Emerging—characterized by awareness building, primarily through name recognition.
2. Maturing—when growth and expansion were reinforced through advertising.
3. Mature—when differentiation was emphasized, particularly through product innovation and communications through new media.

In effect, Visa shifted over time from simple awareness building toward differentiating their brand from the competition, including strategies to extend the benefits of the Olympic sponsorship before and beyond the 17 days of the Olympics itself. As a key Visa senior marketing executive stated in 2003,

> Our campaign for the 1988 Calgary Olympics was all about branding and we focused on the 17 days surrounding the games. Then in 1994, we saw that Visa was going to have to adapt its marketing to make it closer to tourism and spread its efforts over a much longer period. We realized that we had to work with the Olympic city before, during, and after the Games in order to derive the best benefits for our members. We asked ourselves why host cities bid for the games and we realized the answer came down to showcasing the city to the world. Not only do the games bring tourists to the Olympic city, but also create a large halo effect that lasts beyond the games. Prior to the 1992 Olympics, Barcelona was the 16th most popular tourist destination in Europe. In 1993, it was the third. There was a similar kind of lift in Australia after the 2000 games.[2]

For example, at the 2000 Sydney Olympics Visa launched a four-year destination marketing program that created $40 million in additional marketing value in Australia and led to a 7 percent rise in tourism.[3] According to a 2003 Stanford Business School case study, "Unaided consumer awareness of Visa's sponsorship after Sydney was an unprecedented 72%, and research shows sponsorship awareness drives Visa brand preference."[4] These initiatives reflected the company's plan to shift from a commodity to a specialty position, a concept also known as the *bent arrow theory of marketing*, shown in Figure 16.1.[5]

The bent-arrow theory is a simplification of the S-curve (also called the lifecycle graph) familiar to business students everywhere, which stylizes the stages of growth for a brand, business, or product, as shown in Figure 16.2.

Branding success in most businesses is dependent on clear differentiation that customers recognize and find relevant. As one can imagine, this is a common but challenging objective to execute, particularly in the

Specialty   Commodity

Figure 16.1   Bent Arrow Marketing

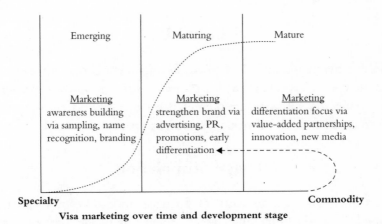

Visa marketing over time and development stage

Figure 16.2   Lifecycle with Bent Arrow Overlay

Strong Member Interest   Brand Fit   Usage Stimulation

Ease of Implementation   Event History/ Credibility

Event's Marketing Plan   Broad Reach

Low Risk   Governing Body Control

Advocacy Creation

Figure 16.3 Visa Sponsorship Criteria[6]

payment services industry, where products are often seen as inter-changeable and new features are easily and rapidly matched. Differen-tiation for Visa was therefore based on associating with the Olympics as a renowned, external event with a prestigious reputation and exclusive stature. Management hoped the positive brand attributes of the Olym-pics would create a halo effect over Visa. Visa did not approach this naively or with false hope. Management saw many parallels between the Olympics and Visa. Visa established sponsorship selection criteria to ensure the Olympics and any other company sponsorships had the right ingredients to support a large marketing investment (Figure 16.3). These criteria are a useful starting point for almost any company considering a sports sponsorship investment.

Brand Fit

Effective marketing includes reasonable alignment between the sponsor and the event. Visa believed that the two organizations were leaders in their respective categories, represented excellence, and enjoyed wide-spread awareness, global reach, and local impact.

Usage Stimulation

Visa's members are a network of financial institutions and merchants around the world. Attracting customers and convincing them to buy are two of the key imperatives of most marketing campaigns. Visa saw the

Olympics sponsorship as a catalyst for inspiring consumers to use the card more frequently and would, directly, benefit Visa's members as a consequence.

Event History and Credibility

Consumers today are more skeptical of traditional marketing, perceiving it as insincere and slick. Therefore, marketers must study the event they wish to sponsor to assess its reputation and whether sponsoring it would be consistent with their own company's reputation. The rich and storied history of the Olympics discussed in this book provides readers with a greater appreciation for the appeal of the modern Games. Visa, too, understands this history and sees its sponsorship as benefiting from the event's 2,700 years of tradition.

Broad Reach

In advertising terms, *reach* refers to the total number or percentage of an audience reached by a single ad or exposure during a specified time. With respect to the Olympics, broad reach describes the size of the total audience that will see the Olympics at least once during the duration of the event. Of course, most fans watch multiple events throughout the 17 days, creating a much larger cumulative reach, representing a significant audience for Visa to establish, solidify, and enhance its position.

Governing Body Control

Marketers must ensure their counterparts at the event under consideration are reliable and effective. A strong, competent governing body conveys professionalism and gives sponsors confidence that the event will be well-managed. Visa makes a sizable investment in each Olympic quadrennial, so governing body control provides the company with reassurance that sponsorship commitments will be honored and, more broadly, that the integrity of the Olympic Games remains strong and intact.

Advocacy Creation

Marketing success relies on strong market support in which individuals and societal institutions perceive the event favorably. The Olympic movement has been a driving force for developing grassroots support for the Olympics throughout much of the modern era. Furthermore, the Olympics are deeply meaningful to fans and athletes, creating a powerful emotional connection that reinforces the Olympic ideal.

Low Risk

Well-run events with positive reputations and respected governing bodies create an attractive, low-risk investment opportunity for sports marketers. Sponsors face risks related to their own management of their event marketing effort, including unclear objectives, misalignment between the sponsor and the event, and poor marketing execution. Marketers must be accountable for their activities, as should any manager. Visa's 25-year sponsorship of the Olympics has grown in sophistication, minimizing the investment risk, even as the Olympics have confronted challenges including scandals. Fortunately, the IOC has demonstrated reasonable competence in addressing these challenges and preventing any lasting harm to the Olympic brand.

Event's Marketing Plan

The event's management must present a clear plan that describes how they will market the event and how they will use the sponsorship monies. The IOC has developed a detailed, methodical plan for marketing the Olympic movement overall and each Olympics quadrennial, including sponsorship levels and criteria, strict Olympics-related identity usage and guidelines, and general quality control in marketing communications. Visa is familiar with the IOC, NOCs, and OCOG and their role in supporting and marketing each Olympics globally, nationally, and at the host city, which gives the company added confidence in proper and professional execution of the Olympic image.

Ease of Implementation

Sports events are complex. Coordinating premarketing, athletes, event timing, sponsors, venue logistics, fan movement, ticketing, food, security, scoring, officiating, and more for thousands of people requires extraordinary management skill and deft planning. Most Olympics are well-run, successful events despite the innumerable variables that can affect the smooth operation of the Games. The 116 years of experience in the modern era have developed practices and controls enabling each succeeding Olympiad to operate relatively smoothly. This success reflects well on Olympic management and governing body control. As sponsors, Visa wants to ensure that its own marketing efforts are equally well run.

Strong Member Interest

Obviously, a successful sports event should attract the attention of fans. The Olympics' broad range of sports and the thousands of participating athletes offer something for almost every kind of sports fan. For Visa, Olympic fans are prospective future customers. Therefore, Visa's sports sponsorship must be seen as beneficial and actively supported by its member institutions. Fortunately, the Olympics are a well-known sports event, clearly understood, and they have strong values with universal appeal. Visa's member institutions derive significant benefit, underscored by their ongoing support the past 25 years.

Assuming a sport meets Visa's sponsorship criteria, the company then leverages the investment across several marketing *platforms*, which are a modified version of classic marketing techniques. These platforms provide Visa with a framework, shown in Figure 16.4, for dividing their marketing efforts into specific activity areas in each phase: pre-, during, and post-Olympics:

Advertising

The objective of Visa's advertising platform is to build awareness. Building awareness is, in many ways, an effort to introduce the brand or, in Visa's case, a new storyline, since the company is already known.

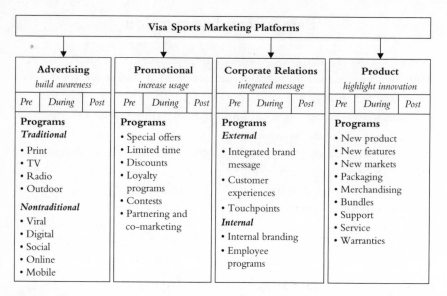

Figure 16.4 Visa Sponsorship Marketing Platform Framework
Note: The bulleted individual tactics are examples of general programs within each marketing category and are not meant to suggest that these are Visa's specific programs.

Promotional

Visa's promotional platform is focused on increasing usage of the Visa payment service and partnering with respected brands, like Disney. The benefits are obvious: Increasing usage improves the financial returns for Visa and its member institutions, and partnering with well-known brands adds credibility to Visa's products. Plus, any promotional activity undertaken by the partner has the potential to benefit Visa as well.

Corporate Relations

The corporate relations platform is used to strengthen the power and impact of Visa's numerous marketing programs (including those outside sports marketing) by integrating them around a more cohesive brand message. This platform also benefits Visa's employees because the company markets its various programs and partnerships to its own employees, a powerful example of company culture building. Visa wants its employees to be aware of its marketing efforts, believing that informed employees work more effectively together, ultimately benefiting member institutions and consumers as a result.

Product

Visa uses this platform to launch new products and technologies. Part of the promotional platform investment discussed earlier implies infrastructure investment to support the anticipated usage increases. These infrastructure investments include the addition of ATMs, transactions and processing equipment, and a combination of new temporary and permanent distribution points and accompanying support for Visa member institutions.

Visa's marketing plans are tailored to each of these platforms, enabling the company's marketers to focus their planning and execution efforts around tightly defined marketing subactivities. Visa's marketing organizational efforts are thorough and precise, affording marketers the luxury of specialized attention and detailed planning specific to the needs of each platform. While such diligent planning does not guarantee success, it reduces uncertainty about direction, and it creates a clear road map about marketing activities and responsibilities. The Olympics sponsorship planning effort engages the marketing organization, sharpening its focus around a single, albeit enormous and complex event.[7]

Has the more than 20-year Olympic sponsorship been worth it? Visa certainly provides one of the more compelling examples of how sports sponsorship can ultimately create value for the company. Let's review Visa's success in the context of Figure 16.5, which outlines four key areas of brand value.

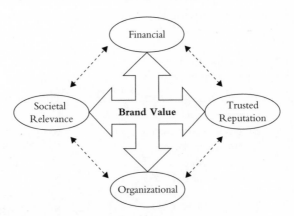

Figure 16.5   The Dimensions of Brand Value[8]

Financial

Table 16.1 summarizes at the TOP program revenues since the mid-1980s.

Simple arithmetic indicates that Visa's Olympic sponsorship since 1986 (the year their Olympic relationship began) has been more than $320 million, assuming the final marketing revenues for the 2009–2012 Vancouver-London Quadrennium total more than $1 billion, as anticipated. But recall that this invested amount only buys *the right* to sponsor the Olympics and that each sponsor spends three to four times that amount in activating its sponsorship properly, including money spent on creative design, media placement, logistics, and implementation. Therefore, one can deduce that Visa's total Olympic investment since 1986 is probably closer to $1 billion, depending on the multiple used.

Visa has witnessed a significant increase in financial and market performance since it initiated its Olympic sponsorship efforts in 1986. Visa's 2010 operating revenues were $8.065 billion,[9] and while figures are not available for 1986, one can surmise that revenues have grown. The number of credit cards issued has grown from 137 million to more than 1.8 billion, and transactions volume (the total amount of payments and cash flowing through Visa payment services) has increased from $111 billion to $5.6 trillion. Since 2002 alone, the total number of transactions using Visa credit cards has grown from $34 billion to over $74 billion. One of Visa's original reasons for sponsoring the Olympics in the mid-1980s was to increase awareness. As of the 2004 Olympic Games in Athens, Visa attained 87 percent consumer awareness, the

Table 16.1   TOP Program Evolution[10]

Quadrennium	Games	Partners	NOCs	Revenue
1985–1988	Calgary/Seoul	9	159	US$96 million
1989–1992	Albertville/Barcelona	12	169	US$172 million
1993–1996	Lillehammer/Atlanta	10	197	US$279 million
1997–2000	Nagano/Sydney	11	199	US$579 million
2001–2004	Salt Lake/Athens	11	202	US$663 million
2005–2008	Torino/Beijing	12	205	US$866 million
2009–2012	Vancouver/London	11	205	TBC

highest level of awareness among all sponsors, indicating the power and strength of the Visa brand and the success of its Olympic sponsorship efforts. Visa was again among the highest in awareness as an Olympic sponsor in Vancouver at 66 percent.[11] Not only was awareness strong but also Visa saw significantly increased market share. Since first sponsoring the Olympics in 1986, Visa's global market share based on total volume had increased 37 percent to 57.3 percent (MasterCard had 31.8 percent share, American Express had 8 percent, and Discover had 1.4 percent in 2010). In March 2008, Visa went from a private company to a public company, with the largest initial public offering (IPO) in U.S. history, valued at $17.9 billion. Visa also reports that for those consumers who use Visa cards, tourism expenditures increased 63 percent in Beijing during the 2008 Olympics as compared to the same period a year earlier, and in Vancouver during the 2010 Winter Olympics, tourism expenditures increased 81 percent over the previous year.[12] As of August 2011, Visa's market capitalization was $62.8 billion, which was more than 11 times 2010 sales. These results are due to more than market momentum, population growth, favorable economic conditions, or dumb luck. Although both MasterCard and American Express enjoyed growth, neither witnessed the same degree of success during this time. MasterCard did have its own successful IPO in May 2006, raising $2.4 billion. MasterCard's 2010 revenues totaled $5.539 billion, and its market capitalization as of August 2011 was $44 billion, eight times its 2010 sales. However, note that MasterCard also lost its sponsorship of the 2010 and 2014 World Cup to Visa.[13]

Trusted Reputation

Since 1986, Visa management has viewed sports as something valued and shared across cultures, bringing people together to celebrate competition and athletic achievement. By closely aligning the company with the Olympics (and Visa's other sports sponsorships—Paralympics, FIFA World Cup, and the NFL), Visa management believes that the halo effect from these renowned megasports events will cast a favorable glow over Visa. Furthermore, Visa gets deeply involved in each community where an event occurs. The net benefit is that Visa has shifted its market position from a commodity product to market leader with a premier reputation, the result of a patient, 25-year strategic Olympic sponsorship effort to position Visa as a reliable, convenient, and vital contributor to the lifestyle of its customers.

Organizational

Organizational value is best exhibited when employees are directly and regularly engaged with their own company and its business activities, can clearly understand what the company is trying to achieve, and can see how, why, and where they fit in. Visa developed internal programs that involved employees in the Olympic effort, including contests to win tickets to various Olympic Games. Visa started sponsoring the FIFA World Cup in 2010 in South Africa and continues through 2014, providing another source of inspiration for its employees, as does the company's aforementioned efforts with the Paralympics and the NFL.

Societal Relevance

Visa's Olympic sponsorship has provided more than $150 million in support for Olympic teams and athletes: 50 individual athletes from around the world, including Russia, China, the United States, Brazil, and New Zealand, and the national teams from more than 20 countries, including the United States, Canada, Brazil, China, Russia, the United Kingdom, and South Africa. In previous Olympiads, Visa created a children's art program called "Visa Olympics of the Imagination." Launched in 1994, the program taught children between the ages of 10 and 14 about the Olympic movement. Concurrently, the children were entered into an art competition, and selected winners had a chance to go to the Olympics, sponsored by Visa. According to company figures, more than 1 million children competed, and 181 children from 48 countries attended the Games. The pictures from this program were a vibrant reminder of the power and imagery associated with the Olympics, with many of the themes already discussed in this book reflected in the descriptions, from unbridled optimism to hero worship to national pride. They also highlighted the vivid imaginations of children as they envisioned the Olympics as a unifying event that allowed the world to forget its troubles, if only for a couple of weeks every two years. Visa's Olympics of the Imagination was also an excellent illustration of nontraditional marketing, connecting children to the Olympics by channeling their energy and creativity for the purpose of conveying a hopeful image of the world, inspired by the possibility of actually attending the Games, yet also enabling Visa to use the resulting artwork to promote both the children's program and the company's support for the Olympics. The launch of the first Youth Olympic Games in Singapore in 2010 had 14- to 18-year-old youth participate in athletic competitions, as well as a new culture and education program (CEP) that encompassed five imaginative themes (Olympus and Olympic values, skill development, well-being and healthy lifestyle, social responsibility, and expression through digital media). The CEP program could be viewed as a successor to the Olympics of the Imagination (albeit a much broader and more complex one), although this has not been stated by either Visa or the IOC.

Equally important, Visa was the first global sponsor of the International Paralympic Committee and continues to support numerous national Paralympic sports federations and individual athletes. Visa's support conveys an inspiring and inclusive message of empowerment.[14] This effort included the first Paralympic web site, usable to people with hearing, sight, and other disabilities (www.paralympic.org/index.html). Visa has actively supported both fan and athlete involvement in the Paralympics. For example, Visa's support of the British Paralympic Association (BPA) sent more than 300 athletes and staff to the 2004 Paralympic Games in Athens. The Athens Games saw Visa partner with regional Paralympic groups to encourage attendance by Visa customers. Additionally, Visa helped provide accessibility to the disabled who attended the 2004 Athens Paralympics.[15]

Visa management acknowledges that a direct link between Olympic sponsorship and performance results is not always perfectly clear, but they firmly believe that the Olympic Games have been an influential factor in their success and growth over the past 25 years. Visa has learned a great deal about sports sponsorships in more than two decades of Olympic efforts, developing expertise in leveraging a trusted event with several thousand years of tradition into an invaluable partnership that has changed the fortunes of the company for the better. Visa's early objectives of developing awareness succeeded and were then superseded by even more ambitious goals of building market share, increasing transactions volume, growing credit cards in circulation, improving its reputation with customers and members, and building measurable brand value, each of which set a firm foundation for growth. As Michael Lynch, head of global sponsorship management at Visa, stated,

> Obviously, not all of that is from the Olympics. But we're finding that those who are aware of our Olympic sponsorship are more likely to use the Visa card than those who are unaware.[16]

Visa's Olympic sponsorship marketing has been ongoing since 1986, and the company's performance during this 25-year period demonstrates many of the benefits they have derived from their carefully crafted Olympic marketing. As Visa looks to the future, the company has developed a foundation of sports sponsorship success, leveraging its 25-year sponsorship of the Olympics, and its more recent sponsorship of the FIFA World Cup, to grow its business around the world. While the Olympics, and sports sponsorships in general, were not the sole focus of Visa's marketing efforts, company leaders strongly indicate that these sponsorships have created a positive and lasting impact. With Visa's Olympic sponsorship continuing through 2020, and its FIFA World Cup sponsorship lasting at least through 2014, the company will continue to benefit by being associated with the world's leading megasports events. As Joseph Saunders, chairman and chief executive officer of Visa, stated in the 2010 annual report about the company's recent use of new media,

> . . . we continued to optimize our media investments based on changing consumer consumption habits. The results of this were evident in our shift towards digital and social media for the Olympic Games and FIFA World Cup. For these two events, we focused our advertising on driving transactions at the point of sale surrounding the Olympic Games and World Cup in relevant geographies. Similarly, we worked with more than 500 of our financial institution and merchant clients in 76 countries, providing them with access to unique platforms that helped generate awareness, excitement and usage with unique offers linked to both events.[17]

Based on his comments, and with the rapid growth of social and digital media, it appears the opportunity is there for Visa to have an even bigger impact on these events and grow their business well into the future.

Questions

1. Does Visa's sponsorship experience with the Olympics provide any lessons for other companies considering a major sports sponsorship investment? What are those key lessons?
2. While the evidence seems to indicate that the Olympics sponsorship has created substantial benefits for Visa over the years, it is much harder to link sponsorship actions with specific results. Why is that? What can be done to improve this? Does this suggest that Visa's Olympic sponsorship results are less than they appear?
3. Use Visa's sponsorship criteria (Figure 16.3) to evaluate Visa's own results as described in this case.
4. Are Visa's products a good commercial fit for the Olympics? Why or why not?
5. CEO Saunder's comments at the end of the case suggest a shift in marketing tactics for the future. How do you think digital media will affect Visa's Olympic sports sponsorship investment and tactics? Should Visa add more marketing tactics? Fewer?
6. How well do Visa's company values match those of the Olympics? Does this matter? Why or why not?

Chapter 17

Section IV Sponsorship Preparation Questions

The sponsorship section discussed the myriad ways that companies structure their TOP sponsorship. There are several important takeaways that can guide marketers as they weigh the pros and cons of their sponsorship decision, including determining the strategic rationale for the sponsorship. If the company intends to use the sponsorship to increase sales in the short run, then the activation planning must reflect the tactical detail such an emphasis requires. Conversely, if the sponsorship is intended to help strategically reposition the company over time, then the activation planning and marketing communications approach needs to outline this. Of course, tactics and strategies are not mutually exclusive and typically go hand in hand. The question is one of degree: how much emphasis is to be placed on boosting sales (which implies a promotion-oriented sponsorship activation plan) and strategy (which suggests communicating messages designed to foster a particular image of the brand). Strategy-based sponsorships can still lead to increased sales, but over a longer time horizon. A common approach by most TOP sponsors is to ensure that whatever decisions they make, brand value is increased. Recognizing the importance of brand value will require sponsors to evaluate their sponsorship on the basis of the dimensions of brand value discussed here. The following questions will help marketers in the preparation of their sponsorship plan.

Sponsorship

1. Review audit questions from other sections to provide context.
2. What is the level of investment being made?
   a. Is the investment for the sponsorship rights only?
   b. How much are you willing to invest to activate the sponsorship?
   c. Have you prepared a budget detailing sources and uses of sponsorship monies?
3. Have you identified who is on the sponsorship team?
   a. Are responsibilities and reporting lines of authority clearly understood?
   b. Are the degrees of decision-making freedom known?
   c. Do any team members have prior sports sponsorship experience of this kind?
4. What are the pre-, during-, and post-sponsorship tactical plans?
   a. What marketing communications programs will be used for each target customer?
      i. What are the objectives/goals for each?
      ii. What message will be used?
      iii. Which media? Traditional? Nontraditional? Both? (see Section V for more details)
   b. How will you determine success?
      i. Identify measures and milestones
         1. Frequency, reach, gross rating points (GRP), other?
         2. Insertion dates?

Four Dimensions of Brand Value
Financial

1. What are your goals in deriving measurable value for the company?
   a. Improve image of the company to develop a more premium image?
   b. Enhance brand value?

2. What are your plans for highlighting the value of the products offered during the sponsorship?
   a. Optimizing price?
   b. Focusing on features?
   c. Differentiation? (Each of these ultimately affects customer perceptions of value, and the Olympics can serve as a platform for product launches, test marketing, or dramatic changes in current pricing structures.)
3. How will we measure return on our sponsorship investment?
4. Do we understand the investment required to protect and reinforce our brand image and support the massive logistics and infrastructure needs?
5. How financially stable is the event?
6. Are there any concerns that the event does not have the required capital to successfully operate?
   a. How do you plan to learn this?

Trusted Reputation

1. What is your reputation with customers? In the marketplace in general?
   a. How do you know your perception is accurate?
   b. How will you convey your reputation?
2. Will you include your best customers as guests at the sponsored event?
   a. Will your best employees and/or partners be there?
3. What is the event's reputation?
   a. What are the factors that have created this reputation (see audit questions at the end of Section I)?

Organizational

1. Do you have recognized support from senior management?
2. Does each person involved have contact information for easy access?
3. Which internal resources/departments will be needed to support each activity?
   a. Can you deliver on support and logistics expectations?
   b. What equipment is needed, and how will you get it?
4. Which outside resources will be needed to support each activity?
   a. Are there contractual relationships with clearly defined expectations and deliverables?

5. How will you communicate your sponsorship plans inside the organization?
   a. Who is responsible for communicating them?
6. What are the timing sequences for involving different resources?
7. How would you rate the event's organization?
   a. Can they provide necessary support?
   b. Who are the key decision makers, and do you have their contact information?
   c. Have they provided clear guidelines and instructions?

Societal

1. What is the societal good your company does overall?
   a. Is this known? If so, how is it known?
   b. How are you getting feedback on the positive contributions your company is making?
      i. Do you need a more formal mechanism for tracking this?
2. What is your company's corporate social responsibility (CSR) plan relative to the sponsorship?
   a. Is it in line with the company's overall CSR efforts, or are these new initiatives?
   b. Do you intend to promote these initiatives? If so, how?
   c. Are you providing resources to get involved in the local community?
3. What is the societal benefit provided by the event?
   a. Community goodwill?
   b. Entertainment value?
   c. Superior sports product?
4. Which aspects are closest in line to your company's expectations?
   a. Is your sponsorship aligned with these?

V

OLYMPIC MARKETING VICTORY

Chapter 18

The Olympic Fans

Congratulations! You have been allocated some of the greatest tickets on earth! This email is from the London 2012 Ticketing team, confirming that your Olympic Games ticket application has now been processed.[1]

This e-mail captures the essence of what sports fans are: exuberant. As any true sports fan knows, their favorite sports, teams, and athletes are a source of inspiration, pride, frustration, and aspiration. Sports fans live and breathe their sports. Fans of the Olympics are the same. This e-mail would certainly seem to be a welcome find for any fan of the Olympics. Of course, there is more behind the story of tickets for London in 2012, as will be discussed, and Olympic ticketing practices overall. In this chapter, we look at Olympic sports fans to paint a more complete picture of who they are and how sponsors can use and improve this information so that their sponsorship activities have a greater chance of success. A sports marketer's dream would be to have the definitive profile of Olympics fans that identifies their characteristics, thereby giving sponsors a better understanding of how to appeal to these fans. Unfortunately, there is no singular Olympic sports fan definition or profile. Sports fans are as varied as the 200 and more countries and territories from where they come. Improving our understanding beyond a superficial generalization that "Olympic fans love sports" requires greater in-depth study on a per-country basis, which is beyond the scope of this book. However, to provide some ideas about Olympic fans, we will draw from a few surveys to give us a reasonable sense of who they are.

The Fans

The TOP sponsors invest enormous sums of money to attract the Olympics fan base. Studies of fans from different countries around the world uncover variations in fan profiles, and the details are important for sponsors intent on marketing specifically to a given country's fans. More generally, there are three layers of Olympics fans, categorized by the intensity of their interest, from most intense in the center to least intense on the outside (but still interested in the Olympics), as represented by Figure 18.1. These designations are not intended to encompass all population segments. There are many more potential populations that are aware of the Olympics and/or sports in general, but their interest intensity is peripheral at best, so we are focusing only on those who, at

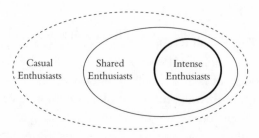

Figure 18.1 Layers of Olympic Fans

some level, are followers of the Olympics, as they are most likely to be of interest to TOP sponsors. The three layers are:

1. Intense enthusiasts
2. Shared enthusiasts
3. Casual enthusiasts

Intense Enthusiasts

Intense enthusiasts (IEs), or avid Olympics fans, are the heart of the fan base. They love the Games and the intensity of the competition, and they will watch hours of Olympic coverage on TV and/or online each day. They may have favorite Olympic sports they prefer watching, but they will also watch other sports simply because they are part of the Olympics. They tend to be athletes themselves, compete in sports leagues and also exercise regularly, and have a strong appreciation for the rules, histories, and techniques of the sports. They are also more comfortable watching the Olympics by themselves, although they will certainly be part of groups watching the same event (but more focused on watching the event than socializing or interacting with others). Intense enthusiasts often enjoy keeping track of statistical detail, from time splits in qualifying events to the total number of medals in each category won by the various countries. They also follow Olympic news in the years between Olympiads. There are, of course, fans in this layer who are less physically active, but whose love of and devotion to the Olympics designates them as IEs as well.

Shared Enthusiasts

Shared enthusiasts (SEs) are the immediate networks of family, close friends, and professional colleagues of IE fans. They love the Olympics as well, although they are less intense than IE fans. However, whereas the IEs may be more individualistic, enjoying watching the Olympics on their own, SEs favor group or shared community experiences (hence their designation). The SEs' relationship to the IE fans is partly what motivates their interest in the Olympics, although their interest is also self-driven because they, too, are athletes and/or at least enjoy staying fit. They are keenly aware of the Olympics, but as opposed to the hours IEs spend watching each day, SEs watch highlights every day or two, increasing their viewing when sports specific to their interests are on and/or as interesting stories in the media spark their interest to pay closer attention, whether during the Games or in the years in between.

Casual Enthusiasts

Casual enthusiasts (CEs) might be connected to the shared enthusiasts through social and/or professional networks, but they are just as likely to be entirely separate from the other two layers. As the designation implies, CEs are more relaxed about their Olympics interests, paying peripheral attention most of the time, but increasing their interest when media coverage and general hype ignite their curiosity, particularly if surprises occur during the Games, or as friends and acquaintances discuss the latest news and results. They tune in to watch the occasional event a few times during the Games but do not follow the Olympics as much in the off years. They might participate in sports and fitness occasionally, but they are just as likely to be nonathletic.

To help the reader develop an appreciation for the challenges of determining general Olympic fan characteristics, and also give insight about narrow groups of fans and their respective characteristics, we will briefly look at three different studies:

1. A European study of sports trends and fans.
2. A study of youth perceptions of the Olympics in the United Kingdom prior to the 2012 London Olympics.
3. Two studies of fans in the United States, one conducted prior to and during the 2010 Vancouver Winter Olympics, and the other well after the conclusion of the Vancouver Olympics, toward the end of 2010.

European Sports Trends

In March 2011 Havas Media, a respected European media company, presented results from its study "The Consumption of Sport in 2011 and Beyond."[2] As the study title implies, the purpose was to understand where trends are going in media consumption and sports fan interest. Among the study's findings were the following insights about European fan interest in the 2012 London Olympics:

- "One out of every ten UK sports fans will NOT follow the Olympic Games compared to 94% of Italians who expect to follow the Games.
- "German fans are most likely to watch at public viewing areas or at work. They are also most likely to join the 23% of Spaniards who expect to watch the Games in a bar.
- "Sports fans focused on viewing quality rather than accessibility when asked what would improve their viewing experience—3DTV (49%) and HD TV (36%) were cited as the technologies which would most improve the viewing experience of the Olympic Games.
- "When sports fans were asked which sports they would most like to watch in 3DTV, Gymnastics got the top slot with swimming, sprint events, diving and field hockey following in the top five.
- "When at home 90% of sports fans will catch the action (or recaps . . . could include news as well) on TV with over 60% predicting that they will at least occasionally listen to the radio.
- "Many of the markets recorded high numbers of student-aged sports fans who are intending to watch the Games—in the UK this was the highest—42% of sports fans between the ages of 12 and 35 years old are under the age of 21.
- "As much of the daytime Olympic action will be taking place during the day, of the students across all markets that plan on following the Games, 59% will do so online and 43% on their smart phones whilst at school."[3]

The findings are interesting for several reasons. First, while the information provided is not extensive, the data do hint that the complexity and diversity of fan tastes and interests vary by country, culture, and demographic. This suggests that TOP sponsors must plan their marketing communication strategy to ensure the right platform carries the most relevant message to the intended audience. A one-size-fits-all approach is likely to struggle, given the fan statistics. Second, a sizable percentage of European youth indicate they view the Games online and via mobile devices. Part of this is explained by the timing of events since many will be held while the students are in school. However, this is valuable knowledge for TOP sponsors as well since they can develop content that works best on those devices. Third, the fans' stated sports preferences for 3DTV should help sponsors determine which events in that media format are likely to be most popular so that their message is maximized accordingly. These reasons only begin to describe how sponsors can interpret fan survey results. Since the TOP sponsors are large global companies, their own marketing research can be used to see where the best marketing areas are to invest, based on the company's overall strategic plan and sponsorship objectives.

Youth Perceptions in the United Kingdom

Youth have been a target of increasing focus by the IOC, as the launch of the Youth Olympic Games demonstrates. With more activities than ever vying for their attention, from digital to television and social media, attracting the attention of youth to the centuries-old appeal of the Olympics is getting more challenging. Like many global marketers responsible for visible brands, the IOC wants to ensure it remains not just relevant, but compelling and exciting for youth to ensure the Olympics have a fan and athlete base for decades to come.

In a related fashion, the London Organizing Committee for the Olympic Games (LOCOG) set an ambitious target: to inspire the nation's youth. While such an exhortation sounds common across many countries and cultures as part of their respective national efforts to get their nation's youth to follow healthier lifestyles, actually making it happen is far more challenging, revealing the possible limits to marketing communications as a vehicle for influencing change. A 2011 survey by Axa Ambitions Awards Scheme revealed that more than 50 percent of UK teenagers (age 11 to 18) were not interested in the London Olympics, despite several years of national and international press coverage. Seventy percent said that the Games had not changed their desire to partake in sport more often than they had intended before, and 5 percent said the Olympics had actually turned them off.

London Olympic organizers have worked hard to overcome this: Half the torch relay runners will be under 24 years old, and more than 200,000 tickets have been reserved for schoolchildren. On the positive side, 5 percent of those surveyed said that the London Olympics had inspired them to participate in more sports activities than ever before, and 20 percent said they would participate a little more. With respect to awareness and enthusiasm, 12 percent of those surveyed did state that they were very excited about the 2012 London Olympics, 37 percent were "a little excited," and 60 percent of UK schools had signed up for the Get Set program, which registers schools for an allocation of tickets. Of the sports the youth found most interesting to try, 27 percent favored archery, 16 percent liked swimming, 15.3 percent were drawn to athletics, 15.1 percent wanted to try badminton, 14.4 percent liked football, 12 percent favored shooting, and another 12 percent were interested in basketball.[4] While a single event may not necessarily transform a nation, the absence of such an effort in support of the Games would seem to be an opportunity wasted. For TOP sponsors, part of their marketing efforts should be based on knowledge of the Olympic fans and target customers, since their biases can help their marketers devise strategies that have a greater chance of inspiring customers. In the case of youth in the United Kingdom, for example, knowing that many remain skeptical or uncertain about participating in sports could compel the sponsors to develop campaigns that appeal to specific emotional triggers and hopefully help change their perceptions, even slightly, of the Olympics and the sponsor's products.

United States Youth Studies

During the 2010 Vancouver Olympics, a survey of U.S. fans was conducted by Turnkey Sports & Entertainment to understand fan recognition of sponsors and also the sports and athletes they followed the most during the Games.[5] These survey results were interesting. The statistics about viewing measured two groups of fans: avid and casual. Using a 5-point scale, those who answered the questions with a 4 or 5 were considered avid fans, and those who responded with a 3 were designated as casual fans. The questions and results were as follows:[6]

Question: **Since the start of the 2010 Winter Olympics, how many hours of Olympic coverage have you watched on average per day on TV or online?**

	Avid Fans	Casual Fans
Less than 30 minutes per day	2.00%	26.80%
30–59 minutes per day	10.60%	32.60%
1–2 hours per day	22.70%	30.50%
2–3 hours per day	28.30%	8.50%
3 or more hours per day	36.40%	1.60%

The viewing pattern data can help sponsors begin to identify the behavioral characteristics of their audience. Additional useful data would be to understand what hours of the day viewers are watching, and which sports during those hours. This information can be useful in determining the final content of advertising messages, depending on the sport, time of day, and audience profile.

Question: **Which of the following members of the 2010 U.S. Olympic team are you familiar with/have you heard of?**

	Avid Fans	Casual Fans
Apolo Ohno	77.80%	68.40%
Bode Miller	74.20%	58.40%
Shaun White	68.20%	59.50%
Lindsey Vonn	67.20%	58.40%
Johnny Weir	58.60%	32.60%
Evany Lysacek	52.50%	29.50%
Shani Davis	50.00%	24.70%
Julia Mancuso	44.40%	22.60%
Kelly Clark	39.40%	19.50%
Chad Hedrick	38.40%	13.70%

Sponsors can use this information to target their marketing communications on television and online approximately when these athletes are competing. Sponsors can also evaluate the effectiveness of their advertising in creating *awareness* (for example) during the performance of these or any other selected athletes. Also, sponsors of these athletes can get a better sense of the *type* of exposure their brand might have gained when their athlete was competing. (For example, did something controversial occur that might affect the sponsor?)

Question: **What sport did you most enjoy watching?**

Males		Females	
Hockey	24.40%	Figure skating	38.60%
Figure skating	13.40%	Hockey	11.40%
No favorite	9.70%	No favorite	9.10%
Snowboarding	9.20%	Ski jumping	8.20%
Curling	8.80%	Snowboarding	7.30%

For sponsors, understanding fan interest patterns can facilitate a deeper understanding of the customers who watched the Olympics, and, conceivably, this knowledge can aid post-Olympics marketing as well. Knowing which sports a particular fan segment watches also helps sponsors determine where and how to allocate their media buys.

This same survey asked fans to identify which companies were the official partners of the United States Olympic Committee (USOC) in 11 different business sectors. Each category included the actual partner and the main competitor. Fortunately for sponsors, in 9 of the 11 categories, the companies identified most frequently were the actual USOC partners. Five of these companies were also TOP sponsors, in addition to being USOC partners: Visa, Coca-Cola, GE, McDonald's, and Acer. The question and results are summarized next:

Question: **Which of the following is an official partner of Team USA?**

		Avid	Casual
Credit card	Visa (1988)*	65.70%	45.80%
	MasterCard	7.10%	4.70%
	I'm not sure	19.20%	41.60%
Soft drink	Coca-Cola (1928)	59.10%	43.70%
	Pepsi	11.10%	12.10%
	I'm not sure	22.70%	38.40%

(*Continued*)

		Avid	Casual
Quick service restaurant	McDonald's	55.10%	35.30%
	Subway	12.10%	10.50%
	I'm not sure	22.20%	48.40%
Consumer packaged goods	Procter & Gamble	35.40%	24.70%
	Clorox	5.10%	1.60%
	Colgate-Palmolive	4.00%	7.90%
	I'm not sure	51.00%	64.20%
Wireless service	AT&T Wireless (1984)	33.30%	20.00%
	Verizon Wireless	16.20%	11.10%
	I'm not sure	37.40%	57.90%
Beer	Anheuser-Busch (1984)	31.30%	23.20%
	Coors	9.60%	6.30%
	Miller	6.10%	5.30%
	I'm not sure	46.50%	62.60%
Technology	General Electric (2006)	29.80%	16.80%
	LG	10.60%	5.30%
	IBM	8.60%	6.30%
	I'm not sure	46.50%	67.90%
Insurance	Allstate (2001)**	13.60%	10.50%
	Aflac	15.70%	3.70%
	Geico	12.60%	8.40%
	Progressive	6.10%	3.20%
	I'm not sure	43.40%	65.80%
Hotel	Hilton (2005)**	11.60%	4.20%
	Marriott	7.10%	3.70%
	I'm not sure	67.70%	78.40%
Airline	American Airlines	13.10%	8.40%
	United (1980)**	10.10%	5.30%
	I'm not sure	57.60%	71.60%
Computer Hardware	Dell	17.20%	12.10%
	HP	7.60%	4.20%
	Apple	6.60%	4.70%
	Acer (2009)	6.10%	4.70%
	I'm not sure	57.10%	71.60%

*The 1988 Seoul Olympics are when Visa first started sponsor-related activities, although their relationship with the Olympics officially began in 1986.
**USOC sponsor, a second-tier designation that is below the TOP program.

The USOC sponsored a different study later in 2010, conducted by Millward Brown, to understand the profile of the most passionate and committed.[7] They hoped to use the information for creating deeper connections with U.S. Olympic fans in the future. The results were also shared with sponsors and the governing bodies of the various sports. In addition, the USOC was developing specific marketing tools that would be more effective and useful in appealing to these fans.

The USOC said there are 131.2 million Olympic fans in the United States, about 42 percent of the population, a sizable number and percentage. But the USOC wanted to learn more about the most dedicated fans, a group they called *fangelists*, totaling about 36.5 million people, or 27.8 percent of U.S. Olympic fans. To identify these 36.5 million people, the study's methodology focused on three factors: viewership, engagement, and level of enthusiasts. These fans are comprised of three unique adult groups and their associated characteristics:

1. Sports enthusiast
   - Youngest of the three groups.
   - Mostly male.
   - Most actively engaged with sports and exercise.
   - Motivated, self-empowered.
   - Loves the Olympics, inspired to become better athletes.
   - Watches the best athletes for technique in order to learn and improve themselves.
   - Less interested in Olympic values or in the purpose of bringing the world together.
   - Spends 50 percent more time on social media and reading magazines than the average American.
   - Follows Olympic movement even when the Games are not taking place.
2. Values-driven fangelist
   - Family-centric, gets happiness from here.
   - Strong believer in holistic mind, body, spirit.
   - Most ethnically diverse.
   - Values-driven.
   - Enjoys watching the participating countries, variety of sports, different athletes.

- Believes Olympics gives them connection to something larger than other sports offer.
- Donates to the Olympics because they are believers.
- Follows Olympic movement even when the Games are not taking place.
3. Flag bearer
   - Most patriotic, strong believer in America—more than other two groups.
   - Expresses strong pride in being American.
   - Slightly older than other two groups.
   - Interested in learning about Olympic sports and athletes in the months before the Olympics.
   - Watches the Olympics to see their athletes win.
   - Less engaged globally.

The study also revealed insights about teen fangelists. They are characterized as:

- Active.
- Eager.
- Ambitious.
- Love everything that they do.
- Like the older sports enthusiasts, the teen fangelists watch Olympic sports to learn.
- Draw significant inspiration from the Olympics.
- Support Team USA.
- Enjoy "discovering" new stars.
- Interested in learning new cultures.
- Believe in travel and exercise—these are fundamental to their values.
- Very social—visits family, friends, places.

This latter study described the customer-profiling approach marketers most commonly use—identifying characteristics and associations that are specific to each customer type. Details like these give marketers much clearer insight into each of the Olympic sports fan groups, albeit for a single country. Each fan group's characteristics help marketers develop communication plans that appeal to each group. One can easily imagine the problems that would ensue if a sponsor used the same communications strategy to reach each of these groups. The flag bearers and the values-driven fangelists have many points of difference between them, so a message common to all may end up appealing to none.

How Sponsors Can Use Fan Data to Improve Their Business

Investing $240 to $360 million on sponsorship, a sizable sum, implies that company management has thoroughly assessed the strategic advantages and disadvantages of being associated with the Olympics and is therefore well aware of the need to fully leverage the sponsorship. Of course, having keen awareness of the sponsorship's importance is only part of the leveraging process. Translating this awareness into an actionable plan, determining objectives, identifying target customers, developing marketing programs, recommending resource needs, and then measuring the results are the key activities that the marketing team must undertake to safeguard the investment and maximize returns. A central challenge is identifying the sponsor's target Olympic customers. The effort required to identify the sponsor's target customers goes beyond the three Olympics fans layers of Intense Enthusiasts, Shared Enthusiasts, and Casual Enthusiasts. Those are important starting points, but sponsors want to know more. Are they athletes? Are they general consumers? Are they sports fans overall? Are they fans of a particular sport? Are they businesspeople or a company? Are they young or old? The answer is yes to all, which can be frustrating to marketers trained to focus on a single target market. But as this book has discussed, the Olympics are a unique sports event that represents an ideal and a set of beliefs and values that embody a sense of hope for humanity, not just a series of athletic competitions. The definition of an Olympic fan, therefore, defies and transcends more traditional business vocabulary that typically defines a company's customers in clinical terms. Olympic customers represent a state of mind, a lifestyle, a love of fair competition, and a belief in international solidarity.

A composite fan description would reasonably define Olympic fans as those who:

- Attend the Games.
- Watch or listen to the Games on broadcasts and/or online.
- Read about the Games.
- Hear about the Games from others.
- Socialize about the Games on social media and similar platforms.

But these descriptions offer little insight beyond the obvious. Marketers for TOP sponsors want to and should know more if they want to take meaningful advantage of this once-every-four-years event. What is it that attracts people to do any of these activities? Most fans know generally that what the athletes are doing is extraordinarily difficult, even if they do not have personal experience doing it, and that the athlete's challenge is magnified by the intensity of the Olympic spotlight and the prestige of the Games. The athlete's performance is also evaluated in the context of the current competition, taking into account event conditions, the other competitors' qualifying heat performances, and even fellow competitors' respective reputations.

Interestingly for TOP sponsors, the CEs represent a larger fan population that may not have detailed knowledge of the Olympics or the athletes within. Many of the athletes and teams in both the Summer and Winter Olympics are not as regularly followed as those in more traditional sports leagues, nor are the Olympic sports in which they compete always widely understood by CEs. The comfort many loyal sports fans find in knowing their athletes, teams, and leagues comes from a lifetime of devotion to attending games, sharing knowledge with fellow fans and friends, and reading the daily results from print media or online. The equivalent level of intimate knowledge of Olympic athletes is mostly known by the IE fans and, perhaps, the SEs, but not as widespread with CE fans or peripheral viewers of the Olympic Games. Knowing the specific sports, while certainly helpful, is not a defining characteristic explaining the global appeal and success of the Olympics, nor is it a requirement to be a fan. The Olympics have risen above being just a sports event, appealing to a higher need in fans—the need to feel fulfilled, entertained, and inspired. This means that the Olympics represent more than just sport—they are a celebration, a happening, and an entertainment vehicle, and they can even represent relief from political tension. The Olympics are an escape from the world as it is to a world as it could be. This combination of factors helps attract fans and should inform sponsors as to how to appeal to Olympics fans.

Corporate sponsors would be making a mistake if they approached the Olympics as if they were conducting a traditional product promotional campaign or appealing only to a narrow fan group. While narrower targeting might eventually reach the intended audience, there is the possibility that such an intensity of focus would risk alienating the broader audience that is also watching the Olympics. In effect, the sponsor would not be taking full advantage of the unique opportunity the Olympics offer to reach a massive, and passionate, fan base. With today's viral marketing tools, from social media like YouTube and Facebook to the millions of blogs and podcasts, company management may quickly find themselves the subject of a viral backlash from disenchanted fans. Worse, the sponsor may simply be ignored. The onus is on marketing and senior management to fully understand the qualitative characteristics of Olympics fans and the Olympic movement to guide their sponsorship activation planning. The following simple questions can help this part of the planning process:

- What do we hope our association with the Olympics will accomplish for us?
- What do we want people to think about us?
- What does our company stand for (values, beliefs), and how do these fit with the Olympic Games and its billions of fans?
- Are we prepared to invest in proper support of our overall marketing theme?
- How will we tailor our message to ensure it is relevant to the Olympic fans we are interested in attracting?

A reasonable percentage of the sponsor's activation planning must emphasize its understanding of the intangible, qualitative aspects of the Olympics in order to develop marketing tactics that resonate with Olympics fans. Yet marketers might be understandably nervous about recommending marketing activities to senior management that favor intangible gains over precise, tangible targets and outcomes. This is not to suggest that marketers dismiss the more tangible aspects of traditional customer planning. Implicit within their marketing planning responsibilities is the fact that sports sponsorships are most effectively maximized when companies connect the high-level strategic, qualitative components of their marketing directly with on-the-ground tactical, measurable activities designed to engage fans directly with the company's offerings. To do this, marketers must understand that their Olympics customers are *fans*, using that knowledge to shape marketing programs geared toward creating memorable fan experiences. Creating fan *experiences* means engaging and interacting with them through multiple touchpoints. These touchpoints include:

- Products (products, services, price).
- People (staff, athletes, suppliers).
- Marketing communications (advertising, PR, promotions, broadcast, online, digital, social).
- Retail environments (atmosphere, merchandising).
- Support (customer service, warranties, guarantees).
- Events (games, contests, drawings, networking, client get-togethers).
- Partnerships/alliances (between companies).
- Media coverage (reporting that shapes public perception).
- Customized activities (sponsor-designed pavilions and Olympics-themed offerings).
- Promotional giveaways (tickets, merchandise).
- Meet-and-greet sessions (with athletes, Olympic officials).

Each of these touchpoints and many more ultimately affect perceptions of a TOP sponsor. From the CEO on down, the entire sponsor organization must be cognizant of the need to create as positive a fan experience as possible. Therefore, marketers must know the profiles of their targeted Olympics fan base and supplement their knowledge with new research information to facilitate their understanding and knowledge of their fans.

At a minimum, useful fan information includes knowing:

- Fan segments and targets (how do the IE, SE, and CE fans fit with the sponsor's strategic branding needs?).
- Relevant fan needs within (what inspires fans?).

- Your market share per fan (how much of your target audience do you own, versus your competitors?).
- Your revenues and profits per fan type (how much does each fan type contribute to your company's financial results?).

These are by no means the only fan profile components marketers should know, but they provide an important starting point for determining whether a fan group is attractive. If so, the marketing team can then develop the most appropriate message.

Fan Segments and Targets

So far we have discussed the three Olympic fan layers: intense enthusiasts, shared enthusiasts, and casual enthusiasts. Sponsor marketers should still rely on traditional marketing frameworks to further deepen their knowledge of target segments. Classic marketing theory says that there are four segmentation approaches:

1. **Demographics:** Age, ethnicity, income
2. **Psychographics:** Behaviors, personality, lifestyle, values
3. **Geographic:** Location: local, regional, national, natural boundaries
4. **Product use:** Matching customer need and product purpose

Marketers use these segmentation approaches separately or in some combination to identify common characteristics that could be exploited in the integrated marketing plan. This first step in customer identification should yield characteristics that a company can compare to their own capabilities, determining if a segment, while attractive at first review, is one that can be reasonably pursued using existing resources. If additional resources are required, then the company must decide whether further investment merits consideration. This is hard to determine without additional information about the customer group, so the marketing team must dig deeper to learn more.

Relevant Customer Needs Within

To begin the customer evaluation process, marketers must gather information about the different customer segments. The reason for doing this is

Table 18.1 Segment Needs

Needs	Intense Enthusiasts	Shared Enthusiasts	Casual Enthusiasts
Service and support	✓		✓
High quality	✓		
Low price		✓	
Loyalty programs		✓	
Lifestyle fit	✓		

to determine the characteristics that differentiate each segment. Market research, either company-initiated or through third-party market research firms, is highly recommended since the resulting information tells marketers if, based on a segment's needs and characteristics, they can appeal to that segment in their sponsorship activation activities. The converse is true as well: The information can help marketers eliminate segments early, before additional time and resources are expended on attracting them.

In this hypothetical example, our sports sponsor has identified three segments (we'll call them Segments IE, SE and CE, to use our familiar designations from earlier in the chapter). Each segment has slightly different needs, as shown in Table 18.1.

Each segment's needs provide insight about the factors the customers view as important, which can help marketers determine the type of marketing program (general advertising awareness, specific sales promotion) and message that will work best. Segment IE is most interested in service, quality, and lifestyle, which signals to marketers that this is a high-end customer group that may be willing to pay a premium for outstanding offerings. Knowing this would guide the marketing team to devise a program that appeals to this segment's needs. Segment SE is attracted to low price and loyalty, suggesting that if they find the right product at an affordable price, they will become regular customers. The marketing team would develop a different marketing program for this customer segment than for Segment IE for obvious reasons: Each segment's interests are both unique and, in this example, in opposition to each other. As a consequence, a marketing message to Segment IE probably won't appeal to Segment SE. Segment CE simply wants great service, and this, too, provides the marketing team with useful information about how to plan a marketing approach that would best appeal to this segment. Interestingly, of the three segments in this example, Segments IE and CE share a common preference for quality service, indicating this is where resources should be devoted. The marketing team would logically deduce that Segment SE may not fit in their sports sponsorship plan at this time, although Segment SE may be a good fit for other marketing programs unrelated to this sports sponsorship.

Resourceful marketers would still want to learn more about their target segments, starting with a closer review of their company's performance in penetrating each segment in the past, using these insights to help determine the potential for future gains. There are several ways to measure existing segment performance and its future potential, but for simplicity, let's focus on three key metrics, then analyze them in greater detail:

1. Market share of each segment.
2. Revenues represented by each segment.
3. Profit represented by each segment.

Market Share of Each Segment

Detailed data about the sponsor's market share in each customer segment can give a good indication of their performance compared to the competition. However, it is not always possible or practical for many companies to know their customer market shares because the company is too small, or reliable statistics are hard to find. Assuming the data are available, marketers need to ask several questions:

- Can we gain market share versus our competitors if we succeed in winning over these customers?
- What are the market share gains, if any, we can reasonably expect?
- Is it reasonable to expect any market share gains in the short term?
- What is our competition doing that is affecting their success with each segment?
- Are there gaps or opportunities in our offering that can be addressed?
- Are the relative market shares indicative of product quality, effective marketing communication, service delivery, or some combination of these?

Armed with this information, marketers can determine how favorably segments might respond to the sponsorship marketing activities. A technique called market share analysis by segment is useful here. To illustrate, let's assume a TOP sponsor is trying to understand how its core customer segments (IE, SE, CE) are doing versus its closest competitors (call them 1, 2, 3).

Keep in mind that this analysis is measuring the TOP sponsor's success in penetrating each segment *in general*, not just during the Olympics. The reason for emphasizing this is that a TOP sponsor's competitors, while not officially allowed to use Olympics-themed marketing, continue to appeal to the same types of fans on an ongoing basis. So the TOP sponsor wants to know how successful it is in winning each segment's business over time, not just during the Olympics. With that said, the TOP sponsor's Olympic-themed marketing can be used to make gains versus its competitors.

Assuming our TOP marketers have research data about their company's customer segments, they can run a simple market share analysis. Knowing the maximum share in each customer segment is 100 percent, our marketers can simply divide their company's sales (in units or currency) in each segment by total market sales in that same segment to determine market share. This same procedure would be repeated for all three customer segments, IE, SE and CE, and is represented by the following equation:

$$\text{Market Share (\%)} = \frac{\text{Total Company Sales to Segment (IE or SE or CE)}}{\text{Total Market Sales to Segment (IE or SE or CE)}}$$

If the company sold $100 to Segment IE, and total market sales to Segment IE were $1,000, then the company's market share of Segment IE is 10 percent:

$$\text{Market Share (\%)} = \frac{\$100}{\$1,000}$$
$$= .10 \text{ or } 10\%$$

The same analysis would apply to measuring the market share Competitors 1, 2, and 3 have in Segment IE. Let's assume Competitors 1, 2, and 3 have the following sales in Segment IE:

Competitor 1: $450
Competitor 2: $290
Competitor 3: $160

Their respective market shares would be:

Competitor 1: $\dfrac{\$450}{\$1,000} = .45$ or 45%

Competitor 2: $\dfrac{\$290}{\$1,000} = .29$ or 29%

Competitor 3: $\dfrac{\$160}{\$1,000} = .16$ or 16%

Knowing one's market share in each segment compared to competitors is important for many strategic reasons, but primarily it signals competitive strength and relative market position. This is summarized in Table 18.2.

This comparative segment share analysis helps our TOP sponsor understand how the company performs against its competitors in attracting these three levels of fans, and the information should help it determine what opportunities exist and how its competitors are performing.

Segment share analysis can also aid our sports marketer's understanding of the percentage of total sales each customer segment represents to the company's overall sales.

Table 18.2 Segment Share Analysis

	Intense Enthusiasts	**Shared Enthusiasts***	**Casual Enthusiasts***
TOP Sponsor	$100/10%	$300/30%	$500/50%
Competitor 1	$450/45%	$250/25%	$120/12%
Competitor 2	$290/29%	$90/9%	$170/17%
Competitor 3	$160/16%	$360/36%	$210/21%

*The figures for SE and CE segments were plugged in to complete the illustration, and total market sales for each were also assumed to be $1,000 to simplify the analysis. The same methodology would apply to calculating their respective shares.

In this case, our sports marketer knows that each of the company's three customer segments have the following sales:

Segment IE: $100
Segment SE: $300
Segment CE: $500

Total Sales $900

Each segment's percentage of total company sales is:

Segment IE : $\dfrac{\$100}{\$900}$ = .111 or 11.1%

Segment SE : $\dfrac{\$300}{\$900}$ = .333 or 33.3%

Segment CE : $\dfrac{\$500}{\$900}$ = .555 or 55.5%

The marketer now knows what percentage each segment contributes to company sales (call this *internal market share* since it is the share each segment represents of the company's total business), which helps signal which customers are most important and/or where opportunities lie. Continuing this internal analysis of segment contribution to company performance, our sports marketer would be able to refine the sponsorship activation plans by adding two other variables:

1. The number of customers in each segment compared to the company's total number of customers.
2. The profitability of each segment.

Let's assume the following about each segment:

Segment IE   40 customers $15 in profits
Segment SE   90 customers $10 in profits
Segment CE   250 customers $5 in profits

We can see that our sports marketer's company has 380 total customers and $30 in total profits. The new information is in Table 18.3.

Our sports marketer now knows how many customers are in each segment and how much each segment contributes to the company's total revenues and profits. The number of customers in each segment

Table 18.3 Segment Contribution Analysis

	Intense Enthusiasts	Shared Enthusiasts	Casual Enthusiasts	Total
Customers	40	90	250	380
Revenues	$100	$300	$500	$900
Profits	$15	$10	$5	$30

is important since this information will probably affect planning for account management, sales force structure, and customer support and service. Also, knowing this reveals not just how well the company is doing in appealing to its customer segments, but whether the financial performance can be improved. Several questions must be addressed:

Revenues

- Is the customer group (either business or consumer) large enough that our success with one or two customers will enable us to continue developing growth opportunities?
- If not, then is the potential for revenue growth large with each individual customer?

Profits

- What is the profit we can earn from these target customers over a given period of time?
- Are these customers high-end, high-margin customers with whom we can cultivate a premium image?
- Or are they volume customers requiring us to secure sizable contracts to ensure a reasonable profit?
- How will winning over these customers affect our brand reputation?

This is a useful exercise because it provides a convenient and informative performance snapshot that can help marketers ascertain which customer segments are performing well and, therefore, which should be emphasized in the marketing activities supporting the sports sponsorship. The decision of which segments to focus on may sometimes be counterintuitive. For example, a customer segment that contributes most of the profits might seem to be a likely candidate for the marketing effort since that high-margin segment is willing to pay a premium. However, management may determine that the weakest-performing segment should receive most of the marketing effort, perhaps because that segment offers the best long-term growth potential despite the lower margins in the short term. Alternatively, a segment might be emphasized because its profile most closely matches that of the sports event's target audience, which the company has identified as an influential segment to capture.

As this illustration demonstrates, evaluating your segments by reviewing revenue and profit contributions can be quite helpful in guiding the final marketing plan for the sports sponsorship. Keep in mind the lesson that marketers must look beyond the summary statistics and dig deeper into the factors that created the financial picture being reviewed. Part of what distinguishes superior marketers from the rest is their ability to see connections and relationships among various data and understand the potential implications, even though this information is not clearly delineated. It is easy to report numbers and describe trends, but it is much harder to explain what the potential causes are and where opportunities exist. Much like a general understanding that the Olympics are a prestigious sports event only scratches the surface and does not reveal the depth of the event's history and traditions, seeing market share, revenue, and profit numbers only provides a glimpse of the customer contribution to company and market performance. They do not explain why these results happened, describe the underlying influences, or overtly review what the broader market context was. For those insights, marketers must look still deeper.

Targeting

Targeting reveals the most attractive, high-potential customers within each segment. Recall the Visa example earlier. While the company's initial overall objectives were to increase awareness and, ultimately, grow their business, a more detailed, descriptive plan was needed to take these objectives from vague generalities to concrete specifics that identified targets, actions, and measures so that everybody within the company could more easily understand where and how they contribute. Arguably, Visa's desire to increase awareness could be in reference to *anybody seeking financial services*, which could also be construed as a segment, however vague it may sound. This would have been insufficient and relatively uninformative since *anybody seeking financial services* would have been too imprecise for making meaningful marketing investment and resource allocation decisions. Within the segment of customers needing financial services are Visa's related subsegments or targets: consumers and member businesses (nonfinancial and financial).

In Visa's situation, for its sports sponsorship investment to be useful in increasing awareness and growing its business, it had to decide which customers appeared to be the most attractive to target, especially in light of these general objectives. Visa's awareness could be raised to all audiences by simply being associated with the Olympics. But the awareness might quickly wear off without marketing programs designed to engage target customers more directly, and any drop-off in awareness would probably not lead to increased growth. Logically, one can assume Visa recognized the importance and interdependence of consumers and member businesses as two of its key target customer groups. Heightened consumer awareness of Visa might reasonably translate to increased demand for Visa-brand financial products, such as credit cards. Consumers might also increase their purchase of products and services from businesses that use the Visa card. In concert with these consumer-led demands might also be a related decline in consumer patronage of businesses that do not honor the Visa card, possibly compelling many of those businesses to begin accepting Visa in hopes of recapturing lost customers and gaining new ones as well.

How should a sponsor determine the most attractive targets within a segment? The answer requires an understanding of marketing planning fundamentals. When launching a new product or a new brand campaign, marketers must first understand their segment evaluation criteria. This includes asking:

1. What are the characteristics of the target segments and/or markets?
   a. Are they large enough to warrant our attention for this event?
   b. Higher revenue/profit potential?
   c. Market share growth potential?
   d. Early adopter/late adopter?
   e. Price sensitive/inelastic?
   f. Better ROI?
   g. High-cost/low-cost entry?

     h. Risk of competitor retaliation?
     i. Fast/slow growing?
     j. Risk-taking/risk-averse?
     k. Limited means/wealthy?
     l. Fair weather/casual/devoted sports fans?
     m. Functional/emotional orientation?
     n. Interests/behaviors/needs?
     o. One-time/loyal?
2. How closely does this segment match our company's capabilities?
     a. Can we deliver on promises we make?
         i. Infrastructure?
         ii. Support?
         iii. Meet demand?
         iv. Necessary financial resources?
         v. Previous experience with this market?
     b. Do our capabilities align (loosely) with the target customer's characteristics?
         i. If so, is the customer aware of this?
         ii. If not, do we believe our efforts will create the awareness needed?
         iii. Do they buy our products currently?
         iv. Will our effort be seen as credible?
         v. Is our reputation positive with this customer? Negative?

These represent a selection of the many questions company management should ask when evaluating their segments to determine the most attractive targets. Once the target customer analysis has been completed, several sets of segment data will be available for a comparison. The marketing team can select the ideal target customer(s) based on the resulting scores. A higher, positive score is obviously desired. There will be a temptation to select all customer groups, particularly with an event like the Olympics, which has a significant global reach and reputation that appeals to a diverse range of people. But on closer examination, as we have discussed, each company uses the sponsorship for a multiplatform approach that reaches both a broad audience and more focused customer groups within. This is an important finding of sports sponsorships, particularly large-scale events. Awareness is created by appealing to a broad audience, often through a lifestyle, feel-good message that reflects the qualities embodied by the sports event. However, as we saw with the TOP program sponsors, their multiplatform marketing effort included a wide range of tactics designed to involve customers more directly with the company's products. Coca-Cola has sold its products throughout the Olympics at various venues and supplements this with unique programs like Olympic Pin Trading that shows consumers a different side of the company. Visa offered host city destination getaways. Samsung used the Olympics to highlight its mobile business. John Hancock brought its local field agents to the Games to meet directly with customers. Lenovo built lounges for athletes and fans to use for their computing needs. Acer uses its sponsorship to demonstrate its technological prowess. In each case, these companies combined the strategic message with tactical programs to create an extensive customer experience.*

This sequence of customer planning around segmentation and targeting may seem like hard work, and it is. To have a chance at sponsorship success requires hard work. But as the saying goes, chance favors the prepared mind—or, in this case, the prepared marketing team. Leveraging the Olympic sponsorship meant that the companies had to think about the best ways to capture the imagination of their customers. Some managers stop when they have developed a clever advertising campaign, thinking that marketing and sports sponsorship is primarily an effort in attaching logos to signs around the event. Of course, that is both limiting and naive. Whether your company has the same resources as the Olympic TOP partners is irrelevant because the key lesson from these companies is not derived from their size, but from their ingenuity and implementation. Arguably, any sports sponsorship should compel companies to undertake similarly thoughtful efforts. Inarguably, a sports sponsorship costs time, resources, and money (or the in-kind equivalent), so it behooves marketers to think thoroughly about their customers and how best to attract them. Knowing your objectives and identifying the best customers then allows the marketing team to focus on creative execution.

---

*Detailed cases about John Hancock's and Lenovo's Olympic sponsorship activities are available for download at www.wiley.com/go/olympiceffect.

Questions

1. Should TOP sponsors focus their activation efforts on specific groups of fans? If so, how would you recommend they decide which groups to target?
2. As a TOP sponsor's head marketer, what kinds of questions would you ask if you wanted to learn more about your target fans? How would you use this information in your activation planning?
3. The customer segment share and customer contribution analyses are designed to help marketers understand the importance different groups of fans have in their company's performance. What are other factors you would consider in evaluating the attractiveness of fans?
4. What risks exist, if any, by relying on generalized characteristics of fan segments? How would you overcome those risks?
5. How would understanding fans' needs help TOP sponsors develop their activation plans?

Chapter 19

The Olympic Creative Execution

Many terrific books have been written over the years about creativity in business, particularly in marketing communications and advertising. This chapter is not intended to rehash those books or provide an exhaustive description of the nuts and bolts of creativity. Instead, this chapter looks at creative execution in the context of the Olympics Games and, specifically, TOP sponsors.

When the business world was simpler (nostalgically and essentially, anytime before the present), the marketer's job was to advertise products using messages created by an ad agency and deployed in print publications or via TV and/or radio broadcasts. Companies had a great deal of power, and consumers did not. Of course, the world has not been that simple for some time, and in recent years, consumers are skeptical of advertising claims, often preferring learning about products through social media networking. Furthermore, consumers are armed with information from Internet searches, blogs, podcasts, and social media well before they decide to purchase a product. They might pay attention to an advertisement, but only after their skepticism has been overcome through their own research. Power has shifted from companies to consumers (or any customer, for that matter), which makes creative execution much harder. In fact, creative execution has expanded from an emphasis on graphic design and ad copy to include an emphasis on innovative distribution, merchandising, corporate identity and logo programs, digital media, mascots and sponsorships (in the case of sports-related marketing), and, more broadly, integrated marketing platforms. A key driver of this shift is the desire to create customer experiences, not just clever advertising, which, in isolation, is not nearly as effective as it was in decades past.

An example of provocative creative execution that is memorable, but with sometimes uncertain results, are the TV ads by GoDaddy during the annual Super Bowl in the United States. GoDaddy has run racy ads on the Super Bowl since 2006, typically featuring attractive women not so subtly flaunting their sex appeal, in an effort to promote the company. Over the years, the ads have had a predictable range of responses, from support (mostly from male fans) to confusion (from many bloggers and media analysts) over what the company actually does. To clarify any reader uncertainty, the company enables users to register Internet domain names affordably. According to Techcrunch, the company's 2011 SuperBowl ads, featuring female racing star Danica Patrick and TV fitness guru Jillian Michaels, were rated in the top three "overall most disliked ads."[1] Conversely, and perhaps to the dismay of detractors, their 2011 ads were their most successful ever.

> In fewer than 15 minutes after Go Daddy's first Super Bowl commercial aired, our domain name registrations shot up more than 466 percent over last year. Go Daddy's first Internet traffic surge hit when the highly-anticipated GoDaddy.CO Girl was unveiled toward the end of the first quarter. The ad quickly helped push Go Daddy over the 46 million mark for domain names under management, which is more than any other registrar by far.[2]

For creative execution to succeed today requires much more than a simple emphasis on bold visuals for building awareness. In fact, bold visuals may have little or no impact, as the dot-com examples illustrate.

As tempting as daring creative execution might be, its use must occur in the context of longer-term strategic objectives. Companies must evaluate their sports sponsorships cognizant of the reasons for investing in the first place and the possible benefits to be derived. The benefits will include increased awareness, and superb creative execution can facilitate this. Coca-Cola's Olympic sponsorship marketing campaigns since 1928 illustrate the many different ways they used creative execution to improve and reinforce awareness. Visa's use of captivating sports imagery was in alignment with both the Olympics and the values of individual achievement that Visa's financial services celebrate. Samsung's laser focus on its mobile telecommunications business has enabled the company to elevate its brand from the unknown to one of the most admired in the world in just over a decade. Acer hopes to convey that its PCs are compelling and distinctive by using the positive associations with the Olympics to help vault the company from being just a PC competitor to being an industry leader. Each of these TOP partner sponsors have used creative marketing tastefully and innovatively but not garishly or in an attempt to shock or provoke the market. When the creative execution is disconnected from the company and/or the event, then any potential benefits rapidly disappear, leaving a cautionary footnote about the dangers to a company's reputation from ill-conceived creative execution, but little or no evidence of success in growing the business or building a brand.

To describe uses of creative execution, we will briefly highlight examples and descriptions of *message, imagery, logos/identities/landmarks,* and *mascots.*

Message

Creative imagery is considered half of the core advertising concept, with the other half represented by the message, often more commonly known as ad copy (the actual verbal descriptions). Well-conceived ad copy says a great deal in a mere few words and does so in a way that paints verbal pictures that complement the imagery used. Simplicity is key. Or to summarize a quote attributed to the American writer Mark Twain,

> I didn't have time to write a short letter, so I wrote a long one instead.[3]

As almost anybody in a professional capacity knows, it is far harder to write or speak concisely (whether the communiqué is an e-mail, a business plan, a proposal, or a verbal presentation) than it is to communicate excessively. Part of the magic in successful message campaigns is creating sweeping, positive themes that attract people magnetically while also presenting a persuasive point of view. Dense, detailed messages may well be informative, but the deep content can be counterproductive.

Marketing messages will differ in execution, depending on whether they are written (print, online) or verbal (broadcast, speaking engagements). Written communication, particularly print advertising, affords greater latitude in message since more detail can be provided. Verbal communication, particularly broadcast (radio, TV), is more appropriate for less verbose messages. However, while these are general guidelines, they are not hard-and-fast rules. With the advent of the Internet and digital tools, traditional guidelines have become increasingly situational, as is discussed in the section on new media marketing.

There are four requirements for developing a successful message: *relevance*, *resonance*, *distinction*, and *simplicity*.

Relevance

The message must connect directly to the target audience. Whether the goal is a simple three-word slogan, a multilayered product description, or even a broader understanding of a company, the customer must be able to clearly understand it and say, "That is important to me." Without relevance, the message is unlikely to be successful, no matter how creative or lyrical it sounds.

Resonance

The message must evoke important and/or emotional imagery or sensation. Customers must *feel* that the message or information is right and has meaning for them.

Distinction

The message must reinforce to customers what distinguishes a company and its products. Furthermore, customers must recognize this distinction.

This is not always a literal description, as it could be a combination of evocative images as well.

Simplicity

The earlier reference to Mark Twain captures the key point—a convoluted or verbose message risks boring or confusing the market.

Focusing on one or two of the requirements for a successful message without the others handicaps the message, making it incomplete. The challenge of developing a successful message should be readily apparent—it is not about being funny, loud, verbose, or different.

Apple is recognized for having all four requirements and for paying attention to Twain's advice. The company's iconic products, from Macs to iPads to iPhones, are relevant to customers who believe that ease of use, cool design, and innovation (such as the App Store) are important to them. Their products resonate because they evoke a sense of personal freedom and use imagery conveying an individualistic lifestyle. Their products are distinctive from visual, functional, and sociocultural perspectives. Apple's messages are simple and often have no words at all, just images that reinforce what the public already associates with the company. When a brand like Apple is so well known that it can develop message campaigns without using words, then it has reached a rare position—that of being universally understood. The Olympics are relevant to fans around the world because of the love of unfettered, genuine athletic competition. They resonate with fans because of the emotional intensity they feel for their favorite athletes and sports. The Games are distinctive because of their unrivaled traditions and diversity of contests. And like Apple, there is little question the Olympics are universally understood, requiring little or no explanation.

For Visa then, designing its marketing activities to attract more consumers and member businesses, the two customer targets discussed in the customer section, was a sensible conclusion. Past Visa Olympic marketing campaigns did just this. With its nearly two-decade marketing campaign *"It's everywhere you want to be,"* Visa was conveying convenience and access. At times, this campaign was supplemented by a message that more businesses accepted Visa cards than any other credit card and that it was the *only* card accepted at the Olympic Village.

The implications of the message were clear: For consumers to ensure financial security, they should have a Visa card, and for businesses to ensure more customers, they should accept the Visa card. This campaign lasted nearly 20 years and saw Visa's market share, revenues, profits, and overall brand reputation grow, while it also diversified its product offerings from consumer products (credit cards, debit cards, prepaid cards) to consumer services (ATM locators, exchange rates, lost cards, lost travelers checks) to commercial solutions (small businesses, medium to large companies, government). In 2006, Visa changed its message to *"Life takes Visa"* to reflect the changing nature of their offerings from simple credit cards to the broader range of financial solutions it had expanded into. The design of the message was deliberately intended to convey that Visa is essential to almost everything in life. Visa also hoped the new message would connect more emotionally with the market.[4]

In 2008, Visa launched its IPO, raising nearly $18 billion. Antonio Lucio was appointed chief marketing officer earlier that same year. With new reporting responsibilities as a public company, budgeting and investment planning changed. Lucio said the company shifted from having no budgets to working closely with finance to ensure that marketing investment decisions were made with an eye toward directly contributing to revenue creation. Shortly after joining, he was surprised to discover that Visa's marketing efforts, as good as they had been, had used multiple messages around the world and were 95 percent delivered through traditional media. In 2009, Lucio launched Visa's first-ever global advertising campaign, called "Go," with the tagline "More people go with Visa," and he allocated 40 percent of its marketing funds to digital. The company created a YouTube channel where fans could see Olympic advertising before it was on TV, vote for it, and then even enter a contest to have their names in the final TV ad.[5] The effort was timed to take advantage of the company's 2010 Vancouver Winter Olympics and 2010 South Africa World Cup sponsorships (the latter was the first of its FIFA World Cup sponsorships, which run through the 2014 World Cup). Visa partnered with Yahoo! for part of the campaign delivery for the Vancouver Olympics. The campaign included Yahoo! home page editorial promotion, medal count section, a customized athletes section, Yahoo! Sports store and Visa cardholder discount, and a Yahoo! mobile promotion. The campaign created 216 million impressions, 50 percent more than Visa targeted. Visitors spent 314 million minutes on the site during the Games, and Visa had more than 1.3 million unique visitors to the Yahoo! Mobile site. More than 60 percent of the purchases in the Yahoo! Sports store were made with a Visa card.[6] Visa's successful customer targeting efforts over the past 25 years, along with its targeted marketing communications, enabled the company to increase its market leadership position as measured by awareness, market share, revenues, profits, total transactions, and number of cards issued.

Coca-Cola's message at the 2010 Vancouver Olympics was "Open Happiness." The company ran a TV ad that showed two Canadian athletes side by side in the Olympic Village, with one drinking a Coke. Snow then fell off the roof above them, knocking the bottle of Coke to the ground. The two athletes looked around to see where the snow came from and spotted athletes from another team, so they threw a snowball at them. This quickly escalated to a large-scale snowball fight with dozens of athletes and teams in good-spirited fun. During the escalation, the Canadian athlete who had the bottle knocked away navigated his way through the snowball fight to a Coca-Cola vending machine. The ad ended with his getting another bottle of Coke from the machine and drinking it while the snowball fight continued all around him. The ad concluded with the message "Open Happiness." The imagery and message were elegantly simple: Coke inspires competitive fun.

To a greater or lesser extent, most TOP sponsors have attempted to create a message for their Olympic sponsorship. Customers ultimately determine each sponsor's success, although a weak message does not portend an unsuccessful sponsorship. By this point, readers should be well aware of the importance of approaching the sponsorship from a multidimensional set of activities and not depending on one or two elements, such as a clever message, for determining success. Each of the TOP sponsors invests in numerous activities, related to its known expertise, to create a memorable experience for Olympic fans, athletes, and business partners.

Imagery

Choice of visual imagery is an important tool in the marketing mix since well-chosen images can become easily recognized as related to a brand. Great imagery is powerful and evocative. This does not mean bright, outlandish images are the only choices that work best in marketing communications, however. Even simple images can have significant influence on awareness and recognition. When determining choice of imagery, note that success here has similar requirements to successful messages, particularly an emphasis on *resonance* and *relevance*. Consider Apple again—its quirky, sometimes minimalist advertising is designed to inspire us. From its iconic 1984 Super Bowl commercial to its late 1990s "Think Different" campaign to its silhouetted iPod users dancing to music, the company's advertising has stood out partly because its message has remained simple and uncluttered, while featuring sophisticated technology devices anybody can use. The TV ads for the iPad 2 show slice-of-life scenes, with the iPad 2 as a veritable companion for capturing memories, learning, and socializing. Nike's advertising imagery is replete with athletic scenes, as are UnderArmor's (a growing athletic apparel and footwear maker). McDonald's is known for showing people, particularly families and kids, enjoying themselves. Disney's Castle and Mickey Mouse are classic images for which the company is widely known, as are many of their best-known characters. Singapore Airlines has the renowned Singapore Girl. Manchester United's ubiquitous red color is used with creative identities targeted to different fan groups, with Fred the Red focused on kids and the Red Devils targeted to adults, not to mention the club's extensive merchandising, advertising, and online communications efforts, all tied together thematically by the color red. Benetton is known for its "United Colors of Benetton" advertising that frequently uses arresting, controversial images. The Olympics, of course, have the flame. The choice of imagery can define a brand, and the consistent use of it in carefully planned and executive marketing communications can make indelible impressions that reinforce brand reputations for years. For the 2008 Beijing Olympics, GE used simple, yet stunning photography of Chinese countryside or iconic Beijing Games venues, but with a visual twist, such as a cloud shaped like a diver arcing gracefully toward the water. Imagery can also create controversy. While Nike is not a TOP sponsor, the company has supported Olympic athletes and teams for decades. In 2000, the company created a TV ad designed to promote sports as a means to extend and improve life, which certainly sounds like a motivational message. The ad featured U.S. Olympic middle-distance star (at that time) Suzy Favor

Hamilton being chased by a chainsaw-wielding, hockey-mask-wearing assailant. Hamilton prevails, outrunning him, and he gives up, exhausted. Viewers protested, saying it promoted violence against women, causing the ad to be pulled, although Hamilton said the ad was inspiring since the female won. Years earlier, Nike's rival, Reebok, confronted a different problem: The imagery it chose featuring two promising American decathletes, Dan O'Brien (then the world record holder) and Dave Johnson, led viewers to ponder which of the two would do better at the 1992 Barcelona Olympics. Unfortunately for Reebok, Dan O'Brien failed to make the team, even though the ad campaign was running at that time. Dave Johnson did make the team and won the bronze medal, and Reebok ran commercials featuring O'Brien cheering on Johnson. O'Brien did win the gold medal at the 1996 Atlanta Olympics.[7]

As TOP sponsors consider their creative execution, there are certainly lessons to be learned, both positive and negative, from many of the world's leading marketers.

Identities/Logos/Landmarks

Imagery encompasses corporate identity marks such as logos. When we see a logo, even without the company name, other images and associations, as well as emotions, bubble to the surface.

Logos are also part of a detailed corporate identity program that describes appropriate use of all logos and trademarks, from corporate stationary to podcast logos to sales literature to advertising. Corporate identities and logos are legally protected from unauthorized or improper use, as designated by each organization. The IOC has strict guidelines for proper and consistent usage of all imagery associated with the Games. Doing so protects the Olympic trademarks and the sponsors since the risk of nonapproved usage is reduced due to the legal penalties for violators, ensuring that official sponsors will have the appropriate support when using Olympic images in their marketing. Even the order of colors in the Olympic rings must be presented a specific way to prevent a multitude of confusing variations in the marketplace (the blue, black, and red rings are always across the top, and the yellow and green rings are along the bottom). Imagery is linked to locations. We do not have to see the name of a city or a country to know its name once we see a world-renowned landmark.

Seeing the names of recognized logos and landmarks immediately conjures up images of their organization and location, triggering a flood of associations. The power of these images acts as an information filter, helping us evaluate how we feel about them. Marketers have a significant opportunity and responsibility to think carefully about how to use imagery to take full advantage of the enormous exposure they will receive when sponsoring the Olympics or any other sports event. An easy starting point for planning imagery is to write down the top two or three associations you would like target customers to have, and then consider the innumerable choices available that convey those associations. Samsung certainly has done this with its Olympic logos that look a bit like a mobile phone.

Mascots

What is the purpose of a mascot? Technically, mascots are intended to help put a colorful, memorable face on the organization it represents. Sports teams, particularly in North America although they are used increasingly around the world, use mascots to inspire fans during games and for public appearances via community outreach events to bring the public closer to the organization. Mascots range from animals (such as the Chicago Bears) to gastropods (the University of California at Santa Cruz Banana Slugs) to birds (Tottenham Hotspur's Chirpy Cockerel). Sports mascots have been a source of controversy, particularly when they appear to be caricatures of an ethnic group, and a few more extreme observers have suggested banning mascots altogether because they serve as little more than a PR stunt that does not affect how players play. Yet no such elimination has occurred.

Consumer marketing has long relied on mascots as a device for attracting young customers. Think of Ronald McDonald and images of a yellow-suited clown in red floppy shoes with flaming red hair instantly appear. Mars M&Ms candy has turned the round candy-coated chocolate treat into a much-sought-after toy, complete with its own web site where visitors can make their own M&Ms characters and then send them to friends (www.mms.com/us/becomeanmm/index.jsp). Mascots, or a variation of them, can go viral, demonstrating another clever method marketers can use to reach the public. Jollibee, a popular Philippine-based fast-food chain, has a giant bee in a red blazer and chef's hat as its mascot and main corporate identity. The Japanese telecommunications company NTTDoCoMo has Docomodake, the smiling mushroom, as its mascot. Disney has perhaps been the company most responsible for turning mascots into their own industry, with stuffed toys, action figures, cartoons, and a dizzying array of related merchandise.

The Olympics have been using mascots since 1968, when Schuss the skier was introduced at the Grenoble Olympic Games. The 2012 London Olympics have two mascots: Wenlock, who represents the Olympics, and Mandeville, who represents the Paralympics. The names sound quintessentially British and whimsical, but they are actually based on U.K. Olympic history. Wenlock is based on a British village called Much Wenlock, which had an early role in the birth of the modern Olympics by hosting the Wenlock Olympic Games in 1850. Mandeville is based on the Stoke Mandeville hospital in Buckinghamshire, which hosted the Stoke Mandeville Games in 1948 for British World War II veterans who had suffered spinal injuries. These Games are considered the forerunner to the modern Paralympics. Using an integrated marketing platform, the London organizers will feature Wenlock and Mandeville animated videos on the web site and YouTube, cross-market them in the Get Set education program that emphasizes Olympic values, have Twitter and Facebook pages devoted to them, and have them as a component of the London 2012 merchandising strategy. They will also be available online for users to customize (much like the M&Ms characters).[8] Despite the positive intentions, historic connections, and integrated multifaceted marketing, Wenlock and Mandeville have met with controversy, like many Olympic mascots. While having an anchor in reality is not a requirement in creating a mascot, having a sense of fun and whimsy apparently is. Critics complained that Wenlock and Mandeville continue a trend of amorphous, overly cute, and stylized hybrid creatures that do little to reflect the culture of the host country in a memorable way. Irrespective of personal preference, Olympic mascots are an important part of the Games marketing communication efforts. They allow organizations to make themselves more playful, perhaps even more human (despite the general lack of anything remotely human in most cases) to endear themselves to fans. Mascots help the Olympics attract younger audiences, add another dimension to each host city's personality, and provide a symbol that loosely represents the host nation's culture. Mascots, of course, can also be turned into merchandise that increases the pool of revenues flowing into the IOC.

For Olympics sponsors, mascots are another Olympic identity that can be leveraged for hospitality events, particularly community outreach programs and youth-oriented activities. Corporate sponsors do not typically design their own mascots for the Olympics, as there really is no justifiable need or reason. Plus, such an effort might serve to undermine the Olympic mascot effort. Table 19.1 summarizes the Olympic mascots since 1968.

Whether they are absurd, surreal, or cute and cuddly, mascots do not originate from a rocket science project designed to inspire deep thinking about the organization it represents. Mascots are simply a marketing device, nothing more or less. They are intended to reinforce the organization's identity by making it more memorable.

Merchandising

The IOC's Olympic merchandise is controlled by its licensing program. Companies that become official Olympic licensees must adhere to the IOC's strict requirements, including product quality, product type, and an approved use of the various Olympic symbols and marks. An ongoing education program informs licensees and the public about the legal protections the IOC has in place, plus enforcement and monitoring procedures. The Olympic licensing program is designed to protect the integrity of the Olympic brand and the rights of licensees and sponsors by ensuring unauthorized knockoffs and copies are kept to a minimum. Tables 12.11 and 12.12 from Chapter 12 describe the licensing revenues since 1988. The strongest performing Olympic licensing program was during the 2008 Summer Olympic Games in Beijing, which generated $163 million. Licensed merchandise revenues from the Winter Olympics were typically in the mid-$20 million range until the 2010 Vancouver Winter Olympics, which generated $51 million.

Table 19.1 Olympic Mascots[9]

Olympic Games	Mascot(s)	Description
1968 Winter Olympics in Grenoble	Schuss	Skiing man, first unofficial mascot
1972 Olympic Games in Munich	Waldi	Dachshund—head and tail were blue and the body had 3 vertical stripes featuring Olympic colors
1976 Winter Olympics in Innsbruck	Schneemann	Snowman
1976 Olympic Games in Montreal	Amik	Beaver—meant to symbolize hard work
1980 Winter Olympics in Lake Placid	Roni	Raccoon—Roni replaced Rocky, an actual raccoon who died just before the Olympics
1980 Olympic Games in Moscow	Misha	Bear—mascot's full name was Mikhail Potapych Toptygin
1984 Winter Olympics in Sarajevo	Vucko	Wolf—representing friendship with animals
1984 Olympic Games in Los Angeles	Sam the Eagle	Eagle—designed to appeal specifically to children
1988 Winter Olympics in Calgary	Hidy and Howdy	Bears—symbolizing Canadian friendliness
1988 Olympic Games in Seoul	Hodori	Tiger—designed to show the friendly side of a tiger . . . and Korea
1992 Winter Olympics in Albertville	Magique	Snow Imp—replaced Chamois the Mountain Goat as the mascot
1992 Olympic Games in Barcelona	Cobi	Surreal dog—became successful TV show
1994 Winter Olympics in Lillehammer	Haakon and Kristin	Boy and girl dolls from Norwegian folklore—two actual children who looked similar traveled the world as Olympic ambassadors
1996 Olympic Games in Atlanta	Izzt	Nondescript blue blob—one of the least understandable mascots
1998 Winter Olympics in Nagano	Sukki Nokki Lekki Tsukki	All 4 are snow owls—they replaced Snowple the Weasel

(Continued)

Table 19.1 Continued

Olympic Games	Mascot(s)	Description
2000 Olympic Games in Sydney	Olly Syd Millie	Kookaburra—representing generosity Platypus—representing the environment Echidna—representing the millennium
2002 Winter Olympics in Salt Lake	Powder Copper Coal	Snowshoe hare—symbolizing speed Coyote—symbolizing highest performance Black bear—symbolizing strength
2004 Olympic Games in Athens	Athena and Phevos	Brother and sister—looked like ancient Greek dolls
2006 Winter Olympics in Torino	Neve Gliz Aster	Snowball Ice cube Snowflake
2008 Olympic Games in Beijing	Beibei Jingjing Huanhuan Yingying Nini	Fish Panda Olympic flame Tibetan antelope Swallow
2010 Winter Olympics in Vancouver	Miga Quatchi Sumi	All three are mythical creatures based loosely on local folklore
2012 Summer Olympics in London	Wenlock Mandeville	Based on historical U.K. connections to the modern Olympics and Paralympics
2014 Winter Olympics in Sochi	The Polar Bear The Hare The Leopard	Decided by national vote on television, the mascots represent the 3 Olympic medals.

For corporate sponsors, merchandise programs can extend into a wide range of offerings, from apparel to office supplies to household items. There is no magic set of guidelines that says which types of merchandise are best and which are to be avoided—each company needs to determine the items that lend themselves most effectively to extending its brand. But there is a possible lesson in the Olympic merchandising experience: Too much can lead to public disenchantment, which might ultimately undermine the image of integrity associated with the Olympics. For companies, a similar effect may very well harm their brand as well.

TOP Sponsor Creative Examples

Creative execution is a key driver of Olympic sponsorship success. A compelling image and a cleverly worded phrase can certainly help position sponsors, but such superficial activation does not take full advantage of the significant opportunity sponsors have to use the Olympics to establish their companies as progressive, innovative, and caring institutions.

Coca-Cola

Coca-Cola wanted to use the emphasis at the Vancouver Olympics to unveil its own sustainability efforts by rolling out 1,400 vending machines in Canada with clean and green cooling technology, part of the company's strategic effort to cease using HFC-based technology that is known to damage the environment. Not only did the company activate its usual wide variety of Olympics marketing tactics, from new products to Olympics pins and new advertising, but it also used the Olympics to make a statement about its commitment to a sustainable and greener future. Part of its marketing activation included development of a social media iPhone app that was a virtual snowball fight. The company also partnered with Olympic broadcaster NBC to create an app that had sounds of Coca-Cola being poured, air horns, and fans cheering. Athletes sponsored by Coca-Cola tweeted to fans throughout the Games.[10]

Omega

Omega used the Vancouver Olympics not only to demonstrate the quality of its timepieces and timing technology but also to convey a sense of prestige and quality. The company built a temporary boutique at the Fairmont Hotel in Vancouver featuring Olympic-themed watches and a selection of its finest models. The location in the Fairmont Hotel reinforced the atmospheric sense of luxury, helping the brand to cover key needs, including reliability and quality.[11] In addition, the company spent three years designing a new starting gun that could get through today's tightened airport security systems without being mistaken as a potential terrorist threat. The company sent 200 timekeepers and 250 tons of supporting equipment to Vancouver, illustrating that being a TOP sponsor requires more than just having your products displayed for sale and advertised on available signage. Omega also had astronaut Buzz Aldrin (who wore an Omega watch on the moon), model Cindy Crawford, and swimmer Michael Phelps walking around the Olympic Village and venues wearing the company's higher-end watches, ranging from $3,000 to $10,000 in price. And while the IOC specifically forbids commercial signage in any Olympic venue, Omega has the benefit of being the only TOP sponsor present because every piece of timing equipment for every event has the Omega name on it.[12]

McDonald's

McDonald's used the 2008 Beijing Olympics to build its presence in China. Its competitor KFC has a much larger presence there, an unusual situation for McDonald's. McDonald's 2010 Vancouver Olympics sponsorship activation also integrated a wide range of elements in reinforcing its creative strategy. McDonald's outlets were built in the athlete's village and were open 24/7. Olympics-themed promotions were featured at McDonald's locations in the region, complemented by an onslaught of TV and radio advertising. The ads featured Canadian Olympic athletes alongside regular McDonald's employees, both excited about the Olympics but for very different reasons. There was criticism since the company's most popular foods, burgers and fries, are not associated with healthy diets. But the company stressed its Olympic sponsorship intentions are not just about food per se (its Olympic advertising often emphasizes the healthier items on its menus), but about the connection to a positive life.[13]

P&G

Procter & Gamble created a four-story P&G Family Home for American athletes and their families. Rooms inside were themed after branded P&G products from health care to food to detergents and more. The Pampers Village (named for the well-known diaper brand) featured a play center for children. A hair salon featured the company's many brands of hair care products. Television advertising was family-centered, with emotional and motivating ads featuring moms taking their kids to sports practices and, later on, competing in Olympic venues. The ads ended with the message "P&G, Proud Sponsor of Moms."[14] It will also partner with other TOP sponsors, including Coca-Cola and GE, to create cobranded opportunities for London 2012. The company overall plans to sponsor athletes' families, and its individual brands would sponsor athletes themselves. The family oriented theme continues the effort they used in Vancouver, even to the point of using moms of famous Olympians in its London 2012 advertising, including Usain Bolt's mother, Jennifer Bolt, and Paula Radcliffe's mother, Pat.[15]

Panasonic

Panasonic used the 2008 Beijing Olympics to promote its HD (high-definition) TV and recorder products through a promotion called "Get your family ready for the first HD Olympics." Panasonic-branded trucks visited retail locations across China in the months leading up to the Olympics, bringing former Olympic athletes and holding contests in which participants could win a new HDTV or even tickets to the Games.[16]

The creative execution will succeed or fail based on the TOP sponsor's ability to integrate the multitude of marketing platforms, both traditional and new media, with an integrated message that is relevant to and resonates with the target audiences. The TOP sponsors are under pressure from shareholders and society to demonstrate financial returns and a sense of responsibility to the world. The demands on them are significant, but the age of new media, with its instant communication and sheer ubiquity, has made hiding from bad decisions and mistakes virtually impossible. Fans everywhere can instantly respond and quickly assemble a viral flash mob that overwhelms a company's positioning efforts. The onus today is on TOP sponsors, and companies anywhere, to use sponsorships and brand building to promote authenticity over hype, responsibility over exemption, integrity over dishonor, and collective good over self-interest. The age of globalization and instant communication means companies cannot rely merely on traditional means to build their brands and reinforce positive reputations. Missteps in sponsoring the Olympics may not be company-ending events, but the sheer magnitude of the Games means mistakes are quickly amplified. As we have seen, TOP sponsors plan carefully for years to activate their sponsorships, adapt plans along the way, use each Games sponsorship to build on the efforts of the last, and thereby reach out more effectively to fans around the world.

Questions

1. Conduct online research into Coca-Cola's many different sponsorship activities over the years. How well integrated was their creative message, and did the company use multiple media in a consistent, brand-building way?

2. Is an Olympic sponsorship a creative challenge, or is it more of a logistical and operational one? Explain.

3. Assess the critical observation that Olympic mascots are too juvenile. In your review, think about who the target audience is. If you decide the critics are correct, then recommend how the Olympic mascot program can be improved. If you disagree with the critics, describe how the mascots fulfill their intended marketing purpose. (You may need to do additional research about Olympic mascots.)

4. Critically assess the creative execution of the TOP sponsors highlighted within this chapter. How successful were they with their Olympics-related creative execution? How would you measure that success? A more in-depth online review of their respective Olympics creative marketing efforts will provide additional evidence to support your assessment.

Chapter 20

The Olympic Marketing Communications

Marketing communications is a broad discipline with numerous tools available for reaching target customers. They encompass *traditional* and *new media* components, ranging from broadcast advertising to blogs. Whereas companies used to treat marketing's different tools as separate areas of expertise, emphasis is now placed on integrating these pieces together. Done well, integrated marketing minimizes the chances of different marketing programs contradicting each other or misrepresenting the company's offerings, since everyone and every tactic is aligned behind a common objective.

As we saw with the TOP sponsors discussed in this book, many of their sponsorship activities were designed around a central theme and then executed differently depending on the marketing tool used. For example, 30-second television spots do not work well on the web. But a short clip with a similar theme might easily go viral on YouTube.

An elegantly worded print ad would not translate well to a billboard, tweet, or SMS text message, yet communication techniques exist that convey the same meaning without verbosity. Sports marketing success is predicated on a marketer's identifying the target audience, selecting a marketing tool to reach them, and adapting the company message to fit that tool. Visa's four marketing platforms—advertising, promotional, corporate relations, product—are broad theme areas under which specific marketing activities support each theme. Its marketing has consistently followed a central theme supported by advertising, PR, merchant programs, hospitality, and destination programs into an integrated program tailored to the Olympics. The advent of new media has given marketers new tools that not only complement existing traditional media but also can be used to more effectively target very specific audiences, allowing sponsors to tailor their messages according to the unique needs of a given customer group.

Traditional Marketing

Traditional marketing represents the classic communication elements most often associated with large-scale media in television, radio, and print, although it also includes additional mix elements like hospitality tents, team sponsorships, and outdoor advertising. Traditional marketing is usually one-way communication from the company to the market, and even with the excitement and rapid growth of new media, traditional marketing remains an important part of sponsor marketing strategies because consumers continue to use it. According to a Nielsen survey, 67 percent of Chinese citizens got their Olympic information from newspapers.[1] While the percentages of traditional media consumption vary depending on the country examined, it is still a potent force in the arsenal of marketing tools.

In preparing for sports sponsorships, marketers often use a planning template. In this hypothetical example, a marketer has determined through research that the primary target audiences (A, B, C) respond to the media marked in Table 20.1. In the real world, it is likely that a target audience would respond to a combination of traditional and new media.

The marketing choices for target audience A pay attention to classic media such as TV, radio, print, and outdoor signage, whereas target audiences B and C respond to different marketing tools. A marketer must develop a communications program that best fits the profile of each audience (assuming the company has the luxury of investing in multiple marketing vehicles to reach different customer groups). Table 20.2 is an example of a marketing activity planning worksheet.

This company has chosen "Go for Gold" as its message for the Olympics, and it uses this theme consistently across the media types targeted to audience A. Note that a key goal is to increase awareness of the company 10 percent by the time the campaign has ended. This can be measured using surveys before, during, and after this marketing campaign. *Reach* measures the number or percentage of people who were exposed to a single ad during a specified period of time.[2] *Frequency* measures the number of times members of the target audience are exposed to the same ad during the specified period of time.[3] *Gross rating points* (GRP) are the result of Reach Frequency, and they describe the total number of ad exposures a marketing campaign will generate during a specified period of time.[4] To calculate these figures requires data about the size of the customer audience from each of the media companies. Insertion date refers to the start date of the particular media type used. Ad length/size is self-explanatory. Total cost includes the cost of creative execution (producing the creative content either in-house or through an outside ad agency), the cost of media (fees charged by the media type to place an ad in a specified size, location, and time slot), and related support costs (other professional services). Determining the project outcome is both science and art. A company may have historical data that show the impact on awareness (or whatever goal is used for the project outcome), which should guide the marketer's goal setting. If the company has historically seen awareness grow 1 percent, then setting a goal of a 95 percent increase in awareness would be too ambitious. But settling for 1 to 2 percent suggests a lack of effort. This is where the art comes in, since part of the entire marketing effort directed to each target audience is predicated on judgment born of other experiences.

The actual cost of TV coverage depends on the size of the expected audience and the demographics of the broadcaster's country of origin. When broadcasters set advertising rates in the United States, for example,

Table 20.1 Traditional Marketing

	TV	Radio	Print	Product	Signage	Outdoor	Tickets	Hospitality	Athlete Team Sponsorship
Target Audience A	✓	✓	✓		✓				
Target Audience B				✓	✓	✓	✓	✓	
Target Audience C						✓		✓	✓

Table 20.2 Marketing Activity Planning Worksheet (Traditional Marketing)

Media Type	Target Audience	Message	Reach	Frequency	Insertion Date	Ad Length or Size	GRP (gross rating points)	Total Cost (creative, media buy)	Project Outcome
TV	A	"Go for Gold"	20%	6x	August 1	30 sec.	225	$3 M	10% ↑ awareness
Radio	A	"Go for Gold"	40%	12x	July 1	15–30 sec.	300	$300k	10% ↑ awareness
Print	A	"Go for Gold"	25%	8x	June 15	1 page	75	$225k	10% ↑ awareness
Signage	A	"Go for Gold"		3-month contract	June 1	5 billboards	unknown	$125,000	10% ↑ awareness

they base the rates on the size of the expected audience at each viewing time. The most expensive TV advertising time slots in the United States are during prime time, between the hours of 7 and 11 P.M., when most Americans tend to watch TV. Viewing habits in the United States have changed significantly over the past 25 years due to the advent of more choices, such as cable, the Internet, and mobile streaming, while the traditional big television networks (ABC, CBS, NBC, and Fox) have seen steady viewership declines. Nevertheless, the big networks broadcast the Olympics and have added to their core media business by acquiring or adding cable- and Internet-based offerings. Table 20.3 shows the changes in U.S. television coverage, along with the growth of the Olympics.

Historically, the prime time ratings for Olympiads held outside the United States decreased due to time zone changes, so that many U.S. fans ended up watching tape-delayed rebroadcasts or skipped viewing events entirely unless it was both of interest and shown live during prime time hours. There has been a significant jump in the total network hours broadcast in the 2000s, starting with the 2004 Olympics in Athens. The increase has been due to NBC's choosing to broadcast 24 hours a day, seven days a week, using the network's various broadcast, Internet, and cable properties. The 2010 Vancouver Olympics' network hours broadcast was double the coverage in Turin in 2006. The network broadcast hours for the 2012 London Olympics are estimated to total 4,675 hours, representing a substantial increase in coverage. For the first time, NBC will broadcast all 2012 Olympic events live, a change that will undoubtedly affect the viewing habits of U.S. Olympics fans. Corporate sponsors are understandably attracted to the size of the U.S. television audience. The challenge for sponsors is timing their ads during peak viewing hours. However, with more broadcast choices available now, this increases the complexity of the sponsor's advertising mix, including reach and frequency decisions. Corporate sponsors may also buy advertising time on foreign broadcast networks, assuming they sell commercial airtime, which many do not. But the total possible range of TV advertising options is large. Beyond the United States, global TV coverage has also grown substantially. The IOC estimated that the 2010 Vancouver Winter Olympics had more than 24,000 hours of TV coverage worldwide, a nearly 50 percent increase over the 2006 Turin Winter Olympics.[5]

Table 20.3 Olympic Games since 1960 and U.S. Television Coverage[6]

Olympics	U.S. TV Network	Average Prime Time Rating*	Total Network Hours	Number of Nations Competing	Number of Olympic Events
1960 Winter Olympics in Squaw Valley	CBS	NA	NA	30	27
1960 Summer Olympics in Rome	CBS	NA	20	83	150
1964 Winter Olympics in Innsbruck	ABC	NA	17.5	36	34
1964 Summer Olympics in Tokyo	NBC	NA	14	93	163
1968 Winter Olympics in Grenoble	ABC	13.5	20	37	35
1968 Summer Olympics in Mexico City	ABC	NA	43.75	112	172
1972 Winter Olympics in Sapporo	NBC	17.2	26	35	35
1972 Summer Olympics in Munich	ABC	24.4	62.75	121	195
1976 Winter Olympics in Innsbruck	ABC	21.5	27.5	37	37
1976 Summer Olympics in Montreal	ABC	23.9	76.5	92	198
1980 Winter Olympics in Lake Placid	ABC	23.6	35	37	38
1980 Summer Olympics in Moscow	NBC	**	**	80	203
1984 Winter Olympics in Sarajevo	ABC	18.4	41.5	49	39
1984 Summer Olympics in Los Angeles	ABC	23.2	180	140	221
1988 Winter Olympics in Calgary	ABC	19.3	95	57	46
1988 Summer Olympics in Seoul	NBC	17.9	176	159	237
1992 Winter Olympics in Albertville	CBS	18.7	107	64	57
1992 Summer Olympics in Barcelona	NBC	17.5	148	169	257
1994 Winter Olympics in Lillehammer	CBS	27.8	110	67	61
1996 Summer Olympics in Atlanta	NBC	21.6	164	197	271
1998 Winter Olympics in Nagano	CBS	16.3	124	72	68
2000 Summer Olympics in Sydney	NBC	14.2	441	199	300

2002 Winter Olympics in Salt Lake	NBC	16.9	375.5	77	78
2004 Summer Olympics in Athens	NBC	15.5	1,210	201	301
2006 Winter Olympics in Torino	NBC	12.2	416	80	84
2008 Summer Olympics in Beijing	NBC	16.2	3,600	204	302
2010 Winter Olympics in Vancouver	NBC	13.8	835	82	86
2012 Summer Olympics in London	NBC	TBD	4,675 (est.)	204 (est.)	302 (est.)

*Average prime time rating; Each point represents 1.1 million U.S. households.

**The United States boycotted the 1980 Summer Games; NBC's coverage was limited to highlights and two anthology-style specials after the Games were completed, though the network still paid the full rights fee.

Marketers must plan each activity carefully, starting with strategic objectives—such as Visa's initial desire to raise awareness in the 1980s—and then setting tactical goals that identify specific marketing programs targeted to specific audiences with a message designed to yield a specific outcome—such as Visa's increases in transactions volume, credit cards issued, and increased financial institution membership.

New Media Marketing

The growth of new media has led to a tremendous power shift from companies to customers. More consumers around the world are opting for the newer communications tools as they slow their usage of traditional media. The 24,000 hours of worldwide TV coverage was indeed a substantial increase at the 2010 Vancouver Olympics. But even more impressive was the rapid growth of digital media coverage, which was equal in hours to the TV coverage in Vancouver. Mobile's growth was also impressive, accounting for 25 percent of the digital coverage in Vancouver.[7]

New media tools can be less expensive up front. For example, many blog and podcast applications are available free or at very low prices, reducing the expense of media placement (in the case of these two media types). New media have required companies to rethink their marketing approaches if target customers are to find the message credible. New media marketing is two-way and often simultaneous. The public increasingly views traditional marketing with skepticism since one of its key tools, advertising, is the company's effort to push its message across to customers with no direct feedback (in the short term); therefore, it is often perceived as unsubstantiated claims in the eyes of consumers. New media marketing can be started anywhere by anybody—it does not have to be generated by the company. Customers view new media marketing as more genuine and authentic because it is unedited communication among and between people, sharing opinions. When good (or bad) news is reported about a company and its products, new media marketing enables the message to grow virally extremely quickly, and, conceivably, reputations grow or change rapidly as well. The important point for sports marketers is to use both traditional and new media in their sponsorship planning since the world is comprised of audiences familiar with each, but some are more comfortable with one versus the other. Furthermore, successful integrated marketing is about leveraging a common theme across a variety of marketing programs, and combining traditional and new media marketing can offer the potential for maximum impact with target audiences.

Returning to our earlier example, the marketer has determined that target customers X, Y, and Z respond to new media marketing best, as shown by Table 20.4.

In this example, a marketer would create a worksheet for each media type (web, banner, and so on), with specific metrics as goals for the specific sports sponsorship campaign. The company, in this case, is using the "Go for Gold" message in its new media marketing tactics, just as it did with traditional marketing, and this worksheet displays a possible way to evaluate the performance of the sponsorship's Web-specific campaign. The web site campaign choices range from special sports-specific offers on the company's existing web site to an entirely new and separate web site (or a site within a main web site). A campaign planning worksheet is shown in Table 20.5.

The company's marketers have set specific goals using select web metrics. *Direct URL access* describes the number of customers who access the company's web site by directly entering its URL, versus a link to it from another site. This can tell marketers how well known and sought after their company is. The company wants to increase the number of people who visit the site using direct URL access by 5,000 per week. *Engagement* refers to the length of active time a visitor spends on a web site (versus idle time, indicated by a page that sits for hours because a user has walked away). Our company wants their sports sponsorship web site to drive a 20 percent increase in engagement (as compared, for example, to other company web sites unrelated to the sports sponsorship). *Abandonment* describes people who abandon a web site after a short time or in the act of ordering a product.[8] Here, the company is targeting a 15 percent decrease in shopping cart abandonment (perhaps a feature of the shopping cart has been improved that streamlines the ordering process).

Each new media tool will have its own goals and objectives because each is used differently. Blogs are another fast-growing activity. For example, many of the most popular blogs are comprehensive, lengthy

Table 20.4 Nontraditional Marketing

	Multimedia	Web Site	Banner	Blogs	Podcasts	Social Media	Mobile	SMS
Target Audience X	✓	✓	✓	✓				
Target Audience Y		✓		✓	✓	✓		
Target Audience Z		✓					✓	✓

Table 20.5 Marketing Activity Planning Worksheet (New Media Marketing)

	Target Audience	Message	Direct URL Access	Engagement	Abandonment	Cost	Purchase Goals
Web	X	"Go for Gold"	5k↑ per week	20%↑ in time spent on site	15%↓ in shopping cart abandonment	$250k	15%↑ in purchases

pieces. Of course, blogs are not usually used like traditional print advertising. But bloggers often discuss companies, products, services, politics, and much more. Also, the most popular blogs have thousands or even millions of fans and readers who regularly spread the message from the blogs through online sharing, also called viral marketing. Viral marketing is a form of marketing, but it is not easy for companies to control. Nevertheless, it has become one of the by-products of the new communication tools in recent years.

A blog's success can be analyzed using web site metrics plus a review of changes to the number of RSS feed subscribers, the number of RSS to e-mail subscribers, top posts, top feed readers, trackbacks, and replies (RSS is short for Really Simple Syndication, and it is an easy way for people to be automatically notified of content changes to their favorite blogs and web sites without initiating their own search). Podcasts may use a mix of classic measures (total subscribers) with new media digital metrics (viral adoption rates). YouTube provides statistics on views and even a basic five-star viewer ratings system. During the years Lenovo was an Olympic TOP sponsor (primarily during the 2006 Turin and 2008 Beijing Olympics), a small group of Lenovo employees produced several short, whimsical video spots about the superior qualities of their laptop computers that they uploaded to YouTube (such as the "Lenovo Sky-walker" video). They set a goal of getting around 900,000 views (200,000 views is considered very good and 1 million views is considered excellent) and did not inform their colleagues or senior management about their project. Total views came to more than 3 million, indicating a major success. Senior management then noticed, illustrating to them the potential power and reach of new media marketing.

New media's growth has been impressive, driven by enormous changes in the way individuals and companies consume information. Global advertising patterns are changing due to the advent of new media marketing tools. ZenithOptimedia, a media research firm, cites the following general advertising trends:[9]

- Ad expenditure growth would return to prerecession levels in 2011.
- Ad expenditure growth will be 5.9 percent worldwide, with Eastern Europe growing 9 percent, Latin America 6.7 percent, Asia Pacific 5.9 percent, Western Europe 3.3 percent, North America 2.3

Table 20.6 Global Advertising Spending by Medium[10]

	2009	2010	2011	2012	2013
Newspapers	97,354	95,945	93,750	93,253	92,892
Magazines	43,776	43,810	43,201	43,094	42,992
Television	163,484	179,601	189,412	202,712	214,968
Radio	31,917	32,259	33,025	34,397	35,604
Cinema	2,099	2,310	2,440	2,593	2,746
Outdoor	27,830	29,926	31,721	34,042	35,689
Internet	54,700	63,690	72,176	82,818	94,967
TOTAL	**421,161**	**447,541**	**465,724**	**492,910**	**519,857**

Note: Figures shown are in millions of US$ using 2006 currency average rates.

percent, and the Middle East a 12.1 percent decline due to the turmoil of recent years, particularly from the Arab spring of 2011.

- China's ad market is growing rapidly, gaining on number two Japan. In 2005, China's ad market was 23 percent of Japan's; in 2013, it is forecasted to be 83 percent of Japan's.
- Through 2013, 49 percent of new ad dollars will come from TV.
- Internet advertising will grow 14.2 percent through 2014, up from 9.7 percent of total global ad expenditures in 2008 and 12.3 percent in 2010.

The trends in advertising medium spending are depicted in Table 20.6. A quick calculation shows that Internet ad expenditure growth is expected to grow 74 percent by 2013, from 2009 levels, the largest percentage growth rate of all media.

New Media Tools Growth Areas

Broadband penetration rates around the world are interesting because they can help sports marketers determine if the use of a particular new medium is likely to be noticed by the target audience, wherever they are in the world. To illustrate, let's look at broadband data in Figure 20.1.

Broadband penetration rates have been growing dramatically around the world. Canada is ranked 24th with a broadband penetration rate of 85.7 percent, the United Kingdom is 27th with 79.3 percent

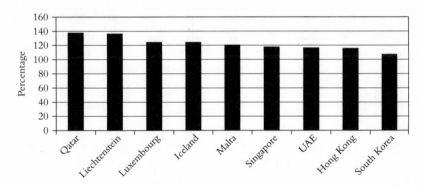

Figure 20.1 Broadband Penetration by Household in Q1 2011[11]

penetration, and the United States is ranked 28th at 77.5 percent. Now marketers should turn their attention to learning why customers are online, what they are doing, and which applications should be considered in a marketing campaign. (This rationale is not limited to broadband, as marketers would conduct a similar analysis for other new media, as well as traditional marketing areas.) Knowing how target customers spend their time online helps marketers determine the type of message, which web sites, and message location. Varying the message and location by web site can provide additional detailed data on which approach yielded the most effective response rates from customers.

From here, marketers should look at the specific target audience profiles in the key countries where the marketing effort will concentrate and try to link target customer profiles to advertising trends to see if there is a large enough audience to justify the marketing investment and choice of medium. Of course, online usage is one of the many new marketing tools. Mobile entertainment and social media have become standard marketing tools in the late 2000s.

Mobile Entertainment

According to Juniper Research, mobile entertainment is forecasted to grow to $38.4 billion in 2011–2012 from $33.2 billion in 2010. Projections for 2015 show the market increasing to $54 billion. China and the Far East are the largest markets, followed by Western Europe. Sports marketers may consider developing marketing programs that work effectively in mobile entertainment, such as games, small-profile videos, and real-time delivery of sports statistics, along with the sponsorship message.[12]

Social Media

The changes in this sector have been extraordinary, even since the first edition of this book came out in 2008. Twitter, founded in 2006, has grown dramatically. The number of registered users in spring 2011 was officially stated by Twitter as 200 million, although some analysts say the number is closer to 360 million. Every day 50 million people use Twitter and send more than 350 million tweets (compared to 5,000 tweets per day in 2007). Twitter is one of the promising young social media companies that investors are watching carefully. While official figures are not available since Twitter is a private company, estimates indicate their 2011 revenue is approximately $140 million, with $360 million in funding, and an estimated value of $7.8 billion.[13] Facebook has enjoyed significant growth as well. From 12 million users in 2006, the company grew to more than 800 million as of September 2011, with 75 percent of them outside the United States. Facebook is available in 70 languages. Facebook's users are dedicated to the site. More than half of Facebook's users log onto the site every day. Facebook launches new features regularly, most of which grow quickly. As an example, a feature launched in 2009 is called Like. As of September 2011, more than 2 billion posts on Facebook are now Liked every day. New apps are installed by users 20 million times each day. The company has announced it would launch its IPO (initial public offering) by April 2012, and analysts have predicted its valuation could exceed $100 billion when it goes public. If this proves true, then this, too, would represent astonishing growth (in value), from a mere $23 billion in June 2010. Like Twitter, Facebook is not public and does not release official financials. However, industry analysts indicate the company generated $2 billion in revenue in 2010 and will more than double that amount in 2011.[14] YouTube continues to be impressive in its own right, with its 2010 statistics indicating more than 2 billion views per day. The site is localized in 23 countries and 24 languages. Like Facebook, more than 70 percent of traffic is from users outside the United States. Even more interesting:[15]

- Ninety-four of *AdvertisingAge*'s 100 top advertisers placed ad campaigns on YouTube.
- More than 1,000 major corporate partners use YouTube's Content ID, a free service that allows companies to have control over their content.

Why are the social media sites growing so rapidly? One of the key factors is the *network effect*, which means that the value of a network grows as more people are added to it. With the Internet's ubiquity, once a social network grows past a certain point, each user adds his or her own network, so the numbers grow exponentially. The immediacy of response and the relative authenticity of the communications have also appealed to users around the world, enabling social media networks to become the new way people around the world increasingly socialize. Social media have not replaced face-to-face get-togethers or actual human contact, but it has complemented the way people interact with others, and it has become a more credible mechanism for people to get *real* information in a globalized world in which many increasingly see advertising as suspect. As a consequence, companies have found this very attractive as well. In the United States, more than 83 percent of Fortune 500 companies use at least one social media site for some form of corporate communications and relationship development. Popular social media choices are Facebook, LinkedIn, Twitter, and Foursquare. Seventy-one percent of the Inc. 500 have company Facebook sites, with 44 percent of them citing it as their best networking platform. Nearly 60 percent of the Fortune 500 have corporate Twitter accounts. Blogs, once among the fastest growing areas of the online world, have slowed in popularity, although they still grew 5 percent between 2009 and 2010, with half of the Inc. 500 using a corporate blog.[16]

2008 Summer Olympic Games in Beijing

Let's look at the U.S. market to understand new media usage for the Olympics, specifically Beijing in 2008. (The United States has extensive consumer and media statistics, and both the data collection and analytical techniques have been refined over decades.) According to Scarborough

Sports Marketing, 57 percent of U.S. adults followed the progress of the 2008 Beijing Olympics overall. NBCOlympics.com stated that more than 1.2 billion web pages were served, plus 72 million video streams. These numbers indicated a more than doubling of the *combined* traffic for both the 2004 Athens and 2006 Turin Olympiads. Nielsen Online said that daily average unique audience traffic for Olympics content visited was as follows: Yahoo!Olympics (4.73 million), NBC Olympics (4.27 million), AOL Olympics (1.32 million), Sports Illustrated Olympics (704,000), ESPN Olympics (676,000), Beijing2008.cn (515,000), New York Times Olympics (461,000), and USAToday Olympics (239,000).[17] Online media complemented, and did not substitute for, traditional media, allowing fans to stay on top of the latest updates from the Games.

In advance of the 2008 Beijing Olympics, the nation's preoccupation with using the Olympics to reintroduce China to the world included ongoing national promotions to generate fan interest and inspire patriotic and nationalistic tendencies. Chinese citizens were surveyed, and many suggested that they would alter their lifestyles to accommodate watching the Games.

And with a line up of world-class events over the coming three weeks, Chinese people are eagerly adjusting their lifestyles to fit in with the Olympic schedule. To ensure they don't miss a thing, nine in 10 Chinese said they would be adapting their personal schedules to accommodate the Games, and seven in 10 will change their working hours—while 30 percent intend to watch Olympics coverage at work, with many Chinese companies making special arrangements to keep them happy.[18]

Figure 20.2 on the next page shows the complete survey results.[19]

New media tools played a role in how the Chinese chose to follow the Games. Ninety-six percent of those surveyed said they would watch the Games on TV, an expected percentage, to be sure, due to TV's dominance as a mature, preferred medium. Interestingly, 74 percent said they would video stream the Games online, and another 27 percent said they would stay informed through their mobile devices. This usage information is highly useful for sports marketers. Conducting additional customer research would undoubtedly help marketers

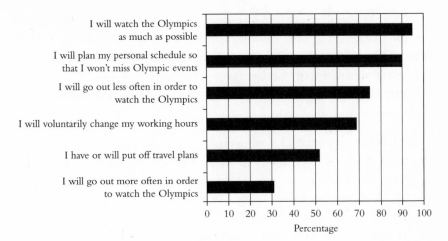

Figure 20.2 "Please state whether you agree or disagree that the following statements reflect your intention to follow the Olympic Games" Response = Agree

uncover more details about the Chinese fans, including demographic, psychographic, and geographic information, all of which could then be used to fine-tune marketing campaigns on multiple platforms. The full survey results are in Figure 20.3.[20]

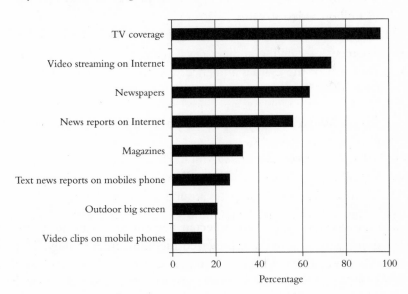

Figure 20.3 "Which media do you intend to use to watch the 2008 Beijing Olympic Games?"

More generally, paying attention to audience media usage will inform marketers about possible trends that might require a shift in marketing communication planning for subsequent campaigns. The following summary of media usage statistics from the 2008 Beijing Olympics offers useful insights about traditional marketing and new media usage:[21]

- 4.3 billion potential TV viewers.*
- Estimates that 3.6 billion people watched at least 1 minute of Olympics coverage.
- 61,700 hours of TV coverage, of which 72 percent was over free TV channels (versus cable).
- Total broadcast exceeded coverage from the 2004 Athens Olympics by 40 percent and doubled the coverage from 2000 Sydney.
- Opening Ceremonies had 1,144 hours of global TV coverage, of which 54 percent was live.
- Global reach of Opening Ceremonies (defined as viewing at least one minute) reached 1.5 billion viewers.
- 1.4 billion viewers watched at least 15 minutes of Olympics coverage.
- 8.2 billion page views of the official Beijing 2008 web site.
- 628 million video streams.
- IOC's official YouTube channel received 21 million video views.
- 53 percent of viewing audience was male.
- 45 percent of the Games audience was under 45 years old.

2010 Winter Olympic Games in Vancouver

The 2010 Vancouver Winter Olympics final report stated that more than 3.5 billion viewers watched the Games, which were broadcast on 300 TV channels and 100 web sites around the world. Using the United States again as an example, 190 million viewers watched the Vancouver

---

*Note that TV coverage for the Olympics is usually described as "potential" audience, meaning the total number of people with access to a TV showing official broadcasts. Refining this to a precise figure is not possible without the use of technology that accurately measures actual viewing habits and records the results—a daunting technological undertaking that is unlikely to occur anytime in the near future. Therefore, TOP sponsors have to be content with the potential audience figures to determine how attractive TV is as a marketing medium.

Games, and the average prime time audience rating was 24.4 million. Nielsen reported that 56 percent of the viewers were female and the overall viewing audience skewed older, with ratings from those age 55 and above 82 percent higher than the national average for past prime time Olympics broadcasts, whereas teenagers were 57 percent lower. Those between 18 and 49 years were 20 percent lower than the average. Looking more deeply, the viewing data for specific audiences versus the national average are even more insightful:[22]

- African American and Hispanic American viewers were each 74 percent below the national average.
- Asian American ratings were 15 percent below.
- The West Central region was 24 percent higher.
- The Southwest was 28 percent lower.
- Fifty-five percent of Olympic viewers were in HD-capable/ receivable homes, and the viewing in these homes was 14 percent higher than the national average.
- Forty-one percent of Olympic viewers were in DVR homes and had ratings 12 percent higher.

Not surprisingly, new media were important components of the overall marketing mix in the 2010 Vancouver Olympics as well:

- More than 3.5 billion potential TV viewers
- 47 percent more global TV coverage than for the 2006 Turin Winter Olympics, representing 26,000 hours of coverage
- 300 TV stations and 100 web sites worldwide
- 6,000 hours of mobile coverage
- 50,000 total broadcast hours on all media, worldwide
- 1,500 appearances of the Olympic Games mascots
- 78 million unique visitors to the Vancouver Olympics web site
- A record 9,185,306 unique visits in a single day broke the previous mark of 8,797,614 set in Beijing in 2008
- 19.1 percent of people across North America visited the site using Internet access
- 4.6 percent of people worldwide with Internet access visited the site during the Olympics
- 14,000 followers on Twitter

- 1.25 million downloads for the official mobile spectator guide
- 1.1 million Facebook fans, more than four times the total from Beijing

Singapore 2010 Youth Olympic Games in Singapore

The first YOG was held in Singapore in 2010. The IOC used the lessons learned about new media from Beijing and Vancouver for the media strategy for the first YOG. The young athletes (only 14- to 18-year-olds could participate) were given guidance on how to use various social and digital media to connect with fans, giving early advice to these future potential stars about how to build relationships with their fans, share emotional insights, and generally show their human side. Julian Lim was in charge of the YOG social media effort in Singapore:

> Social media presents a valuable channel for athletes to connect with their fans and those who are interested in their sports . . . we were heartened to see that athletes were interested in learning about social media applications. They attended workshops where they learnt about free, web-based applications that could help them with photo editing, micro-blogging, information resources, file-sharing, and even where to stream music legally. With that, we hope we've done our part to create an even more social media-savvy generation of athletes.[23]

Major social media, including Twitter and Facebook, were used by the YOG athletes, as well as blogs. The YOG now has more than 70,000 fans on Facebook worldwide, and Facebook was used for fans to vote on the 2012 YOG Winter Games in Innsbruck mascot. A Chinese version of Twitter called Weibo has garnered roughly 1 million YOG followers. The media coverage had a reach of 266,379,343 people. The marketing value of the media coverage was $45,105,814. As an inaugural event, the multiplatform statistics were strong:[24]

- 400+ hours of live coverage
- 8 live feeds

- 20–30 video clips per day on YouTube
- 29 rights-holding broadcasters
- 160 territories broadcast YOG on TV
- 4,400,000 video views on www.youtholympicgames.org
- 341,773 unique visitors to www.youtholympicgames.org and 799,038 *peak* unique visitors
- 6,300,000 video views on YOG YouTube channel
- 247 million TV viewers
- 19,100,000 page views of the Singapore 2010 web site
- 530 articles published
- 5,982 Twitter updates and 4,042 tweets
- 14,488 Flickr image uploads and 2,898,384 views
- 82,745 Likes Facebook updates
- 64,050 blog entries

2012 Summer Olympics in London Expectations

The London organizers anticipate a continuation and expansion of the multiplatform media approach that has been evolving since 2000. More than 20,000 press and media are expected to participate, and in excess of 9 million tickets are going to be sold. Additional information about London's marketing and new media is discussed briefly elsewhere in this book, to the extent that advanced information about marketing and new media was available and relevant.

Other data shows that fans from the United Kingdom and Spain have increased their interest in new media for getting their Olympic news, using their mobile phones as one of the key media platforms. The same is true for American fans. New media has fast become an essential choice for fans seeking Olympics coverage.[25] In effect, Olympics fans are staying more consistently connected to their news, whether watching on TV or while in transition, using their mobile devices to keep them up-to-date in real time. These statistics from the Olympics in Beijing, Vancouver, Singapore, and London and from the Nielsen surveys are a proverbial gold mine for TOP sponsors and sports marketers seeking to profile their target audiences and tailor their sponsorship programs accordingly.

The IOC, too, has increased its promotional usage of social media and integrated marketing to good effect. Each year on June 23, the IOC promotes a daylong celebration called Olympic Day, the anniversary of the founding of the modern Olympics, encouraging people around the world to participate in sports or fitness. For the 2011 Olympic Day, the IOC used Facebook, Twitter, and YouTube to spread the word about the day and encourage people to share stories, videos, photos, and text messages of their favorite sports memories. To prepare for Olympic Day 2011, the IOC started using a cross-platform digital strategy at the beginning of June, including overhauling its main web site. The new web site provided a global map showing where Olympic Day sports activities were occurring in different locations around the world. Contests were held on Twitter, Facebook, and YouTube asking fans to describe their sports activity for that day. Those who participated in the Twitter contests were eligible for a complimentary trip to the 2012 London Olympic Games, and Facebook contestants could win a trip to Lausanne, headquarters of the IOC, and the Olympic Museum. You-Tube contestants were eligible to win a trip to the 2012 Winter Youth Olympic Games in Innsbruck, Austria. The IOC has more than 4 million fans on Facebook and 110,000 Twitter followers, and the IOC web site had more than 7 million visits. Commenting on the IOC's social media strategy, IOC President Jacques Rogge said,

> Through our digital platforms, the IOC wants to reach out to young people using their own language and channels of communication. I am thrilled to see how many people are embracing the spirit of Olympic Day and sharing their sporting moments with us. This is what the IOC has always strived to achieve: to get people active regardless of their age, gender or athletic ability. Thanks to our initiatives in social media, we are reaching out to an even greater number of people around the world and spreading the values of sport.[26]

For sports sponsors, knowing that a large number of customers are using online media for reasons of trust should inspire thinking and planning on how to use these social media tools to connect to these customers.

Questions

1. Given the shifting demographics of the world's sports population, what should TOP sponsors do with their marketing communications to effectively attract youth?

2. What controls would you recommend, if any, to ensure that TOP sponsors are able to maintain message consistency over multiple marketing platforms (traditional and new media), yet convey authenticity?

3. Pick one of the TOP sponsors discussed earlier in this book and develop a marketing communications strategy for them for London 2012. What will you do to ensure your marketing choices are consistent with the company's target audience and brand reputation?

4. Discuss differences you foresee with respect to marketing communications strategies for TOP sponsors in London 2012, compared to Beijing 2008.

5. The IOC's Olympic Day celebration is embracing new media. Can the IOC do more to improve its use of new media, plus expand its marketing and attract global fan support, yet not risk overly commercializing the Olympics? What would you recommend?

Chapter 21

The Olympic Sponsorship Checklist

Your Company's Competitive Fitness

The audit questions at the end of Sections I through IV are a highly recommended starting point for assessing your company's competitive fitness. It may seem like a lot of work, and it is. But so is the preparation and work an Olympian does before competing in the Games, let alone winning a medal, as is the effort the TOP sponsors put in to create a successful sponsorship. As described within this book, successful sponsorships are multipart, multiyear commitments. Only a few organizations end up putting in the rigor required to succeed. But for those that do, the rewards can be substantial.

Sports Sponsorship Checklist

Three areas should be on every company's sports sponsorship checklist:

1. Objectives
2. Deliverables
3. Postevent Evaluation

1. Objectives   Management must ask itself why it wants to sponsor a sports event, whether the Olympics or otherwise. Answering this question will begin the process of identifying what are sensible and practical objectives to set forth for guiding the sponsorship. These will vary according to each company's individual needs, but may include:

- Revive, renew, or enhance company reputation.
  Sports events are visible, and established ones like the Olympics have the potential to cast a favorable glow over the sponsoring company.
- Grow awareness.
  Awareness includes recall (can the company be named without prompting?) and recognition (is the company remembered once a respondent is prompted?).
- Improve sales.
  Sales can be measured in units or dollars and are frequently an objective. The challenge is tying long-term sponsorship efforts to short-term sales expectations. It may be better to measure sales over the long term unless a specific offer is made during the sponsorship event.
- Convert new customers.
  Awareness helps attract customers, so a logical objective would be converting the newly aware to actual customers.
- Reinforce company personality.
  Consumers connect to companies that exhibit a human face. Use the sponsorship to foster a more genuine, likable company image.
- Expand social responsibility efforts.
  Help the public see a different side of the company by demonstrating community involvement, society-building, and/or environmental programs.
- Inspire employees.
  Successful brand building requires a strong internal organization that rallies behind and supports company objectives. A sports sponsorship

is a fun and engaging way to increase employee interest and involvement in the company.

- Distinguish from competitors.
  Associating with a major sports event creates a visible and memorable distinction from competitors.
- Become part of the social milieu
  Social media is how an increasing majority of people around the world are getting their information, developing social networks, and generally talking about topics of the moment. To be a meaningful part of this social universe means social media users have to believe in you. If they do, your company's (or your company's products) stand a better chance of being seen as authentic, and not pretenders.

2. Deliverables   Exhibit 21.1 will help companies identify deliverables they should consider as they investigate and negotiate their sponsorship contract. There are many other possible benefits a sponsor may seek, but Exhibit 21.1 provides a useful starting point.

Exhibit 21.1   Sports Sponsorship Deliverables[1]

Pre-Event Deliverables

- Access and usage of event images and trademarks
- Publicity support by event management
- Detailed event and venue guidelines for signage and other sponsorship exposure vehicles

Event Day and Related Deliverables

- Tickets/tickets in preferred zones
- Hospitality suites/facilities
- Access to off-limit areas
- Access to event management, support, and logistics

Association Type Deliverables

- Name association recognition—"official sponsor"
- Sport association recognition

Athlete/Team/Facility Deliverables

- Athlete appearance deliverables
- Athlete endorsement deliverables

(Continued)

- Athlete association recognition
- Confidence that the event will ensure a high-quality, high-integrity event

Visual Image Deliverables
- At event site
- At event surroundings
- On direct transmission of event
- On replays of events
- Use in advertisements and promotions

- Athlete image deliverables
- Use of facilities for corporate events

Ambush Marketing Protection
- Aggressive stance against ambushers

Postevent Deliverables
- Review and audit with event management
- Preparation for next event/stage in relationship

3. Postevent Evaluation The pre-event objectives serve as the guide for setting detailed performance goals. Each of the objectives is reviewed, along with the more specific tactical programs that were deployed in support of the sponsorship. Actual results compared to projected results should be closely reviewed to see what lessons can be learned. Aside from reviewing pre-event objectives, additional measures might include:

- Marketing communications effectiveness
  This includes all media used, comparing media placement metrics with actuals. Surveys of consumer feedback will supplement this review.
- Market share (a longer-term measure)
  One-time sponsorships are not likely to create market share gains, but sustained sponsorships, such as the TOP sponsors, can track changes over time.
- Brand value (a longer-term measure)
  Similar to market share, appreciable changes are more likely to occur over time than overnight. Determining if the sponsorship is the sole driver of brand value changes is less likely to be confirmed, but part of the entire sponsorship effort discussed in this book is a microcosm of ongoing corporate brand-building activities anyway, so a well-run sponsorship may noticeably accelerate brand value changes.

Chapter 22

The Olympic
Sponsorship Lessons

Benefits to Olympic Sponsors and
Non-Olympic Sports Sponsors

Respect and Honor Traditions

The 2,700-year review of Olympic highlights that started this book is intended to show the enormous diversity of influences that shaped the traditions we now commonly associate with the Olympics. While other sports do not have thousands of years of history, most have rich traditions that have carried on for decades, inspiring generations of fans. Understanding the traditions will help companies develop a sponsorship plan that does not violate society's understanding of the sport and its deeper meaning. Athletes pursue the Olympics because they love what being an Olympian means and what it might confer on them.

Seek Common Values

Every organization stands for something far beyond making money. Each athlete has a personal code of conduct and a set of values by which to live. Identifying and knowing core values of both the company and the sports event will help avoid artificial or forced matchups.

Self-Assess

As athletes become more successful, they specialize. Over time, they have built a skill set and expertise in their event. Business schools teach the virtues of developing a recognized expertise and a set of skills and competencies to support it. Knowing what you are good at doing will assist the process of identifying sports sponsorship opportunities that offer the best potential. Tobacco companies, for example, would have a hard time developing a convincing sponsorship plan if they were to sponsor the Olympics. While they may share a few values in common, such as desire to be the best, their expertise would be in contradiction to that of the Olympics.

Focus on Strategic Benefits

The long term is important. Short-term sales and profits can be increased but are often temporary in the absence of a guiding set of objectives that provide a sense of direction. An athlete looks at long-term goals, such as winning a gold medal, and keeps that objective foremost in mind, where it serves as inspiration. Looking at a sponsorship as a strategic investment in the growth and development of the firm's value ensures that the sponsorship is supported and viewed seriously, rather than as a one-time expendable tactic. Adjustments can and should be made, as was shown with the TOP sponsors—all made changes in their event-specific marketing programs as they learned more about which activities worked best—but they should be made in the context of moving toward the long-term objective.

Develop a Pre-, During, and Postevent Activation Plan Outlining Tactical Implementation

This is where daily accountability is rooted. Long-term strategy is realized when short-term tactics are executed effectively. Mistakes will be made, but successes must outweigh failures for a strategy to work. Athletes know that aiming for a gold medal does not make it happen. They have to train rigorously, vary their preparation, compete against the very best along the way, and perform in different locations and challenging conditions, all in an effort to achieve their strategic goals. The athlete's daily training routine is the equivalent of a company's sponsorship marketing tactics: Individually, each activity strengthens a different part of the athlete or company; collectively, the tactics add up to a systematic approach for achieving the objectives. This is where many managers and marketers get into trouble. Successful planning requires not just descriptions of what is to be done, but assigning responsibility, setting deadlines and accompanying deliverables, establishing measures of success, preparing options if and when programs need adjusting, and aligning the individual tactics in a way that ensures they are all moving in the same direction. Managers must own their piece of the plan, and teammates must be accountable to each other and to the company's overall objectives. Reviews of the plans at predetermined stages must occur if accountability is to be realized and final results *owned*.

Be Flexible, but Don't Compromise Core Principles

Every plan faces risks, challenges, and possible disappointments. Planning a risk- or failure-free event may be politically attractive, but it is impractical, if not impossible. Instead, the options mentioned previously may be put to use here. Alternatively, and more likely, the hundreds and thousands of judgment calls made every day will determine success. The only rule of thumb is a simple one: If it is illegal, unethical, immoral, or simply against the organization's normal principles, then don't do it—no matter how attractive the short-term benefits might be. Athletes know there are no compromises or shortcuts that can be made to achieve their ambitions. When compromises are made, then the long-term dream suffers, such as from using performance-enhancing substances, or may even be irreparably damaged, as happened to the U.S. sprinter Marion Jones. The Olympics have a formidable reputation because, fundamentally, its caretakers over time have kept Olympic ideals at the forefront of their decisions and the Olympic movement. When crises occur, the collective strength of the Olympic movement and the support of public opinion simply won't let the Olympics be compromised. You know you have a strong brand when your own customers, your fans, help keep you focused on the ideals for which you stand.

Commit to Excellence

Sports sponsorships are unlikely to fail when organizations and responsible people within them commit overtly and privately to excellence. There is a simple choice each one of us faces every day, as do, more broadly, our organizations: You can choose to be world class. Or not. Success comes when people dedicate themselves to being world class. Just ask any Olympic athlete.

Questions

1. Review and compare the Olympics to other megasports events (choose one or two of the following: World Cup, F1, Rugby World Cup, Cricket World Cup, UEFA Champions League, EPL Football, Super Bowl, World Series, America's Cup, NBA Championships, Stanley Cup, Tennis' Grand Slam, Golf's Four Majors).
   a. How important is the event's history to its current success? Justify.
   b. What are the event's most important qualities and characteristics. List and explain why.
   c. How is their revenue model structured (sponsorships, ticketing)?
   d. How has the event changed over the past 20 to 30 years? Discuss.
   e. Are sponsors doing anything differently than Olympics sponsors? What are those differences?
   f. Describe their fan profile. What characteristics do they share with Olympics fans? Where do they differ? What do sponsors see as appealing about this fan base?

Chapter 23

Section V Sponsorship Preparation Questions

The questions throughout this book are designed to stimulate and provoke sponsorship thinking and evaluation. Before embarking on a sponsorship agreement, prospective sponsors should begin at the beginning and ask a few very simple questions, as outlined here. The answers should guide toward either additional analysis or agreement that the sponsorship should not be pursued. Sports sponsorships, particularly Olympic TOP sponsorships, involve substantial commitments in time, money, resources, planning, execution, and follow-up.

Questions

Purpose
1. Why is the sponsorship attractive?
2. What purpose does it serve?

3. What benefits are possible?

4. What risks are there?

5. How committed is the organization?

Fans

1. What segments are you targeting?
  a. What do the fans have in common?
2. What do you know about them?
  a. What are their needs?
  b. Your market share?
  c. Their contribution to revenues/profits?
  d. Does the segment match our ability to deliver?
3. Have you evaluated each fan target and scored/rated them?

Creative Execution

1. Is your message clear?
  a. Is it designed to be funny/memorable/professional/instructional/ other?
2. Is your message succinct?
  a. Can you describe it in a few words or seconds?
3. Is it relevant to the needs of the target customers?
  a. How do you know?
4. Does it resonate with them?
  a. How do you know?
5. Is the message distinctive?
  a. Is the distinction recognized by customers?
6. Is it simple?
  a. Do people get it?
7. What images/imagery do you want associated with the message and your company (follow the previous relevance/resonance/distinctiveness guidelines)?
8. What logos and trademarks will be used?
  a. How will they be used?
  b. Are they following corporate guidelines?
9. Mascots and merchandise
  a. Will you be using either or both?
  b. What is the purpose of the mascot in your specific situation?
    i. Will it enhance or help your sponsorship plan?

    c. How is the merchandise plan being handled?
- i. Design
- ii. Vendors
- iii. Quantities
- iv. Quality
- v. Price
- vi. Distribution

10. What are the equivalent answers to these questions for the event and for other sponsors?

    a. Are you comfortable with how these activities and plans are unfolding (as far as you known them)?

Traditional and New Media Marketing

1. What is your mix of traditional and new media marketing?

    a. How will they be deployed?

    b. Who is in charge of media planning and purchase decisions?

    c. Is there a media insertion schedule?
- i. Who is responsible for it?
- ii. Who monitors the execution?

    d. Do you have digital media expertise in-house, or do you need to source for it?

    e. Are all logos and trademarks designed in appropriate formats for use in all media?

    f. Is your corporate and/or product image being properly conveyed?

2. Are your various marketing media integrated?

    a. Who oversees and coordinates this effort?

3. What are your contingency plans if a media provider does not deliver?

4. What is your perception of the event's equivalent marketing efforts?

    a. Are you confident the event can deliver a great overall message in support of the sport?

Final Word

While this book was written in a specific sequence to provide a proper contextual backdrop for evaluating sports sponsorship opportunities, the audit questions at the end of each part may ultimately be addressed in a different order. The questions in this book are not exhaustive, and you will undoubtedly create your own list. Obviously, it is important to know your target customers as you plan, so the questions you ask and the data you receive may come earlier in the planning process. Perfect planning, with all information known up front and all potential problems addressed before they start, is not a reasonable expectation. Such analysis-paralysis thinking will miss any marketing opportunity. The most important point is to *keep asking questions* as you go through the sponsorship planning and execution process. Remember, since it is a sports event you will be sponsoring, part of sponsorship success is understanding fans, so be a fan of the event being sponsored, and of your own effort to make the sponsorship successful.

About the Companion Web Site

The companion web site for this book can be found at www .wiley.com/go/olympiceffect. This site contains two additional sponsorship case studies from the original edition of the book but not included in the second edition because the two companies, Lenovo and John Hancock, ended their Olympic sponsorship after the 2008 Beijing Olympics. However, both case studies contain updated data that came out after the first book and remain useful examinations of Olympic Games sponsorship planning and results.

The two case studies are:

1. Case study about Lenovo's TOP sponsorship for the Summer and Winter Olympic Games from 2004 to 2008.
2. Case study about John Hancock's TOP sponsorship for the Summer and Winter Olympic Games from 1993 to 2008.

Notes

Introduction

1. IOC web site: www.olympic.org/sponsorship.
2. Burt Helm, "An Olympic PR Challenge," *BusinessWeek,* June 21, 2007: www
   .businessweek.com/globalbiz/content/jun2007/gb20070621_511854.htm.
3. IOC web site: www.olympic.org/sponsorship.
4. Olympic Marketing Fact File, 2011 Edition, pp. 20–28: www.olympic.org.
5. NPD, "NPD Releases Global Sports Market Estimate 2010," August 3, 2010:
   www.prweb.com/releases/NPD/Global-Sports-Estimate/prweb4343944
   .htm; and Trevor Slack, *The Commercialization of Sport* (London: Frank Cass,
   2003).

Chapter 1   The Olympic Dream

1. "Vancouver 2010 Olympic Winter Games," *Canada Post,* January 12, 2010:
   www.canadapost.ca/cpo/mc/personal/collecting/stamps/2010/2010_Olympic_
   Winter_Games.jsf; and Eric Blais, "Quebec and 2010," *Marketing Magazine,*
   112, no. 21 (2007).
2. George Foster and Victoria Chang, *Visa Sponsorship Marketing.* Case: SPM-5,
   p. 5. Stanford University Graduate School of Business ©2003.
3. David Cushnan, "Vancouver 2010: An Olympic Investment," *SportsPro online,*
   February 16, 2010: www.sportspromedia.com/notes_and_insights/vancouver_
   2010_an_olympic_investment/.

4. Clare Ogilvie, "Sponsors Spend Millions to Be Part of 2010 Games," *Vancouver Province*, August 27, 2008: www.canada.com/story_print.html?id=fcae10e1-86a2-4850-958e-1223fe6b65db&sponsor=.

5. "The Ancient Athlete: Amateur or Professional?" Tufts University, Perseus Data Base: www.perseus.tufts.edu/hopper/text?doc=Perseus%3Atext%3A1999.01.0162&redirect=true.

6. Tom Kuntz, "The Guy Who Ate a Cow and Other Olympic Stars," *New York Times*, July 14, 1996: www.nytimes.com/specials/olympics/cntdown/0714oly-review.html.

7. J. W. Cohoon, trans., *Dio Chrysostom, I, Discourses 1–11, Dio Chrysostom* (Cambridge, MA: Loeb Classical Library, Harvard University Press, 1932): www.hup.harvard.edu/catalog/L257.html.

8. Robin Fowler, "Pherenike the Trainer": ancienthistory.suite101.com/article.cfm/pherenike_the_trainer.

9. Donald G. Klye, "Winning at Olympia," *Archaeology*, April 6, 2004: www.archaeology.org/online/features/olympics/olympia.html.

10. Joseph B. Verrengia, "The Ancient Olympics Had Its Own Scandals," July 28, 2004: www.cnbc.com/id/5467740/Ancient_Olympics_had_its_own_scandals.

11. University of Pennsylvania Museum of Archaeology and Anthropology, "The Athletes: Amateurs or Pros?": www.penn.museum/sites/olympics/olympicathletes.shtml.

12. David C. Young, "Imagine That! Olympic Games in Greece!" speech at Columbia University: www.greekembassy.org/Embassy/content/en/Article.aspx?office=1&folder=30&article=11574&hilite=David%20Young.

Chapter 2   The Olympic Experience

1. Sophie Hardach, "Weightlifting—Grieving Steiner Wins Gold," Reuters, August 19, 2008: http://in.reuters.com/article/2008/08/19/idINIndia-35083120080819.

2. David Wallechinsky and Jaime Loucky, *The Complete Book of the Winter Olympics Turin 2006 Edition* (Toronto: Sports Media Publishing, 2006), 3–10.

3. Ibid.

4. Official web site of the Olympic Movement (n.d.): www.olympic.org/uk/games/pastindex_uk.asp?OLGT=2&OLGY=2006.

5. Kasef Majid, Ramdas Chandra, and Annamma Joy, "Exploring the Growing Interest in the Olympic Winter Games." *Sport Marketing Quarterly* 16, no. 1 (2007): 30.

6. John A. Davis, *Competitive Success—How Branding Adds Value* (Singapore: John Wiley & Sons (Asia), Pte, Ltd., 2010), 15.

7. Majid, Chandra, and Joy, "Exploring the Growing Interest in the Olympic Winter Games."

8. Barry Smart, "Not Playing Around: Global Capitalism, Modern Sport and Consumer Culture," in *Globalization and Sport*, ed. Richard Giulianotti and Roland Robertson (Oxford: Wiley-Blackwell, 2007), 10.

9. Conrado Durantez Corral, *Pierre De Coubertin, The Olympic Humanist* (Lousanne: The IOC and the International Pierre De Coubertin Committee, 1994), 65.

10. Carl Diem Institute, ed., *Pierre De Coubertin, The Olympic Idea* (Karl Hofman Verlag, 1967), 100.

11. Majid, Chandra, and Joy, "Exploring the Growing Interest in the Olympic Winter Games."

12. Ibid.

13. Majid, Chandra, and Joy, "Exploring the Growing Interest in the Olympic Winter Games."

14. Barry Smart, "Not Playing Around," 10.

15. IOC web site: www.olympic.org/uk/athletes/profiles/bio_uk.asp?PAR_I_ID=43395, supplemented by http://news.bbc.co.uk/sport2/hi/olympics 2000/bbc_team/859595.stm, www.timesonline.co.uk/tol/sport/article537461 .ece, and www.independent.co.uk/news/people/sebastian-coe-you-ask-the-questions-556162.html.

16. David C. Young, "With Hands or Swift Feet—The Ancient Greek City-States Were Rarely as United as They Were at the Olympic Games," *Natural History Magazine* 113, no. 6 (July/August 2004): 24–30.

17. "The Ancient Athlete: Amateur or Professional?" Tufts University, Perseus Data Base: www.perseus.tufts.edu/olympics/amat.html.

18. Young, "With Hands or Swift Feet."

19. Walter Woodburn Hyde, "Greek Literary Notices of Olympic Victor Monuments outside Olympia," in *Transactions and Proceedings of the American Philological Association* 42 (1911): 53–67: www.jstor.org/stable/282573.

20. Michael B. Poliakoff, "Melankomas, ek klimakos, and Greek Boxing," *American Journal of Philology* 108, no. 3 (Autumn, 1987): 511–518: www.jstor .org/pss/294676v.

21. George E. Mylonas, "The Bronze Statue from Artemision," *American Journal of Archaeology* 48, no. 2 (April–June, 1944): 143–160: www.jstor.org/pss/ 499921.

22. T. F. Carney, "Content Analysis and Classical Scholarship," *Journal of Hellenic Studies* 88 (1968): 137–138: http://uolibraries.worldcat.org/title/content-analysis-and-classical-scholarship/oclc/486654087&referer=brief_results.

23. "America's Shame—Review of *Heroes without a Country: America's Betrayal of Joe Louis and Jesse Owens* by Donald McRae," *Journal of Blacks in Higher Education*, no. 45 (Autumn, 2004): 125: www.jstor.org/stable/4133637.

24. Frank Litsky, "Bob Mathias, 75, Decathlete and Politician, Dies," *New York Times*, September 3, 2006: www.nytimes.com/2006/09/03/sports/othersports/03mathias.html.

25. Larry Schwartz, "Boy-Wonder Mathias Elevated Decathlon," *espn.com*: www.espn.go.com/sportscentury/features/00016202.html.

26. IOC web site: www.olympic.org/jean-claude-killy.

27. IOC web site: www.olympic.org/nadia-comaneci; Toby Miller, "Competing Allegories: An Introduction," Social Text No. 50, *The Politics of Sport* (Spring 1997): 1: http:jss.sagepub.com/content/23/2/126.abstract; and bartandnadia.com/.

28. IOC web site: www.olympic.org/sebastian-coe, supplemented by news.bbc.co.uk/sport2/hi/olympics2000/bbc_team/859595.stm, www.timesonline.co.uk/tol/sport/article537461.ece, and www.independent.co.uk/news/people/sebastian-coe-you-ask-the-questions-556162.html.

29. www.olympic.org/earvin-johnson; www.olympic.org/michael-jordan; and www.nba.com/history/dreamT_moments.html.

30. www.olympic.org/katarina-witt; www.katarina-witt.de/.

31. www.olympic.org/uk/athletes/profiles/bio_uk.asp?PAR_I_ID=20272; www.facebook.com/michaelphelps?sk=info; and www.michaelphelpsfoundation.org/about1.php.

Chapter 3 The Olympic Dynamics

1. NBC Sports, "Qatar Lures Athletes with Citizenship, Cash—Country Importing Athletes to Help Win Medals at Asian Games," December 8, 2006: nbcsports.msnbc.com/id/16113525/.

2. Chris Isidore, "Time to Pay Olympic Winners: U.S. Medal Winners Get Prize Money, but Most Olympians Are True Amateurs Who Get Nothing for a Win," August 20, 2004: money.cnn.com/2004/08/19/commentary/column_sportsbiz/sportsbiz/index.htm.

3. Jeff Lee and Gary Kingston, "Win Medals, Earn \$\$\$; Canada Joins Other Countries with 'Money for Medals' Policy for Olympic Winners," CanWest News, November 20, 2007; and Mark Brennae and Meagan Fitzpatrick, "Canadian Athletes to Get Cash for Olympic Success," CanWest News, November 19, 2007: www.canada.com/globaltv/national/story.html?id=2a36c58a-ac62-4815-8d56-d815d71d9843&k=69958.

4. David Williams, ". . . But Golden Wonders of China Will Be Set Up for Life," *Daily Mail*, August 13, 2008; BBC Sports, "Russian Winners Promised Windfall," July 12, 2000: news.bbc.co.uk/sport2/hi/athletics/830528.stm.

5. "Sport Minister: Amount of Bonuses for Olympic Champions," *Ukraine Business Daily*, February 3, 2010; BBC Sports, "Russian Winners Promised Windfall."

6. "Comaneci No Longer Inspires Romanian Gymnasts," *ChinaDaily*, March 27, 2008: www.chinadaily.com.cn/sports/2008-03/27/content_6569757.htm.

7. Singapore National Olympic Council, "Multi-Million Dollar Awards Program": www.snoc.org.sg/mmdap.htm; Williams, "But Golden Wonders of China."

8. "JAAF Offers Rewards for Medal Winners," *Japan Times*, June 15, 2004: search.japantimes.co.jp/cgi-bin/so20040615a1.html.

9. Williams, "But Golden Wonders of China."

10. Scott Taylor, "Slow Swimmer a Crowd Favorite," *Deseret News*, September 20, 2000: www.deseretnews.com/article/195015385/Slow-swimmer-a-crowd-favorite.html.

11. Mark Baker, "Olympics 2004: For Some Athletes, behind the Medals Lies Real Gold," RadioFreeEurope/RadioLiberty, August 6, 2004: www.rferl.org/content/article/1054208.html.

12. Williams, "But Golden Wonders of China."

13. Ibid.

14. "UAE to Offer Cash Rewards to Medalists at Beijing Olympics," Xinhua General News Service, July 30, 2008.

15. Dipesh Gahder, "Beijing Olympics: Athletes to Get an Alfa with Their Medals," *Sunday Times*, August 13, 2008: www.timesonline.co.uk/tol/sport/olympics/article4449540.ece.

16. William J. Kole, "Olympics: The Spoils of Victory; Athletes Cash in on Olympics," *Herald-Sun* (Durham, NC), August 19, 2004: findarticles.com/p/news-articles/columbian-vancouver-wash/mi_8100/is_20040819/olympics-spoils-victory-athletes-cash/ai_n51291814/.

17. Biathlon World web site: www.biathlonworld.com/en/press_releases.html/do/detail?presse=1334; http://translate.google.com/translate?hl=en&sl=de&u=http://www.michael-greis.de/&sa=X&oi=translate&resnum=1&ct=result&prev=/search%3Fq%3Dmichael%2Bgreis%26hl%3Den.

18. www.olympic.org/uk/athletes/profiles/bio_uk.asp?PAR_I_ID=20272; www.facebook.com/michaelphelps?sk=info; www.michaelphelpsfoundation.org/about1.php; John Henderson, "Phelps Ready to Strike More Gold," *Denver Post*, April 12, 2008: www.denverpost.com/sports/ci_8907515.

19. Jonathan Tait, "Shaun White Unveils Major Sponsorship Deal," *SportsPro*, August 17, 2011; Tom Love, "Shaun White Endorses Chewing Gum Brand Stride," *SportsPro*, March 8, 2011; ABCNews, "Olympic Endorsements: Who Will Cash In?" March 1, 2010: abcnews.go.com/Business/olympic-endorsements-cash/story?id=9961545.

20. ABCNews, "Olympic Endorsements"; BusinessWire, "Peyton Manning Tops Bloomberg Businessweek.com's Power 100 Ranking of the Most Powerful Athletes in Sports," January 27, 2011: images.businessweek.com/slideshows/20110124/power-100-2011/; Tom Love, "The World's 42nd Most Marketable Athlete—Lindsey Vonn," *SportsPro*, May 18, 2011: www.sportspro media.com/notes_and_insights/the_worlds_42nd_most_marketable_athlete_-_lindsey_vonn/.

21. "Usain Bolt Signs New US$20 million Deal with Puma . . . Bolting to Bank," *Urban Islandz*, August 24, 2010: http://urbanislandz.com/2010/08/24/usain-bolt-signs-new-us20-million-deal-with-puma-bolting-to-the-bank/; Tom Love, "The World's Most Marketable Athlete—Usain Bolt," *SportsPro*, May 27, 2011: www.sportspromedia.com/notes_and_insights/the_worlds_most_marketable_athlete_-_usain_bolt/; "Usain Bolt's Net Worth 2011": www.filipinoster.com/sports/usain-bolt-net-worth/.

22. IOC Charter, "Programme of the Olympic Games," 80–83: www.olympic .org/Documents/olympic_charter_en.pdf.

23. IOC web site: www.olympic.org/Documents/Commissions_PDFfiles/Programme_commission/INFO_New_sports_sochi.pdf; "New Events for the 2014 Olympic Winter Games in Sochi," *BBCSport*, July 8, 2005: http://news .bbc.co.uk/sport2/hi/other_sports/olympics_2012/4658925.stm; IOC web site: www.olympic.org/uk/games/index_uk.asp; "IOC Approves New Sports for Beijing Olympics," *CBCSports*, October 27, 2005: www.cbc.ca/sports/story/2005/10/27/iocmeetings051027.html.

24. IOC web site, "Youth Olympic Games": www.olympic.org/yog-presentation.

Chapter 4   The Olympic Host Cities

1. David Gilman Romano, "The Politics of the Olympic Games," from *The Real Story of the Ancient Olympic Games:* www.penn.museum/sites/olympics/olympicpolitics.shtml.

2. Frank J. Nisetich, "Olympian 1.8–11: An Epinician Metaphor," *Harvard Studies in Classical Philology* 79 (1975): 55–68: www.jstor.org/pss/311128; "Are Today's Olympians Too Commercial? Depends," from *The Real Story of the Ancient Olympic Games*: www.penn.museum/sites/olympics/olympic commercialism.shtml.

3. Rick Burton, "Olympic Games Host City Marketing: An Exploration of Expectations and Outcomes," *Sport Marketing Quarterly* 12, no. 1 (2003): 37–47; IOC web site, "117th IOC Session Candidate Procedure for the 2012 Olympic Games": www.olympic.org/Documents/Reference_documents_Factsheets/2012_Olympic_Games_Bid_Procedure_QRef_june2010.pdf.

4. IOC web site: www.olympic.org/olympic-games.

5. Ibid.

6. Martin Wolk, "Games Hold Allure for Would-Be Host Cities," *MSNBC News Headlines*, August 30, 2004: www.mail-archive.com/dailynews@lists .msnbc.com/msg00616.html.

7. Jeffrey Owens, "The Economic Significance of the Beijing Olympic Games": www.youtube.com/watch?v=gDmUqLuNc2Y.

8. G. Andranovich, M. Burbank, and C. Heying, "Olympic Cities: Lessons Learned from Mega-Event Politics," *Journal of Urban Affairs* 23, no. 2 (2001): 124: www.blackwellpublishing.com/content/BPL_Images/Journal_Samples/ JUAF0735-2166 ~ 23 ~ 2 ~ 079%5C079.pdf.

9. Liu Jie, "No Worries to Post-Olympic Slowdown," *China Daily*, April 14, 2008: www.china.org.cn/business/news/2008-04/14/content_14949930.htm. The article did not indicate which host countries did not experience a post-Olympics slowdown.

10. The data of Beijing 2007 and 2008 come from *China Statistical Yearbook* 2009; the 2009 data are from the 2009 *Statistics Bulletin of the National Economic and Social Development;* and Liuqian Huang, "Research on Effect of Beijing Post-Olympic Sports Industry to China's Economic Development Energy," *Energy Procedia* 5 (2011): 2097–2102: www.sciencedirect.com/science/article/pii/ S1876610211012987.

11. Y. Fan, "Branding the Nation: What Is Being Branded?" *Journal of Vacation Marketing* 12, no. 1 (2006): 9–10: jvm.sagepub.com/content/12/1/5.short? rss=1&ssource=mfc.

12. Heather Timmons, "Corporate Sponsors Nervous as Tibet Protest Groups Shadow Olympic Torch's Run," *New York Times*, March 29, 2008: www .nytimes.com/2008/03/29/business/worldbusiness/29torch.html.

13. IOC web site: www.olympic.org/uk/games/index_uk.asp.

14. "Beijing Officials Say Air Quality Improved during Trial Olympic Traffic Ban," *International Herald Tribune*, August 21, 2007: www.nytimes.com/2008/ 07/09/sports/olympics/09beijing.html?scp=1&sq=Beijing%20officials%20say %20air%20quality%20improved%20during%20trial%20Olympic%20traffic% 20ban&st=cse&gwh=8520C202140A64E2DDAD1981036C9871.

15. Anita Elberse, Catherine Anthony, and Joshua Callahan, "The Vancouver 2010 Olympics," Case 9-507-049, p. 16. Revised October 5, 2007. Harvard Business School. ©2007 President and Fellows of Harvard College. Originally adapted from IOC reports and Holger Preuss, "The Economics of Staging the Olympics," 2004. The 1980 Games in Moscow are excluded for lack of data.

16. Ibid., 12.

17. Ibid.

18. Oriol Nel-lo, "The Olympic Games as a tool for Urban Renewal: The Experience of Barcelona '92 Olympic Village," in *Olympic Villages: A Hundred Years of Urban Planning and Shared Experiences: International Symposium on Olympic Villages, Lausanna 1996*, ed. Miquel de Moragas Spá and Miquel Botella, 2–9 (Lausanne: International Olympic Committee, 1997); Jennifer Baliko, "Turin's Turnaround Olympic Games Spark an Industrial City's Makeover," *Daily Herald*, December 5, 2005: http://goliath.ecnext.com/coms2/gi_0199-5070752/Turin-s-turnaround-Olympic-Games.html.

19. Ferran Brunet, "An Economic Analysis of the Barcelona '92 Olympic Games: Resources, Financing and Impacts." In *The Keys of Success: The Social, Sporting, Economic and Communications Impact of Barcelona '92*, ed. Miquel de Moragas Spá and Miquel Botella, 10 (Bellaterra: Servei de Publicacions de la Universitat Autonoma de Barcelona, 1995).

20. Frank C. Zarnowski, "A Look at Olympic Costs," *Journal of Olympic History* 1, no. 1 (1993): 16–26: www.la84foundation.org/SportsLibrary/JOH/JOHv1n1/JOHv1n1f.pdf.

21. Brunet, "An Economic Analysis of the Barcelona '92 Olympic Games," 10.

22. Ibid., 13. Brunet noted the table was supplemented with additional data from the IOC, the SOOC, and the COOB'92.

23. Burton, "Olympic Games Host City Marketing"; IOC, Auditor-General's 2002 Report to Australian Parliament, vol. Two.

24. *Games of the XXI Olympiad Montréal 1976 Official Report*, 54–62: http://olympic-museum.de/o-reports/report1976.htm; "Olympic Games May Be Close to Being Buried," *Peterborough Examiner*: www.peterboroughexaminer.com/PrintArticle.aspx?e=993090; Michel Gar, "Legacy of the Olympic Games in Montreal: An Introduction," April 27, 1996: www.montrealolympics.com/mg_legacy.php.

25. Brunet, "An Economic Analysis of the Barcelona '92 Olympic Games," 11; Lance Morrow, "Feeling Proud Again," *Time*, January 7, 1985: www.time.com/time/magazine/article/0,9171,956226,00.html.

26. Alan Riding, "Rivalry in '92 Barcelona Olympics Starts Early," *New York Times*, September 26, 1989: http://query.nytimes.com/gst/fullpage.html?res=950DE4D71F3DF935A1575AC0A96F948260.

27. "Olympics: A Pre-Olympic Gold Drain as Budget Surplus Dwindles," *New York Times*, January 25, 1994: http://query.nytimes.com/gst/fullpage.html?res=9405E6D71130F936A15752C0A962958260.

28. Jere Longman, "Atlanta Games, a Celebration for 197 Nations, Close," *New York Times*, August 5, 1996: http://query.nytimes.com/gst/fullpage.html?res=9B0DEED81E3FF936A3575BC0A960958260&sec=&spon=&pagewanted=all.

29. Jere Longman, "Olympics: Nagano 1998; Cold Shoulder Turns into Warm Embrace," *New York Times*, February 6, 1998: http://query.nytimes.com/gst/fullpage.html?res=9B0DE2D8123DF935A35751C0A96E958260.

30. David Armstrong, "Reinventing the Rings—Sydney Olympics Depends Less on Commercial Sponsorship, More On Responsible Financing." *Sydney Examiner*, January 10, 1998: http://olympics.ballparks.com/2000Sydney/index.htm; Mark Landler, "Sydney 2000; Sydney Anticipates Long-Term Boon," *New York Times*, October 3, 2000: http://query.nytimes.com/gst/fullpage.html?res=950CE2DD133DF930A35753C1A9669C8B63.

31. Winter Olympics 2010 presentation. Slide 6. authorstream.com: www.authorstream.com/presentation/HannahBanana-64394-2010-vancouver-olympics-sports-mkting-pres-education-ppt-powerpoint/.

32. Chi-Chu Tschang, "An Olympic Glitch in China," *BusinessWeek*, November 12, 2007: www.businessweek.com/magazine/content/07_46/c4058040.htm.

33. Morrow, "Feeling Proud Again."

34. John A. Davis, *Competitive Success—How Branding Adds Value* (Singapore: John Wiley & Sons (Asia) Pte. Ltd., 2010), 374.

35. "Beijing to Unveil Olympics Budget in May," March 6, 2008: http://news.xinhuanet.com/english/2008-03/06/content_7734331.htm; "China Invites the World to Olympics," August 8, 2007: www.chinadaily.com.cn/olympics/2007-08/08/content_6017952.htm; Vasily Zubkov, "How Much Will Beijing Pay for the Olympics," May 28, 2007: www.spacedaily.com/reports/How_Much_Will_Beijing_Pay_For_The_Olympics_999.html.

36. Tom Van Riper, "Host City Curse," *Forbes*, February 8, 2006: www.forbes.com/2006/02/08/host-city-olympics_cx_tvr_0208olympiccity.html.

37. BOCOG/Beijing Budget: http://images.beijing2008.cn/upload/lib/bidreport/zt5.pdf.

38. Ibid.

39. Michael F. Martin, *China's Economy and the Beijing Olympics*, CRS Report for Congress: www.dtic.mil/cgi-bin/GetTRDoc?Location=U2&doc=GetTRDoc.pdf&AD=ADA486071; Raymond Li, "1b Yuan Olympics Excludes Venues' Construction Costs," *South China Morning Post*, June 20, 2009.

40. Jon Tiegland, "Mega-Events and Impacts on Tourism: The Predictions and Realities of the Lillehammer Olympics," *Impact Assessment and Project Appraisal* 17, no. 4 (1999): 305–317: www.ingentaconnect.com/content/beech/iapa/1999/00000017/00000004/art00006; Jeffrey G. Owen, "Estimating the Cost and Benefit of Hosting Olympic Games: What Can Beijing Expect from Its 2008 Games?" *Industrial Geographer*, Fall 2005: http://igeographer.lib.indstate.edu/owen.pdf.

41. "Chief Auditor: Beijing Olympics' Profit Exceeds 1 Bln Yuan," June 19, 2009: www.gov.cn/english/2009-06/19/content_1344813.htm.

42. "Games Torch Relay Cost £746,000," BBCNews, April 22, 2008: http://news.bbc.co.uk/2/hi/uk_news/england/london/7360156.stm; "Olympic Relay in Beijing Climax," BBCNews, August 6, 2008: http://news.bbc.co.uk/2/hi/asia-pacific/7544252.stm.

43. "Paris Protests Force Cancellation of Torch Relay," Associated Press, May 6, 2008: http://nbcsports.msnbc.com/id/23978408/.

44. Katrin Bennhold and Elisabeth Roesenthal, "Olympic Torch Goes Out, Briefly, in Paris," *New York Times*, April 8, 2008: www.nytimes.com/2008/04/08/world/europe/08torch.html?pagewanted=all.

45. Ibid.

46. N. Madden, J. Mullman, and C. Brodesser-Akner, "China Earthquake Tragedy Recasts Olympics Sponsors," *Advertising Age* 79, no. 21 (2008): 3–32.

47. Ibid; GE web site: www.ge.com/foundation/disaster_relief/index.jsp.

48. Belinda Goldsmith, "Beijing Opening Night Lures 15% of World," *Reuters*, August 11, 2008: www.reuters.com/article/2008/08/11/us-olympics-viewers-idUSPEK15134720080811.

49. IOC web site. "Olympism in Action": www.olympic.org/olympism-in-action.

50. Committee of 100, "Survey on American and Chinese Attitudes toward Each Other," 2007: www.Committee100.org.

51. Richard Wike, "The Pew Global Attitudes Project: Global Public Opinion in the Bush Years (2001–2008)," Pew Research Center, 2008, p. 12: www.pewglobal.org/2008/12/18/global-public-opinion-in-the-bush-years-2001-2008/.

52. Program on International Policy Attitudes, 7. BBC World Service Poll 2009. Washington, DC: PIPA.

53. "The 2010 Winter Olympics and Paralympic Games," *City Mayors Sport Report:* www.citymayors.com/canada/vancouver_olympics.html.

54. Anita Elberse, Catherine Anthony, and Joshua Callahan, "The Vancouver 2010 Olympics," Case 9-507-049, p. 10. Revised October 5, 2007. Harvard Business School. © 2007 President and Fellows of Harvard College. The 1980 Games in Moscow are excluded for lack of data.

55. VANOC Olympic Games web site, "Revised Budget": www.vancouver2010.com.

56. Budget from www.vancouver2010.com; Jay Gladish and Adam Gable, "The Effect of the 2010 Olympics on the Economy of the Greater Vancouver Area," 4–6: web.unbc.ca/~chenj/course/project/Vancouver_2010_Olympics.doc.

57. PricewaterhouseCoopers, "The Games Effect," March 31, 2010, 6: www.pwc.com/ca/en/events/2010-games.jhtml; VANOC Olympic Games web site, "Revised Budget."

58. Jeff Lee, "Olympics Impact to Be Felt on Vancouver for Years to Come," *Postmedia News*, February 11, 2011: www.skyscrapercity.com/showthread .php?t=1320997; and Petti Fong, "Are the Olympics Worth It? Costs and Benefits of the Games Won't Be Known for a Long Time Afterwards and Maybe Never," *Toronto Star*, January 30, 2010. www.globe-net.com/ articles/2010/january/31/are-the-olympic-games-really-worth-it/?sub=.

59. VANOC Annual Report, "Consolidated Financial Statements: Vancouver Organizing Committee for the 2010 Olympic and Paralympic Winter Games," December 17, 2010, 17. www.fin.gov.bc.ca/reports/2010_ VANOC_Financial_report_English.pdf.

60. Ibid., 18. In thousands of Canadian dollars, except where indicated:

Note a. *IOC Contribution:* Pursuant to the Host City Contract, the IOC provides contributions to VANOC as consideration for VANOC's role in planning, organizing, and staging the Games. At July 31, 2010, $33,343 is receivable from the IOC, $5,865 of which is intended for VANOC's dissolution expenses subsequent to July 31, 2010 and has been recorded on the consolidated statement of financial position as a deferred IOC contribution as at July 31, 2010. Subsequent to July 31, 2010, VANOC received $29,993 from the IOC.

Note b. *Sponsorship Revenues:* The sponsorship revenues received by VANOC under its domestic sponsorship program and the IOC's international sponsorship program are as follows:

Cumulative Period from Inception September 30, 2003 (Incorporation) to July 31, 2010

	Operating Fund $	Venue Development Fund $	Total $
IOC international sponsorship			
Cash	36,500	—	36,500
VIK	137,058	1,414	138,472
Sub total	**173,558**	**1,414**	**174,972**
Domestic sponsorship			
Cash	431,427	—	431,427
VIK	298,730	10,392	309,122
Sub total	**730,157**	**10,392**	**740,549**
Total sponsorship revenues	**903,715**	**11,806**	**915,521**

Note c. *Marketing Rights Royalties*: The marketing rights royalties recorded are as follows:

Cumulative Period from Inception September 30, 2003 (Incorporation) to July 31, 2010

	Operating Fund $	Venue Development Fund $	Total $
IOC marketing royalties *(a)*	73,573	574	74,147
COC marketing royalties *(b)*	108,658	1,342	110,000
IPC marketing royalties *(c)*	4,442	—	4,442
CPC marketing royalties	86	—	86
Total marketing royalties	**186,759**	**1,916**	**188,675**

(a) Pursuant to the terms of the Host City Contract, VANOC is required to pay the IOC a 7.5 percent royalty on the value of any cash consideration received and a 5 percent royalty on any VIK contributions received pertaining to any element of commercial exploitation of VANOC's marketing rights. To date, VANOC has recorded royalties to the IOC in the amount of $66,469 in respect of cash and VIK acquired, of which $25,400 is payable at July 31, 2010. Pursuant to the terms of the Marketing Plan Agreement between the IOC and VANOC, VANOC is required to pay the IOC a management fee calculated based on the value of any amounts received by VANOC under the IOC international sponsorship program. At July 31, 2010, VANOC had recorded $7,678 in respect of management fees, of which $3,608 is payable at July 31, 2010. Subsequent to July 31, 2010, VANOC paid all marketing royalty amounts and management fees owing to the IOC.

(b) Pursuant to the Joint Marketing Programme Agreement ("JMPA") between the Canadian Olympic Committee ("COC") and VANOC, pays a 16 percent royalty on the value of cash consideration received and a 12 percent royalty on VIK contributions received pertaining to any commercial exploitation of VANOC's marketing rights to the COC. The royalties payable are subject to a minimum payment of $73,500 to a maximum payment of $110,000. At July 31, 2010 VANOC had paid a total of $63,000 and accrued $47,000 owing to the COC, the maximum amount owing under the JMPA. Subsequent to July 31, 2010, VANOC paid its obligation to the COC as disclosed in note **.

(c) VANOC paid $4,442 ($4,000 USD) to the International Paralympic Committee ("IPC") in exchange for all rights with respect to the domestic marketing and worldwide broadcasting and ticket sales programs related to the Paralympic Winter Games.10(c)VANOC pays to the COC marketing royalties under the JMPA and also sells certain VIK goods and services to the COC at fair value. To July 31, 2010, VANOC had incurred $110,000 of marketing royalties payable of which $47,000 was accrued but unpaid (note b above). To July 31, 2010, VANOC had sales of $4,631 of VIK goods and services to the COC, of which $1,754 was receivable at July 31, 2010. In connection with VANOC's dissolution plan, VANOC has negotiated with the COC the assignment and sale of future cash receipts committed but not yet due under VANOC's sponsorship agreements for a fair value exchange amount of $37,190. On a net basis, the amount owing by VANOC to the COC at July 31, 2010 was $8,056 which has subsequently been paid in full.

61. PricewaterhouseCoopers, "The Games Effect," 14, 17.

62. Lee, "Olympics Impact to Be Felt on Vancouver."

63. "Vancouver's Olympic Hangover: Up False Creek, The Cost of a Property Deal Gone Sour," *Economist*, January 13, 2011: www.economist.com/node/17906069.

64. Pricewaterhouse Coopers, "The Games Effect," 11.

65. John Iaboni, "Vancouver 2010," AIPS, December 28, 2010: www.aipsmedia .com/index.php?page=news&cod=5356&tp=n.

66. Robin Morris, "Rogge Hails 'New Chapter in History of Olympic Movement' as First Youth Olympics Games Open in Singapore," AIPS, August 15, 2010: www.aipsmedia.com/index.php?page=news&cod=4917&tp=n&allcomm=1.

67. IOC web site; "YOG DNA Showcased at IOC Session," July 7, 2011: www .olympic.org/media?articlenewsgroup=-1&articleid=133150&searchpageipp= 10&searchpage=1.

68. Alan Abrahamson, "2018 Youth Games: Calling Mr. T," August 26, 2010: http://3wiresports.com/2010/08/26/2018-youth-games-calling-mr-t/.

69. "Papering over Youth Olympics Budget Mistakes," *Yawning Bread*, September 17, 2010. http://yawningbread.wordpress.com/2010/09/17/papering-over-youth-olympics-budget-mistakes/; *MyPaper*. www.mypaper.com.sg.

70. Singapore 2010 Youth Olympic Games Official Report, March 23, 2011: http://app1.mcys.gov.sg/Publications/BlazingTheTrailSYOG2010Official Report.aspx.

71. Kenny Lim, "YOG Sponsorship Drive Still on the Starting Line," *Campaign Asia Pacific*, April 23, 2009: www.brandrepublic.asia/Media/print.php?id= 35426.

72. "Visa Spending during YOG Rose 38% on Same Period Last Year," *Channel NewsAsia*, September 1, 2010: www.channelnewsasia.com/stories/singapore localnews/view/1078517/1/.html.

73. IOC YOG: www.olympic.org/yog#/side12.

74. Keir Radnedge, "London 2012 Olympic Stadium Marks 1 Year to Go to the Olympic Games," *AIPS*: www.aipsmedia.com/index.php?page=news&cod= 6203&tp=n.

75. "Cost of 2012 London Olympics Falls," thetimes.co.uk, May 13, 2011; Owen Gibson, "Cost of Building Olympic Venues Falls to £7.25bn and Nears Completion," *Guardian*, July 19, 2011: www.guardian.co.uk/sport/2011/jul/19/london-olympics-2012-sebastian-coe.

76. Matthew Beard, "£750M Spending Spree Set to Put 2012 Games in Class of Its Own," *Evening Standard* (London), July 11, 2011: www.thisislondon.co .uk/standard/article-23968826-pound-750m-spending-spree-set-to-put-2012-games-in-class-of-its-own.do.

77. Jane Wardell, "Weighing Pros and Cons of London Olympics," Associated Press, July 6, 2005: www.highbeam.com/doc/1P1-110791249.html.

78. "Visa Europe: A Golden Opportunity–London 2012 Olympic and Paralympic Games Expenditure and Economic Impact," July 11, 2011: www.visaeurope.com/en/newsroom/olympics_impact_report.aspx.

79. Vanessa Kortekaas, "London 2012 Nears Funding Finishing Line," *Financial Times*, July 24, 2011: www.ft.com/cms/s/0/3c2fbf6c-b490-11e0-a21d-00144feabdc0.html#ixzz1UqkKE7ln.

80. *Government Olympic Executive London 2012 Olympic and Paralympic Games Annual Report February 2011*, 36: www.culture.gov.uk/publications/7800.aspx.

81. "Olympic Charter in Force as from 8 July 2011," 91: www.olympic.org/Documents/olympic_charter_en.pdf.

82. Graham Ruddick, "Will Britain Benefit from the £9.3bn Olympic Budget?" *Daily Telegraph*, April 1, 2011; Graham Ruddick, "London 2012 Olympics: North-South Divide Exists on Whether Games Will Benefit Whole of UK," *Daily Telegraph*, April 1, 2011: www.telegraph.co.uk/finance/london-olympics-business/8419670/London-2012-Olympics-North-South-divide-exists-on-whether-games-will-benefit-whole-of-UK.html.

83. Sochi 2014 Olympics web site: http://sochi2014.com/en/.

84. Cushman & Wakefield, "Sochi: The Impact of the 2014 Winter Olympic": www.cushwake.com/cwglobal/jsp/kcReportDetail.jsp?Country=GLOBAL&Language=EN&catId=100005&pId=c10800020p.

85. SBRnet–Sports Business Research Network, "Deal of the Month," July 2011.

86. Martin Müller, "Measuring the Regional Economic Impact of Mega-Events: What Are the Benefits of the 2014 Olympics for Sochi?" In *Professional Training for the XXII Olympic and XI Paralympic Winter Games: Problems and Perspectives*, 192–201 (Sochi: Sochi State University for Tourism and Recreation, 2009): www.alexandria.unisg.ch/publications/57540/L-en.

87. Alan Abrahamson, "Sochi at the Halfway Point and a 'New Russia,'" October 14, 2010: http://3wiresports.com/2010/10/14/sochi-at-the-halfway-point-and-a-new-russia/.

88. "Russia: Sochi Olympic Spending Bypasses Finance, Economics Ministries—Daily," BBC Monitoring International Reports, June 14, 2011: www.access-mylibrary.com/article-1G1-205027197/russia-2014-olympics-face.html.

89. Cushman & Wakefield, "Sochi: The Impact of the 2014 Winter Olympic," 13.

Chapter 5 Section I Sponsorship Preparation Questions

1. John A. Davis, *Competitive Success: How Branding Adds Value* (Chichester, UK: John Wiley & Sons, 2010), 126–127.

Chapter 6 The Olympic Stage

1. *Olympic Marketing Fact File*, 2008 Edition, 25: www.olympic.org. Note that the *Olympic Marketing Fact File*, 2010 Edition (p. 25) describes the Average Minute Rating as follows: "*Average Minute Rating measures the number of viewers watching a typical minute of Olympic Games television coverage. The global figure is calculated by combining the average minute rating of dedicated Games coverage aired by official broadcasters.*"
2. IOC Marketing Report Vancouver 2010, 30–34: www.olympic.org.
3. www.olympic.org/Documents/IOC_Marketing/IOC_Marketing_Fact_File_2010%20r.pdf.
4. Olympic Marketing Fact File, 2011 Edition, 23–27: www.olympic.org/Documents/IOC_Marketing/OLYMPIC_MARKETING_FACT_FILE_2011.pdf.
5. Ibid., 32–38.
6. Ibid., 32–37.
7. Auditor General New South Wales, *Auditor-General's Report to Parliament 2002*, vol. 2, April 22, 2003. Archived Auditor's report, pages 10–11.
8. "Athens Olympics Cost May Top $14.6 Billion," *USA Today*, November 18, 2004; "Athens Olympics Seen Costing More Than Double Initial Target," Reuters/Fox News, August 25, 2004: www.foxnews.com/story/0,2933,130057,00.html.
9. "Beijing 2008 Olympic Budget Unveiled," *People's Daily*, February 24, 2001: http://english.peopledaily.com.cn/200102/24/eng20010224_63279.html.
10. Matthew Forney, "Beijing Bags It," *Time*, July 15, 2001: www.time.com/time/arts/article/0,8599,167611,00.html.
11. "Olympics Budget Rises to £9.3 billion," BBCNews, March 15, 2007: http://news.bbc.co.uk/2/hi/uk_news/politics/6453575.stm.
12. Olympic Marketing Fact File, 2011 Edition, 25.
13. Richard Sandomir, "NBC's Olympic Run Is Extended to 2012 with $2 Billion Bid," *New York Times*, June 7, 2003: www.nytimes.com/2003/06/07/sports/olympics-nbc-s-olympic-run-is-extended-to-2012-with-2-billion-bid.html.
14. "NBC Retains US Olympic Broadcast Rights in Mammoth Four-Games Deal," *Sport Business*, June 8, 2011: www.sportbusiness.com/news/183748/nbc-retains-us-olympic-broadcast-rights-in-mammoth-four-games-deal.

15. Alan Abrahamson, "NBC's $4.38 Billion Knockout Punch," June 7, 2011: http://3wiresports.com/2011/06/07/nbcs-4-38-billion-knockout-punch/.

16. Author's Note: Watching the 2004 Olympic Games in Athens from Singapore, where I had just moved a few months before, was a great example of regional programming preferences. While each day's broadcast brought coverage of the various sports, much of the Olympics coverage centered on badminton and table tennis, two enormously popular sports in Asia. The fans for these sports are no less passionate than those of the more recognized sports, such as swimming, track and field, gymnastics, and basketball. Indeed, Singaporeans in 2004 watched with rapt attention the fortunes of Li Jiawei, their women's table tennis sensation. She finished fourth, just out of the running for a medal, but her performance endeared her to Singaporeans, and the television coverage of her throughout the Olympics captured the collective attention of this small city-state. The local media featured extensive profiles of her athletic achievements, her family, and her long-term ambitions, creating a more human and emotional connection between Li Jiawei and Singaporeans.

Chapter 7   The Olympic Halo

1. Coca-Cola web site: www.thecoca-colacompany.com/heritage/olympic games_difference.html.

2. "Acer Aims to Be Faster, Higher, Stronger," *Globe and Mail*, December 7, 2007: www.theglobeandmail.com/search/?q=acer+aims+to+be+faster& searchField=keywords&searchQuery=*%3A*.

3. Ibid.

4. Susan P. Douglas, Samuel C. Craig, and Edwin J. Nijssen, "International Brand Architecture: Development, Drivers and Design," 1999: http://pages .stern.nyu.edu/~sdouglas/rpubs/intbrand.html; "Samsung–The TOP Brand in the World": www.123helpme.com/view.asp?id=47241; "Samsung Extends Sponsorship of Olympic Games until 2016," *Sport Business*, April 24, 2007: www.sportbusiness.com/news/161740/samsung-extends-sponsorship-of-olympic-games-until-2016.

5. Seeking Alpha, "Coca-Cola Company Q1 2010 Earnings Call Transcript": http://seekingalpha.com/article/199745-coca-cola-company-q1-2010-earnings-call-transcript.

6. John Davis, *Measuring Marketing: 103 Key Metrics Every Marketer Needs* (Singapore: John Wiley & Sons (Asia) Pte. Ltd.), 253.

7. Douglas, Craig, and Nijssen, "An International Brand Architecture"; "Samsung—The TOP Brand in the World"; "Samsung Extends Sponsorship."

8. "Sponsor Joins in Games Support," *China Daily*, August 2, 2011: http:// europe.chinadaily.com.cn/sports/2011-08/02/content_13032400.htm.

9. Davis, *Measuring Marketing*, 66, 71.

10. George Foster and Victoria Chang, *Visa Sponsorship Marketing*, Case: SPM-5, p. 15. Stanford University Graduate School of Business ©2003; "Olympics, What Olympics? Sponsors, What Sponsors?" Performance Research Independent Studies. Performance Research conducted 509 pre-event (January 12–13, 1994) and 268 postevent (February 28, 1994) random nationwide telephone interviews. The margin of error is +1 percent. In "Top Line Results: Performance Research-Survey Sampling 2010 Olympic Viewership Study": www.performanceresearch.com/olympic-sponsorship-vancouver.htm.

11. Ibid.

12. Ibid.

13. Bien Perez, "Acer to Take Olympic Lead from Lenovo," *South China Morning Post*, December 7, 2007: www.eurochina-ict.org/documents/newsattachment071207.doc.

14. Coca-Cola Canada web site. "Vancouver 2010 Olympic Winter Games and Olympic Torch Relay Sponsorship Drives Gold Medal Results for Coca-Cola Canada," February 25, 2010: www.cocacola.ca/pr_20100225-1.htm.

15. H. I. Ansoff, "Strategies for Diversification," *Harvard Business Review* 35, no. 2 (1957).

16. Ibid.

Chapter 8   The Olympic Spirit

1. "Whatever Happened to Vera Caslavska (TCH)?": www.olympic.org/vera-caslavska; www.gymn.ca/gymnasticgreats/wag/caslavska.htm.

2. E. M. Swift, "A Reminder of What We Can Be," *Sports Illustrated*, February 21, 1994: http://sportsillustrated.cnn.com/features/cover/news/2000/02/17/a_reminder_of_what_we_can_be/; Bruce Lowitt, "Do You Believe in Miracles?" *St. Petersburg Times*, December 26, 1999: www.sptimes.com/News/122699/Sports/_Do_you_believe_in_mi.shtml.

3. Lowitt, "Do You Believe in Miracles?" Video footage on YouTube features multiple samples of the famous Al Michaels's sports cast in which he clearly excitedly calls the end of the U.S.-Soviet hockey game: www.youtube.com/results?search_query=miracle+on+ice&search_type=.

4. "Flying High," *Guardian*, September 3, 2007: http://film.guardian.co.uk/news/story/0,,2161238,00.html.

5. Ibid.

6. "Eddie the Eagle: 20 Years on," BBC Gloucestershire, February 13, 2008: www.bbc.co.uk/gloucestershire/content/articles/2008/02/13/eddie_the_eagle_feature.shtml.

7. Interview by Jonathan Sale, "My First Job: Eddie the Eagle, the Olympic Ski-Jumper, Was a Plasterer," *Independent*, December 13, 2007: www

.independent.co.uk/student/career-planning/getting-job/my-first-job-eddie-the-eagle-the-olympic-skijumper-was-a-plasterer-764891.html.

8. Mike Dodd, "Jamaican Bobsled Team Story Continues to Inspire," *USA-Today*, February 23, 2006: http://content.usatoday.com/topics/topic/Cool+Runnings.

9. "Winter Olympics; Russia Surprises Russians," *New York Times*, February 28, 1994: www.nytimes.com/1994/02/28/sports/winter-olympics-russia-surprises-russians.html; "Fall of the Soviet Union," The Cold War Museum: www.coldwar.org/articles/90s/fall_of_the_soviet_union.asp.

10. "Karnam Malleswari": www.olympic.org/karnam-malleswari; "Olympics 30 Great Olympic Stories, Karnam Malleswan": www.olympics30.com/30greatest/karnam-malleswari-weightlifting.asp; "Sports Reference/Olympic Sports": www.sports-reference.com/olympics/athletes/ma/karnam-malleswari-1.html; "Wowtelugu": www.wowtelugu.com/telugupeople/Sportsstars/Karnammal leswari.asp.

11. "Steiner Steals Gold for Germany," Associated Press. August 19, 2008. www.2008.nbcolympics.com/weightlifting/news/newsid=235388.html#steiner+steals+gold+germany; Simon Barnes, "Matthias Steiner's Triumph Is Worth the Wait," *Sunday Times*, August 20, 2008; Sophie Hardach, "Weightlifting—Grieving Steiner wins gold," Reuters, August 19, 2008: www.reuters.com/article/2008/08/19/idINIndia-35083120080819; "Matthias Steiner Wins Heavy Gold for Germany," August 19, 2008: http://the.hono luluadvertiser.com/article/2008/Aug/19/br/hawaii80819019.html; Randall J. Strossen, "The Super Men at the Olympics" http://imbodybuilding.com/articles/super-men-at-olympics/.

12. Christa Case Bryant, "Petra Majdic Gives Slovenia Its First-Ever Cross-Country Medal," *Christian Science Monitor*, February 17, 2010: www.csmonitor.com/World/Olympics/2010/0217/Petra-Majdic-gives-Slovenia-its-first-ever-cross-country-medal; Mark Lamport-Stokes, "I Can Ski, Says Broken Majdic," Reuters, February 24, 2010: www.reuters.com/article/2010/02/24/us-olym pics-crosscountry-majdic-intervie-idUSTRE61N1BG20100224; "An Ode to Those Moving On: 2011 + Veerpalu," April 14, 2011: http://nordicxplained .wordpress.com/category/petra-majdic/.

13. Julie Mancur, "Kim Yu-na Wins Gold in Figure Skating," *New York Times*, February 26, 2010: www.nytimes.com/2010/02/26/sports/olympics/26skate.html?pagewanted=all.

14. Malcolm Kelly, "An Inside Look at Joannie Rochelle's Brave Olympic Odyssey," CBCSports, March 22, 2010: www.cbc.ca/sports/figureskating/story/2010/03/21/sp-rochetteperron.html; Jeer Longman, "Through Grief and Tears, a Triumph on the Ice," *New York Times*, February 24, 2010: www.nytimes.com/2010/02/25/sports/olympics/25longman.html; Kelly Whiteside.

"Rochelle 'Tried to Make My Mother Proud,'" *USAToday*, February 26, 2010: www.usatoday.com/sports/olympics/vancouver/figureskating/2010-02-26-rochette_N.htm; Lori Culbert, "Joannie Rochelle Carries Canada's Colours into Olympic Closing Ceremony," *Vancouver Sun*, February 28, 2010: www.vancouversun.com/Joannie+Rochette+named+Canada+flag+bearer/2624610/story.html; Ken MacQueen, "An Act of Courage," *Macleans*, March 18, 2010: www2.macleans.ca/2010/03/18/an-act-of-courage/#more-113633.

Chapter 10 The Olympic Challenges

1. Eugene N. Borza, "Athenians, Macedonians, and the Origins of the Macedonian Royal House," *Hesperia Supplements* 19, *Studies in Attic Epigraphy, History and Topography Presented to Eugene Vanderpool* (1982), 7–13.

2. Andrew Strenk, "What Price Victory? The World of International Sports and Politics," *Annals of the American Academy of Political and Social Science* 445, Contemporary Issues in Sport (1979): 128–140: www.jstor.org/stable/1042961; "Emperor Nero—Olympic Champion," January 2, 2001: www.bbc.co.uk/dna/h2g2/A493689; Herbert W. Benario, "Nero (54–68 A.D.)" (2006): www.roman-emperors.org/nero.htm.

3. Peter Andrews, "The First American Olympics," *American Heritage* 39, no. 4 (1988): www.americanheritage.com/content/first-american-olympics.

4. Aaron Kuriloff, "25 Great Hoaxes, Cheats and Frauds in Sport," *ESPN*, April 17, 2005: http://proxy.espn.go.com/oly/columns/story?id=2039471.

5. Christine Brennan, "TV Ratings Slip as Figure Skating Loses Its Edge," *USAToday*: www.usatoday.com/sports/columnist/brennan/2008-01-23-skating_N.htm.

6. "Three-Year Ban for Skating Judge," BBCSport, April 30, 2002: http://news.bbc.co.uk/sport2/hi/other_sports/1959181.stm.

7. Mark Starr, "Scoring without Scandal?" *Newsweek*, February 27, 2006: www.thedailybeast.com/newsweek/2006/02/13/scoring-without-scandal.html; Candus Thomson, "Revised System Born in Scandal," *Baltimore Sun*, February 1, 2006: http://articles.baltimoresun.com/2006-02-01/sports/0602010042_1_pelletier-international-skating-union-figure-skating. Readers may find the International Skating Union web site, www.isu.org, worth visiting for additional detail on the scoring system.

8. John A. Clendenin and Stephen A. Greyser, *Tarnished Rings? Olympic Games Sponsorship Issues*. Case 9-599-107, pp. 1, 5. Revised August 4, 2004. Harvard Business School. © 1999 President and Fellows of Harvard College.

9. Ibid., 6.

10. Ibid.

11. Ibid.

12. "S.L. Bid Scandal Leads to Olympic Reforms," *Deseret News:* www.deseret news.com/oly/view/0,3949,30000166,00.html; "Samaranch Leaves Mixed Olympic Legacy," CNN.com: http://m.si.com/news/wr/wr/detail/2547643/2;jsessionid=61FA0CAD0218070823911C757C768088.cnnsi2.

13. David Wallechinsky and Jaime Loucky, *The Complete Book of the Winter Olympics*, Turin 2006 edition (Miami: Sports Media Publishing, 2006), 8–9.

14. "Kwan Withdraws from Olympic Winter Games: U.S. Olympic Committee Report," *US Figure Skating*, February 12, 2006: www.usfigureskating.org/Story.asp?id=33082.

15. Darren Rovell, "There Will Be Some Awkward Moments for Coke, Visa," ESPN.com, February 13, 2006: http://sports.espn.go.com/oly/winter06/figure/columns/story?id=2328319.

16. "Protestor Ruins Marathon," BBCSport, August 29, 2004: http://news.bbc.co.uk/sport2/hi/olympics_2004/athletics/3610598.stm.

17. Kashef Majid, Ramdas Chandra, and Annamma Joy, "Exploring the Growing Interest in the Olympic Winter Games," *Sport Marketing Quarterly* 16, no. 1 (2007), 31.

18. Crouse, Karen. "Scrutiny of Suit Rises as World Records Fall," *New York Times*, April 11, 2008: www.nytimes.com/2008/04/11/sports/othersports/11swim.html?_r=3&ref=sports&oref=slogin&oref=slogin&oref=slogin; "Critics Claim NASA Swimsuit Is 'Technological Doping,'" CNN.com, April 30, 2008: www.tsn.ca/chl/story/?id=234029.

Chapter 12   The Olympic Opportunity

1. Richard Sandomir, "In NBC's Shadow, Comcast Ponders an Olympic Plunge," *New York Times*, December 28, 2010: www.nytimes.com/2010/12/29/sports/29olympics.html.

2. Olympic Marketing Fact File, 2011 Edition, 6: www.olympic.org.

3. Ibid.

4. Ibid., 17.

5. Ibid.

6. Ibid., 30.

7. Ibid.

8. "About Tickets": www.tickets.london2012.com/about_tickets_p2.html; "2012 London Olympic Games Ticket Prices Released," October 15, 2010: www.bbc.co.uk/news/uk-england-london-11546228.

9. "Fans Furious as 'Lucky' Ticket Applicants Find Out What They'll Be Watching at London Olympics," Mail Online, June 22, 2011. www.dailymail.co.uk/sport/olympics/article-2006745/London-2012-Fans-furious-lucky-ticket-applicants-theyve-got.html#ixzz1YbpXR1pi.

10. Mark Tran and Sam Jones, "London 2012 Olympic Games Ticket Prices Revealed," *Guardian*, October 15, 2012: www.guardian.co.uk/uk/2010/oct/15/london-2012-olympics-ticket-prices.

11. "2012 London Olympic Games Ticket Prices Released."

12. www.vancouver2010.com; "A Look at What It Will Cost to Attend Various 2010 Olympic Events at Vancouver," Canadian Press Newswire, October 11, 2008: www.lexisnexis.com/hottopics/lnacademic/?.

13. "Tickets to the Singapore 2010 Youth Olympic Games on Worldwide Sale," April 30, 2010: www.prnewswire.com/news-releases/tickets-to-the-singapore-2010-youth-olympic-games-on-worldwide-sale-92509214.html.

14. Ibid.

15. "Olympic Tickets, Same Price for All," February 16, 2007: http://en.beijing2008.cn/90/05/article214020590.shtml; Consulate-General of the People's Republic of China/Manchester, April 16, 2007: http://manchester.chineseconsulate.org/eng/xwdt/t312263.htm.

16. Ibid., 31. Table 12.6 license revenues table (and forward from here). Use Olympic Marketing Fact File, 2011 Edition, 31.

17. Ibid.

18. www.olympic.org/sponsorship.

19. Ibid.

20. Brian Gomez, "Tough Economy Not Slowing Olympic Sponsorships," *Gazette*, October 21, 2010: www.gazette.com/articles/usolympiccommittee-106635-usoc-internationalolympiccommittee.html; Howard Berkes, "Olympic Sponsors Go for the Golden Image," NPR, February 25, 2010: www.npr.org/templates/story/story.php?storyId=124068024; Jonathan Birchall, "Olympic Sponsorship Is P&G's Track to a Billion New Customers," *Financial Times/beyondbrics*, July 28, 2010: http://blogs.ft.com/beyond-brics/2010/07/28/olympic-sponsorship-is-pgs-track-to-emerging-markets/#axzz1Y9bscODc; Stephen Wilson, "Procter & Gamble Is Latest Global Olympic Sponsor," *Huffington Post*, July 28, 2010: www.huffingtonpost.com/huff-wires/20100728/oly-ioc-sponsor/; "P&G Sponsors the U.S. Olympic and Paralympic Teams," *Holmes Report*, April 15, 2011: www.holmesreport.com/casestudy-info/10160/PG-Sponsors-The-US-Olympic-And-Paralympic-Teams.aspx; David Lieberman, "USAToday CEO Forum: GE Sees Growth Opportunities," *USA Today*: www.usatoday.com/money/companies/management/2007-12-13-immelt-ge_N.htm; Normandy Madden, "Sponsoring the Games: Marketing

Plans Shaping Up," *Ad Age*, February 14, 2007: www.plasticsnews.com/
china/olympics/english/headlines2.html?id=1175176784; "Kodak Ends Olympic
Sponsorship after Beijing Games," National Press Photographers Association,
October 16, 2007: www.nppa.org/news_and_events/news/2007/10/kodak
.html; "Coca-Cola Extends Olympic Sponsorship," *Atlanta Business Chronicle*,
August 1, 2005: http://atlanta.bizjournals.com/atlanta/stories/2005/08/01/
daily4.html; "Olympic Sponsor—Omega Contract Extended to Include the
London 2012 Olympic and Paralympic Games," 2010 Commerce Centre BC
Olympic and Paralympic Winter Games Secretariat, May 16, 2006: www
.2010commercecentre. com/news.aspx?articleID=85; "Manulife-Sinochem
Announces Long-Term Partnership with Olympic Taekwondo Gold Med-
alist, Luo Wei," September 29, 2006: www.manulife.com/public/news/
detail/0,,lang=fr&artId=144325&navId=630002,00.html; "McDonald's Signs
Eight-Year Olympic Deal to Include Turin, Vancouver Games," *Ski Racing*,
June 7, 2004: www.skiracing.com/index.php?option=com_content&task=
view&id=1581&Itemid=38; "Atos Origin Becomes Worldwide Partner of
the International Paralympic Committee," January 28, 2008: www.atosorigin
.com/en-us/Newsroom/en-us/Press_Releases/2008/2008_01_29_01.htm.

21. "London 2012 Olympics Sponsor Dow: Don't Judge Us on Bhopal Deaths,"
August 4, 2011: www.metro.co.uk/news/871416-london-olympics-sponsor-
dow-dont-judge-us-on-bhopal-deaths; Jack Kaskey, "Dow Chemical Agrees
to Worldwide Sponsorship through 2020," July 16, 2010: www.bloomberg
.com/news/print/2010-07-16/dow-chemical-agrees-to-worldwide-sponsor
ship-of-olympics-through-2020.html.

22. www.olympic.org/sponsorship.

23. www.olympic.org/sponsorship?tab=1.

24. Ibid.

25. Olympic Marketing Fact File, 2011 Edition, 12.

26. "2006 FIFA World Cup™ Broadcast Wider, Longer and Farther Than Ever
Before," February 6, 2007: www.fifa.com/aboutfifa/organisation/marketing/
news/newsid=111247.index.html. Note that the Olympics changed its
tracking of viewing audience from cumulative viewing audience to cumulative
viewing hours in 2000. The last Olympiads that tracked cumulative viewing
audiences were the 1996 Atlanta Olympics (cumulative viewing audience of
19.6 billion) and Nagano in 1998 (cumulative viewing audience of 10.7 billion) (see Olympic Marketing Fact File 2008 Edition, 24). These figures
compare to cumulative viewing audiences of 24.7 billion for the 1998 World
Cup and 28.8 billion for the 2002 World Cup, respectively.

27. John A. Davis, "Brand Value," chap. 2 in *Competitive Success: How Branding
Adds Value* (Chichester, UK: John Wiley & Sons, 2010), 33.

28. Speech by David Haigh at BrandFinance Forum in Asia, March 2008, Singapore Management University.

29. "Best Global Brands 2010": http://interbrand.com/en/best-global-brands/Best-Global-Brands-2010.aspx.

30. Visit the BrandFinance web site to see various brand surveys and results: www.brandfinance.com/images/upload/brandfinance_global500_2011_web.pdf.

31. Olympic Marketing Fact File, 2011 Edition, 6.

32. Asís F. Martínez-Jerez and Rosario Martínez de Albornoz, *Hala Madrid: Managing Real Madrid Club de Fútbol, the Team of the Century*, Case 9-105-013, p. 4. Revised June 8, 2006. Harvard Business School. © 2004 President and Fellows of Harvard College.

33. Antonio Davila and George Foster, *Futbol Club Barcelona: Globalization Opportunities*, Case SPM-33, p. 2. February 1, 2007. © 2007 by the Board of Trustees of the Leland Stanford Junior University.

34. "Starbucks, Fair Trade and Coffee Social Responsibility" guidelines, published March 7, 2006. Visit www.starbucks.com/responsibility for more information.

35. Bill Carter, "Super Bowl Ratings Cap Record Year for N.F.L.," February 7, 2011: http://mediadecoder.blogs.nytimes.com/2011/02/07/super-bowl-ratings-cap-record-year-for-n-f-l/.

36. Vikas Bajaj and Peter Edmonston, "ETrade Struggles to Avert Big Write-Down as Shares Tumble," *International Herald Tribune*, November 13, 2007: www.iht.com/articles/2007/11/13/business/etrade.php.

37. Warren Berger, "Hot Spots!" *Wired*: www.wired.com/wired/archive/8.02/commercials_pr.html.

38. "The Olympics . . . Greatest Show on Earth?" Synovate Change/Agent, November 2007: www.synovate.com/changeagent/index.php/site/full_story/the_olympics_greatest_show_on_earth.

39. "Issue: Adidas' Challenge: Sprinting Ahead in China," *BusinessWeek*, August 7, 2008: www.businessweek.com/managing/content/aug2008/ca2008087_756565.htm.

40. "Who Were the Real Winners of the Beijing Olympics?" Just Ask Nielsen, September 2008. http://cn.en.nielsen.com/site/documents/Olympic_en.pdf.

41. Hongbum Shin, Soonhwan Lee, Hyun-duck Kim, and Nicholas Zumbrun, "The Relationship between Sponsorship and Customers' Buying Intention: The Case of the Beijing 2008 Summer Olympic Games," presented at the 2009 Sport Marketing Association (SMA) Conference, (Cleveland, OH, October 28–30, 2009), 4.

42. "Top Line Results: Performance Research-Survey Sampling 2010 Olympic Viewership Study": www.performanceresearch.com/olympic-sponsorship-vancouver.htm.

43. Lara O'Reilly, "Coca-Cola 'Most Recognized' 2012 Olympic Sponsor," *MarketingWeek* May 31, 2011: www.marketingweek.co.uk/disciplines/sponsorship/coca-cola-"most-recognised"-2012-olympic-sponsor/3026917.article.

44. Matthew Davis, "Games' Eagle-Eye Sponsor Police," *BBCNews*, August 14, 2004: http://news.bbc.co.uk/2/hi/europe/3565616.stm.

45. Pippa Collett and Nick Johnson, "Don't Be Ambushed in 2012," Brand Strategy, February 2006: www.mad.co.uk/Main/News/Disciplines/Marketing/IndustryIssues/Articles/8f6b68250fa54bdf9da452af2c22a0ba/Don't-be-ambushed-in-2012.html.

46. Holger Preuss, Kai Gemeinder, and Benoit Seguin, "Ambush Marketing in China: Counterbalancing Olympic Sponsorship Efforts," *Asia Business & Management* 7 (2008): 243–263: www.palgrave-journals.com/abm/journal/v7/n2/full/abm20083a.html.

47. A. Kingston, "The Outlaws," *Maclean's* 123, no. 8 (2010), 48–49: http://search.ebscohost.com/login.aspx?direct=true&db=aph&AN=48373457&site=ehost-live&scope=site.

48. "Brand Protection Guidelines," 5: www.london2012.com/documents/brand-guidelines/guidelines-for-non-commercial-use.pdf.

Chapter 13   The Olympic Sponsor Case Brief: Acer

1. Acer corporate web site: www.acer-group.com/public/Sponsorships/olympics.htm.

2. Jonathan Tait, "Acer to Supply 2012 Olympics," *SportsPro*, August 2, 2011.

3. "Sponsor Joins in Games Support," *China Daily*, August 2, 2011: www.chinadaily.com.cn/cndy/2011-08/02/content_13029199.htm.

4. "Acer Becomes IOC TOP Sponsor for 2009-2012," *Sports Business*, July 7, 2007: www.sportbusiness.com/news/163074/acer-becomes-ioc-top-sponsor-for-2009-2012.

5. Patrick Seitz, "Samsung, Panasonic, Acer, Atos Seek Olympic Branding Gold," *Investors Business Daily*, February 19, 2010: www.investors.com/NewsAndAnalysis/ArticlePrint.aspx?id=521686.

6. "Acer Becomes IOC TOP Sponsor for 2009–2012."

7. "Acer Becomes IOC TOP Partner after 2009," *TMC News*, December 7, 2007: www.tmcnet.com/usubmit/2007/12/07/3147872.htm.

8. Lester Haines, "Acer Inks Olympic Partner Deal," *Register*, December 6, 2007: www.theregister.co.uk/2007/12/06/acer_olympic_deal/print.html.

9. Bien Perez, "Acer to Take Olympic Lead from Lenovo," *South China Morning Post*, December 7, 2007.

10. "Taiwanese Computer Maker Acer Sees Profits Surge," BBCNews Business, August 4, 2010: www.bbc.co.uk/news/business-10865915; Bill Wilson, "Acer Signs 2012 Sponsorship Deal," *BBC News*, December 6, 2007: http://news.bbc.co.uk/2/hi/business/7130551.stm; Acer corporate web site "Olympic Spirit": www.acer-group.com/public/Sponsorships/olympics.htm.

11. Patrick Seitz, "Samsung, Panasonic, Acer, Atos Seek Olympic Branding Gold," *Investors Business Daily*, February 19, 2010: www.investors.com/NewsAndAnalysis/ArticlePrint.aspx?id=521686.

12. Julian Lee, "Viewers Cool on Winter Games Ads," *Sydney Morning Herald*, April 9, 2010: www.smh.com.au/business/viewers-cool-on-winter-games-ads-20100408-rv21.html.

13. Daniel Eran Dilger, "IDC: Apple Hits 8.7% Share as Fastest Growing PC Maker in US 4Q Sales," *Apple Insider*, January 12, 2011: www.appleinsider.com/articles/11/01/12/idc_apple_hits_8_7_share_as_fastest_growing_pc_maker_in_us_4q_sales.html; "PC Market Returns to Positive Growth in Line with Expectations, Though Gains Remain Small, According to IDC," July 13, 2011: www.idc.com/getdoc.jsp?containerId=prUS22937811.

14. Mark Lee and Janet Ong, "Acer Sets Sights on Apple, HTC after HP Chase Stumbles," *BusinessWeek*, April 1, 2011: www.businessweek.com/news/2011-04-01/acer-sets-sights-on-apple-htc-after-hp-chase-stumbles.html.

15. "Olympic Stock Prices; IOC Marketing Chief on Sponsorship; Apple, Samsung, Battle," *Around the Rings*, April 23, 2011. www.aroundtherings.com/articles/view.aspx?id=36857.

16. Paul Knurl, "Acer Slashes Tablet Forecast, Banks on Notebooks," *Channel Register*, June 15, 2011: www.channelregister.co.uk/2011/06/15/acer_cuts_tablet_forecasts/.

17. "UPDATE 1-Olympics-GE Extends Sponsorship Deal to 2020," Reuters, July 29, 2011: www.reuters.com/article/2011/06/29/olympics-sponsorship-ge-idUSLDE75S0Q520110629.

Chapter 14   The Olympic Sponsor Case Brief: Samsung

1. "Samsung Concludes Contract with the International Olympic Committee to Sponsor Olympic Games through 2016," April 23, 2007: www.samsung.com/us/news/newsRead.do?news_seq=3687&page=1.

2. Interbrand, "Best Global Brands 2010": www.interbrand.com/en/knowledge/best-global-brands/best-global-brands-2008/best-global-brands-2010.aspx.

3. "Samsung Concludes Contract with the International Olympic Committee."

4. Elizabeth Woyke, "Samsung Goes for Olympic Gold," *Forbes*, June 16, 2008: www.forbes.com/2008/06/15/samsung-olympics-wireless-tech-wireless08-cx_ew_0616samsung.html.

5. Ibid.

6. "WOW Factor: Samsung Unveils '10 Olympic Games Marketing Plan," *SportsBusiness Daily*, June 24, 2009: www.sportsbusinessdaily.com/Daily/ Issues/2009/06/Issue-192/Olympics/WOW-Factor-Samsung-Unveils-10- Olympic-Games-Marketing-Plan.aspx.

7. "Samsung Announces Plans to Participate in London Olympic Torch Relay Sponsorship," May 26, 2010: http://pages.samsung.com/canewsroom/article? articleId=36.

8. "WOW Factor."

9. "Samsung, Iginla and Wickenheiser Get Closer Together for the Game," September 7, 2008: http://pages.samsung.com/ca/hockey/en/pdfs/Press Release_en.pdf.

10. Rachel Donachie, "Samsung Unveils New Olympic Campaign Logo," *MarketingWeek*, June 13, 2011: www.marketingweek.co.uk/sectors/telecoms- and-it/samsung-unveils-new-olympic-campaign-logo/3027367.article.

11. Dan Butcher, "Olympic Sponsors Samsung, Visa Team Up to Power Mobile Payments," *Mobile Commerce Daily*, April 1, 2011: www.mobilecommercedaily .com/2011/04/01/olympic-sponsors-samsung-visa-team-up-to-power-mobile- payments.

12. "Samsung Gets Jump on Olympic Sponsorship," *Sports Info Business*, May 8, 2011: www.sportsinfo101.com/olympics/samsung-gets-jump-on-olympic- sponsorship.

13. Roger Blitz, "Samsung Calls for Olympic Anti-Ambush Ads Push," *Financial Times*, June 13, 2011: www.ft.com/intl/cms/s/0/851f3e3c-95e1-11e0-ba20- 00144feab49a.html#axzz1YWIAihhM.

14. "President Approves Samsung Probe," BBC News, November 27, 2007: http://news.bbc.co.uk/2/hi/business/7114644.stm.

15. Woyke, "Samsung Goes for Olympic Gold."

Chapter 15 The Olympic Sponsor Case Study: Coca-Cola

1. "The Real Thing: Coca-Cola Extends Sponsorship of Olympic Games through 2020," *BrandWeek*, August 1, 2005: www.brandweek.com/bw/ news/recent_display.jsp?vnu_content_id=1001001168.

2. Scott Simpson, "Coca-Cola Uncaps 12-Year Fizz in Olympics Deal," *Vancouver Sun*, August 2, 2005: www.skyscrapercity.com/showthread.php? t=241195.

3. Widen & Kennedy, "Advertising Plan for the Coca-Cola Company 1996 Summer Olympic Games," www.unc.edu/~jdee/adplan.html; Jere Longman, "On the Playing Field, Atlanta Games Were a Success," *New York Times*,

August 6, 1996: www.nytimes.com/specials/olympics/0805/oly-rdp.html; Glenn Collins, "Coke's Hometown Olympics: The Company Tries the Big Blitz on Its Own Turf," *New York Times*, March 28, 1996: www.nytimes .com/1996/03/28/business/coke-s-hometown-olympics-the-company-tries-the-big-blitz-on-its-own-turf.html.

4. Coca-Cola corporate web site, 2008 Annual Report, 41, www.thecoca-colacompany.com/investors/pdfs/2008_annual_review/2008_annual_review_ Operating_Group_Highlights.pdf.

5. Ibid.

6. Coca-Cola 2010 Annual Review, 5: www.thecoca-colacompany.com/ ourcompany/ar/pdf/TCCC_2010_Annual_Review.pdf; Yahoo! Finance. Retrieved periodically from December 3, 2010, to February 2, 2011, from http://finance.yahoo.com/q?s=ok.

7. "Partnership History," Coca-Cola corporate web site: www.thecoca-colacompany.com/heritage/olympicgames.html.

8. "The Olympic Games," Coca-Cola corporate web site: www.thecoca-colacompany.com/heritage/olympicgames_difference.html.

9. Ibid.

10. Ben Berkon, "Coca-Cola Comes Clean about Going Green at Olympic Games," *BrandChannel*, February 1, 2010: www.brandchannel.com/home/post/ 2010/02/01/Coca-Cola-Comes-Clean-About-Going-Green-At-Olympic-Games.aspx.

11. "Coca-Cola's Delivery Fleet Will Run on Biomethane," *NGVJournal*, July 7, 2011: www.ngvjournal.com/en/vehicles/item/5675-coca-colas-delivery-fleet-will-run-on-biomethane.

12. Coca-Cola corporate web site, "What Steps Is Coca-Cola Taking towards Improving the Carbon Footprint of Its Olympic Sponsorship?" www.coca-cola .co.uk/faq/olympic-games/how-is-coca-cola-improving-the-carbon-footprint-of-its-olympic-sponsorship.html.

13. Coca-Cola corporate web site, 59: www.thecoca-colacompany.com/citizen-ship/pdf/SR07_OG_56_62.pdf; www.olympic.org/marketing-commission? articleid=55118.

14. Coca-Cola corporate web site: www.thecoca-colacompany.com/heritage/ pdf/Olympics_Partnership.pdf.

Chapter 16   The Olympic Sponsor Case Study: Visa

1. George Foster and Victoria Chang, *Visa Sponsorship Marketing*, Case: SPM-5, p. 3. Stanford University Graduate School of Business © 2003.

2. Ibid.

3. John T. Amis and Bettina Cornwell, *Global Sports Sponsorship* (Oxford: Berg, 2005), 187; Visa corporate web site: www.corporate.visa.com/about-visa/brand-and-sponsorships/olympics.shtml.

4. Foster and Chang, *Visa Sponsorship Marketing*, 15.

5. Robert T. Davis, *Marketing in Emerging Companies* (New York: Perseus, 1984). Author's Note: This book was written by my dad, Bob Davis, who was the Sebastian S. Kresge Professor of Marketing at Stanford Graduate School of Business until his death in 1995.

6. Foster and Chang, *Visa Sponsorship Marketing*, 4.

7. Ibid., 5–6.

8. John A. Davis, *Competitive Success: How Branding Adds Value*, 34.

9. Visa Annual Report 2010, 2: http://phx.corporate-ir.net/External.File?item=UGFyZW50SUQ9NzM5MjV8Q2hpbGRJRD0tMXxUeXBlPTM=&t=1.

10. Olympic Marketing Fact File, 2011 Edition, 11.

11. "Top Line Results: Performance Research-Survey Sampling 2010 Olympic Viewership Study": www.performanceresearch.com/olympic-sponsorship-vancouver.htm.

12. "Generating Visitor Spending: Mega-Sporting Events 2011," 26: http://blog.visa.com/wp-content/uploads/mega-sporting-events-report.pdf.

13. MasterCard Annual Report 2010, 2: http://phx.corporate-ir.net/External.File?item=UGFyZW50SUQ9OTUzMDh8Q2hpbGRJRD0tMXxUeXBlPTM=&t=1.

14. "Visa Extends Support of Paralympic Games Through 2012," January 19, 2010: http://corporate.visa.com/media-center/press-releases/press977.jsp.

15. Ibid.

16. Foster and Chang, *Visa Sponsorship Marketing*, 1–15; Ben Woolsey and Matt Schulz, "Credit Card Industry Facts and Personal Debt Statistics" (2006–2007): www.creditcards.com/statistics/credit-card-industry-facts-and-personal-debt-statistics.php.

17. Visa Annual Report 2010, 6.

Chapter 18   The Olympic Fans

1. "Fans Furious as 'Lucky' Ticket Applicants Find Out What They'll Be Watching at London Olympics," *Daily Mail*, June 22, 2011: www.dailymail.co.uk/sport/olympics/article-2006745/London-2012-Fans-furious-lucky-ticket-applicants-theyve-got.html#ixzz1YbpXR1pi.

2. Havas Media, "The Global Sports Forum Barcelona Presents the Study 'The Consumption of Sport in 2011 and Beyond,'" March 8, 2011: www.havas-media.com/2011/03/the-global-sports-forum-barcelona-presents-the-study-%E2%80%9Cthe-consumption-of-sport-in-2011-and-beyond%E2%80%9D/.

3. Ibid.

4. Jacqueline Magnay, "London 2012 Olympics: British Youth Not Inspired by Games, Survey Shows," *Telegraph*, June 21, 2011: www.telegraph.co.uk/sport/olympics/8588728/London-2012-Olympics-British-youth-not-inspired-by-Games-survey-shows.html.

5. David Broughton, "Visa's Visibility Recognized by Olympics Fans," *Sports Business Journal*, March 5, 2010: www.sportsbusinessdaily.com/Journal/Issues/2010/03/20100315/Sponsor-Loyalty-Data/Visas-Visibility-Recognized-By-Olympics-Fans.aspx.

6. Ibid.

7. Nicole Saunches, "U.S. Olympic Committee Commissions Study to Profile Most Passionate Olympic Fans," USOC, December 2, 2010: http://pressbox.teamusa.org/Pages/U-S--Olympic-Committee-Commissions-Study-to-Profile-Most-Passionate-Olympic-Fans.aspx#.

Chapter 19   The Olympic Creative Execution

1. Robin Wauters, "Tech Super Bowl Ads Didn't Hit Home-Salesforce and Go Daddy Most Disliked," *TechCrunch*, February 7, 2011: http://techcrunch.com/2011/02/07/tech-super-bowl-ads-didnt-hit-home-salesforce-and-go-daddy-most-disliked/. See Youtube.com for samples of GoDaddy's television commercials, including their 2011 Super Bowl TV commercials referenced in this section.

2. "Godaddy on Tonight's Super Bowl Commercials: Registrations Up 466% over Last Year; Traffic Doubled & Now Over 45 Million Domains," February 7, 2011: www.thedomains.com/2011/02/07/godaddy-on-tonights-super-bowl-commercials-registrations-up-466-over-last-year-traffic-doubled-now-over-45-million-domains/.

3. "Mark Twain (Samuel Clemmons)," *Senior Magazine:* www.seniormag.com/whitt/mark_twain.htm.

4. George Raine, "Visa Is Putting New Life in Advertising Theme, 'It's Everywhere You Want to Be' Ends after 20 Years," *San Francisco Chronicle*, February 8, 2006: www.sfgate.com/cgi-bin/article.cgi?file=/chronicle/archive/2006/02/08/BUGIIH4FD21.DTL&type=business.

5. Bruce Horowitz, "Marketers Play Social Game for Olympics; Sponsors Urge Consumers to Mingle with Brands Online," *USA Today*, February 12, 2010:

www.usatoday.com/printedition/money/20100212/olysocial12_st.art.htm; "Antonio Lucio Talks about the Go Campaign": http://corporate.visa.com/about-visa/brand-and-sponsorships-index.shtml.

6. Yahoo! Advertising Solutions, "Visa Case Study: Visa Finds Digital Gold with 'Go World' Campaign," September 2010: http://advertising.yahoo.com/industry-knowledge/visa-case-study.html.

7. Peter Hartlaub, "The Top 8 Olympic Marketing Screw-Ups," MSNBC, August 6, 2008: www.msnbc.msn.com/id/26001006/ns/business-business_of_the_olympics/t/top-olympic-marketing-screw-ups/#.Tn-E3OtQb28.

8. "London 2012 Unveils Games Mascots," May 20, 2010: www.marketingweek.co.uk/news/london-2012-unveils-games-mascots/3013695.article.

9. To read about the mascots and their histories, visit the IOC web site at www.olympic.org/uk/games/index_uk.asp.

10. Charlene Rooke, "Brand Olympics: The Best Marketing Campaigns of the 2010 Vancouver Winter Games," February 1, 2010: http://sparksheet.com/brand-olympics-the-best-marketing-campaigns-of-the-2010-vancouver-winter-games/; Bruce Horovitz, "Marketers Play Social Game for Olympics; Sponsors Urge Consumers to Mingle with Brands Online," USA Today, February 12, 2010: www.usatoday.com/printedition/money/20100212/olysocial12_st.art.htm.

11. Andrew Wilis, "Under the Gun, Omega Delivers for Vancouver; Watch Maker Unveils Starting Pistol for Terrorist-Sensitive Age," Globe and Mail, February 17, 2010: www.theglobeandmail.com/globe-investor/investment-ideas/streetwise/under-the-gun-omega-delivers-in-vancouver/article1470481/.

12. "Omega Olympics: Omega Olympic Games Boutique," January 15, 2010: www.sweetspot.ca/SweetLife/shops_and_services/14353/omega_olympics/.

13. Howard Berkes, "Olympic Sponsors Go for the Golden Image," NPR, February 25, 2010: www.npr.org/templates/story/story.php?storyId=124068024.

14. Ibid.

15. Jennifer Whitehead and John Reynolds, "P&G to Partner Coke for Olympic Games activity," Marketing Magazine, August 4, 2010; Antony Yung, "Panasonic vs. LG: Who Delivered the Sharper Image in Media?" AdAge, June 11, 2009: http://adage.com/article/mediaworks/panasonic-lg-delivered-sharper-image-media/137199/.

16. Ibid.

Chapter 20   The Olympic Marketing Communications

1. Agnes Hui, "Let the Games Beijing—As Chinese Audiences Prepare to Go Multimedia for their Olympic Viewing," August 8, 2008: http://ir.nielsen.com/phoenix.zhtml?c=211455&p=irol-newsArticle&ID=1461214&highlight=.

2. John A. Davis, *Measuring Marketing: 103 Key Metrics Every Marketer Needs* (Singapore: John Wiley & Sons (Asia) Pte. Ltd., 2006), 183.

3. Ibid., 185.

4. Ibid., 188.

5. Michael Hiestand, "Coverage of Games Keeps Growing," *USA Today*, February 25, 2010: www.usatoday.com/SPORTS/usaedition/2010-02-26-olymedia26_ST_U.htm.

6. "Olympic Games": www.olympic.org/olympic-games; LA84Foundation, *Official Reports*, vols. 1, 2, and 3: www.la84foundation.org/6oic/Official Reports/2010/2010v2.pdf; IOC Marketing Fact File 2011, 20–29; IOC Marketing Fact File 2010, 22–39; IOC Marketing Fact File 2008, 21–35; Rachel Cohen, "NBC to Offer All 2012 Olympics Events Live," TVNews Check, August 30, 2011: www.tvnewscheck.com/article/2011/08/30/53608/nbc-to-offer-all-2012-olympics-events-live.

7. Ibid.

8. Rohit Bhargava, "Analysis: The Top 10 Most Underappreciated Metrics to Track in 2008," *Influential Marketing Blog*, December 18, 2007: http://rohitbhargava.typepad.com/weblog/2007/12/the-top-10-mo-1.html.

9. ZenithOptimedia, "Global Ad Expenditure to Return to Pre-Recession Peak Level This Year," 1, July 13, 2011: www.zenithoptimedia.com/files/media/Press%20releases/Adspend%20forecasts%20July%202011.pdf.

10. Ibid., 4.

11. Fiona Vanier, "World Broadband Statistics: Q12011," 7, June 2011: http://point-topic.com/dslanalysis.php.

12. John Levett, "Press Release: Mobile Entertainment Service Revenues to Reach $54 Billion by 2015 Propelled by Surge in Consumer Smartphone Adoption," Juniper Research, March 2, 2011: http://juniperresearch.com/viewpressrelease.php?pr=233; John Levett, "Press Release: Mobile Entertainment Market to Grow by 15% in 2011 Despite Global Economic Uncertainty, Juniper Report Finds," Juniper Research, April 6, 2011: http://juniperresearch.com/viewpressrelease.php?pr=238.

13. Jay Yarow, "Twitter Getting 460,000 New Accounts Daily," *Business Insider*, May 14, 2011: www.businessinsider.com/twitter-stats-2011-3; Claudine Beaumont, "Twitter Users Send 50 Million Tweets Per Day," *Telegraph*, February 23, 2010: www.telegraph.co.uk/technology/twitter/7297541/Twitter-users-send-50-million-tweets-per-day.html; Jeff Bullas, "11 New Twitter Facts, Figures and Growth Statistics Plus": www.jeffbullas.com/2011/09/21/11-new-twitter-facts-figures-and-growth-statistics-plus-infographic/.

14. Mariel Loveland, "Facebook Reveals New Stats about the Social Network's Growth," September 23, 2011: www.scribbal.com/2011/09/facebook-reveals-new-stats-about-the-social-networks-growth/; Kelly Fiveash, "Facebook

Value Hits $100 Billion, to Go Public in Q1, 2012," *Register*, June 14, 2011: www.theregister.co.uk/2011/06/14/facebook_ipo/.

15. "Five Years of YouTube: Statistics and Infographics," *Online Marketing Trends*, January 24, 2011: www.onlinemarketing-trends.com/2011/01/five-years-of-youtube-statistics-and.html.

16. Nora Ganim Barnes, "The Fortune 500 and Social Media: A Longitudinal Study of Blogging, Twitter and Facebook Usage by America's Largest Companies," November 2010, UMass Dartmouth; "The 2010 Inc. 500 Update: Most Blog, Friend and Tweet but Some Industries Still Shun Social Media," January 2011. Both at www.umassd.edu/cmr/studiesandresearch/bloggingtwitterandfacebookusage/.

17. "Fans around the World Following the Olympics Online: Nielsen Online Analyzes Web Usage across Ten Countries and Host Country, China," August 20, 2008: www.nielsen-online.com/pr/pr_200808_HK.pdf; Michael Sachoff, "Fans Flock Online for Olympics Coverage," *Web Pro News*, August 19, 2008: www.webpronews.com/fans-flock-online-for-olympic-coverage-2008-08; Robert Seidman, "190 Million People Watched Olympics in US, 2nd Most Watched Winter Olympics in History," March 1, 2010: http://tvbythe numbers.zap2it.com/2010/03/01/190-million-people-watched-olympics-in-us-2nd-most-watched-winter-olympics-in-history/43448/.

18. The Nielsen Company, "Let the Games Beijing—As Chinese Audiences Prepare to Go Multimedia for Their Olympic Viewing," August 8, 2008: http://ir.nielsen.com/phoenix.zhtml?c=211455&p=irol-newsArticle_print&ID=1461214&highlight=.

19. Agnes Hui, "Let the Games Beijing—As Chinese Audiences Prepare to Go Multimedia for their Olympic Viewing," August 8, 2008: http://ir.nielsen.com/phoenix.zhtml?c=211455&p=irol-newsArticle&ID=1461214&highlight=.

20. Ibid.

21. "Sponsorship Intelligence: Games of the XXIX Olympiad, Beijing 2008 Global Television and Online Media Report," September 2009: www.olympic.org/Documents/IOC_Marketing/Broadcasting/Beijing_2008_Global_Broadcast_Overview.pdf.

22. "The Vancouver 2010 Olympic Winter Games: By the Numbers," *Canada NewsWire*, February 28, 2010: www.newswire.ca/en/releases/archive/February2010/28/c5535.html.

23. "Fresh Tracks," 45, *Olympic Review* 78, January–March 2011: http://view.digipage.net/?id=olympicreview78.

24. *Singapore 2010 Youth Olympic Games Official Report*, 199–200: http://app1.mcys.gov.sg/Publications/BlazingTheTrailSYOG2010OfficialReport.aspx.

25. Hui, "Let the Games Beijing."

26. AIPS, "Social Media Activating People on Olympic Day," June 23, 2011: www.aipsmedia.com/index.php?page=news&cod=6016&tp=n.

Chapter 21   The Olympic Sponsorship Checklist

1. Adapted and augmented based on information from George Foster, Stephen A. Greyser, and Bill Walsh, "Sports Marketing: Advertising, Sponsorship, and Endorsements," Section 6 in *The Business of Sports: Text and Cases on Strategy and Management* (Cincinnati, OH: South-Western College Publishing, 2005), 237.

Index